"The relationship between John Wesley and the growing numbers of evangelical clergy within the Church of England is a subject much in need of fresh treatment. Despite the fact that it seems obvious that ecclesiastical and theological differences in eighteenth-century England need to be located in rich social and political contexts, few scholars on either side of the Atlantic seem able or equipped to write in this inclusive way. Ryan Danker is an exception. He combines theological literacy with historical sophistication and serious research with accessible prose."

David Hempton, dean of the faculty of divinity, McDonald Family Professor of Evangelical Theological Studies, John Lord O'Brian Professor of Divinity, Harvard University

"Challenging the 'standard line' that Wesley's relationship with those evangelicals who remained in the Church of England during the eighteenth century was one despoiled largely by theological considerations, that is, *his* Arminianism and *their* Calvinism, Danker has carefully weaved social, political and ecclesiastical threads to offer a far more sophisticated and ultimately convincing picture. This is a splendid book on so many levels: creatively conceived, deftly contextualized and wonderfully executed. I highly recommend it."

Kenneth J. Collins, professor of historical theology and Wesley studies, director of the Wesleyan Studies Summer Seminar, Asbury Theological Seminary

"This is a most welcome study, greatly advancing our understanding of the warm, yet often heated relationships between John Wesley and other evangelical clergy in the Church of England. It demonstrates that while theological factors played an important role, much more was involved in the growing divergence among the broad evangelical camp. In the process it sheds new light on continuing debates about the very nature of evangelicalism, and where (or whether) Wesleyanism may fit within that stream of the Christian community. Highly recommended!"

Randy L. Maddox, William Kellon Quick Professor of Wesleyan and Methodist Studies, Duke Divinity School

"*Wesley and the Anglicans* is an important and timely discussion of the context and content of ecclesial shifts attributed to John Wesley and the rise of Methodism. Avoiding easy discourses with familiar anecdotes pitting Wesley against Calvin, Danker does the historical work to reintroduce the pressing issues of church, society and politics in the eighteenth century. Anyone interested in discovering or rediscovering how Wesley initiated and sustained an evangelical witness, both within the church and outside it, should read this book. Maybe these echoes of Wesley's disdain for settled ministry can revitalize evangelical Christianity again."

Joy J. Moore, assistant professor of preaching, Fuller Theological Seminary

"The last three decades have seen a revolution in scholarship on the eighteenth-century Church of England. Ryan Nicholas Danker's *Wesley and the Anglicans* finally places John Wesley squarely and critically within the context of the vibrant and thriving eighteenth-century Church of England that newer scholarship has described. Danker's highly nuanced historical narrative offers a fresh perspective on the Wesleyan movement—actually, on the 'John-Wesleyan' movement, since Danker is also conscious of Charles Wesley's sharply delineated variance from John Wesley's ecclesial vision. This is a must-read for serious students of the Wesleys and Methodist origins."

Ted A. Campbell, professor of church history, Perkins School of Theology, Southern Methodist University

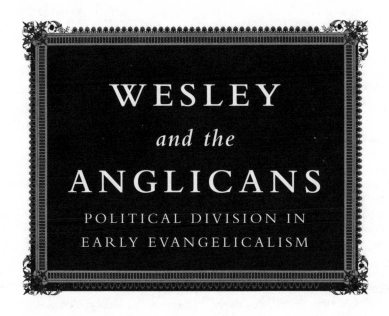

WESLEY
and the
ANGLICANS
POLITICAL DIVISION IN
EARLY EVANGELICALISM

RYAN NICHOLAS DANKER

IVP Academic

An imprint of InterVarsity Press
Downers Grove, Illinois

InterVarsity Press
P.O. Box 1400, Downers Grove, IL 60515-1426
ivpress.com
email@ivpress.com

InterVarsity Press® is the book-publishing division of InterVarsity Christian Fellowship/USA®, a movement of students and faculty active on campus at hundreds of universities, colleges and schools of nursing in the United States of America, and a member movement of the International Fellowship of Evangelical Students. For information about local and regional activities, visit intervarsity.org.

Scripture quotations, unless otherwise noted, are from the New Revised Standard Version of the Bible, copyright 1989 by the Division of Christian Education of the National Council of the Churches of Christ in the USA. Used by permission. All rights reserved.

Cover design: Cindy Kiple
Interior design: Beth McGill
Images: church service: A Service in Old Cripplegate Church. English School / Private Collection / Bridgeman Images
        certificate border: blackred/iStockphoto

ISBN 978-0-8308-5122-5 (print)
ISBN 978-0-8308-9964-7 (digital)

Printed in the United States of America ∞

Library of Congress Cataloging-in-Publication Data

Names: Danker, Ryan Nicholas, 1979- author.

Title: Wesley and the Anglicans : political division in early evangelicalism / Ryan Nicholas Danker.

Description: Downers Grove : InterVarsity Press, 2016. | Includes bibliographical references and index. | Description based on print version record and CIP data provided by publisher; resource not viewed.

Identifiers: LCCN 2016009333 (print) | LCCN 2016007924 (ebook) | ISBN 9780830899647 (eBook) | ISBN 9780830851225 (pbk. : alk. paper)

Subjects: LCSH: Wesley, John, 1703-1791. | Methodist Church—Relations—Anglican Communion. | Anglican Communion—Relations—Methodist Church. | Methodist Church—History—18th century. | Anglican Communion—History—18th century. | Christianity and politics—England. | Evangelicalism—History.

Classification: LCC BX8495.W5 (print) | LCC BX8495.W5 D36 2016 (ebook) | DDC 287.09/033—dc23

LC record available at http://lccn.loc.gov/2016009333

P	23	22	21	20	19	18	17	16	15	14	13	12	11	10	9	8	7	6	5	4	3	2	1
Y	35	34	33	32	31	30	29	28	27	26	25	24	23	22	21	20	19	18	17	16			

To David Hempton, Richard Heitzenrater,

Randy Maddox and Karen Westerfield Tucker

Mentors and friends

CONTENTS

ACKNOWLEDGMENTS

LIKE SO MANY LARGE-SCALE PROJECTS, this book has taken on a life of its own. The project began as an independent study at Duke, became the topic of my doctoral dissertation at Boston, and now after numerous revisions, additions, subtractions and a good amount of time, has become the book you now have before you. In the course of over a decade of conversations, presentations and engagements, I have amassed various and sundry debts to many. Special thanks goes to Duke Divinity School and Asbury Theological Seminary, where I participated in both the Duke Summer Wesley Seminar and the Asbury Wesley Summer Seminar and had full access to their library facilities and the insights that come from prolonged engagement with one's colleagues. Also, thanks to the librarians at the Boston University School of Theology, the Boston Athenaeum, Wycliffe Hall, Oxford and the Oxford Centre for Church History and Methodism at Oxford Brookes University.

Throughout the writing process friends and colleagues have provided insight into early evangelicalism, English history, Wesley studies and the world of academic publishing. Others have provided necessary encouragement to complete the project. I would like to specifically thank those who have contributed directly to the work, including Glen Messer, Stephanie Budwey, Donald Chase, Peggy Joyner, Bill Ellison, Peter Forsaith, Bill Gibson, Joel Scandrett, Russ Richey, Bryan Stone, Christopher Brown, Kenneth Collins, Ted Campbell, Rex Matthews, Daniel Malotky, Lawrence Czarda, Justyn Terry, Jonathan Powers, Donald Dayton, Matthew McCormick, Allan Warren and Gary Waller.

Thanks are due to my editors, Andy Le Peau and Drew Blankman, for their patience and insight and for believing that this project was worthy of a larger audience. Also, thanks to the two scholars who anonymously reviewed the work, bringing a wealth of knowledge in the field of evangelical studies and a keen awareness of historical nuance and detail. The staff at IVP Academic has been wonderful to work with from start to finish.

My parents, Terry and Carol Danker, have been, as always, a great support throughout this entire process. Colleagues at both Greensboro College and Wesley Theological Seminary have been exceptionally supportive.

I have dedicated this book to mentors who have made me the scholar I am today, whose friendship I treasure, whose work inspires me, and for whom I am thankful: David Hempton, Richard Heitzenrater, Randy Maddox and Karen Westerfield Tucker. My hope is that this small gesture might in some way show them my gratitude.

In the end, my aim in writing this book was to bring greater historical clarity and context to early evangelicalism, and to understand the forces that unite and divide evangelicals to this day. Additionally, I wanted to more fully grasp the life and thought of Wesley and the nuances of early Methodism, a person and a movement to which I am more than casually attached, and a movement and a theological perspective that I believe more vitally necessary today than ever.

Ryan Nicholas Danker
Alexandria, Virginia

ABBREVIATIONS

DEB	Donald M. Lewis, ed. *Dictionary of Evangelical Biography, 1730–1860.* 2 vols. Grand Rapids: Baker Academic, 2004.
Letters	John Telford, ed. *The Letters of John Wesley.* 8 Vols. London: Epworth, 1931.
Works	Frank Baker and Richard P. Heitzenrater, eds. *The Works of John Wesley.* Bicentennial ed. 35 vols. planned. Nashville: Abingdon, 1984–.
Works (Jackson)	Thomas Jackson, ed. *The Works of John Wesley.* 3rd ed. 14 vols. London: Wesleyan Conference Office, 1872. Reprint, Kansas City: Beacon Hill, 1978.

INTRODUCTION

JOHN WESLEY'S RELATIONSHIP WITH evangelical clergymen of the eighteenth-century Church of England is a historical topic that has been too little studied in its fuller context. This work is an attempt to understand that relationship and the gradual divide that took place between Wesley and fellow evangelicals within the Church of England. The standard line has been that Wesley's Arminianism clashed with the dominant Calvinism of eighteenth-century evangelical Anglicans and caused a rift in the Evangelical Revival in England. In this book I will attempt to provide a counterargument, formulating a more coherent description of the larger picture and of the events and issues that led some evangelical clergy to disassociate with Wesley and Wesleyan Methodism.[1] My approach in this book is that social, political and ecclesiastical issues have not been given proper weight in the discussion. When considered in isolation, the theological questions raised by the participants in this slow divide simply do not provide the necessary rationale for a division of English evangelicalism.

Because there are various ways that scholars use the term *Evangelical/ evangelical* it is essential at the beginning to define the term. Henry Rack argues for the use of the capitalized form to distinguish "Evangelicals"

---

[1]The use of the term *Wesleyan Methodism* is meant to delineate that portion of the larger revival specifically under the oversight of the Wesley brothers and especially John Wesley. This should be seen as a fluid designation. Readers with an understanding of British Methodist history are cautioned to avoid linking this group with the later Wesleyan Methodist denomination of the nineteenth century, although there are historical connections. My use of the term here is an attempt to classify one relational group within a larger and fluid revival, not to designate a denomination.

within the Church of England from evangelical dissenters, those who found objection with the established Church, primarily among Presbyterian, Baptist and independent congregations.[2] David Bebbington uses the capitalized form to designate "any aspect of the movement beginning in the 1730s."[3] D. Bruce Hindmarsh argues that the use of capitalization to differentiate churchman from dissenter encourages an all-too-clean demarcation that was not easily discernable in the early period.[4] With a nod to both Bebbington and Hindmarsh, I have chosen to follow Rack's usage as a means of providing clarity to a picture that is undoubtedly murky, yet still capable of cautious categorization. When referring to the broader movement inside and outside the Church, I use the lowercase form.

The Evangelical Revival—which included early Methodism, roughly beginning in the mid-1730s and ending with the deaths of its last first-generation leaders, Wesley and Lady Huntingdon, in 1791—was varied and should be understood in terms of broader movements or a conglomeration of movements together responding to larger societal realities.[5] Early Methodism was not an organizational structure tightly knit to the wish and whim of John Wesley. Ironically, given its name, early Methodism often lacked formal structure. Methodism included but was not limited to those clergy, lay preachers and laity in association or relationship with John Wesley, but as a revivalistic movement early Methodism continuously rejected Wesley's attempts to control it. There were Methodists in England in this early period with no connection to Wesley whatsoever. Despite the establishment of the Methodist Conference in 1744, Methodism would remain a fluid association throughout most of the century.[6]

---

[2]Henry D. Rack, *Reasonable Enthusiast: John Wesley and the Rise of Methodism*, 3rd ed. (Philadelphia: Trinity Press International, 2002), xii.

[3]David Bebbington, *Evangelicalism in Modern Britain: A History from the 1730s to the 1980s* (Boston: Unwin Hyman, 1989), 1.

[4]D. Bruce Hindmarsh, *John Newton and the English Evangelical Tradition: Between the Conversions of Wesley and Wilberforce* (Grand Rapids: Eerdmans, 2001).

[5]W. R. Ward, *The Protestant Evangelical Awakening* (New York: Cambridge University Press, 2004); and David Hempton, *Methodism: Empire of the Spirit* (New Haven, CT: Yale University Press, 2005).

[6]For a fuller description of authority within early Wesleyan Methodism see Adrian Burdon, *Authority and Order: John Wesley and His Preachers* (Burlington, VT: Ashgate, 2005), especially the introduction.

Rack has described the Methodist movement in the eighteenth century as composed of various revivals with different wings, some under Wesley's direct influence and others not.[7] This broad revival included Arminians and Calvinists, Anglicans and dissenters, enthusiasts and rationalists. At the same time, given its relational character, the movement was often ascribed to George Whitefield or the Wesleys by association.[8] Wesley's relationship to Evangelical clergy in the Church was often marred by the experience of itinerant preachers trudging through Church parishes, whether they had been appointed to do this by Wesley or not. The Methodist preacher in Lincolnshire, due to the socially disruptive nature of his itinerant preaching, may have left an impression in the local parish that would affect the parish priest's impression of the broader movement. The term *Methodist* was often attached to those with no association to the movement's leaders; instead it was used as a term of derision for those with evangelical or irregular tendencies, actions bathed in volatile political and social meaning.[9] The varied nature of the Methodist movement makes any attempt to describe

---

[7]See Rack, *Reasonable Enthusiast*, 171-80; or Henry D. Rack, "Survival and Revival: John Bennet, Methodism, and the Old Dissent," in *Protestant Evangelicalism: Britain, Ireland, Germany and America c. 1750–c. 1950, Essays in Honour of W. R. Ward*, ed. Keith Robbins (New York: Basil Blackwell, 1990), 2-3.

[8]At times, the revival is seen to reside outside the official structures of the Church of England and exclusively with Wesley and Whitefield's innovative efforts. Despite its thorough (and necessary) grasp of the trans-Atlantic nature of the revival, Carla Gardina Pestana's *Protestant Empire: Religion and the Making of the British Atlantic World* (Philadelphia: University of Pennsylvania Press, 2009) describes the revival in England without any mention of evangelical work within the structures of the Church itself. She does, however, provide keen insights into the challenges and opportunities faced by the revival in the Church of Scotland. See her chapter on the spread of evangelicalism, 187-217.

Also, some readers may wonder why I have not spent more time on Whitefield. The focus on this work is Wesley's relationship to the regular Evangelicals. Whitefield was an Evangelical clergyman, but distinctly unique among them. He did not serve within the parish structure of the Church and spent much of his ministry in the American colonies working as much or more among dissenters than he did among Anglicans. He was anything but regular. For a recent work on Whitefield particularly insightful in its description of his character and his American ministry, see Thomas Kidd's *George Whitefield: America's Spiritual Founding Father* (New Haven, CT: Yale University Press, 2014).

[9]See for example, Edmund Gibson, *The Case of the Methodists Briefly Stated: More Particularly in the Point of Field-Preaching* (London: Printed for Edward Owen, 1744); and his *Observations Upon the Conduct and Behaviour of a Certain Sect, Usually Distinguished by the Name of Methodists* (London: printed by Edward Owen, 1743 or 1744).

a break between one portion of the movement with another a topic to be approached with due caution.[10]

The Church of England in the eighteenth century was a church free of the parties that would come to dominate it subsequent to the Tractarian movement of the next century. The Evangelical clergy in the eighteenth century as a group were a small, nascent conglomeration of friends and acquaintances, or even, as I describe them later in this work, an Evangelical fraternity.[11] There was no official party line, as was also the case for Methodists under Wesley's conference system. None of the clergy could speak for the group. What primarily distinguishes these Evangelicals from the majority of those within Wesleyan Methodism was their determination to remain within the "regular" ministry of the Church of England. (*Regular* and *irregular* were general terms used to distinguish religious work. A regular ministry, such as that preferred by the Evangelicals as the century progressed, was a ministry performed within the established norms of the state church, while irregularity generally signified innovative measures such as extemporaneous prayer or field preaching.) Polity and method would play a large role in Evangelical arguments with Wesley, especially for Samuel Walker and Thomas Adam, and to a certain extent William Grimshaw, one of Wesley's most ardent Evangelical supporters. These issues alone, however, do not explain the gradual shift that took place as Methodism and Evangelical Anglicanism diverged.

The varied historical picture forces the historian to look at broader cultural movements and issues and to simultaneously emphasize the importance of personal relationships. Group pronouncements do not suffice to describe diverse movements. Neither should ideological argu-

---

[10]J. H. Overton, in his *Evangelical Revival in the Eighteenth Century* ([London?]: Longmans, 1900), 44, writes that "Methodism and Evangelicalism were both parts of one great religious movement; and it is perhaps only by reading events of the eighteenth century in the light which the nineteenth throws upon them that the two can be separated by any very strong line of demarcation."

[11]The Evangelical clergy in the eighteenth century were a small and embattled minority and should be seen as such. They were not the powerful lobby that they would become a century later. In regard to Wesley, this work assumes that he became an evangelical by 1738 without placing too much emphasis on the Aldersgate experience of that year as a "conversion." A list of Evangelical Anglican clergy serving during John Wesley's lifetime is provided as an appendix.

ments be allowed to trump political and social considerations when discussing group dynamics. Thus the insights of the social historian looking at seemingly impersonal forces must be brought into conversation with the intimacy of the historical biographer in order to capture the insights provided by both. The repercussion of Bishop Lavington's claims that Wesley was a cheap, beer-guzzling seducer of barmaids cannot be overlooked when discussing Wesley's relationship with evangelical clergy in Cornwall. Likewise, the effects of ecclesiastical strictures on Evangelicals beginning as early as the 1740s should not be ignored. Episcopal pressure on an Evangelical cleric with sympathies for irregular Methodism was often swift, impersonal and unsympathetic, yet the repercussions were often personal, as they placed deeply held theological considerations in conflict with the practical needs of family and employment.

As a result of movements in the 1760s to alter ecclesiastical admission standards at Oxford and Cambridge, the rise of conservative politics under an ascendant Toryism, and the reaction of the establishment to those who continued to challenge Anglican hegemony, the relationship between Wesley and the Evangelicals became increasingly strained. By the end of the decade, it was hard to see either group working in tandem with the other. Although John Wesley, and specifically Charles, remained in contact with a number of Evangelicals in the Church and even employed a few of them in London, the differing trajectories of Evangelical Anglicanism and Wesleyan Methodism became distinctly apparent.[12]

This book is divided into nine chapters, arranged thematically. The issues that divided the Evangelicals and Wesley, taken together, paint a picture in which the division of the two is almost inevitable. I encourage the reader to see the issues thematically and to move away from a timeline that ends with the Calvinist controversies of the 1770s. By the 1770s the controversies over predestination appear to be fought between opposing groups that had already taken divergent paths.[13]

---

[12]In order to provide clarity to the text, I have at times referred to Charles Wesley by his first name. Throughout the text "Wesley" refers to John Wesley because he is the focus of the study. This is in no way meant to slight Charles Wesley, who, if he were the focus of the work, would be referred to more formally and customarily by his last name.

[13]There is no doubt that the Calvinist controversy was one of the great mudslinging episodes of

The first chapter, "Identity and Challenge," delves into the character-istics of early English Evangelicalism and its place in the larger Evan-gelical Revival. The chapter serves to define the parameters of the book while highlighting the theology, social status, geography and principal characters of the movement. I designate Evangelicals within the Church as an "Evangelical fraternity" in an attempt to show the loose but organic connection that grew up among them as experience and opposition served to solidify group identity.

Chapter two examines John Wesley himself to show how he fit within the larger picture of English Evangelicalism. One primary goal of the chapter is to outline the tension inherent in Wesley's own evolving eccle-siological understanding as an Anglican and as an Evangelical. Despite his firm commitment to core evangelical doctrines, he also embraced a lingering high churchmanship that often left him at odds with other Evangelical Anglicans. In the chapter I place his conversion experience at Aldersgate, where his heart was "strangely warmed," within the larger international revival, a sweeping movement that the revival's participants would never fully understand.

The third chapter, "Propaganda and Power," looks at public tracts, whether produced by the Wesley brothers or by their opponents, which were printed regularly during the early period of the revival in England and served to form public impression of the broader evangelical movement. This propaganda served to complicate the relationship be-tween John Wesley and the regular Evangelical clergy. Public pressure on Evangelicals was great, and they struggled to remain within the struc-tures of the Church as an already marginalized group.

"Politics and Polity," the fourth chapter, examines the political ramifi-cations of Methodist irregularity in post-Restoration England with its long historical memory. Methodism often raised suspicion of rebellion

---

the Evangelical Revival. Rack notes that Wesley brought the Calvinist Augustus Toplady "to gibbering fury" at one point during a period in which intense personal abuse was common on both sides. See especially Rack's treatment in *Reasonable Enthusiast*, 450-61. Essential primary sources include the 1770 minutes found in *Works* 10, *The Methodist Societies, The Minutes of Conference*; John Fletcher's *Checks on Antinomianism* (1770–1775); Richard Hill's *Monthly Review* (1772) and Toplady's *Historic Proof of the Calvinism of the Church of England* (1774).

much akin to the Cromwellian revolution that overthrew Church and Crown in the previous century. Methodists, particularly those connected to Wesley, were thought to be setting up "conventicles" throughout England that would undermine the regular clergy and perhaps the Crown. Methodist practices, and especially those promulgated by Wesleyan Methodists such as lay preaching and society and class meetings, were controversial and affected the relationship between Wesley and his Evangelical colleagues.

Chapter five explores Evangelical enclaves and Methodist incursions. Many of the complaints lodged against Wesley by the Evangelical clergy center on Wesley's use of lay preachers and their work within parishes with an already established Evangelical Anglican presence. Anglican Evangelicals were an embattled minority group, and one with established regional centers or strongholds, and so the influx of Wesleyan Methodist lay preachers into these enclaves served to place embattled minority against embattled minority, although with different stakes for each group.

In chapter six, "Eucharist and Ethos," I explore the collision of the continued suspicion of schism and the attempt on the part of many of Wesley's lay preachers to administer communion, or the Lord's Supper. Many within the Evangelical "party" saw lay administration of communion as the end of their association with Methodism. William Grimshaw, Wesley's close associate and head of the Methodist work in the north of England, warned Wesley that any attempt on the part of lay preachers to administer the sacraments would drive him from Methodism. Eucharistic practice, a theological issue as much as an issue of church polity and authority, was seen by many to determine the true trajectory of Wesleyan Methodism's place in the Church. The debate also highlights Charles Wesley's high churchmanship, a theme that runs through many of the chapters but is most obvious in chapters five and six. Charles Wesley was instrumental in maintaining his brother's connections to the Evangelicals. Without Charles's incessant cry against schism, Wesley would have been left bereft of one of his most ardently conservative voices. Both Samuel Walker and John Fletcher, two leaders of the Evangelicals, corresponded with Charles in order to curtail John's maverick interpretation and use of Church polity. Charles is essential to understanding Wesley's relationship to the Evangelical clergy.

The seventh chapter, "Hegemony and Casualties," describes the repercussions of changing political tides in the 1760s under George III and the influence of a changing political environment on evangelicalism. In 1768 six students were expelled from Oxford for "methodistical practices" as a part of a larger attempt within the university to curtail the activities of evangelicals. Outside the university there was pressure to allow admission without subscription to the Church of England's Thirty-Nine Articles. The reaction in the university was a call for stricter adherence in the face of these challenges. Evangelicals became targets and soon found themselves further marginalized.

Evangelicals as a group had difficulty attaining holy orders and livings, and the expulsions from Oxford denied Evangelicals access to one of the two universities in England and thus in a certain sense to the prospects of ordination. Evangelicals were faced with the repercussions of close association with Methodism in stark terms if their movement was to work within the regular systems of the Church of England. These expulsions can be seen as a watershed moment in Methodist/Evangelical relations and as a prime example or source of Methodist/Evangelical tensions.

"Vision and Divergence," the eighth chapter, attempts to create an entirely new historiographical paradigm in which to place Wesley and the Evangelical clergy. Looking for the principles with which each defined their ministry, the chapter describes Wesley the high churchman, influenced by the nonjurors and the Caroline divines and their emphasis on the early church fathers, in stark contrast to his Evangelical colleagues, influenced by the revival of the "Old Divinity" of the Puritans and the English Reformers. This theological map provides a key to the theological debates that flared up between these groups throughout the revival.

Finally, in "Constrained to Deviate," I discuss Wesley's last efforts at union with the Evangelicals. In the 1760s Wesley attempted for the last time to form an Evangelical union based on shared theological principles.

His efforts met with little success and seem to have been his last attempt to create a lasting link with his Evangelical colleagues. This concluding section describes these attempts on Wesley's part and identifies the reasons why such an attempt had little or no chance of bearing fruit given the overall trajectory outlined in the preceding chapters. By 1770 there was a discernible, although amiable, divide between the two groups that will remain throughout the rest of Wesley's lifetime.

1

IDENTITY AND CHALLENGE

Defining Early English Evangelicalism

IN 1799 JOHN NEWTON WROTE a biography of his late friend and colleague William Grimshaw, one of the great Evangelical leaders in Yorkshire, in the form of six letters to Henry Foster. In these letters Newton captures much of Grimshaw's passion and eccentricity. In one he describes a visit by George Whitefield. The scene, perhaps unique in its bluntness, was characteristic of the passion behind the Evangelical Revival in England. Whitefield had been invited by Grimshaw to preach in his church and began his sermon, as G. R. Balleine recounts, "in his suave and conciliatory way," with kind words to the congregation.[1] This, as Newton records, "roused Mr. Grimshaw's spirit, and, notwithstanding his great regard for the preacher, he stood up and interrupted him, saying with a loud voice, 'Oh, sir, for God's sake do not speak so. I pray you do not flatter them: I fear the greater part of them are going to hell with their eyes open.'"[2]

All these men—Newton, Grimshaw, Foster and Whitefield—were clergy in the Church of England and participants in the eighteenth-century Evangelical Revival. Grimshaw's behavior would have been

---

[1]G. R. Balleine, *A History of the Evangelical Party in the Church of England* (London: Longmans, Green, 1909), 68.

[2]John Newton, *Memoirs of the Life of the Late Rev. William Grimshaw, A. B., Minister of Haworth, in the West-Riding of the County of York; With Occasional Reflections* (London: W. Baynes and Son, 1825), 109.

distinct among the Evangelicals in the Church—he was known for his unique methods—but his desire to promote a message of conversion, or New Birth, would not have set him apart from his fellow Evangelicals.[3] Like them, he was convinced that the experience of the New Birth lay at the heart of authentic Christianity, and he used any number of means to convey that message, even interrupting visiting preachers. That uniformity of intention, however, could not mask the complexities of the larger revival, which was anything but uniform. At the same time, as Carla Gardina Pestana has noted, "the revivals created a sudden and intense sense of linkages" across numerous divides.[4] Unity and diversity met within the revival, however, with varied results. The Evangelical Revival, trans-Atlantic in scope, was a volatile world composed of localized revivals, old and new practices sometimes embraced for their efficiency and other times opposed as zealotry, and leaders from across the theological spectrum.

This diversity of practice and theological persuasion, despite core convictions about the need for conversion, marked the earliest period of the Evangelical Revival in England and was one of the primary contexts in which Wesley and his Methodists engaged Evangelicals in the Church. The context often defies characterization. The term *Methodist*, for example, could be applied to those connected to Wesley or even those who had no connection to him at all.[5] Although the term *Methodist* is now

---

[3] Newton comments, "It was [Grimshaw's] frequent and almost constant custom to leave the church while the psalm before sermon was singing, to see if any were absent from worship, and idling their time in the church, the street, or the alehouses; and many of those whom he so found he would drive into the church before him" (ibid., 84).

[4] Carla Gardina Pestana, *Protestant Empire: Religion and the Making of the British Atlantic World* (Philadelphia: University of Pennsylvania Press, 2009), 197.

[5] See L. E. Elliott-Binns, *The Early Evangelicals: A Religious and Social Study* (London: Lutterworth, 1953), especially 446-49, where Elliott-Binns describes the efforts of Evangelicals post-1789 to separate themselves more firmly from the title *Methodist*. George Whitefield had for a long time been perhaps the most widely known "Methodist" in Britain. Whitefield was, it could be argued, more aware of the power of that term than even Wesley. See especially George Whitefield, *An Answer to the First and Second Part of an Anonymous Pamphlet, Entitled, Observations upon the Conduct and Behaviour of a Certain Sect Usually Distinguished by the Name of Methodists. In Two Letters to the Right Reverend the Bishop of London, and the Other the Right Reverend the Bishops Concern'd in the Publication Thereof* (London: 1744). Whitefield (p. 6) saw very plainly the political ramifications of the pamphlet and insinuated that *Observations* was written to push the Methodists out of the Church into dissent, thus relegating its potential to cause civil and political uprising.

thought to be synonymous with Wesleyanism, at the beginning of the Evangelical Revival in England it was an elusive term.[6] The title was often used as a derogatory term to slander anyone who espoused aspects of an evangelical theology or who participated in "methodistical" activities such as field preaching or attendance at evangelical society meetings.[7] In his *Force of Truth: An Authentic Narrative* (1778) Thomas Scott writes, "Methodist, as a stigma of reproach, was first applied to Mr. Wesley, Mr. Whitefield, and their followers; and to those who, professing an attachment to our Established Church, and disclaiming the name of Dissenters, were not conformists in point of parochial order, but had separate seasons, places, and assemblies of worship."[8] The designation *Methodist*, however, was regularly applied outside Scott's parameters not only to the followers of John and Charles Wesley or Whitefield but also to evangelicals both Arminian and Reformed, regular and irregular, Anglican and dissenting.

The elastic nature of the term *Methodist*, for those in England's evangelical uprising, is fitting to describe not only a movement whose parameters are often muddled and whose adherents included a unique breadth of classes, professions and religious backgrounds, but also whose leaders spanned a spectrum from the mentally unstable enthusiast to members of the aristocracy.[9] The Evangelical Revival in England included leaders as divergent at the establishmentarian Thomas Adam and the self-made prophet Thomas Maxwell. The revival included recognizable figures such

---

For a contemporary example of the term used against all those involved in the revival, see as an example Philadelphus, *Remarks on a Pamplet, Intitled, A Dialogue Between a True Methodist and an Erroneous Methodist* (London: 1751). Arguing for a broader understanding of the theological diversity of early Methodism, Joanna Cruickshank, in *Pain, Passion, and Faith: Revisiting the Place of Charles Wesley in Early Methodism* (Toronto: Scarecrow, 2009), esp. 169-70, provides further analysis of the theological diversity of early Methodism through Charles Wesley's emphasis on suffering. Cruickshank argues that Charles Wesley should be seen as a theologian in his own right within a theologically diverse movement.

[6]For this very reason, David Hempton refers to "Methodisms" in his book *Methodism and Politics in British Society 1750–1850* (London: Hutchinson, 1984), 11.

[7]For a discussion of the term *Methodist* as applied to Oxford Methodism, see Richard P. Heitzenrater, *Wesley and the People Called Methodists*, 2nd ed. (Nashville: Abingdon, 2013), 50-51.

[8]Thomas Scott, *Force of Truth: An Authentic Narrative* (1778), part l, *sub finem*.

[9]William Cowper, for example, a well-known hymn writer connected with John Newton, was known to have mental health issues. Lady Selina Huntingdon and Lord Dartmouth were the best-known aristocrats engaged in the work of the revival.

as the Wesleys and Whitefield but also the little-known but influential headmaster of the Truro Grammar School, George Conon.[10]

In this chapter I will attempt to describe the Evangelical clergy within the Church of England in order to begin to understand their relationship to John Wesley. The historiographical difficulty of categorizing persons and movements in this period complicates the picture but also highlights the reality that singular causes are not sufficient to describe the complex relationship between Wesley and his Evangelical Anglican colleagues within the Church.[11] Peter Nockles writes that in the eighteenth-century Church "neat categorizations and labels ought to be curbed, if not avoided."[12] There were distinctions in the eighteenth-century Church between those evangelical leaders who were ordained and those who were not, those who worked within the parish structures of the Church, the "regular" clergy, and those who chose to work via "irregular" means. A "regular" could become "irregular" or vice versa. He could dabble in a mixture of regular and irregular methods, but the distinction between an ordained priest in the established Church and an ordained minister of one of the dissenting bodies is easily identifiable. Likewise this is generally true of laypersons, although scholars have shown that attending Church services did not always preclude attendance at chapel meetings, and some, such as the early Wesleyans, were categorized subjectively based on differing perceptions of churchmanship.

---

[10]See G. C. B. Davies, *The Early Cornish Evangelicals 1735–60: A Study of Walker of Truro and Others* (London: SPCK, 1951), for an overview of Conon's influence, especially related to his influence on Samuel Walker, the later leader of the Cornish revival within the Church of England.

[11]The international, pan-denominational and yet oddly unified nature of the revival is evident in contemporary works such as the anonymous *The Christian History, Containing Accounts of the Revival and Propagation of Religion in Great-Britain & America. For the Year 1743* (Boston: 1744–1745). This work not only describes trans-Atlantic events but uses key evangelical nomenclature such as *awakened* to describe the New Birth. The work contains sections titled "Concerning those who have been awaken'd and appear now to be converted in a silent unobserved Manner" (94-95) and "Concerning them who cried out when they were awakened, or made Application to me from Time to Time, under their spiritual Distress; but were not under any bodily Affections" (98-103).

[12]Peter Nockles, "Church Parties in Pre-Tractarian Church of England, 1750–1833: The 'Orthodox'—Some Problems of Definition and Identity," in *The Church of England, c. 1689–c. 1833: From Toleration to Tractarianism*, ed. John Walsh, Colin Haydon and Stephen Taylor (New York: Cambridge University Press, 1993), 334.

From the beginning evangelicals could often be identified by their vocabulary. The experience of evangelical conversion, and particularly descriptions of those experiences, provided a common experiential framework or language that united the various arms of the revival both within and outside the established Church. An "evangelical language" arose to describe the experience of conversion. But even this common language did not overcome issues of polity and politics entrenched in England's ecclesiastical soil. After centuries of often bloody ecclesiastical and political dispute, shared experience alone was not sufficient to conquer entrenched patterns of social life.

The English Civil War of the previous century had not been forgotten. Memories of the war were connected with ecclesiastical and political issues common to English life since the Reformation. Presbyterian George Lawson rightly captured the intertwined nature of secular and religious interests when he wrote that "Poltiks both civil and Ecclesiastical belong unto Theologie, and are but a brand of the same."[13] John Locke captured the sentiments of the period, writing that "all those flames that have made such havoc and desolation in Europe, and have not been quenched but with the blood of so many millions, have been at first kindled with coals from the altar."[14] The preface of the 1662 Book of Common Prayer makes reference to the "late unhappy confusions" and connects the Interregnum's disruption of English ecclesiastical and political life and the zealotry that ensued to the need for liturgical uniformity accompanied by the restoration of the monarchy.[15] As Evangelical

---

[13]George Lawson, *Politica Sacra & Civilis: or, A Modell of Civil and Ecclesiastical Government* (London: 1660), 29, as quoted in J. C. D. Clark, *English Society, 1660–1832: Religion, Ideology, and Politics During the Ancien Régime* (New York: Cambridge University Press, 2000), 99.

[14]John Locke, *Two Tracts on Government*, ed. Philip Abrams (New York: Cambridge University Press, 1967), 211.

[15]For contemporary sources that connect the English Civil War to the need for religious and political moderation, see Bruno Ryves, *Mercurius Rusticus: Or, the Country's Complaint of the Barbarous Outrages Begin in the Year 1642, by the Sectaries of this Late Flourishing Kingdom*, 5th ed. (London: 1732). Originally printed in 1685, Ryves's piece includes a description of the parliamentarians as "Schismaticks" and the war as "unnatural." As an example of an explicitly religious connection, see J. H. and A. B., *Gratitude to God the Surest Defence Against Future Dangers. A Sermon Preached to a Selected Audience, on Thursday October 9, 1746. Being the Day Appointed for a General Thanksgiving for Our Happy Deliverance from the Miseries of the Late Unnatural Rebellion* (London: 1746).

initiatives gained popular notice in the 1730s, many saw the movement as another form of the same religious enthusiasm that threw the nation into disarray under the banner of Puritanism and brought on those "unhappy confusions."[16] Whether this particular form of religious enthusiasm came from the altar, the pulpit or in small, secretive meetings was of little importance.

THE EIGHTEENTH-CENTURY CONTEXT

The eighteenth century has been judged for many years in light of nineteenth-century expectations, and only recently has it come to be understood in its own terms.[17] The negative assumptions of later low church Evangelicals and their high church Tractarian adversaries in the nineteenth century came to dominate eighteenth-century studies.[18] Through the 1740s eighteenth-century England was coming to terms with the political and social turmoil of the previous century. At the same time, however, great effort was made by both Whigs and Tories under newly defined versions of the "divine right of kings" to secure the new Protestant dynasty. Within this context, eighteenth-century leaders actively fought against continued efforts by the Stuarts and their Jacobite allies in both 1715 and 1745 to undermine what in many ways was the ascendency of the Church over the monarchy, a shift in the *ancien régime* that would last until the Reform Acts of the late 1820s. The English approach to governance in the eighteenth century, while cautious early on with a focus on restorationism by the later part of the century, had embraced an expansionist policy both economically and geographically. Despite the loss of the American colonies, and seven large-scale conflicts

---

[16]See Clark, *English Society.*

[17]See William Gibson, *The Church of England 1688–1832: Unity and Accord* (New York: Routledge, 2001), especially his chapter "Historians and the Eighteenth-Century Church," in which Gibson describes historiographical approaches of the period and efforts to rescue it from negative Victorian assessments (4-27).

[18]See not only Gordon Rupp's *Religion in England, 1688–1791* (New York: Oxford University Press, 1986) but also Robert G. Ingram's *Religion, Reform and Modernity in the Eighteenth Century: Thomas Secker and the Church of England,* Studies in Modern British Religious History 17 (Woodbridge, UK: Boydell, 2007) on renewal in the eighteenth-century Church as examples of this new perspective.

with the expansion of British imperialism,[19] by century's end the Hanoverian dynasty was secure and with it a Protestant England ready to compete with Roman Catholicism in a colonizing race safely situated outside the British Isles.

Within the *Pax Anglia* the Church of England flourished. Recent historians such as Jeremy Black, J. C. D. Clark, William Gibson and Nigel Yates, among others, have begun the long process of correcting the perception that the Church in the eighteenth century was decrepit. Black notes that "there is copious evidence both of massive observance of the formal requirements of the churches and of widespread piety."[20] Echoing Black, Yates claims that religion in England, and its established Church, was much healthier than has been previously acknowledged.[21] With the cooperation of what Clark terms the Church-Whig alliance under the first two Georges, he asserts that "in the face of an assertive Anglicanism, the number of Dissenters and Roman Catholics in England was each roughly halved in the years c. 1690–1740."[22] At the same time, the Church of England understood, as much of Europe did after the Peace of Westphalia in 1648, the repercussions of theologically inspired warfare. The resulting caution that such knowledge engendered has been misinterpreted as weakness but produced growing toleration and stability. Revolutionary sentiments on the Continent and the phantom of Oliver Cromwell with the image of a beheaded Charles I, however, represented lasting images of zealotry in the imagination of English churchmen.

The English Civil War and its repercussions continued to haunt the Church for over a century after the regicide of Charles on January 30, 1649. Despite the complexity of the war, or even wars, and its multiple causes—which had as much or more to do with power struggles between king and Parliament as it did between Laudian and Reformed "parties"

---

[19]James Horn, "British Diaspora," in P. J. Marshall, ed., *The Oxford History of the British Empire*, vol. 2, *The Eighteenth Century* (New York: Oxford University Press, 1998), 33.

[20]Jeremy Black, *Eighteenth-Century Britain, 1688–1783*, 2nd ed. (New York: Palgrave Macmillan, 2008), 136.

[21]See Nigel Yates, *Eighteenth-Century Britain: Religion and Politics 1714–1815* (New York: Longman, 2008), esp. 4, for a discussion of religion in England as positive in the eighteenth century.

[22]Clark, *English Society*, 99.

within the Church—on the ground the nuances of history were regularly overlooked. Often the complexities of the Civil War period were replaced in the eighteenth century by a common fear of any real or supposed challenge to the *Pax Anglia*. Clark has written extensively on the struggles faced by Church and society not only because of the Civil War but also after the Glorious Revolution and the ramifications of a potentially resurgent Catholic dynasty.[23] Alan Harding writes that although the Church of England was the "victor" of seventeenth-century struggles, it came away from that victory with definite scars.[24] Within this context the uprising now known as the Evangelical Revival was anything but a welcome addition to eighteenth-century England. That Evangelicals remained within a Church that in so many ways thought them malevolent and fanatical is a story worth telling all on its own.[25]

THE ELUSIVE NATURE OF EVANGELICALISM

W. R. Ward writes, "Evangelicals, in the Anglo-Saxon sense of the word, seem generally to have found it easier to recongise each other than others have found it to categorize them."[26] Sectarian interests have often inspired attempts to neatly write the story of this early period.[27] Revival

---

[23]See especially ibid., 43-124.

[24]Alan Harding, *The Countess of Huntingdon's Connexion: A Sect in Action in Eighteenth-Century England* (New York: Oxford University Press, 2003), 6.

[25]The standard work on English evangelicalism remains Balleine's *History of the Evangelical Party*. Recent works include David Bebbington, *Evangelicalism in Modern Britain: A History from the 1730s to the 1980s* (London: Unwin Hyman, 1989); and Kenneth Hylson-Smith, *Evangelicals in the Church of England, 1734–1984* (Edinburgh: T&T Clark, 1988). Works that include England but cover a broader geographic spectrum include Mark Noll, *The Rise of Evangelicalism: The Age of Edwards, Whitefield, and the Wesleys*, History of Evangelicalism (Downers Grove, IL: InterVarsity Press, 2004).

[26]W. R. Ward, *Early Evangelicalism: A Global Intellectual History, 1670–1789* (New York: Cambridge University Press, 2006), 6.

[27]Later evangelical identity in the nineteenth century will be fused on the battlefield, first with the High Church Party and subsequently against the higher critics or liberal Protestants of the later part of the century. This ecclesiastical battlefield will not only create identifiable parties within the Church, as shown in the work of Norman Sykes, but will also change the very nature of evangelicalism. For example, Methodism will, under Jabez Bunting and other post-Wesley leaders of the newly formed church, begin to ignore John and Charles Wesley's sacramental and liturgical theological emphases in the face of what they saw as high church extremism or abuse of these more catholic elements of the Christian tradition. In so doing, Methodism will not only define itself apart from the high church's sacramental and liturgical revival but also will actually alter the Wesley brothers' vision of Methodism itself. The early Methodist clamoring for the

participants were labeled or claimed titles that often deviate from later expectations. John Fletcher, for instance, was both an Anglican and a Methodist; so were John and Charles Wesley, William Grimshaw, George Whitefield and Lady Huntingdon. All of the early Evangelicals were called "Methodist" or "methodistical" by their opponents. Some claimed the title for themselves, such as Fletcher, who wrote to Charles Wesley in 1758 that "I find my heart strongly attached" to the Methodists and who was fearful of leaving them to "stand alone in the midst of so many dead people."[28]

For many, Methodism was simply another form of enthusiasm, an elusive term used for political reasons. The Evangelical John Berridge was convinced that talk of God was enough to rouse the suspicions of some. He wrote that "to talk of God upon a visit, would turn the hearers sick or sour, and brand the speaker for a rude man or a methodist."[29] The charge of enthusiasm could range from simple rudeness to insanity. Dewey Wallace describes the rise of antienthusiasm campaigns beginning in the 1650s. He highlights Henry More's *Enthusiasmus Triumphatus: Or, a Discourse of the Nature, Causes, Kinds, and Cure of Enthusiasme* (1662) as "an early anatomy of enthusiasm." More wrote in the 1650s and for political reasons left the Puritans out of his equations. What he described as enthusiasm would define the term for decades. His definition included "dabblers in alchemy and magic" and those overwhelmed by delusions and mental disorders. His examples included a nobleman who thought he was made of glass and a woman who thought she was a

---

sacrament, an essential element of the early Wesleyan understanding of the process of sanctification, will subside with the passing cadence of the Corpus Christi procession of the Tractarians and find an alternative outlet among the rambunctious cacophony of the revival meeting. See, for example, Mats Selen, *The Oxford Movement and Wesleyan Methodism in England 1833–1882: A Study in Religious Conflict*, Bibliotheca Historico–Ecclesiastica Lundensis 30 (Lund, Sweden: Lund University Press, 1992).

[28]Fletcher's letter to Charles Wesley, Tuesday, December 26, 1758, in Peter Forsaith, ed., *Unexampled Labours: Letters of the Revd John Fletcher to Leaders in the Evangelical Revival* (London: Epworth, 2008), 56-57. See also Peter Fosaith and Geordan Hammond, eds., *Religion, Gender, and Industry: Exploring Church and Methodism in a Local Setting* (Eugene, OR: Wipf and Stock, 2011). David R. Wilson's essay "Church and Chapel" in this volume is particularly helpful for understanding the context of Fletcher's ministry.

[29]John Berridge, *The Christian World Unmasked. Pray Come and Peep. By John Berridge, A. M. Vicar of Everton, Bedfordshire; Late Fellow of Clare-Hall, Cambridge* (London: 1773), 15.

cat and pounced on mice. Wallace notes that More helped set the stage for an antienthusiasm campaign.[30]

Methodism, however, included many who did not fall under the term *enthusiast* and was distinctly diverse. Many were identified as Methodists for their use of the society model, or a variation of it, commonly used in the Restoration period but increasingly identified with evangelicalism as the century went on. Lady Huntingdon had a connexion of Methodists, and so did Wesley and Whitefield. Samuel Walker allowed small group meetings in his parish, as did Fletcher, Newton and Berridge. And yet Wesley had difficulty, and ultimately failed, in his attempts finally to relinquish Methodist societies under his control within the Evangelical parishes administered by Edward Stillingfleet and Henry Venn.[31] These men were all a part of a larger movement, and their common allegiance to the New Birth served to solidify them within a milieu that found their ideas troubling if not outright dangerous.[32]

DEFINING EVANGELICALISM

In order to understand early English evangelicalism, attachment to the primacy of theological systems should be tempered by the inclusion of practical considerations: church polity, liturgical practice and an emphasis on the need for the experiential. Peter Forsaith claims that "'Evangelical' at this time referred to being evangelistic rather than to doctrinal position."[33] While pointing to one of the defining characteristics of evangelical practice, the "being evangelistic" must also be understood as the outgrowth of a theological viewpoint calling for such drastic behavior.

---

[30]See Dewey A. Wallace, *Shapers of English Calvinism 1660–1714: Variety, Persistence, and Transformation* (New York: Oxford University Press, 2011), 39.

[31]Frank Baker, *John Wesley and the Church of England* (London: Epworth, 1970), 185-86. The issue came to a head at the conference of 1761, and a compromise was agreed on in the case of Venn's parish. Venn had an amicable relationship with the Wesleyans, but those under Wesley's care were afraid of losing contact with Wesley if their society was under the control of Venn. Such concerns show the relational nature of early evangelicalism in Britain.

[32]See, for example, George Swathe, *Enthusiasm No Novelty, or, The Spirit of the Methodists in the Year 1641 and 1642* (London: Printed for T. Cooper, 1739), which explicitly compared Methodism to the parliamentary forces of the seventeenth century; and Joseph Trapp, *The True Spirit of the Methodists, and Their Allies (Whether Other Enthusiasts, Papists, Deists, Quakers, or Atheists) Fully Laid Open* (London: Printed for Lawton Gilliver and sold by T. Cooper, 1740).

[33]Forsaith, *Unexampled Labours*, 24n71.

David Bebbington's fourfold definition of modern evangelicalism is the most useful place to begin to define the evangelical movement of this period. Bebbington's definition has become the standard defining principle of current evangelical scholarship.[34] He summarizes his "four qualities" of evangelical religion, which include: "*conversionism*, the belief that lives need to be changed; *activism*, the expression of the gospel in effort; *biblicism*, a particular regard for the Bible; and what may be called *crucicentrism*, a stress on the sacrifice of Christ on the cross," claiming that "together they form a quadrilateral of priorities that is the basis of Evangelicalism."[35] Bebbington's categories provide an elastic description of evangelicalism broadly conceived from 1730 up to the present. Their elasticity rightly matches the elasticity of the movement they attempt to define.

These four qualities are evident in the theology and practice of evangelicals in the earliest period. Of the four, however, conversionism reigns supreme. Thomas Adam, one of the early Evangelical Anglicans, whose penchant for writing more than made up for his lackluster pulpit performance, highlighted this evangelical trait in his 1767 *Practical Lectures on the Church-Catechism*. Adam questions "whether religion, according to the plain meaning of the Bible, is not *Conversion?* and whether any kind of religion, which leaves him just where it found him, without working any change of his tempers, and affections, can be pleasing to God, or a ground of his present and future happiness."[36] This conversion-dominated theology runs throughout Adam's *Lectures*, a work that was widely praised and widely used by the Evangelicals.[37]

Using language to emphasize the experiential nature of the Christian faith, Adam claims that "the end of all divine knowledge is practice

---

[34]Bebbington's definition is the standard used for the inclusion of persons in the *Dictionary of Evangelical Biography* and is also used by David Hempton and Mark Noll, among other leading scholars of the field. For example, David Hempton and Myrtle Hill, *Evangelical Protestantism in Ulster Society 1740–1890* (New York: Routledge, 1992), 14; and Noll, *Rise of Evangelicalism*, 16.

[35]Bebbington, *Evangelicalism in Modern Britain*, 2-3.

[36]Thomas Adam, *Practical Lectures on the Church-Catechism. By Thomas Adam. The Fifth Edition. To Which Is Now Added, An Exercise, by Way of Question and Answer, Preparatory to Confirmation* (London: 1767). Available in *Eighteenth Century Collections Online*, Gale Group, vi. See also 64.

[37]Adam's *Practical Lectures* was widely sold. The copy now held at Lambeth Palace includes Archbishop Secker's personal bookplate, indicating that the work was in the archbishop's personal library.

and self-application."[38] The experience of conversion was the "touch-stone of the heart" or the foundation on which the awakened soul could rest. Closely aligned with this emphasis on the experience of conversion, the doctrine of assurance was not simply a matter of concern for Wesleyans and Moravians but a natural extension of an experiential theology.[39] Adam writes that in this heartfelt experience the Spirit of God would "do its work in us," and in this experience "we must work with *it*."[40]

The call to conversion was at the heart of what it meant to be an evangelical. Adam said it distinctly when he wrote, "The one thing necessary is conversion; I mean, as begun, and carried on, by the Holy Spirit."[41] Wesley's now-famous dictum that he had nothing to do but save souls summarized the watchword and song of these men. Although Bebbington's fourfold definition appears at first glance to be a quadrilateral of equal sides, it was this experience of the New Birth, or conversion, that more than anything defined the outlook of these early evangelists. For Wesley the New Birth and justification by faith were the two doctrines that "may be properly termed fundamental."[42] This one "side" of the quadrilateral outweighed the rest and was the cornerstone, rather than an equal partner with the others.[43]

THE EVANGELICAL FRATERNITY

John Walsh describes the Evangelicals as "remarkably unorganized, sprinkled thinly and haphazardly across the parochial map of

---

[38] Adam, *Practical Lectures*, 8.

[39] See *Works* 19, *Journals and Diaries II (1738–1743)*, 152-62, for Wesley's view of the Stillness Controversy, which ultimately split the Wesleyan Methodists and the English Moravians.

[40] Adam, *Practical Lectures*, 8.

[41] Ibid., 10.

[42] John Wesley, "The New Birth," *Works* 2:187.

[43] This emphasis on conversion can be seen throughout the primary sources, including George Whitefield, *The Almost Christian: A Sermon Preached to a Numerous Audience in England* (London: 1739); Martin Madan, *Justification by Works: and Not by Faith Only, Stated, Explained, and Reconciled with Justification by Faith, Without Works. Being the Substance of a Sermon on James ii.24. Preached at St. Vedast's Church, Foster-Lane, February 8, 1761* (London: 1761); and in John Wesley's sermons including: "Salvation by Faith," "'Awake, Though That Sleepest,'" "Justification by Faith" and "The Marks of the New Birth," among others (*Works* 1).

Anglicanism."[44] Bebbington describes them as "few and scattered."[45] These men did not form a party, as they would later in the next century. Parties were anathema in this period of English history and were viewed as divisive and unpatriotic. Nockles did not deny the existence of church parties in "the pre-Tractarian Church of England" but argues that they "formed part of a broadly based theological consensus which the Tractarians destroyed, and which according to Avis 'may be likened to a series of mutually overlapping circles.'"[46] The Evangelical "circle" overlapped with various forms of dissent, specifically Presbyterianism and Wesleyan Methodism.[47] The Evangelical circle, however, is unique, as the Evangelicals of this period of the revival are best understood in relational terms, even as a fraternity.

The Evangelicals were not connected like Wesley's "sons in the gospel" but rather through an interlocking series of friendships forged in the shared experience of opposition to their conversionist message. This opposition had the effect of uniting Evangelicals and spearheading efforts to find likeminded colleagues. G. C. B. Davies notes, "An interesting feature of the Evangelical revival of the eighteenth century is the fact that so many of these 'enlightened' clergy and laity in all parts of the country were acquainted with each other."[48] Beginning in the 1750s in the Evangelical strongholds of Cornwall and Yorkshire, and later in various parts of the country, they formed clerical associations.[49] Samuel Walker, perpetual curate in Truro and unofficial leader of the Cornish Evangelicals,

---

[44]J. D. Walsh, "The Anglican Evangelicals in the Eighteenth Century," in *Aspects de L'Anglicanisme*. Travaux du Centre D'Etudes Supérienures Spécialisé D'Historie des Relgions de Stausbourg (Paris: Presses Universitaires de France, 1974), 90.

[45]Bebbington, *Evangelicalism in Modern Britain*, 31.

[46]Nockles, "Church Parties in Pre-Tractarian Church of England," 336.

[47]This overlap with dissent is noteworthy in that many Evangelicals, according to Overton, were more comfortable relating to avowed dissenters than they were to the ecclesiologically elusive Wesleyan Methodists. Taking Evangelical discomfort into consideration, Overton writes that the Evangelicals "foresaw the inevitable break which must occur at Wesley's death, if not before, between Methodists and the Church of England, and they strongly objected to being thought to be in any way mixed up with a movement which was leading to a separation which they would sincerely deplore." *Evangelical Revival in the Eighteenth Century*, ([London?]: Longmans, 1900), 51.

[48]Davies, *Early Cornish Evangelicals*, 167.

[49]For studies particularly devoted to early Evangelicalism in Cornwall and Yorkshire, see Davies, *Early Cornish Evangelicals*; and John Walsh, "The Yorkshire Evangelicals in the Eighteenth Century: With Special Reference to Methodism," PhD thesis (Cambridge University, 1956).

formed such a society around 1750. Kenneth Hylson-Smith calls Walker the "prime mover" of the society whose purpose was "to increase the efficiency and usefulness of each of the members within their own parishes as a consequence of the mutual exchange of ideas and opinions."[50] Hylson-Smith sees this clerical society as yet another means by which Walker, a staunch churchman and friendly critic of Wesleyan irregularity, attempted to work within the parochial structures of the established Church as an Evangelical; clerical societies had been common within Anglicanism well before this time.[51]

Walker was not the only Evangelical clergyman who set up an early society to connect with fellow Evangelicals. John Fletcher created a similar group in Shropshire in the spring of 1765. He describes the group to Charles Wesley in a letter shortly after their first meeting. The group of six Evangelical churchmen included Edward Davies of Bengeworth; a "Mr Baily of Pashur," who is thought to be Thomas Beale of Pershore; Edward Stillingfleet of West Bromwich; John Riland, who although connected with Huddersfield at this time had family connections near Shropshire; Thomas Biddulph then of Worcester; and William Talbot, vicar of Kineton, Warwickshire. Two of the members were absent for the first meeting, "one on business and another with a bad leg." They agreed to meet together four times per year.[52]

Similarly, Newton's Olney parish became a center of evangelical activity, both established and dissenting: Newton attracted local Evangelicals in an association much like Fletcher's and Evangelicals from throughout England who would make pilgrimage to the Olney rectory. Hindmarsh notes that within six months of Newton's arrival as curate in Olney in 1764, Newton started a monthly meeting of six or seven Evangelical clergy in "the adjoining counties."[53] This meeting soon included

---

[50]Hylson-Smith, *Evangelicals in the Church of England, 1734–1984*, 23-24.
[51]Ibid.
[52]Forsaith, *Unexampled Labours*, 210 (letter to Charles Wesley, April 28, 1765). See also Fletcher's letter to George Whitefield dated May 28, 1768, in which Fletcher mentions "our meeting of the clergy in Birmingham." Whether this is the same group described to Charles Wesley is not clear.
[53]D. Bruce Hindmarsh, *John Newton and the English Evangelical Tradition: Between the Conversions of Wesley and Wilberforce* (Grand Rapids: Eerdmans, 2001), 207-11.

evangelicals of various denominations, an innovative move among the early Evangelical Anglicans, yet not out of character with Newton's local ecumenism. Even into the nineteenth century, Newton's society remained a regular and important clerical meeting.[54]

The formation of clerical societies in a formal sense and the letters between the Evangelical clergymen on a more personal level show a sincere filial bond. They also help map out the varied connections among the 170 or so clergy in the Church of England during the life of John Wesley who were identifiably Evangelical.[55] Charles Wesley's letters to John Fletcher of Madeley, although perhaps more intimate than most, provide a window into this social network. Charles and Fletcher maintained a close friendship throughout most of the revival. Forsaith writes that for Fletcher, "if John Wesley was a father in God, Charles was a brother in Christ."[56] This close bond would wane with Charles's later inattention to it. As pivotal as both men were to the Wesleyan arm of the revival, their letters to each other describe an Evangelical network larger than that represented at Wesley's conferences.[57] A letter from Fletcher to Charles Wesley in the summer of 1761 describes the interaction common among these clergymen and their supporters and also the ecclesiastical battle lines common among them. Every person mentioned is either an Evangelical clergyman or a member of an aristocratic family friendly to their cause. Fletcher writes:

---

[54]Ibid.

[55]There are various estimates given for the number of Evangelical Anglican clergy in this period. Frank Baker identifies 112 Evangelical Anglicans during Wesley's lifetime; see Baker, *John Wesley and the Church of England*. My own estimate, working principally from the *Dictionary of Evangelical Biography*, is that the number of Evangelical clergy during the life of Wesley is closer to 170. John Walsh argues that by the end of the century there were between three hundred and five hundred Evangelicals. See Walsh, "Anglican Evangelicals in the Eighteenth Century," 102.

[56]Forsaith, *Unexampled Labours*, 27. See appendix to this book.

[57]See *John Bennet's Copy of the Minutes of the Conferences of 1744, 1745, 1747, and 1748; with Wesley's Copy of those of 1746* (London: Wesley Historical Society, 1896–1904) for notes on the earliest conferences. Also see *Minutes of the Methodist Conferences, from the first, held in London, by the late Rev John Wesley, A.M., in the year 1744* (London: John Mason at the Wesleyan Conference Office, 1862–1864). Wesley's *Journal*, especially when describing the earliest conferences, is short on detail. Ward notes that it was later Methodist ecclesiology that emphasized the importance of the earliest conferences. See, for instance, *Works* 20:34 for Wesley's journal account of the 1744 conference.

Last [S]unday I made a visit to Mr. Stillingfleet[,] Lord Dartmouth's Chaplain and minister of Bromwich, I offered him my pulpit as if to a Deputy who also preaches Christ with daring. He is on close terms with Mr. Downing and resembles him by his gentleness and his modesty: He is so afraid of acting the part of a Methodist although he preaches their doctrines that I doubt if he will accept my offer. He took me to dine at Lord D[artmou]th's who was that day with Milady [Lady Huntingdon] at his country seat, if I converse often with him he would soon render me a churchman in all respects: What a difference between Mr. Berridge and him! He read me the details of Mr. Walker his close friend: What a loss for the little flock of Christ![58]

This one quotation, not uncommon in these letters, names four Evangelicals and the two leading evangelical aristocrats around whom a coterie of Evangelicals often gathered. They were from the Midlands, Essex, Yorkshire and Cornwall, nearly representing the four corners of England. The letter also mentions the argument over irregularity that would become one of the principal causes of friction and separation. The conservatives Walker and Stillingfleet and the maverick Berridge were on opposing sides of this debate.

THE "METHODIST DESERT"

As late as 1885, the term *Methodist desert* was used to describe the southern counties of England.[59] The fraternity of Evangelical clergy in this early period formed a company that was, like the Wesleyans themselves, a fraternity on the fringe of the English establishment. These men were not dissenters, yet neither were they at the centers of traditional Anglican life. They may have drawn large crowds of curious spectators from time to time, even collecting wayward parishioners on Sunday mornings, but they did not reside in the places of power. Yorkshire and

---

[58]Forsaith, *Unexampled Labours*, 135. As noted in the text, a cadre of Evangelical clergy can be found throughout Charles's and Fletcher's letters. For further examples where Evangelical connections are mentioned, see Fletcher's letters to Charles on March 1, 1760, and May 6, 1760.

[59]See W. W. Pocock, *History of Wesleyan Methodism in Some of the Southern Counties of England* (London: Wesleyan Conference Office, 1885). For a larger picture of English religious geography, see J. D. Gay, *The Geography of Religion in England* (London: Duckworth, 1971).

Cornwall, as already noted, served as their initial strongholds, far from the power structures of London and Oxbridge. The Evangelicals retained an ebbing presence among the academics of Oxford and Cambridge but were nearly absent from London throughout most of this period. With one-tenth of the nation's population, London not only served as the capital but defined much of the culture of the nation.[60] For years not one Evangelical inhabited a pulpit in London, and only with the use of lectureships and propriety chapels did they begin to gain a foothold there.

The now-famous struggles of William Romaine as, for a time, the lone Evangelical Anglican in a London parish need not be reiterated here. His struggles have certainly been embellished for the sake of evangelical hagiography.[61] But Romaine and those who came to hear his Sunday evening lecture were faced with opposition from the start. Not until Romaine was established as the rector of St. Andrew's and St. Anne's, Blackfriars, in 1766, an appointment that had to make its way through legal challenges, was he able to preach uninhibited.

What would become one of the principal strongholds of London Evangelicalism was a chapel attached to the Lock Hospital, built for the treatment of venereal diseases in the 1740s. The Lock Hospital receives mention in that notorious publication listing eighteenth-century London prostitutes, *Harris's List of Covent Garden Ladies*.[62] The "list" was a bestseller in multiple editions for over thirty-eight years and included the names, locations and prices of London's "ladies of pleasure." The Lock Hospital was the seat of Martin Madan's ministry in London from 1755 to 1780, and under his supervision a long list of Evangelical clergy served as curates and chaplains. Madan was a prolific author whose work included numerous hymns, translations of Juvenal and

---

[60]See Black, *Eighteenth-Century Britain*, esp. 118-20, for a fuller description of the hegemonic role played by London during the eighteenth century.

[61]The story of Romaine's struggles was early on made part of the Evangelical canon. Evangelical Anglican Thomas Haweis wrote his biography of Romaine, *The Life of William Romaine, M. A.: Late Rector of St. Ann's, Blackfriars, and Lecturer of St. Dunstan's*, as early as 1797.

[62]For a recent reprint see Hallie Rubenhold, *The Harlot's Handbook: Harris's List* (Stroud, UK: Tempus, 2007). Rubenhold's edition contains a helpful introduction to the work, the full text of the 1793 edition and selections from the editions of 1761-1791.

Persius, and traditional evangelical treatises such as those on the doctrine of justification by faith.[63] Only after Madan's 1780 publication *Thelyphthora; or, a Treatise on Female Ruin, in its Causes, Effects, Consequences, Prevention, and Remedy*, which called for the legalization of polygamy, was Madan forced to resign.[64] Madan believed that biblical polygamy could be used as a means to get women off the streets. As an avid writer, he retired and spent the last decade of his life writing on the periphery of the revival.[65]

The Lock Hospital chapel served as a way station for many Evangelical clergy without parochial appointments. Securing the rectorship of a parish or chapel not only gave an Evangelical power over the local church, pulpit and liturgical practices but also provided curacies for the newly trained Evangelicals graduating from Oxford and Cambridge. Without these curacies, and seen in light of recurrent episcopal opposition to the ordination of those with evangelical or "methodistical" tendencies, the Evangelical movement within the Church of England would have come to a quick end. Curacies at Haworth, St. Ann's, Blackfriars, Clapham and the Lock Hospital provided stepping stones for those who in the next century would become the leaders of a powerful church party. The Lock Hospital curates included clergy such as Charles Edward de Coetlogon, who would later become chaplain to the Lord Mayor; John Crosse, a convert of Methodism who almost joined the Wesleyans over opposition to his evangelical preaching within the Church; and Thomas Haweis, a leading Evangelical voice who came to the Lock Hospital after opposition to his curacy at St. Mary Magdalene Oxford.

---

[63]See among Madan's works: *Justification by Works: and Not by Faith Only, Stated, Explained, and Reconciled with Justification by Faith, Without Works. Being the Substance of a Sermon on James ii. 24. Preached at St. Vedast's Church, Foster-Lane, February 8, 1761* (London: 1761); *A Treatise on Christian Faith, Extracted and Translated from the Latin of Hermannus Witsius* (London: 1761); and *A Scriptural Comment upon the Thirty-Nine Articles of the Church of England* (London: 1772).

[64]Madan had been for years an advocate for women who desired to leave prostitution. See his *Account of the Triumphant Death of F. S. A Converted Prostitute, Who Died April 1763, Aged Twenty-Six Years* (London: 1763).

[65]The disastrous reception of Madan's *Treatise on Female Ruin* did not stop him from continuing to promote his controversial ideas. In 1782 he plunged headfirst back into the debate that had cost him so much by writing his *Letters on Thelyphthora: With an Occasional Prologue and Epilogue* (London).

London may not have been a stronghold of Evangelical activity like Bristol, Truro or Huddersfield, but it was not entirely devoid of an Evangelical presence in this period. Those who would trumpet the life of William Romaine and the opposition he endured often make it appear that he spent his entire ministry as a lone voice in an ecclesiastical wilderness. In order to find fellowship with those of a similar mind, the London Evangelicals had to stay connected to clergymen outside the capital. Romaine, for instance, visited Samuel Walker in Cornwall for encouragement, and according to Walker's correspondence with Adam would have left the Church had it not been for Walker.[66] But there were sparks of Evangelical fervency in London during this period. Thomas Jones, who was converted in 1754 and served as the chaplain to the bishop of London, is a perfect example. For a few years he, like Romaine, was the only beneficed Evangelical in the capital. However, Jones was not alone in London throughout his entire ministry. Martin Madan knew Jones and even preached his funeral sermon, in June 1762.[67] Thomas Broughton, an Oxford Methodist, was another London Evangelical and served as secretary of the Society for the Promotion of Christian Knowledge, and from 1755 until his death in 1777 he was rector of All Hallows, Lombard Street.[68]

All the same, the proportion of the British population living in London and the low number of Evangelical clergy in the area is an indication of Anglican Evangelicalism's place on the fringe of English life. The number of Wesleyan Methodists in London, or even those who followed George Whitefield and filled his Spitalfields Chapel, although impressive compared to other areas of the country during the eighteenth century, should

---

[66] As recorded in Davies, *Early Cornish Evangelicals*, 178.

[67] See Martin Madan, *A Funeral Sermon on the Much Lamented Death of the Rev. Mr. Thomas Jones, M. A.* (London: 1762).

[68] Broughton wrote many works intended to serve as a defense of Christianity against deism and other forms of theological liberalism. These included his *Christianity Distinct from the Religion of Nature, In Answer to a Late Book, Entitled, Christianity as Old as the Creation* (London: 1732); *The Inspiration of the New Testament Asserted: The Integrity of the Sacred Writers Vindicated* (London: 1739); and *A Defense of the Commonly-Received Doctrine of the Human Soul* (Bristol: 1766). One of his most popular works was *The Christian Soldier: Or, The Duties of a Religious Life Recommended to the Army, from the Example of Cornelius: in a Sermon* (London: 1738). This work went through eight editions by 1800. It is noteworthy in that one of the major avenues of Methodist expansion was through the conversions of so many in the military. See David Hempton, *Methodism: Empire of the Spirit* (New Haven, CT: Yale University Press, 2005), 20-21.

be seen in light of London's expansive population. London was an area of relative evangelical weakness. Walsh has pointed out that the Methodist message found fertile soil outside the hearing of church bells. London's ecclesiastical structure was nothing like the open spaces where Methodism flourished. Neither does it appear to have been entirely open to the very similar message of the Evangelicals.

PRODUCING DISSENT

As members of a fringe movement, the Evangelicals were in a precarious position. The ecclesiastical hierarchy saw them as little better than dissenters. Even after ordination—a process that could take years—many Evangelicals had difficulty finding employment within the Church. Romaine was not the only Evangelical to find opposition when appointed to a parish. Thomas Haweis encountered a similar situation in Northamptonshire that broke out into a public pamphlet war over his fitness for the position.[69]

Evangelical clergy status within the establishment made many of their converts uneasy about following their footsteps within the Church. Many Evangelical leaders were concerned that their efforts were producing the next generation of dissenting leadership.[70] Evangelicals were commonly accused of making dissenters, and in many cases the accusation was ac-

---

[69]See the case of the parish in Aldwincle, Northamptonshire, where Haweis was initially kept from the living for his Evangelical tendencies. Primary sources for the episode include Martin Madan, *An Answer to a Pamphlet, Intitled, a Faithful Narrative of Facts Relative to the Late Presentation of Mr H—s, to the Rectory of Al— W—le, in Northamptonshire* (London: Printed for E. & C. Dilly, J. Robson and J. Matthews, 1767); and Thomas Haweis, *A Supplement; Or, the Second Part of an Epistolary Correspondence Relative to the Living of Aldwinkle. Containing Several Important Letters, Now Forced to Be Made Public to Vindicate Injured Characters, and to Undeceive the Friends of Religion* (London: Printed for J. Wilkie and J. Walker, 1768). It should be noted that both of these sources were printed after Haweis had attained the living in 1764. He would remain there until his death in 1820.

[70]The ministry of Charles Simeon, which took place predominantly after the period under discussion here, can be seen in many ways as a response to this tendency to produce dissenters through an Evangelical ministry. See especially H. C. G. Moule, *Charles Simeon* (London: Methuen, 1892); William Carus, *Memoirs of the Life of the Rev. C. Simeon* (London: J. Hatchard and Son, 1846); Arthur Pollard and Michael Hennell, *Charles Simeon (1759–1836): Essays Written in Commemoration of His Bi-Centenary by Members of the Evangelical Fellowship for Theological Literature* (London: SPCK, 1959); and Charles Smyth, *Simeon and Church Order: A Study of the Origins of the Evangelical Revival in Cambridge in the Eighteenth Century* (Cambridge: Cambridge University Press, 1940).

curate. Yates writes that "without the Evangelical Revival it is likely that 'old dissent' would have been in terminal decline by 1815."[71]

Given the number of converts who became dissenters, many Evangelical leaders feared that the movement would end up outside the Church it meant to reform and move from a fringe movement of the Church to a fringe movement of the culture.[72] Charles Wesley opposed any action taken by Wesleyan Methodists that appeared to take them further afield from the regular ministry of the Church of England, and his views were commonplace among the Evangelicals of the parochial system.[73]

Henry Venn saw firsthand how his own ministry within the Church produced dissenting ministers. Hylson-Smith writes that out of Venn's ministry in Huddersfield "came twenty-two ordinands with working-class backgrounds," all of whom were unable to gain admittance to a university and who were subsequently "lost to the Church of England."[74] It was this loss of clerical candidates that was at the heart of the launch of the Elland Society, whose purpose was to promote and fund the education of Evangelical Anglicans seeking orders.[75] Venn, a key supporter of the society, was influential in the lives of the next generation of Evangelical leaders. His appointment to Yelling, with its proximity to Cambridge, enabled Venn to be instrumental in the lives of William Farish, Thomas Robinson, John Flavel, Charles Jerram and Charles Simeon, the latter one of the greatest leaders of the next generation.

---

[71]Yates, *Eighteenth-Century Britain*, 62. Watts makes the same claim in his three-volume work on the history of dissent (Michael R. Watts, *The Dissenters*, 3 vols. [New York: Oxford University Press, 1985–2015]). Rupp provides an alternative reading of the new rise of dissent, calling the theory that the Evangelical Revival gave dissent new birth "a half truth" (*Religion in England*, 486). What he does not provide, however, is the full defense that such a statement would require. His argument that revivals and dissenting academies untouched by evangelicalism gave rise to dissent in the later part of the century does not fully address the dearth of dissent before the revival and the blossoming of it afterward and in many of the locales where evangelicalism made great inroads. Walsh, for instance, claims that Methodism gave life to pockets of dissent, some of which remained in Methodism. A perfect example of this would be John Bennet's work in the north of England and his societies' history with Wesleyan Methodism.

[72]As examples of the creation of dissent out of the work of established clergy, both Samuel Walker's and Thomas Haweis's parishes spawned dissenting congregations following their departures.

[73]See Charles Wesley, *An Epistle to the Reverend Mr. John Wesley, by Charles Wesley, Presbyter of the Church of England* (London: 1755).

[74]Hylson-Smith, *Evangelicals in the Church of England*, 47.

[75]The papers of the Elland Society are soon to be published with an introduction by John Walsh.

Venn's congregation at Huddersfield left the Church after Venn left the parish, a result that greatly disturbed him.[76] His high estimation of the Church of England is obvious in his writings and especially his sermon "The Duty of a Parish Priest" (1760). He describes the duties of parish priests who have the care of souls and the Church of England as "a most benevolent institution of God; an Institution designed to diffuse the Knowledge of Himself; his Son, his Spirit, and his gospel; and by that Knowledge to make his Reasonable Creatures Holy and Happy." In Venn's words, "whoever is found frustrating, within the Compass of his own Province, an Institution of this Kind, is chargeable with a Crime, as much greater than that of Unfaithfulness to a Civil Trust, as the Salvation of Immortal Souls is more to be prized than the Things of Time."[77]

REVIVALISTS FOR THE CHURCH

An increase in the number of Evangelical clergy was essential to the survival of Evangelicalism, for at its very core it was a movement attached to the structures of the Church. Walsh writes that "only when it could capture some of the ordinands pumped out annually along the parochial arteries of the Church, could Anglican Evangelicalism make very much headway."[78] Walsh notes that the number of Evangelicals and their own security within the establishment were intimately connected.

> As the number of Evangelicals grew, so did their self-confidence and loyalty to the Church. They no longer despaired of Anglicanism as a Church populated by "heathenish priests and mitred infidels." They were less inclined to accept the embraces of Methodists, or to copy their irregular methods. They were more hopeful that the leaven of the Gospel would permeate the Anglican lump.[79]

---

[76]Hylson-Smith, *Evangelicals in the Church of England*, 47-48. For a fuller description of Venn's life and ministry, see John Venn, *Memoir of the Rev Henry Venn* (London: John Hatchard and Son, 1834).

[77]Henry Venn, *The Duty of a Parish-Priest; His Obligations to Perform It; and the Incomparable Pleasure of a Life Devoted to the Care of Souls. A Sermon, preach'd at a Visitation of the Clergy, held at Wakefield, July 2, 1760. H. Venn, A.M. vicar of Huddersfield, and late fellow of Queen's College, Cambridge. Published at the Request of Many of the Fearers* (1760), 10.

[78]Walsh, "Anglican Evangelicals in the Eighteenth Century," 90-91.

[79]Ibid., 91.

The ever-growing fraternity of Evangelical clergymen brought familiarity and normality to the once ragtag band. Their concern for clerical recruits was another indication, however, that they envisioned their ministry within the Church from the very beginning.

This Evangelical fraternity depended on an Evangelical network of clerical organizations, letters, itinerancy and to some extent the work of aristocrats converted to their message. Opposition to the movement was found throughout the ecclesiastical landscape. This opposition fueled fear among Evangelicals that they would create a movement detached from the Church. Driven by this fear, the clerical organizations they founded to create and sustain fraternal bonds specified rules identifying membership in the society as recognition of and participation in the established Church and its practices.[80] Wesley claimed similar restrictions and ultimately failed to convince his Methodists of the essential connection of the United Societies and the Church. Yet the spirit in which the Evangelicals promoted their cause differed from Wesley's because they refused to envision their work apart from the larger efforts of the Church.

The Evangelical Anglican desire to remain within the Church and eschew the second-class status of dissent was no act of Evangelical cowardice, however. Evangelicalism was seen as dangerous regardless of whether it functioned within the Church or not. As the closest, and therefore easiest, targets of Anglican concern over conversionist theology and practice, the Evangelicals were the first to feel the effects of censure. While Whitefield and Wesley were the most noted purveyors of a conversionistic theology, the Evangelical clergy, connected so much more intimately to the power structures of the Church, were likely to face hardships to which Wesley and Whitefield were immune. Some Evangelicals, such as William Jesse, came from aristocratic stock and had no reason to worry about the clash between their message and their means. Most were not in Jesse's situation but served as curates or perpetual curates with limited incomes.

---

[80]See the rules of Samuel Walker's societies and clerical bands in Samuel Walker, *Fifty Two Sermons, on the Baptismal Covenant, the Creed, the Ten Commandments, and Other Important Subjects . . . To Which Is Prefixed a Preface* (London: 1763), 1:xxx.

As the revival continued to unfold throughout the rest of the century, those in the Evangelical fraternity would serve as Wesley's closest allies within the parochial structures of the Church of England. They would also begin to pull away from Wesleyan Methodism as it developed an ethos all its own. Yet it was of this group of Evangelicals that Wesley saw himself a part, and even more so his brother.

2

MOVEMENT AND CONVERSION

Wesley in the Trans-Atlantic Revival

WESLEY'S EVANGELICAL CONVERSION should give any author pause. His relationship to Evangelicals in the Church of England, however, hinges to a great extent on a right historical interpretation of Wesley's Aldersgate experience. At Aldersgate Wesley was caught up in the larger sweep of the Evangelical Revival. Situating Wesley's conversion within the context of the revival enables the historian to see Wesley's place among the evangelicals of his day and their shared, but subjective, religious experiences.

The evangelical conversion stories so common among early evangelicals helped to spread the evangelical message and gave this international movement a common language.[1] Wesley scholars have rarely attempted to see Wesley or his conversion within the overarching context of the revival, and yet it is by such a placement that one begins to see Wesley the evangelical and the forces that shaped his evangelical impulse. Such a placement also highlights the currents that aided his ultimate separation from so many Evangelicals within the Church.

I explored how the term *evangelical* had multiple layers of meaning in the introduction. Within the emerging movement, just beginning to

---

[1]This common language and interdenominational appeal can be seen clearly in the response to Jonathan Edwards's *Faithful Narrative* (1737). George Marsden writes that "Edward's astonishing narrative created an immediate stir. It served as an inspiration for revivals in both Scotland and England" (*Jonathan Edwards: A Life* [New Haven, CT: Yale University Press, 2003], 172-73).

form a core set of leaders, the experience that identified evangelicals was their common experience of conversion. Bruce Hindmarsh describes this defining experience when he writes, "The consequence of the shared experience of conversion on the part of these leaders was that they discovered a common mission."[2] Additionally, these evangelical leaders "found their identities in their religious experience" and even defined themselves "by telling the stories of their conversions."[3] The Aldersgate experience of May 24, 1738, then, was not only Wesley's entrance into a larger spiritual movement but Wesley's evangelical conversion.[4]

As an evangelical conversion, the question is not whether John Wesley was a Christian before or after. Such a question is not necessary to the historical enterprise. Within Anglicanism the question of whether one was a Christian would have been directly related to baptism. Modern evangelicalism, mostly devoid of Anglicanism's sacramental theology, has been perplexed by the nature of Wesley's "conversion" in part because of an inability to place Wesley within the context of his Anglican heritage.

Wesley's experience and subsequent personal interpretations of the Aldersgate event provide necessary clues to Wesley's evangelical pedigree, and yet these personal accounts should be seen as the initial and then corrective interpretations of an experience that Wesley would attempt to come to terms with for the rest of his life. Aldersgate, seen as a conversion to evangelical Christianity, became the impulse behind Wesley's evangelistic efforts. The evangelical movement, defined by conversionism, was marked and would continue to be marked by the various and sometimes divergent interpretations of these transformational episodes.[5]

---

[2]D. Bruce Hindmarsh, *The Evangelical Conversion Narrative: Spiritual Autobiography in Early Modern England* (New York: Oxford University Press, 2005), 91.

[3]Ibid., 10. See David Hempton, *Methodism: Empire of the Spirit* (New Haven, CT: Yale University Press, 2005), 60-68, for a description of the place and use of personal stories of conversion and death scenes in the spread of Methodism. These narratives became ubiquitous in publications such as Wesley's *Arminian Magazine*.

[4]I emphasize the term *evangelical conversion* in order to stay clear of the theological debates surrounding the moment of Wesley's "conversion" to Christianity. As will be evident in the remainder of this chapter, I see little benefit to the debates that have surrounded that question. The use of the term *evangelical conversion* is an attempt to remain within the confines of what can objectively be said about the Aldersgate experience and the effect of the experience.

[5]The theological divide between Arminians and Calvinists was, at its root, a differing interpretation of the experience of conversion. See D. Bruce Hindmarsh, *John Newton and the English*

Placed within the trans-Atlantic revival, we can juxtapose the Aldersgate experience with similar experiences and the social and geographical movements that took place during the period. Such an interpretive lens provides insight not only into the felt spontaneity of the experience but also the centrality of the experience for the beginning of Wesley's revivalistic efforts. Ironically, debates over the meaning of Wesley's Aldersgate experience, especially among Methodist scholars, tend to locate the episode in isolation. Within this isolation it becomes possible to find ways to create an Aldersgate paradigm that looks more and more like the high church, low church or revivalist inclinations of the modern interpreter.[6]

To a large extent, Wesley retained his high church theological tendencies.[7] J. Ernest Rattenbury wrote in the first part of the last century:

> There is no greater mistake than to suppose that Wesley ceased to be a High Churchman after 1738. The popular argument that the Wesley before 1738 and after were two different men, with different views, is a modern Methodist myth which serious investigation proves to be without foundation. There were certain puerilities of his early ministry which Wesley

---

Evangelical Tradition: Between the Conversions of Wesley and Wilberforce (Grand Rapids: Eerdmans, 2001), 50-51, in which John Newton is quoted as arguing that Calvinism is the logical theological rationale for the evangelical experience of conversion. Henry Venn makes a similar claim when he writes that his Calvinism came from "a practical sense of his own unworthiness" (*The Letters of Henry Venn, with a Memoir by John Venn* [Carlisle, UK: Banner of Truth Trust, 1835, 1999], 31-32). For a discussion of the effect of this emphasis on a conversion experience on later generations and issues of generational transmission, see Glen Alton Messer II, "Restless for Zion: New England Methodism, Holiness, and the Abolitionist Struggle, Circa 1789–1845," ThD thesis (Boston University School of Theology, 2006), esp. 122.

[6]Scholars from the late nineteenth century provide the most obvious example of this reading. See L. Tyerman, *The Life and Times of the Rev. John Wesley, M.A., Founder of the Methodists*, 2nd ed. (New York: Harper, 1872) for a dissenting/low church reading. See D. Urlin, *The Churchman's Life of Wesley* (New York: SPCK, 1880) for a high church reading. More recently, see A. Skevington Wood, *The Burning Heart: John Wesley, Evangelist* (Minneapolis: Bethany Fellowship, 1967, 1978) for a revivalist/Wesleyan Holiness reading of the Aldersgate experience.

[7]Writing in 1938, J. Ernest Rattenbury says, "About seventy years ago Dr. J.H. Rigg, in opposition to [the view that Wesley was a high churchman] seems to have been chiefly responsible for the quite undemonstrable but popular modern Methodist opinion, that John Wesley changed from a High Church sacramentalist in 1738 to an evangelical preacher. This antithesis is really meaningless, and the references that Dr. Rigg made to Wesley's sacramentalism are often misleading" (*The Conversion of the Wesleys* [London: Epworth, 1938], 216-17). The debates in the late nineteenth and early twentieth centuries over Wesley's churchmanship often hinged on a particular author's view of the Oxford Movement.

outgrew, and the importance of certain beliefs and practices were seen in a new perspective, not merely by the illumination of his conversion, but by his practical experiences and busy occupation with affairs.[8]

This does not set him apart from every Evangelical. Thomas Adam had similar sympathies, as did many Oxonians, among whom high churchmanship has often found a home. Yet Wesley's high churchmanship offers a clue to his distinctiveness, and I will discuss it in terms of its political and theological implications in a later chapter.[9] What united Wesley to his Evangelical colleagues was that he, like them, was swept up into a larger movement that neither he nor they were ever able to grasp in its entirety. Wesley's evangelical perspective is made clear by his own experience of conversion, the message of his field preaching and the community he began to create within the Church.

THE EVANGELICAL SWEEP

There has been a recent push among scholars of the Evangelical Revival in England, especially by John Walsh, to free the revival from captivity to the British Isles.[10] W. Reginald Ward, following in the footsteps of W. Frank Swift and others, exposed an intercontinental—both European and North American—evangelical movement marked by ideological and physical movement. His work provides an historiographical approach to the sweep of evangelical revivalism from the Alps to the Appalachians.[11]

---

[8]Ibid., 175-76.

[9]The high church designation in the eighteenth century can largely be ascribed to those who gave preferential treatment in their arguments to the church fathers. The term is often confused with the later characteristics of the nineteenth-century Tractarians. In terms of high church political ambitions, the battles between Catholic and Reformed elements within English culture are well known. From Henry VIII up to Victoria's reign, the arguments between high and low churchmen, and their dissenting partners, were enmeshed in competing perspectives, both political and theological.

[10]See especially John Walsh's essay, "'Methodism' and the Origins of English-Speaking Evangelicalism," in Mark A. Noll, George A. Rawlyk and David W. Bebbington, eds., *Evangelicalism: Comparative Studies in Popular Protestantism in North American, the British Isles, and Beyond, 1700–1900* (New York: Oxford University Press, 1994).

[11]For another view of this sweep, one that takes seriously Ward's work, see Hempton, *Methodism*, esp. 13-16, 46; and Hempton, *The Church in the Long Eighteenth Century* (New York: I. B. Tauris, 2011), 40-45.

Ward's sweeping narrative provides a framework in which to interpret the importance of Aldersgate. This evangelical sweep was propelled out of the pressure cooker of central European political and religious conflict created by the clash of Lutheran Orthodoxy and a resurgent Tridentine Roman Catholicism.[12] It was this conflict that, in the case of the Protestant Salzburger diaspora of 1729, inadvertently spread a form of pietistic religion well beyond the Pietist strongholds of Halle and Teschen. Ward argues that the beginning of the populist religious movement known as the Evangelical Revival can be traced to Pietism and specifically to its metamorphosis in the face of political initiatives that caused Pietists to move across Europe and even the Atlantic in search of warmer ecclesiastical climates.

Piestism itself was created in ecclesiastical tension. According to Ward, the movement known as Pietism began as a reaction to criticism of Philip Spener's *Pia Desideria*. Pietists were led to the formation of a group of opposition to the opposition.[13] Spener's ideas of *collegia pietatis* initially found favor in Saxony and among Leipzig theologians. His hope of bringing reform to theological training spearheaded a lay-led movement that turned from Aristotelian logic, foundational in Lutheran and Roman Catholic theology, to an emphasis on the priesthood of all believers. Ward writes that this turn toward a universal priesthood led the newly formed Pietists well beyond Spener's original intentions.[14]

Persecution in Leipzig did not squelch this drive for piety but served to spread the movement further. In turn, opposition to Spener's efforts led his followers to achieve group cohesion apart from established ecclesiastical structures. The movement Spener started, much like the movement John Wesley would start in England, was not firmly wedded to the ecclesiastical structures he had wished to reform.

When Pietism was faced with religious persecution, the ensuing explosion of geographical displacement, revival and expansion spear-

---

[12]W. R. Ward, *The Protestant Evangelical Awakening* (New York: Cambridge University Press, 2004), 16.
[13]W. R. Ward, *Christianity Under the Ancien Régime, 1648–1789* (New York: Cambridge University Press, 1999), 77.
[14]Ibid.

headed a revivalistic movement that appears to have revived a Protestant world slowly losing steam. The unfortunate circumstances of the displaced Pietists gave Protestant Europe an issue around which to form a rallying cry, undermining the psychological effects of a Jesuit-inspired Roman Catholic resurgence that had dramatically cut into Protestant numbers. Ward writes that "everyone knew that the Protestants had lost perhaps half their numerical strength; and almost every change seemed to be for the worse."[15] J. C. D. Clark describes the situation in terms of a Roman Catholic counter-reformation that on the European continent was "everywhere on the offensive," with "Protestantism in retreat, and Protestants subject to the most lurid fears for the future."[16] Protestant malaise was felt from Prussia to the American colonies. As Roman Catholicism spread alongside the rise of both Spanish and Portuguese colonial enterprises, Protestantism had not only stalled but declined on account of forces both internal and external.[17] The Catholic "menace," however, was caught up in its own struggles both within the church and among the Catholic powers. The imagined Roman threat far outpaced the actual threat of Jesuit efforts within the strongholds of Protestant Germany and England. Its power to unite Protestantism, however, was as real as the actual threat was imaginary.[18]

---

[15]Ward, *Protestant Evangelical Awakening*, 16.

[16]J. C. D. Clark, *English Society, 1660–1832: Religion, Ideology, and Politics During the Ancien Régime* (New York: Cambridge University Press, 2000), 67.

[17]Some missiologists argue that Protestant theological interest in predestination also created an antimissionary spirit within it that kept it out of the mission fields where Roman Catholics found fertile soil for native conversions. This, in turn, fed the already depressed mood of European Protestantism as it began to feel more and more the minority. See Justo L. González, *The Story of Christianity*, vol. 2, *The Reformation to the Present Day* (New York: HarperCollins, 1985), 208. See also Andrew Porter, *Religion Versus Empire? British Protestant Missionaries and Overseas Expansion, 1700–1914* (New York: Manchester University Press, 2004), esp. 17-20, and the first page of the preamble to the charter of the Society for the Propagation of the Gospel, which specifically emphasizes the danger of English colonists being caught up in "Popish superstition and idolatry."

Linda Colley writes that "the overwhelming Catholicism of large parts of Continental Europe, and especially France and Spain, provided a newly-invented Britain with a formidable 'other' against which it could usefully define itself," and one that ultimately "allowed the different Protestant traditions of Scotland, Wales, and England to come together in a common union of self-preservation, anxiety, and defiance" (*Britons: Forging the Nation, 1707–1837*, 2nd ed. [New Haven, CT: Yale University Press, 2005], xvi).

[18]Ward calls the Jacobites—who would make two attempts to overthrow the Hanoverians during

The united Protestant voice opposing Roman Catholic persecution of the Pietists led to the Swedish invasion of central Europe under Charles XII on a crusade to "save Protestantism" but also to the outbreak of religious revival oftentimes attached to movement.[19] As those displaced by religious persecution left their homes, local revivals sprang up with their passing cadence. And with the rise of print culture and voluminous letter writing across confessional, national and continental lines, the story of the Pietist march across Europe spread like wildfire.[20]

The printed word was vital to spreading news of the displaced Pietists and their message of heart religion. One famous print that left a lasting impression on European Protestantism was the image of a displaced Salzburg woman trudging through muddy roads with eyes set on a new home, a child under one arm and her Luther Bible firmly clasped under the other. Ward writes that in Germany "by reprint, quotation and reference, as far away as America, the language of hyperbole, if not of miracle, was standard form. The newspaper press had a field day, and sermons and pamphlets are reckoned to have run to 500 titles."[21]

The print culture of early eighteenth-century Europe and North America would play an essential role in the spread of Pietism and evangelicalism.[22] Albert Outler argues that Wesley's reading of Jonathan Edwards's account of the revival in New England was as pivotal to Wesley's development as the Aldersgate experience itself![23] Wesley, perhaps even more so than his Anglican colleagues, understood the

---

the first half of the eighteenth century and who held prominent positions in Oxford and Manchester and throughout Scotland—a real "menace." See Ward, *Protestant Evangelical Awakening*, 17. See James Axtell, *The Invasion Within: The Contest of Cultures in Colonial North America* (New York: Oxford University Press, 1985), for Protestant efforts in New England to combat Jesuit influence from Canada.

[19]See the effects of movement on trans-Atlantic Methodism in Hempton's *Methodism*, especially his chapter "Competition and Symbiosis."

[20]Ward, *Protestant Evangelical Awakening*, 105-6.

[21]Ibid., 105.

[22]See Isabel Rivers, ed., *Books and Their Readers in Eighteenth-Century England* (Leicester, UK: Leicester University Press, 1982); and *Books and Their Readers in the Eighteenth Century: New Essays* (New York: Continuum, 2001).

[23]Albert Outler, ed., *John Wesley* (New York: Oxford University Press, 1964), 15. See also Marsden, *Jonathan Edwards*, 173.

importance of printing the accounts of personal transformation.[24] Conversion, it appears, often accompanied the spread of these conversion stories.[25]

Hindmarsh describes the "voluminous correspondence of the evangelicals" as the "paper parallel to their restless itinerancy," linking both written and homiletical discourse within the same common evangelistic impulse.[26] Similarly, Susan O'Brien describes the correspondence among Calvinist evangelicals of the time as creating a trans-Atlantic evangelical consciousness. This consciousness was encouraged by print culture, but more specifically through personal correspondence that promoted the creation of evangelical networks and spread the message of the movement. "Minister and lay promoters extended the correspondence into a reliable, nonpersonal system of contacts, which they developed into a number of procedures for spreading the news from individuals to groups of committed laity and beyond to a wider lay audience."[27] Isolated correspondents discussed practical and theological issues with likeminded evangelicals on both sides of the Atlantic. O'Brien claims that "it is not too much to say that through the exchange of ideas and materials Calvinist revivalists of the mid-eighteenth century built a 'community of saints' that cut across physical barriers and, on occasion, theological divisions."[28]

Like the impact of correspondence on the revival and the creation of evangelical networks, the knowledge of the Salzburgers' plight engen-

---

[24]For example, Wesley's continued printing of Methodist death accounts can only rightly be seen as an evangelistic tool to spread an evangelical theology of experience and assurance. Such assurance of salvation, based often on the experience of the New Birth, was said to give Methodists peace even in the face of death.

[25]As an example, see Mark Noll's description of the impact of Jonathan Edwards's *Faithful Narrative,* and especially its publication in London, in *The Rise of Evangelicalism: The Age of Edwards, Whitefield and the Wesleys* (Downers Grove, IL: InterVarsity Press, 2003), 90-92. In terms of the Wesleys' conversions themselves, John's conversion was spurred on by Charles's conversion three days previous, and both of the Wesleys were spurred on by George Whitefield's conversion experience. For a description of Whitefield's conversion, see Harry S. Stout, *The Divine Dramatist: George Whitefield and the Rise of Modern Evangelicalism* (Grand Rapids: Eerdmans, 1991), 26-29.

[26]Hindmarsh, *Evangelical Conversion Narrative,* 74.

[27]Susan O'Brien, "A Transatlantic Community of Saints: The Great Awakening and the First Evangelical Network, 1735–1755," *The American Historical Review* 91 (October 1986): 813.

[28]Ibid.

dered renewed passion among Protestants. Ward describes the impact of the Salzburgers' expulsion:

> The religious shock administered by the Salzburgers' march across Europe was tremendous. The simple knowledge that they were coming inspired "moving awakenings" (*bewegliche Erweckungen*); the enthusiasts who stood at the fountainhead of religious revival in the west of the Empire now held that the secret increase of the hidden kingdom of God had reached the point where outbreaks might be expected anywhere.[29]

This "simple knowledge" was a distinctly replicable component. The experiential nature of the revival appeared to be replicable through means of communication. And it was replicable through something as personable as a private letter, the narration of a conversion account or the efforts of an evangelist proclaiming the New Birth in the English countryside.[30]

MOVEMENT AND FERVOR

The movement of persons has recently been described as one major factor that propelled the Evangelical Revival and made possible its international reach. Hempton describes a triangle composed of the Pietist strongholds of Halle and Teschen, London and Oxford, and colonial Georgia as the three corners of an evangelical frontier in which religious experience was traded much like a commodity. He writes that in the early eighteenth century "an unlikely combination of Moravian and Anglican enthusiasm for mission on the frontier of Britain's new American empire soon opened up a more benign religious version of the infamous triangular trade of slavery and cotton that fueled the economics of empire."[31] Hempton's description of Methodism as an "empire of the Spirit" can easily be ascribed to the work of evangelicalism within and without Wesley's authoritarian reach.[32]

---

[29]Ward, *Protestant Evangelical Awakening*, 106.

[30]See, for example, William Grimshaw's conversion narrative in William Myles, *The Life and Writings of the Revd. William Grimshaw* (London: Printed at the Conference Office by Thomas Cordeaux, 1813). Grimshaw was converted by hearing the sermon of a lay preacher.

[31]Hempton, *Methodism*, 13.

[32]However, in Hempton's work, the "empire" that Wesley built is much more easily identifiable in that Wesley and his ecclesiastical heirs built a movement and subsequent church structure in line with the organizational characteristics of empires.

Wesley visited one corner of Hempton's evangelical triangle and lived in the other two. The Society for the Propagation of the Gospel, formed in 1701, brought both John and Charles Wesley to the American colonies, and it was en route to their appointments that the brothers first encountered Moravianism.[33] The Wesleys, however, were not devoid of experiential religion before this encounter with Pietism.[34] The idea that Wesley was brought up in the Church of England with a bland form of religious piety is erroneous. The dying words of John and Charles's father, Samuel Wesley Sr., spoke to the centrality of experience in the Christian life when he said that the "inward witness" was "the strongest proof, of Christianity."[35]

Yet it was in the religiously diverse context of colonial Georgia that Wesley first encountered a form of experiential religion that challenged the definition of "Christian" for the Oxford don turned frontier missionary.[36] Ward writes that "virtually all the clergy serving in America (outside New England) in the early eighteenth century were brought in from abroad, whether from England, Scotland, Ireland, Sweden, Germany, the Netherlands or Switzerland."[37] Georgia and the Carolinas were prime examples of this clerical diversity. The Moravian settlement of Wachovia served as a Pietist stronghold in the region. Additionally, Roman Catholics in Florida and the Mississippi River valley surrounded English settlements. This made for a form of religious diversity but also caused concern over the spread of "popery" and the influence of competing European powers.

---

[33] *Works* 18:137.

[34] See original manuscript letter, in which Charles describes his ailing father and the comfort a Christian should have in the face of death. This letter, written three years before Charles Wesley's evangelical conversion, is loaded with the language of experiential religion. Charles Wesley to The Revd Mr Wesley [Samuel Jr.], Devon; Dated March 25, 1735, from Ch[rist] Church, in Wesley Historical Society Library at Oxford Brookes University, Oxford, UK.

[35] *Works* 26:289. Interestingly enough, the Charles Wesley letter of 1735 referenced in the previous footnote conveys a picture of Samuel's death that shows that Samuel's assurance in the face of death as seen in John's 1747 letter was either overstated or was something Samuel attained in his last month.

[36] See Geordan Hammond, *John Wesley in America: Restoring Primitive Christianity* (New York: Oxford University Press, 2014). Hammond provides the most comprehensive treatment of Wesley's missionary endeavor in Georgia and particularly Wesley's intent to create a center of "primitive Christianity" in colonial Georgia.

[37] Ward, *Protestant Evangelical Awakening*, 5-6.

During this period nonjuroring Anglicanism and heart-warmed Moravians of the Pietist diaspora held the attention of Wesley. It would be the amalgamation of high churchmanship and heart religion that would define Wesley's theological outlook and evangelistic impulses throughout the rest of his life. Walsh describes Wesley's "rubrical High Churchmanship" as having been "cross-fertilised by the heart-religion of the Germans."[38] It was heart religion, however, not high churchmanship, that propelled Wesley into the fields by 1739, and this propulsion only took place subsequent to Wesley's evangelical conversion. This phenomenon of a high churchman and Tory acting the part of a Puritan from the previous century was only made possible by Wesley's conversion experience.

Garth Lean's description of the Aldersgate experience as "destiny accepted" rightly connects Wesley's conversion with the evangelical impulse that followed.

> While it is true that Wesley's basic characteristics remained constant—such characteristics are generally heightened or re-directed rather than obliterated by conversion—the words "psychological reassurance" seem strangely inadequate to describe the effect on Wesley. For Bready is unquestionably right when he says in his massive study that if Wesley had died in his thirty-fifth year he would have been "an unremembered man—capable, methodical, hard-working, but pedantic, legalistic, irascible; unloved and well-nigh unlovable."[39]

The sweep of the Evangelical Revival thrust Wesley and his fellow evangelicals out, literally, proclaiming a gospel of personal transformation marked by the experience of the New Birth.

CAUGHT UP IN THE SWEEP

A historiographical approach to John Wesley's place in the revival should begin by locating Wesley within the equalizing context of revivalism. To

---

[38]John Walsh, *John Wesley 1703–1791: A Bicentennial Tribute* (London: Friends of Dr. William's Library, 1993), 9.

[39]Gareth Lean, *John Wesley, Anglican* (London: Blandford, 1964), 34-35.

set Wesley up, for instance, as the father of English evangelicalism[40] or as the exclusive father of Methodism is to miss the larger picture. The leaders, like the single female Methodist, were propelled by a conversion experience. Wesley, like his band member, should be seen as a part of a larger egalitarian narrative of revivalistic fervor. The conversion experience and the propulsion that followed, nurtured by other conversionists, marked one as an evangelical in this earliest period of the revival.

Placing Wesley within the larger conversionistic movement rescues the revival from national or denominational dependency. Yet given the emphasis on conversion experiences, individual characteristics must be taken into account. The characteristics, assumptions and ecclesiastical loyalties that each person brought with them into the revival added depth to the inchoate movement and would also provide later points of conflict.[41] Theologically, Evangelicals within the Church did not take a uniform stance apart from justification, the New Birth and the need for holy living. Wesley brought with him both his high churchmanship and his Jacobite tendencies, and these would help lay the basis for his divergence from Evangelical Anglicans. Ward describes Wesley's Jacobite tendencies and their source in his upbringing in no uncertain terms:

> There is no doubt that this upbringing marked Wesley lifelong. Born into a Jacobite milieu, the younger brother of a (non-Methodist) collaborator of Bishop Atterbury, Wesley did not adopt the world as his parish; indeed his one substantial trip abroad was to a nest of Jacobites in Georgia, headed by General Oglethorpe, who had been christened James Edward for the Old (Jacobite) Pretender.[42]

---

[40]See G. R. Balleine, *A History of the Evangelical Party in the Church of England* (London: Longmans, Green, 1909). Balleine begins his history of the movement not with larger intercontinental movements of the Spirit but with Oxford Methodism and the meetings held in John and Charles Wesley's Oxford rooms. This is a standard historiographical interpretation of the rise of evangelicalism in Britain.

[41]Wesley points to the influx of dissenters into Wesleyan Methodism as the principal reason behind Methodism's gradual divergence from the Church of England late in his life. See his sermon "On Attending the Church Service," *Works* 3:466. See also in *Works*, sermon no. 32, "Sermon on the Mount, XII," I.7 and n.; see also no. 107, "On God's Vineyard," II.8. For what Outler describes as "the notion that nonconformity was imported into what had been Anglican societies" (*Works* 3:466 n.7), cf. Wesley's letter to Henry Brooke, June 14, 1786.

[42]W. R. Ward, *Early Evangelicalism: A Global Intellectual History, 1670–1789* (New York: Cambridge University Press, 2006), 119.

Debates between Tractarians and Methodists over "rights" to Wesley in the 1870s were grounded in the apparent dichotomy of evangelicalism and high churchmanship that collided in him.[43]

THE ALDERSGATE EXPERIENCE

The purpose of this chapter is to assess Wesley the evangelical. Yet Wesley the maverick Anglican with both high church and evangelical tendencies complicates the picture. The obvious place to further pursue such an assessment is Wesley's conversion narrative itself.[44] Wesley recorded the experience in his journal in words that came to define the Wesleyan movement worldwide. As part of a much larger entry he wrote:

> In the evening I went very unwillingly to a society in Aldersgate Street, where one was reading Luther's Preface to the Epistle to the Romans. About a quarter before nine, while he was describing the change which God works in the heart through faith in Christ, I felt my heart strangely warmed. I felt I did trust in Christ, Christ alone for salvation, and an assurance was given me that he had taken away *my* sins, even *mine*, and saved *me* from the law of sin and death.[45]

This was Wesley's entrance into evangelicalism. By faith in Christ alone he had been granted assurance of salvation. Yet, what it meant was not clear for Wesley even then.

---

[43]See Rattenbury's comments in *Wesley's Legacy to the World*, especially his chapter "The Wesleys and Modern Religious Movements" (J. Ernest Rattenbury, *Wesley's Legacy to the World: Six Studies in the Permanent Values of the Evangelical Revival* [London: Epworth Press, 1928]). Full-length biographies, such as R. D. Urlin's the *Churchman's Life of Wesley*, were written to claim Wesley for the high church/Anglo-Catholic parties of the later nineteenth century, to the horror of many a Methodist.

[44]Historical-theological analyses of the Aldersgate experience seen apart from the Aldersgate experience's placement among the many conversions of the period, the larger picture of political and social movements, and the critical objectivity necessary to describe the event have created or encouraged hagiographical and problematic sketches of Wesley's life. A. Skevington Wood's description of Wesley's Aldersgate as "epoch-making" (*Burning Heart*, 59-69), and Rupert Davies's description (Rupert Davies, *Methodism* [London: Epworth, 2003], 57-60) of a total change after Aldersgate of Wesley's experiential, psychological and theological outlook, for example, overdramatize the experience and all too easily fit revivalist patterns prevalent in later Methodist practice that do not fit the historical context of the experience itself.

[45]*Works* 18:249-50.

Ward states the case distinctly: "There can be no agreement as to whether Wesley's conversion experience was a conversion or not as long as there is no agreement about what constitutes conversion."[46] Even the Wesleys altered their basic understanding of conversion. Early on they conjoined the conversion experience with that of assurance. In later life they saw this as a humorous mistake.[47] Their description of communion as a "converting ordinance" is indication that Wesley used the term in multiple ways, including a move from a less "serious" to a more "serious" form of Christianity. The stories of English evangelicals' conversions often describe a transition from nominal to experiential Christianity. Ward writes that the historian's task is "to assess what the practical effect of the experience was" and goes on to give a "slightly polemical edge" to Henry Rack's arguments in *Reasonable Enthusiast* to claim that "Wesley's conversion was a failed attempt to become a Moravian."[48] With blunt wit he writes:

> [Wesley's] failure to become a High-Church Pharisee, and his failure to become a successful working mystic and Indian missionary, has been followed by a failure to undergo a Moravian conversion. In the event this was no great loss, since it is impossible to imagine Wesley and Zinzendorf cooperating in the same religious community for long.[49]

[46]Ward, *Early Evangelicalism*, 126. In regard to the word *conversion*, volumes have been written on its definition within the Wesleyan tradition. See, for example, Kenneth J. Collins and John H. Tyson, *Conversion in the Wesleyan Tradition* (Nashville: Abingdon, 2001), for a collection of essays on this highly debated topic.

[47]See Henry D. Rack, *Reasonable Enthusiast: John Wesley and the Rise of Methodism*, 3rd ed. (Philadelphia: Trinity Press International, 2002), 393. This change should come as no surprise. Richard Heitzenrater in his article on the Aldersgate text, in a volume edited by Randy L. Maddox (*Aldersgate Revisited* [Nashville: Abingdon, 1990], 49-91), argues persuasively that Wesley's Aldersgate experience was his experience of the evangelical doctrine of assurance. I have here argued that in the general sweep of the Evangelical Revival, Aldersgate was Wesley's "evangelical conversion," and I see no conflict with that terminology and Heitzenrater's assessment. If the experience of assurance created John Wesley the Evangelical, so be it. Maddox's volume of essays contains primarily theological-historical attempts to place Wesley's Aldersgate within the context of Wesley's life and subsequently in the life of later Methodist Christians. The preface of the work provides the focus of the collection, described as questions related to "the dynamic spirituality of Wesley and his early followers" and how "such vital Christian commitments [can] be renewed today." The book was written in the aftermath of the 250th anniversary of Wesley's Aldersgate experience and debates within United Methodism. Not all historical-theological analysis has provided such careful reading of texts, and not every essay in the collection is helpful to the historian's task.

[48]Ward, *Early Evangelicalism*, 127.

[49]Ibid.

The marks of these "failed" conversions appear in Wesley's theological works and practical endeavors throughout his life. The amalgamation of high church, Pietest and evangelical elements within Wesley would often put him at odds with each of these groups. Ward ultimately locates Wesley's conversion with his embrace of the practice of field preaching.[50] Such placement, if seen in conjunction with Wesley's encounter with international Pietism, his search for assurance and the Aldersgate event itself would make sense. As shown in the Aldersgate experience's placement in the public *Journal* as the culminating experience of his early ministry followed by other conversion accounts, it should be seen as Wesley's evangelical conversion experience. Aldersgate became the pattern that Wesley promoted throughout his ministry.

H. Bruce Hindmarsh, in his book *The Evangelical Conversion Narrative*, supplies the most comprehensive analysis of the Aldersgate experience within the context of eighteenth-century conversion narratives. Taken together with Ward's concept of an evangelical trans-Atlantic awakening, Hindmarsh's analysis provides a needed perspective on Aldersgate that looks beyond historical-theological arguments over text analysis.

Hindmarsh begins his work with a discussion of the place of "conversion" in English Christianity in the eighteenth century and particularly narratives of spiritual autobiography as they fed into the Evangelical Revival. These streams included a "native tradition of Puritan and Nonconformist spiritual autobiography and teaching about conversion," along with British, American and Continental Pietism.[51] What Hindmarsh finds is "discernible continuity in evangelical experience that recalled Puritan teaching and practice."[52] This continuity with Puritanism appears in the patterns of the revival, through the spread of revival accounts, the eighteenth century's rise of print news, letter writing and movement. Within the context of expectation and revivalistic fervor,

---

[50]Ibid., 128.
[51]Hindmarsh, *Evangelical Conversion Narrative*, 59.
[52]Ibid., 62.

"narratives of conversion by men and women, leaders and laypeople, published and unpublished, began to multiply."[53]

Alongside these evangelical conversion narratives, Wesley's Aldersgate narrative becomes one conversion narrative among many across the trans-Atlantic world. Mark Noll and Hindmarsh describe the conversions of the leaders of the Evangelical Revival in relative isolation from one another.[54] Yet the picture of Ward's "sweep," Hempton's picture of Pietist/evangelical movement, and the renewal of Puritan patterns of spiritual narrative autobiography, as outlined by Hindmarsh, provide interconnectedness to what appear to be episodic conversions. John Wesley's conversion was inspired by his encounter with Peter Böhler and the Moravians, George Whitefield's 1735 conversion and his brother's conversion a week before his own.[55] These conversions did not happen in isolation but had a spontaneity that undermines any attempt to place a restrictive pattern on their interrelatedness.

Hindmarsh provides text analysis that considers the structure of the *Journal* itself and the larger streams of piety informing the rise of early evangelicalism in Britain. Wesley's *Journal* was not an autobiography but a polemical narrative on the Evangelical Revival and Wesleyan Methodism's place within it.[56] Hindmarsh describes Wesley's *Journal* as not "a subjective autobiography in any thoroughgoing sense" but one that "contained passages of reflexive narrative and self-interpretation."[57] Similarly, Ted Campbell describes Wesley's *Journal* as "apologetic literature published at very particular moments in his career."[58] Thus the *Journal* should be seen within the controversies that had embroiled Wesley; it was written not only for a public audience that read Wesley's accounts but also his opponents, to whom Wesley often replied through the print *Journal*.

---

[53]Ibid.

[54]Ibid., 91; Noll, *Rise of Evangelicalism*, esp. 76-99.

[55]See S. T. Kimbrough Jr. and Kenneth G. C. Newport, *The Manuscript Journal of the Reverend Charles Wesley, M. A.* (Nashville: Kingswood Books, 2007), 1:106-8.

[56]See the introduction to Wesley's *Journal* in *Works* 18:37-61.

[57]Hindmarsh, *Evangelical Conversion Narrative*, 117.

[58]Ted A. Campbell, "John Wesley as Diarist and Correspondent," in *The Cambridge Companion to John Wesley*, ed. Randy L. Maddox and Jason E. Vickers (New York: Cambridge University Press, 2010), 137.

The episodes that mark the earliest installment of Wesley's *Journal* included colonial battles over Sophey Hopkey and Wesley's Jacobite-inspired liturgical experiments in Georgia;[59] the William Morgan affair at Oxford, in which early Methodist practice was thought to lead to Morgan's early death; charges of "enthusiasm" from colleagues and ecclesiastical elites; rumors that Wesley was a Papist; the "free grace" controversy that broke out with the followers of Whitefield; and finally the Wesleyan/English Moravian split over quietism. The journal account of Aldersgate was not published until these events were all in public view.[60] Within this context, the Aldersgate experience forms the crux of Wesley's first three journal installments and his own theology of conversion. Hindmarsh notes:

> It is significant that the second *Journal* appeared only four months after the first. No subsequent *Journals* were printed so closely together, and most appeared at intervals of two or three years. The second *Journal* was unmistakably the sequel to the first. That the theme of this second *Journal* would be conversion is evident not only from the motto and from the incompleteness, or even the note of suspense, of the first *Journal*, but also from the manner in which Wesley's experience on 24 May 1738 is set off as momentous, and the fact that this second *Journal* concludes with no less than eleven specimen conversion narratives that Wesley recounts from interviews conducted at Herrnhut.[61]

Wesley's view of Aldersgate, despite his later corrections to the text, provides a paradigm of conversion. The construction of the narrative is indicative of Wesley's intentions for the text. As Hindmarsh writes, Wesley's Aldersgate experience "was not an isolated or passing experience: it was a model."[62] That, as Ward writes, Aldersgate was a "failed" Moravian conversion is also informative. Wesley's failure to become a Moravian is due to the lasting, formative effect of Wesley's Anglican heritage.

Wesley experience had to be put into the terminology of the Anglican high churchmanship that continued to be the bedrock of his theological

---

[59]See especially Frank Baker's analysis in *John Wesley and the Church of England* (London: Epworth, 1970), 39-57.
[60]See Hindmarsh, *Evangelical Conversion Narrative*, 116.
[61]Ibid., 119.
[62]Ibid., 125.

outlook. Wesley was an English Christian shaped by the history, liturgy and terminology of English Christianity. Such crucial elements of his theology as his definition of grace can be found in the "Collect for Grace" in the Prayer Book's Morning Prayer service. Even his justification of his ordinations in 1784 for the Methodist work in America was informed by Anglican authors Stillingfleet and King, as well as the debates within English Christianity over the nature of clerical orders. Wesley's Aldersgate narrative provided early Methodism with a conversionist model using the terminology of Anglicanism, a vision made possible because of his heartwarming experience.

A RELIGIOUS POLLEN FACTORY: THE FETTER LANE SOCIETY

In his book *Methodism: Empire of the Spirit*, Hempton provides a socio-historical account of the rise of trans-Atlantic Methodism. He also describes the Fetter Lane Society, with which Wesley was affiliated during the time of his evangelical conversion. Hempton describes the society as a "religious pollen factory," an apt title that encapsulates the volatile nature of early evangelicalism in London and the setting in which Wesley's conversion needs to be seen. Heitzenrater describes Fetter Lane as a community with a soteriological agenda, one where "the spiritual health of the participants" was its primary focus.[63] This "religious pollen factory" was the local outpost of the larger movement. Specifically, it was the locality able to spawn such evangelical luminaries as the Wesley brothers and George Whitefield, among others.

Hempton's list of the characters involved in the Fetter Lane Society rightly points to the religious and geographical conglomeration that was Fetter Lane. His list includes "German visitors to London, Calvinist evangelicals, Welsh revivalists, French Prophets, London's artisan pietists, and English High Churchmen like the Wesleys."[64] From its inception Fetter Lane had been at the crossroads of Pietistic movement. As Colin Podmore makes clear in his work on English Moravianism of the

---

[63]Richard P. Heitzenrater, *Wesley and the People Called Methodists*, 2nd ed. (Nashville: Abingdon, 2013), 87.
[64]Hempton, *Methodism*, 14.

period, what led to the founding of the Fetter Lane Society was a visit by four Moravians from the continent, three of whom were traveling to the Moravian settlement in Georgia and a fourth who intended to visit "the remnant of a German society founded by Zinzendorf in 1737."[65] One of these four, Peter Boehler, had been commissioned by Zinzendorf to visit Oxford's students—thus Boehler's connection to John Wesley.[66] Podmore describes a fraternal network that would overlap with the Evangelical fraternity, a network of evangelicals of various stripes connected to the Wesleys, Whitefield and James Hutton through the religious societies that existed in 1730s London, all of whom would form the core of the Fetter Lane Society.[67]

Wesley's conversion should first be approached within the context of international movement. To approach his conversion exclusively through the *Journal* account or the later corrections he imposed on the narrative is to miss the fact that Wesley was swept up by something perhaps difficult for the individual participant to conceive. Hindmarsh asserts that John Wesley's first *Journal* illustrates this movement of people well, "since it was on ship and in remote Georgia in 1736 that Wesley, an English clergyman, was provoked to spiritual anxiety by the questions of believers whose religious fervour had originated deep in central Europe."[68]

Included in this international context, both of the Wesley brothers' conversions were part of a wave of religious and political shifts colliding in contexts such as Fetter Lane. These larger religious and political shifts included fears of deism on one side and a resurgent post-Tridentine Catholicism or English Jacobitism on the other. It must be remembered that deism was seen as a soulless invention and that, until the Catholic Emancipation Act of 1829, Britishness and Protestantism went hand in hand. Contemporary fears included frustration born of an antiquated ecclesi-

---

[65]Colin Podmore, *The Moravian Church in England, 1728–1760* (Oxford: Clarendon, 1998), 30. Podmore's larger description of the social, religious and political context in which the Fetter Lane Society was located is very useful to understanding its connection to Wesley and other Evangelicals.

[66]Ibid., 32.

[67]For Podmore's description of Fetter Lane's connection to these societies, see esp. 34-36.

[68]Hindmarsh, *Evangelical Conversion Narrative*, 70.

astical structure in the Church, as well as pamphlets and reports from religious outbursts and persecutions from the Alps to the Appalachians.[69] The intensity of small groups such as Fetter Lane challenged the brothers' assurance of salvation and added additional spark to a volatile situation. Wesley's warmed heart was the natural outgrowth of a culture that had reached the boiling point both politically and spiritually and provided fertile soil for the continental message of heart religion.

The Fetter Lane period of Wesley's life and the "pollen factory" have been described by Rack as "a highly-charged charismatic atmosphere in which [Wesley] thought he saw the scenes of the Acts of the Apostles, reproduced with all the strange gifts of the apostolic age, repeated: not only instant conversion but visions, demon-possession and healing."[70] The nature of the Fetter Lane Society appears to have been widely known. John Clayton, the inspiration behind much of Oxford Methodism's interest in early church practice—a high church characteristic—wrote a letter to Wesley on the day of his evangelical conversion. Clayton was concerned that Wesley was showing marks of an enthusiast.

> Indeed we are greatly afraid for you, and doubt that you are running yourself into difficulties beyond your strength to bear. We all see and rejoice at your sincerity and zeal, and pray fervently for your perseverance therein. But we think ourselves likewise obliged to beseech Almighty God to give you a right judgment in all things, that so your zeal may be tempered by prudence, and you may have the light of the gospel as well as the heat.[71]

Typical of the period and its calls for reason and moderation, the letter, written very near the Jacobite stronghold of Manchester, is proof that Wesley's plunge into the world of evangelicalism was public knowledge. Clayton's view is typical of the view that will come to define Wesley's

---

[69]The best known of these publications is likely Jonathan Edwards's *A Faithful Narrative of the Surprising Work of God*, describing the revival that took place in New England in the 1730s. Published journals, such as Wesley's and Whitefield's, also served later to promote revivalism in print in a very similar way.

[70]Rack, *Reasonable Enthusiast*, 187.

[71]*Works* 25:538-39 (letter to John Wesley from the Revd. John Clayton, Salford [May 1, 1738]).

image in the minds of many a parish priest in the Church of England.

John Wesley was not the only Wesley brother to receive such pleas from concerned friends. Charles Wesley experienced what he called his "Pentecost" on May 21, 1738. The next day he recorded in his journal that "an old friend called to see me under great apprehensions that I was running mad."[72] This unnamed friend, likely an Oxford colleague, had heard that Charles had embraced experiential religion and pleaded with him to leave London. It appears from Charles's journal that some within the Wesleys' circle were well aware of the religious zealotry stemming from the Fetter Lane Society. Charles records:

> His fears were not a little increased by my telling him the prayer of faith had healed me, when sick at Oxford. "He looked to see the rays of light about my head," he said, and more to that purpose. I begged him for his own sake not to pass sentence till he had his full evidence concerning me. This he could not promise, but faintly prayed me to flee from London and in despair of me took his leave.[73]

Concern for the Wesleys' spiritual and even mental health remained a recurring theme well into the 1770s. This "old friend" represents many who would "pass sentence" on the Wesleys' brand of evangelical religion. Not all such sentences, however, would be done with such a kindhearted visit.

WESLEY THE EVANGELICAL

The Wesleys would not long remain under the influence of Moravianism, although it is obvious that Charles remained open to their message longer than his brother. Moravianism would continue to have an influence on English evangelicalism out of proportion to their numbers. However, the Wesleyan split from Fetter Lane in 1739 marks the beginning of what would ultimately become the United Societies under the headship of John Wesley. In a show of Wesley's lingering high churchmanship, he would reject the quietism of English Moravianism.[74] This

---

[72]Kimbrough and Newport, *Manuscript Journal of the Reverend Charles Wesley*, 1:109.
[73]Ibid.
[74]See especially Wesley's "To the Moravian Church, More especially that part of it now or lately residing in England," *Works* 19:115-18.

rejection of quietism was an indicator of Wesley's perennial attachment to Catholic elements within Anglicanism's via media, combined with his desire to describe the soteriological transformation he saw taking place.

Wesley's high churchmanship would continue to raise its head, although his practices would become an amalgamation of high church, Pietist and Puritan influences. This combination created a Wesleyan Methodist ethos that left some of his colleagues in the Church confused, distant or even hostile. An example of his high churchmanship can be seen in his choice of language to describe his Puritan-inspired use of lay preachers. Most eighteenth-century evangelicals seldom if ever used the term *evangelical*. Hindmarsh writes that evangelicals "often spoke of the gospel and pressed 'gospel' into service as an adjective."[75] It was common to use terms such as *gospel preachers*, *gospel sermons* and *gospel conversions*. Wesley knew full well that such terms were, as Hindmarsh points out, "equated narrowly with the Reformers' teaching about atonement and justification by faith."[76] Thus Wesley told his lay preachers that "we are no gospel preachers." His concern lay in what he saw as a lack of emphasis on holy living and a rejection of humanity's required reaction to God's movement of grace, another area where the nature of Wesley's vision marked him as distinct from the evangelicals as a group.

Wesley was united with his Evangelical colleagues on essentials such as the experience of the New Birth, justification by faith and holy living. Yet a movement defined by a subjective experience of the Spirit will inevitably provide varying interpretations of individualistic encounters. Wesley's attempts to describe and then reproduce his own conversion experience put him at odds with others in the movement whose experience of conversion produced different narratives and differing allegiances to Wesley's connectionalism and drive to perfection. Narratives of human participants with their own geographical, ecclesiastical, political and social allegiances produced differing interpretations of this central soteriological event, and subsequent division was the outcome.

---

[75]Hindmarsh, *Evangelical Conversion Narrative*, 14.
[76]Ibid.

Wesley would continue to create a Methodist structure that cannot be understood properly apart from his desire to recreate some form of the Aldersgate experience. He believed he was called to promote this transformational event. That neither he nor any of the participants in the revival understood the larger sweep and the social causes carrying them into such a countercultural movement should come as no surprise. They were united by a trans-Atlantic movement that only with hindsight could be grasped. Likewise, their ultimate division would come about by social, political and theological concerns much larger than their particular spheres, a story that unfolds as Wesley's relationship to his evangelical colleagues develops with the continued spread of the revival.

3

PROPAGANDA AND POWER

The Revival Under Fire

The Evangelical Revival, which swept up figures such as the Wesley brothers, Lady Huntingdon and George Whitefield, was not always met with appreciation. Those who opposed the new evangelical work included many of the leading figures of the Church of England, men and women who cared deeply about the future of the Church and the needs of English society. This chapter will look at the effects of Methodism's opponents on the relationship of John Wesley to his regular Evangelical colleagues. Specifically, it will attempt to describe how anti-Methodist propaganda, in its various forms, helped to create a context in which connection to the Wesley brothers became a liability to Evangelical work within the established Church.

Evangelicals within the Church could little afford further stigma. They were already opposed by many on the basis of their core principles. It is little wonder that anti-Methodist propaganda would affect any relationship they would have with Wesleyan Methodism. The Wesleyan Methodists were notorious for their evangelical message, but also because they created a separate ecclesiastical structure. They renewed efforts to test out the idea of "occasional conformity" in competition with the establishment.[1] This context of vulnerability separated the Wesley

---

[1]One means by which the Wesleyan Methodists attempted to display their loyalty to the Church was by not holding Methodist meetings during "church hours." They were not, however, the first

brothers from some of the Evangelical clergy, but it also was the context for continuing tensions—theological, ecclesiological and political—between the regular and irregular elements of the revival. By the latter third of the century, regular and irregular would, for the most part, represent Evangelicals and Wesleyan Methodism respectively.

Their economic and social location was one thing that made most Evangelicals unable to afford further stigma. In the eighteenth century scandalous or libelous literature was extremely popular.[2] While Wesleyan Methodists were negatively affected by social stigma, the Evangelicals, in their attempts to remain within the Church, had much more to lose. The greatest difference between the Evangelicals and the Wesleyan Methodists in terms of negative press came down to economics. Attachment to the zealotry of Methodism held little, if any, benefit to a group of men already on the fringes of the establishment. Wesley's preachers were funded primarily through the conference. Evangelicals in the parish system were subject to the demands of a diverse constituency and a complex financial structure often attached to aristocratic landowners.

Thus, from an economical or social perspective, attachment to Wesley's Methodism had no benefit whatsoever to an Anglican clergyman trying to remain within the bounds of the parish system and the established Church. Methodist society meetings were held mostly on the outskirts of parishes and even by Wesley's death contained a fraction of Britain's population. Methodists under Wesley's control could have easily

---

group to initially place their own meeting times at a different time from Church meetings as a sign of partial conformity. Dewey Wallace notes that "Many Presbyterians avoided separate meetings during the Sunday morning services of the established church and thought of their private meetings as supplementing the spiritual diet of the Church of England" (Dewey A. Wallace, *Shapers of English Calvinism 1660–1714: Variety, Persistence, and Transformation* [New York: Oxford University Press, 2011], 23). See also John D. Ramsbottom, "Presbyterians and 'Partial Conformity' in the Restoration Church of England," *Journal of Ecclesiastical History* 43 (April 1992): 249–70. The Church of England was keenly aware of early attempts at what was known as "occasional conformity" but, according to J. S. Simon, by 1712 even "occasional conformity" was not enough to hold public office. "Non-conformists who had conformed by taking the Sacrament in the Church were expected to refrain from participation in non-conformist meetings while in office." See J. S. Simon, "The Conventicle Act and Its Relation to the Early Methodists," *Proceedings of the Wesley Historical Society* 11 (1918): 92.

[2]See Robert Shoemaker, *The London Mob: Violence and Disorder in Eighteenth-Century England* (New York: Hambledon Continuum, 2004), especially his chapter on print, 241-74.

received little notice from theologically sympathetic clergymen with responsibilities for the running and maintenance of an English parish.[3] In the eyes of many in the public, however, the difference between regular and irregular parties in the unfolding revival was easily overlooked. Propaganda from presses across England grouped them together with impunity and often defined public perception. Brett McInelly remarks that given the small number of Methodists during the century, "Many, if not most, of the general populace were as likely, if not more so, to encounter a Methodist caricature in the pages of a novel or on the British stage as they were of meeting a Methodist in real life."[4] Within this environment Wesley's socially disruptive practices, although not unprecedented, could easily undermine Evangelicals in the Church.

This context—primarily a combination of factors most prevalent during the first part of the revival—was made possible on the fertile soil of recent English political unrest. Opposition to Wesley's practices was fueled by anti-Methodist propaganda and the common fear of enthusiasm, and through the censure and ire of episcopal leadership.

METHODISM AND ITS DETRACTORS

Public opposition to Methodism was complex and voluminous. Criticism of "enthusiasm" was common from the episcopal desk to the theater stage. The critics were not the only ones producing sharply worded public propaganda. The stage, for instance, fought back against Methodist claims that made the theatrical world seem an immediate shortcut to one of Dante's levels of hell.[5] In 1740 actors gathered outside Charles Wesley's home, threatening to burn it down.

---

[3]It is even argued that the Evangelicals as a group were among the hardest-working clerics in the country. The drive to promote the New Birth may have been a part of this work ethic, along with the desire to negate any suspicion they were under because of that very insistence on an evangelical conversion experience.

[4]Brett McInelly, *Textual Warfare and the Making of Methodism* (New York: Oxford University Press, 2014).

[5]Wesley referred to the theater as "what Satan esteemed his own ground." See *Works* 20:485 (April 29, 1754); and also 20:3-4; 21:287, 365; and 23:312. Wesley was not alone in his criticism of the theater as destructive of Christian virtue. See, for example, George Anderson, *A Reinforcement of the Reasons Proving That the Stage Is an Unchristian Diversion* (Edinburgh and London: 1733).

According to Charles, the revival had cut off their livelihood. He wrote in his journal that "the ground of their quarrel with me is that the gospel has starved them."[6]

Many clergymen were equally defensive in response to Wesley's diatribes against the "practical atheism" of much English Church life.[7] Methodism challenged aspects of civic life through its pietistic message and expanding structure. As such, the Methodists, as Walsh writes, were "whipping-boys for those who felt a compelling need to demonstrate in aggressive fashion their loyalty to traditional national values."[8]

Henry Rack provides five categories in which to place anti-Methodist propaganda. Although he claims that the distinctions are not precise, he outlines them as: (1) the charge of "enthusiasm," (2) specific theological criticism aimed at "Methodist teaching generally related to the process of salvation, (3) breaches of church order, (4) social disruption, and finally (5) political subversion especially during times of public anxiety."[9] Hempton notes that the "early Methodists were looked upon as 'disturbers of the world,' the new Levellers, and were thus victims of remarkably resilient Civil War memories."[10] They also ignored numerous boundaries in their drive to preach the New Birth with, as Hempton notes, itinerant, lay and female preachers who "crossed traditional boundaries of hierarchy, law, sex, age, wealth, education and religious vocation."[11] Rack describes the charge of enthusiasm as the true "bugbear" that often included all other charges. Enthusiasm could be seen by contemporaries as that which propelled any amount of seemingly irrational, and therefore irregular, behavior on the part of the overly zealous. Misty

---

[6]See S. T. Kimbrough Jr. and Kenneth G. C. Newport, *The Manuscript Journal of the Reverend Charles Wesley, M. A.* (Nashville: Kingswood Books, 2007), 2:290 (Nov. 18, 1740).

[7]See esp. John Wesley's sermon 2, "The Almost Christian," in *Works* 1. Wesley preached this sermon before a congregation in the University Church, St. Mary's, Oxford, in 1741. The sermon was the last he was allowed to preach at St. Mary's, afterward being taken out of the rotation of fellows preaching to the university.

[8]John Walsh, "Methodism and the Mob in the Eighteenth Century," *Studies in Church History* 8 (1972): 227.

[9]Henry D. Rack, *Reasonable Enthusiast: John Wesley and the Rise of Methodism*, 3rd ed. (Philadelphia: Trinity Press International, 2002), 275.

[10]David Hempton, *The Religion of the People: Methodism and Popular Religion, c. 1750–1900* (London: Routledge, 1996), 149.

[11]Ibid.

Anderson captures this popular concern for Methodist enthusiasm, describing Methodism "popularly conceived" as "an illustration of a modern self unmoored."[12]

John Walsh highlights two aspects of Wesleyan Methodism that gave rise to alarm: first, "in an age when the agencies of government were decidedly weak and decentralised, Methodism looked the more sinister because of its highly articulated and nation-wide organisation."[13] This organization, although regarded by the Methodists as entirely benign, was thought to challenge localized authority. Walsh argues, second, that this challenge to local authority was not only addressed "primarily to the poor" but addressed to poor persons "whom it drilled into disciplined cadres which owed their allegiance to leaders far beyond the reach of any local authority." This combination of decentralized national authority and local organization of the lower orders run by "itinerant agents, whose origins were unknown, whose persons were obscure, and who appeared to have no formal authorisation whatever" threatened to disrupt the authority of parson and squire and create a combustible combination.[14]

Criticism was at times aimed at "Methodism" as a whole to include anyone of an evangelical bent.[15] At other times this opposition was aimed at specific leaders of the revival.[16] In still others, critics meant simply to warn the public of the dangers of sectarian religionists, reminiscent of those who had stripped England of its crown, faith and glory in just the last century.[17] Bishop Edmund Gibson was keen to point out the

---

[12]Misty G. Anderson, *Imagining Methodism in Eighteenth-Century Britain: Enthusiasm, Belief, and the Borders of the Self* (Baltimore: Johns Hopkins University Press, 2012), 38.

[13]Walsh, "Methodism and the Mob," 218.

[14]Ibid.

[15]See, for example, Anonymous, *The Question Whether It Be Right to Turn Methodist Considered: In a Dialogue Between Two Members of the Church of England* (London: Printed for M. Cooper, 1745); Edmund Gibson, *Observations Upon the Conduct and Behaviour of a Certain Sect, Usually Distinguished by the Name of Methodists* (London: Printed by Edward Owen, 1743 or 1744); John Downes, *Methodism Examined and Exposed, or, The Clergy's Duty of Guarding Their Flocks Against False Teachers: A Discourse Lately Delivered in Four Parts* (London: Printed for John Rivington, 1759).

[16]John Parkhurst, *A Serious and Friendly Address to the Reverend Mr. John Wesley: In Relation to a Principal Doctrine Advanced and Maintained by Him and His Assistants* (London: Printed for J. Withers, 1753).

[17]George Swathe, *Enthusiasm No Novelty, or, The Spirit of the Methodists in the Year 1641 and 1642* (London: Printed for T. Cooper, 1739).

similarities between the eighteenth-century Methodists and the sectarians of the previous century.[18]

Gibson is a unique figure. His efforts to censure the Methodist revival
provide an opportunity to see the effects of ecclesiastical censure on Wesleyan and Evangelical cooperation. Gibson was a noted churchman,
having played a significant role in ecclesiastical discussions during the
reigns of William and Anne relative to the rights and privileges of convocation. His two-volume 1713 folio, the *Codex juris ecclesiastici Anglicani*,
marked him as one of the most astute students of English canon law.
Etched in stone on his funerary monument is praise for "His Lordship's
peculiar Care and Concern for the Constitution and Discipline of the
CHURCH of ENGLAND" as "eminently distinguished" by "his In-
valuable Collection of HER LAWS" and "by his prudent and Steady Opposition to every Attack made upon Them."[19]

In 1742 Gibson wrote a letter to the clergy of the diocese of London.
He highlighted his recent publication against the Methodists and their
practices and reminded the clergy: "It is now an hundred Years since the
like Clamours were raised and propagated throughout the Nation against
the established Clergy; as a Body lazy and unactive in the Work of Religion, and whose Defects in the Discharge of their Duty did greatly need
to be supply'd by Itinerant Preachers."[20] Gibson was convinced that both
the enthusiasm and the practices of Methodism were detrimental to the
Church and the state as seen from lessons learned in the previous century.
He wrote, "We cannot have a more pregnant Testimony, how mischievous
such Practices are to Religion, and how productive not only to Confusion, but of Blasphemy, Profaneness, and the most wicked and destructive Doctrines and Practices, than these and the like Effects which
they then had; as they are set before us at large, in the Histories of those
Times."[21] Walsh notes that to many "the Methodists looked alarmingly

---

[18]See his *Observations Upon the Conduct and Behavior of a Certain Sect, Usually Distinguished by the Name of Methodists*.

[19]Gibson's funerary monument is located at All Saints, Fullham, London.

[20]Edmund Gibson, *The Charge of Edmund, Lord Bishop of London, to the Clergy of His Diocese, in His Visitation Begun in the Year 1741, and Finish'd in the Year 1742*, 10.

[21]Ibid.

like the harbingers of a second and perhaps a more proletarian puritan revolution."[22] An anonymous set of letters printed in the early 1760s simply laid the charge bare: "The schismatic leaders spoke then the same language, which the Methodist teachers now use."[23]

Critics of a high church persuasion took aim at Methodism's sectarian tendencies and its ability to seduce the weak from the salvific world of sacrament, order and apostolic succession within the Church.[24] Latitudinarians took aim at Methodism's excessive demands on its adherents and the incessant use of experience to justify its networks of societies. Even Archbishop Thomas Secker, a church reformer, felt that Methodism in its various forms had become incapable of participating in the reform of the Church. As sectarians with a separate ethos and a self-designed structure that functioned independently of the Church, they had relinquished their seat at the table.[25]

One should not assume that the Methodists were of one mind concerning the criticism they received. Charles Wesley wrote a piece against his brother when in 1755 he felt that the United Societies were in danger of separating from the Church of England over the issue of sacramental administration.[26] Charles would publish the piece again in 1784 when John ordained Richard Whatcoat, Thomas Vasey and Thomas Coke for the work of the new Methodist church in the United States. Wesley, as a "New Testament bishop," was thought by many, including many

---

[22]Walsh, "Methodism and the Mob," 218.

[23]*An Address to the Right Honourable —: With Several Letters to the D— of —, from the L —, in Vindication of Her Conduct, on Being Charged with Methodism* (London: Printed for W. Sandby, in Fleet-Street, 1761), 6.

[24]See *The Question Whether It Be Right to Turn Methodist Considered*, a document written for those the author thought might be tempted to "leave" the Church in order to join the Methodists. This view, seen as early as 1745, shows just how early fears of schism associated with Methodism ran through public discourse. It was not assumed that the Methodists were, in fact, reform-minded Anglicans, but rather a fringe, and thus dissenting, group attempting to undermine the unity of the Church of England.

[25]For a recent work on Archbishop Secker's view of church reform, see Robert G. Ingram's *Religion, Reform and Modernity in the Eighteenth Century: Thomas Secker and the Church of England*, Studies in Modern British Religious History 17 (Woodbridge, UK: Boydell, 2007). Ingram's work is particularly important to see the efforts of top-ranking ecclesiastical leaders to reform the Church of England in the eighteenth century. The picture of an aloof episcopate mired in the morass of political maneuvering is shattered by Ingram's fresh perspective.

[26]Charles Wesley, *An Epistle to the Reverend Mr. John Wesley, by Charles Wesley, Prebyter of the Church of England* (London: 1755).

Methodists and Evangelicals, to be nothing but a schismatic in Anglican garb.[27] The sharpest criticism he received for these ordinations came from his own brother. One of the earliest challenges to Wesley's claim to be a faithful priest of the Church came from Evangelical clergyman Thomas Adam shortly after the revival began.[28]

Despite this opposition, the underlying experience of the New Birth propelled these various Methodists and Evangelicals. It was the experience of the New Birth that the Evangelical Revival was meant to produce in those who had yet to be "awakened" by the gospel. And while the idea of conversion was not foreign to English Christianity, the understanding of it was never uniform once Reformation ideology—Reformed, Lutheran and even Counter-Reformation—had been unleashed by the court of Henry VIII. No Act of Uniformity ever produced the sort of theological uniformity that had culturally existed in pre-Reformation England.[29] John Wesley may have argued adamantly in his 1777 sermon at the dedication of his City Road Chapel in London that Methodism was nothing but the honest expression of the Bible, the early church and the Church of England, but his amalgamation of these various influences was unique.[30] To some, Wesley's Methodism looked nothing like Anglicanism.

A CLIMATE OF FEAR

The question of monarchical legitimacy within the *ancien régime* that was eighteenth-century Britain lay at the heart of anti-Methodist

---

[27]See Charles's criticism and especially his poetry. It is also notable that in the most up-to-date listing of anti-Methodist publications by Clive Field this item is not listed. Field's methodological approach to the list, like all before it, excludes inner-Methodist arguments published publicly that mirror those of non-Methodist detractors. In the case of Charles Wesley, his desire to publicly criticize his brother and the conference speaks loudly of his own self-perceived ecclesiastical identity and loyalty as a clergyman of the Church of England. Depending on one's historiographical perspective, the limits placed on anti-Methodist publication lists may or may not be helpful. The elusive nature of the term *Methodist* in the early part of the revival makes any listing of anti-Methodist materials an arduous task subject to subjectivity.

[28]G. C. B. Davies, *The Early Cornish Evangelicals 1735–60: A Study of Walker of Truro and Others* (London: SPCK, 1951), 119.

[29]For a description of this cultural context, see Eamon Duffy's *Stripping of the Altars: Traditional Religion in England c. 1400–c. 1500* (New Haven, CT: Yale University Press, 1992). Duffy provides a detailed and valuable description of the Catholic culture that dominated English life before the English Reformation.

[30]Wesley's sermon 112, "On Laying the Foundations," *Works* 3:585-86.

propaganda. The Jacobite rebellions undermined cultural acceptance of Wesley's Methodism. Wesley's reaction to the second rebellion in the 1740s added to underlying suspicions of his commitment to the stability of post-Restoration England. It took both Charles Wesley and Samuel Walker to convince Wesley that he did not need to publish a public letter he had written on behalf of the Methodists in support of the Hanoverian dynasty.[31] This hesitancy stemmed from a desire not to seem too eager to support the current regime such that it could call into question the authenticity of the letter's contents. Caution also avoided the suggestion that Methodism was distinct from the Church of England and therefore in need of making such statements of loyalty.[32] At the same time, Methodist connection to Jacobitism, especially that of the Huntingdons, William Law and others, gives credence to anti-Methodist concerns. Boyd Stanley Schlenther argues that "the common popular fear of Methodism as a socially destructive handmaid to a plot to overturn the Hanoverian monarchy may have had more substance than is generally supposed."[33]

Fear of partisanship was heightened during these Jacobite incursions. Charles and Walker thought the letter would be perceived by the public as sectarian and thus antithetical to Methodist attempts to be seen as a religious movement and not a political one. Their concerns are easily understood. At the beginning of the letter Wesley writes:

---

[31]See *Works* 20:16; 26:104-6. For a fuller description of Wesley's reaction to the 1745 rebellion, see Theodore R. Weber, *Politics in the Order of Salvation: Transforming Wesleyan Political Ethics* (Nashville: Kingswood Books, 2001) and his chapter "Public Political Controversies I: John Wesley and the '45 Rebellion," 69-85.

[32]J. C. D. Clark writes that the very notion of "society" in the eighteenth century was one that described a particular connectedness (i.e., polite society). In terms of national concern the connectedness of the English people to their monarch, or state, was tantamount, the government itself being the fulcrum and unifier of what should be termed English "society." In this light, Walker's and Charles Wesley's adamant insistence that Wesley not publish this tract of loyalty was an insistence that Wesley not set up Methodism as somehow detached as a group of good English people, members of society, rightfully and lawfully connected to their monarch and the state. See J. C. D. Clark, *English Society, 1660–1832: Religion, Ideology, and Politics During the Ancien Régime* (New York: Cambridge University Press, 2000), 3-4.

[33]Boyd Stanley Schlenther, *Queen of the Methodists: The Countess of Huntingdon and the Eighteenth-Century Crisis of Faith and Society* (Durham, UK: Durham Academic Press, 1997), 27. Lord Huntingdon died at age 49, in great part in despair over the failed Stuart campaign of 1745 and the execution of Scottish peers as traitors that same year. See ibid., 30-31.

> So inconsiderable as we are, "a people scattered and peeled, and trodden under foot from the beginning hitherto," we should in no wise have presumed, . . . to open our lips to your Majesty, had we not been induced, . . . by two considerations: the one, that in spite of all our remonstrances on that head we are continually represented as a peculiar sect of men, separating ourselves from the established Church; the other, that we are still traduced as inclined to popery.[34]

Although the sectarian label had merit as Wesley continued to promote the creation of a system of religious societies within the structures of the Church, the second label, that Methodism represented the promotion of popery, was even more dangerous given the ecclesiastical allegiances of the Stuarts. Wesley continued with one of his first public pronouncements concerning the nature of Methodism and its relationship to the Church of England:

> we think it incumbent upon us, if we must stand as a distinct body from our brethren, to tender for ourselves our most dutiful regards to your sacred Majesty, and to declare . . . that we are a part (however mean) of that Protestant Church established in these kingdoms . . . and are steadily attached to your Majesty's royal person and illustrious house.[35]

Wesley adds to this his insistence that the Methodists "detest and abhor the fundamental doctrines of the Church of Rome" to further prove his Protestant credentials.[36] The letter was never sent. It was, however, published in his *Journal* with the note that "upon farther consideration it was judged best to lay it aside."[37]

In some ways, as shown in the above-mentioned letter, it could be said that John Wesley was simply a bad politician. Hempton argues, however, that "Wesley realized perfectly well that early Methodism teetered on the brink of legal irregularities, but he also had respect for English law and for ecclesiastical discipline."[38] This balancing act was not always readily seen in the heat of public debate. Like his parents, Wesley did not have

---

[34]Wesley, March 5, 1744, *Works* 20:16.
[35]Ibid.
[36]Ibid.
[37]*Works* 20:17.
[38]Hempton, *Religion of the People*, 147.

the political flexibility of a Cranmer to make himself amenable to the ever-changing political context of post-Restoration England. His political and theological convictions were much more similar to nonjurors such as Thomas Ken. That Wesley was brought up in such an ideologically stubborn home, and was then surrounded by Jacobites during his education and his American missionary days, did not prepare him to function well as a political figure in a charged political environment, although he was obviously well aware of the ramifications of English law. Hempton and Ward both highlight Wesley's political leanings, both equating Wesley with country Toryism.[39] This political perspective, according to Ward, put Wesley at odds with the government of his day, especially that led by Robert Walpole. With the accession of George III in 1760, the Tories would begin to fare better, but that Wesley was ever seen as acceptable by a larger portion of English society may well be due to his longevity more than any of his attempts to claim continuity with the Church. He simply outlived the majority of his detractors.

Although Wesley's political posturing would become more effective in the 1770s, his understanding of the political climate of the early revival period was colored by his belief that theological issues, and not political ones, were at the forefront of the anti-Methodist challenge. In August 1739 Wesley recorded a conversation in which he defends himself from the charge that he was out to undermine the Church:

> For two hours I took up my cross in arguing with a zealous man, and labouring to convince him that I was not "an enemy to the Church of England." He allowed, I "taught no other doctrines than those of the Church," but could not forgive my teaching them *out of the church walls.* He allowed too (which none indeed can deny who has either any regard to truth or sense of shame) that "by this teaching many souls who till that time were perishing for lack of knowledge, have been, and are, brought from darkness to light, and from the power of Satan unto God." But say, these things ought not to be suffered.[40]

---

[39]Ibid., 80-81. Hempton argues that Wesley put his hope for renewal in the Prince of Wales until the prince's untimely death by tennis ball.

[40]Wesley, August 27, 1739, *Works* 19:89. Baker identifies the man in the journal account as "Th. Robins."

Yet Wesley defends himself in the journal entry not against the charge that his practices were out of line with the cultural norms of his day but against the charge that his theology was Roman Catholic. Arguing that his understanding of the doctrine of justification by faith alone was enough to dispel any question of his loyalty to the Anglican mantle, he nonetheless seemed oblivious to the practical reasons he was accused of disloyalty to the Church. In a strange way, Wesley assumed that his critics' name-calling was grounded in an astute understanding of the finer details of dogmatic theology. The reader is left to wonder whether he is either deflecting the accusations aimed at his irregular methods or simply naive of the implications of his actions within such a charged environment.

Recent scholarship has emphasized the interrelationship of theological foundations and political ideology during the eighteenth century. Hempton writes that eighteenth-century attacks and defenses of the churches of the establishment, for example, were based more on "theological and historical frameworks of understanding than on principles of utility or natural rights," adding that "the most intellectually influential ideas on the relationship between Church and State were not so much based on Locke and Warburton as on Hooker and Filmer."[41] Hempton is not arguing, however, that theological arguments were void of political and social import. Richard Hooker's writings on ecclesiastical polity and Robert Filmer's on the divine right of kings had obvious political repercussions.[42] Wesley, especially during the first two decades of the revival—the period in which most anti-Methodist propaganda was written—at least appeared oblivious to the connection between his own actions and the actions of his fellow evangelicals, with the political uproar that they produced. Whether he actually was oblivious to these connections is hard to tell.

---

[41]David Hempton, *Religion and Political Culture in Britain and Ireland: From the Glorious Revolution to the Decline of Empire* (New York: Cambridge University Press, 1996), 3.

[42]See Richard Hooker, *Laws of Ecclesiastical Polity, Book I*; and Robert Filmer, *The Anarchy of a Limited or Mixed Monarchy* (London[?]: 1648); *The Necessity of the Absolute Power of Kings* (Oxford: 1648); and *Patriarcha* (London[?]: 1680).

EVANGELICALISM AS CROMWELL REBORN

Some critics of the revival attempted to tie the evangelicals directly to the seventeenth-century parliamentarians who fought against the armies of Charles I. Much of the impetus behind these direct attacks was the itinerancy of evangelical preachers. Wesleyan Methodism's attempts to create a category of partial conformity under the Act of Toleration, which would guarantee Methodism the rights of dissenting groups without the second-class citizenship that came along with those rights, were a source of much suspicion.

The Act of Toleration, passed by Parliament in 1689 to make provision within the English legal code for trinitarian Protestant dissenters, made it possible for non-Anglicans to meet legally but created a second class of citizen based on religious practice. The need for this provision arose in the latter part of the seventeenth century, and attempts to evade this religious class system were seen by many to be the first signs of ferment against the government. In his 1744 *Observations Upon the Conduct and Behaviour of a Certain Sect, Usually Distinguished by the Name of Methodists,* Edmund Gibson, then bishop of London, decried the act of holding unlicensed meetings. He wrote vehemently that

> the unbounded Licentiousness of holding Assemblies for Divine Worship, both as to Persons and Places, which had prevailed for some Years before the Restoration, and of which our Histories are full; was a sufficient Warning to the Legislature, to have a watchful Eye over that Spirit, which had caused so much Confusion in the Kingdom; particularly in the publick Worship of God.[43]

It was especially this last point, the "publick Worship of God," that most worried those looking to oppose the return of seventeenth-century extremism. Methodist meetings were held among the working classes and often on the outskirts of parish boundaries. Many were convinced that they were the re-creation of seventeenth-century social and religious unrest. Walsh notes that tension resulted as "preachers, while professing themselves members of the Church of England, drew people away from

---

[43]Gibson, *Observations*, 3.

the parish church and set up, if not as yet altar against altar, at least pulpit against pulpit, pastor against pastor, creating incipient schism in many parishes hitherto united as one flock."[44] Comparisons between Wesley's Methodism and earlier Puritan efforts were easily made.

Even Wesley's evangelical conversion narrative, with its language of a "heart strangely warmed," could be construed as politically subversive when placed alongside similarly worded statements by seventeenth-century pro-parliamentarian clergymen. In an anonymous piece published in 1739 titled *Enthusiasm No Novelty: Or, the Spirit of Methodists in the Year 1641 and 1642,* the author intended to "present the reader with a specimen of that enthusiasm" that eventually "pour'd forth a deluge of misery and confusion over the whole kingdom" in the previous century and show how it was "equally visible in the extempore prayers and sermons of those times, as they are in the field-meetings of Kennington-common, &c. in these our days."[45] The author had no doubt that the social unrest of the past was beginning to show itself in the socially destructive behavior of eighteenth-century evangelicalism.

In an obvious attempt to tie evangelical heart language—and perhaps John Wesley's evangelical conversion account, published the previous year—to historical social unrest, the author of *Enthusiasm No Novelty* provided the following prayer of April 6, 1641:

> Lord, I find now in my heart that inward warmth which I have found in prayer about four several times in a few years last past, which inward warmth of heart now is an undoubted courageous sign of the complete victory of thy saints, thy servants, in this civil war. . . . I pray thee now set up thy standard against the king's standard: do thou stand strongly, courageously in the hearts of our parliament, in the hearts of the citizens of London, in the hearts of the citizens of York, in the hearts of all thy faithful ones, and in the hearts of all those also whom thou hast inclined to favour, to side with, and to stand for the parliament and thy party.[46]

---

[44]Walsh, "Methodism and the Mob," 219.

[45]Anonymous, quoted in Swathe, *Enthusiasm No Novelty*, ii-iv.

[46]Ibid., 13.

Such an obvious correlation of heart language and antigovernment sentiment would have never set well with the eighteenth-century desire for moderation and peace on the home front. Nor would it have made it easier for Evangelicals attempting to become incumbents. The fear that similarly minded clergyman would again inhabit the Church's pulpits explains much of the opposition for regular and irregular evangelicals alike. Charles Wesley in 1738 was actually refused the pulpit by Charles Piers, a fellow Evangelical Anglican, who Charles insisted was driven by "the fear of man." Piers claimed that he was concerned for the "tenderness of his flock," a concern that Charles thought was of little value.[47] That this Evangelical-on-Evangelical rejection took place just two days after the Wesley brothers had been called to answer to the Bishop of London for irregular activities and preaching doctrines that had caused antinomianism "in the time of King Charles" is informative.[48]

The irony is that Wesley amalgamated the theological outlook of the Caroline divines together with the practices of their Puritan and parliamentarian opponents. Combined with his allegiance to Tory politics, this presents Wesley as a confusing picture for admirer and detractor alike. That he would bring this amalgamation to the political context of eighteenth-century England makes the picture anything but simple. Association with Wesley or his movement had its risks regardless of one's own social situation. Wesley's own idiosyncrasies made connection with him problematic for Evangelicals, whose message sounded much like his own, yet who held to the established norms and parochial practices of the Church. The charged political climate simply made evangelicals of any stripe look as though they were dangerous malefactors.

WESLEY AND THE EVANGELICALS UNDER FIRE

Propaganda aimed at Methodism sometimes missed its mark. Evangelicals such as William Romaine of London were caught in the crossfire. Romaine may have been a lightning rod with or without the enthusiasm of the revival, but the vitriolic attacks on his intelligence, fitness for the

---

[47]Kimbrough and Newport, *Manuscript Journal of the Reverend Charles Wesley,* 1:154.
[48]Ibid., 1:150-51.

ministry and sermons, as seen in T. Mortimer's *Die and Be Damned: Or an Anecdote Against Every Species of Methodism; and Enthusiasm*, are rife with the same tone and critical ire that were often aimed at Methodism as a whole.[49] Romaine, a cleric of the Church of England, was called a Methodist, and his suitability for clerical office was called into question, as was his allegiance to the establishment.

Ironically, Wesley complained in 1756 of being criticized for Romaine's actions. In a letter to the *Monthly Reviewers* Wesley wrote: "Gentlemen, for a considerable time I have had a desire to trouble you with a few lines. . . . The question I would propose is this: Is it prudent, is it just, is it humane, to jumble whole bodies of people together and condemn them by the lump?"[50] Apparently, the editors of the magazine had been aggravated by Romaine but took equal aim at Wesley. Their response to Romaine's provocation highlights the connectedness of the revival and the generic use of the term *Methodist*. Wesley responded: "I am not Mr. Romaine; neither am I accountable for his behaviour. And what equity is this? one man has offended you: therefore you fall on another. Will it excuse you to say, 'But he is called the same name'? especially when neither is this his own name, but a term of derision."[51]

Fletcher records in a 1759 letter to Charles Wesley the reaction of the Hill family to his own conversion and concern over further conversions among their family because of his influence. Richard Hill had converted to evangelicalism, and it was feared among family members that Fletcher's continuing association with them might "corrupt" others such that "all the family will be ruined by this Plague of Methodists."[52] Fletcher, who had been a favorite of the matriarch of the family and tutor for her

---

[49]T. Mortimer, *Die and Be Damned: Or an Anecdote Against Every Species of Methodist; and Enthusiasm*, 2nd ed. (London: Printed for S. Hooper and A. Morley, at Gay's-Head near Beauforts-Buildings, in the Strand, 1758). Clive Field notes that Mortimer's piece was written originally in 1758, revised and enlarged the same year, and subsequently published in a third edition in 1761. There was also a Norwich edition of 1828.

[50]*Works* 27:55-58 (John Wesley to the *Monthly Reviewers*, Sept. 9, 1756).

[51]Ibid.

[52]See John Fletcher's letter to Charles Wesley, March 22, 1759, in Peter Forsaith, ed., *Unexampled Labours: Letters of the Revd John Fletcher to Leaders in the Evangelical Revival* (London: Epworth, 2008), 61-62.

children, following his conversion to Methodism became a pariah. Madame Hill informed Fletcher that he could "starve to death without her being troubled" and that he would never be given the living at Madeley. History shows that he was in fact given the living at Madeley; but this sort of personal attack was not particular to John Fletcher.[53]

Association with Methodism posed a risk to anyone with a position of power. In a set of anonymous letters written in the early 1760s and mentioned previously in this chapter, the author wrote to members of the establishment who the author was afraid would lose their clout if their name became associated with the enthusiasm of Methodism. The letters indicate that both the author and the addressee had a sympathetic view of evangelicalism within the Church of England and believed that reform of the Church was necessary for the propagation of the gospel.[54] Methodism posed danger to their efforts.

The author was certain that the Methodists were not a malevolent force and that they, in fact, "do good," but also certain that they did so in "such a way as tends to great hurt, as is likely to introduce a terrible disorder and confusion."[55] The author, however, was not simply content to argue that Methodist practices subverted its productive aspects, but that association with Methodism itself was a detriment that would ultimately undermine the effectiveness of anyone associated with it.

Speaking to a person of rank, with the title "the Right Honourable," the author claims that Methodist practices were not only similar to the practices of seventeenth-century enthusiasts but that "the tenacity which the Methodists' practice has to revive all these mad and mischievous proceedings, and the countenance it has given to the revival of them in many parts of the kingdom, create a very strong prejudice against their advocates; should you be considered as one of these, your weight will be entirely lost."[56] While the author's words of warning border closely on threats, the author's underlying concern for the

---

[53]Ibid.

[54]*An Address to the Right Honourable —: With Several Letters to the D— of—, from the L—, in Vindication of Her Conduct, on Being Charged with Methodism.*

[55]Mortimer, *Die and Be Damned*, 2.

[56]Ibid., 7.

productive influence of the recipient is made plain in pleading words: "If by particular civilities shewn to any Methodist teachers you are thought to favour their proceedings, I beg that you would be pleased to reflect, how much your power to serve the interest of true religion will be hereby weakened."[57] The interests of true religion, even that kind that would bring about needed reform in the Church of England, would be severely hindered by any connection to the socially disruptive behavior of this latest sect of enthusiasts.

Among Evangelicals there was great concern that the Wesleyan Methodists were undermining the larger revival by means of their practices and the widespread suspicion they generated. Thomas Adam and Samuel Walker spoke to Wesley early in the revival. Their concerns would later become the Evangelical party line under leaders such as Charles Simeon. Adam wrote to Wesley in 1755 that he was concerned that talk of Methodist separation from the Church was not only detrimental to Wesley— Adam described the entire situation as "your present embarrassments"— but to "religion in general," a reference to the evangelical aim to bring vital religion to England.[58] Walker's concern about Wesley's actions, described in a letter the same year, was not only for retaining the Methodist witness within the Church but about detrimental effects such actions would make on the Church and the revival. Walker very passionately pleaded with Wesley for "those ministers who are zealous for the power of godliness," arguing that Methodist irregularity and the criticism it was encouraging was going to undermine Evangelical efforts to plant societies in their parishes and only add further proofs to those who opposed them.[59] For Walker there was an obvious public connection between the Methodists under Wesley and the Evangelicals in the Church, such that the actions of one reflected on the other.

The historian should not assume that evangelicals were simply on the receiving end of criticism. The Wesleys and Whitefield often brought on themselves the attention and venom of their ecclesiastical colleagues

---

[57]Ibid., 6-7.
[58]*Works* 26:603.
[59]*Works* 26:585.

and superiors with their own criticism of the establishment. In his 1744 university sermon preached on the Feast of St. Bartholomew, the anniversary of the Great Ejection of 1662, when thousands of nonconformists, including Wesley's grandfather, were ejected from their livings in the Church, Wesley publicly questioned the Christian commitments of Oxford, including its leading figures with, as Outler notes, "scant charity."[60] Wesley was convinced that almost everyone from the heads of houses to the students were Christian in name only. Wesley's approach to "awaken" the clergy of the Church was to write scathing pieces against them such as his *Address to the Clergy* (1756) and to set up unlicensed meetings under his direct control within their individual parishes.[61] The latter action would bring him into direct conflict with Evangelicals, including his brother Charles, as well as Edward Stillingfleet and Henry Venn.[62]

The Revival and Episcopal Power

Gibson and Secker took different routes to combat the perceived excesses of evangelicalism. Secker all but ignored the revival and spent his ecclesiastical career working for the reform of the Church from within and through official channels.[63] Gibson took a more direct role in anti-Methodist propaganda and in the exertion of ecclesiastical power to curb Methodist endeavors. In his own London diocese and in Bristol—thus encompassing the original field of Wesley's United Societies by 1739—ecclesiastical censure was swift and hindered the cooperation of the regular Evangelical clergy with irregulars like the Wesleys and Whitefield.

The radical nature of Wesley's and Whitefield's field preaching and its disregard for parish boundaries brought about rapid action from a Church still suspect of irregularity. Wesley's efforts to build a Methodist substructure within the Church did not stop with field preaching, as he

---

[60]The sermon, "Scriptural Christianity," can be found in *Works* 1:159-80. Outler's description of the context can be found in the same volume, p. 113.

[61]*Works* (Jackson) 10:480-500.

[62]*Letters* (Telford) 4:60-61 (John Wesley to Ebenezer Blackwell, July 16, 1761).

[63]See Ingram, *Religion, Reform and Modernity in the Eighteenth Century*, 2007.

began to send out laymen to do the same. Methodist hagiography has made Wesley's actions look nothing but heroic and in doing so has undermined the radical nature of Wesley actions. I will discuss these practices in detail in the next chapter, but in terms of episcopal censure Frank Baker notes that the "refusal to acknowledge territorial restrictions, whether of parish or of diocese, was allied to a somewhat cavalier attitude to the governing authority of the bishop."[64] It is not entirely clear but likely that this attitude was thought by some on the episcopal bench to be the stirrings of presbyterianism.

The bishops began to answer these challenges to their authority in various ways. One such measure was the Islington Precedent (Ruling), which stated that no one could preach in a church or churchyard without written permission from the bishop. It was applied in London and subsequently in Bristol. Because of the ruling we may never know how many clergy supported Wesleyan Methodism in the earliest stages of the revival.

Wesley's journal entry for March 3, 1742, describes the effect on Methodist preaching and the relationship with Evangelical clergy that these episcopal rulings produced:

> I explained in the evening at Fonmon, though in weakness and pain, how "Jesus saveth us from our sins." The next morning at eight I preached at Bonvilston, a little town four miles from Fonmon. Thence I rode to Llantrisant and sent to the minister to desire the use of his church. His answer was, he should have been very willing; but the bishop had forbidden him. By what law? I am not legally convict, either of heresy or any other crime. By what authority then am I suspended from preaching? By barefaced arbitrary power.[65]

---

[64]Frank Baker, *John Wesley and the Church of England* (London: Epworth, 1970), 63.

[65]John Wesley, March 3, 1742, *Works* 19:255-56. Wesley notes similar instances of episcopal censure in Dublin in 1747. He writes in his journal for the 10th of August of that year: "Between eight and nine I went to Mr. R[oquier] (the curate of St. Mary's) he professed abundance of goodwill, commended my sermon in strong terms, and begged he might see me again the next morning. But at the same time he expressed the most rooted prejudice against lay preachers or preaching out of a church, and said the Archbishop of Dublin [Charles Cobbe, 1687-1765] was resolved to suffer no such irregularities in his diocese" (*Works* 20:187-88).

These episcopal censures were not universally mandated. Wesley notes that "another clergyman immediately offered me his church. But it being too far off I preached in a large room, spent a little time with the society in prayer and exhortation, and then took horse for Cardiff."[66]

Charles Wesley had a similar experience on November 17, 1740. He wrote in his journal that "my mouth was opened to preach the law and the gospel at Llantrisant. Mr [Richard] Harris, the minister, was exceeding civil. He had been dealt with to refuse me the pulpit, but would not break his word."[67] Ward notes that Richard Harris was vicar of Llantrisant, and that the bishop, John Gilbert (1693–1761), who served the diocese of Llandaff (1740–1748), would later become archbishop of York and left a reputation for haughtiness. Gilbert later refused to ordain the Evangelical John Newton.[68]

During the early to middle part of the 1740s, numerous bishops across the country responded in writing to the "new Methodists." These included the archbishop of York, Dr. Thomas Herring, who warned his clergy about Methodism, and Gibson's work already mentioned, which dealt specifically with legal issues. Gibson seemed, according to Baker, "genuinely shocked that such men could pretend to be loyal churchmen."[69]

To the *Charge* of Dr. Richard Smalbroke, the bishop of Lichfield and Coventry, Wesley responded in his *Farther Appeals to Men of Reason and Religion* in December 1744. Baker notes that in refuting Smalbroke, "a bishop who attacked his beloved movement, Wesley was restrained neither by fear of retribution nor hope of favour, nor even by undue reverence for a dignitary thirty years his senior."[70] Smalbroke called Wesley an enthusiast, to which Wesley responded that Smalbroke had a truncated pneumatology.

---

[66]John Wesley, March 3, 1742, *Works* 19:256.

[67]Kimbrough and Newport, *Manuscript Journal of the Reverend Charles Wesley*, 1:288.

[68]John Wesley, March 3, 1742, *Works* 19:255n. For Evangelical John Fletcher's relationship with his bishop, one distinctly different from Newton's own struggles, see William Gibson's chapter, "John Fletcher's Silent Bishop," in Peter Fosaith and Geordan Hammond, eds., *Religion, Gender, and Industry: Exploring Church and Methodism in a Local Setting* (Eugene, OR: Wipf and Stock, 2011), 38-52.

[69]Baker, *John Wesley and the Church of England*, 91.

[70]Ibid., 93-94.

One of the most strongly worded episcopal challenges came from Gibson in his charge to the clergy of his diocese in 1749.

> There is another species of enemies, who give shameful disturbance to the parochial Clergy, and use very unwarrantable methods to prejudice their people against them, and to seduce their flocks from them; the Methodists and Moravians, who agree in annoying the established ministry, and in drawing over to themselves the lowest and most ignorant of the people, by pretences to greater sanctity.[71]

Gibson perceived uniformity among Wesley, Whitefield and the Moravians. Whether they were seen together like this by the majority of society is uncertain, but the bishop's placing them together in this way is an indication that by 1749 such a grouping was acceptable. This also suggests that the breach between Wesley and the Moravians may not have been as perceptible to those outside the revival. The bishop notes that "endeavours [on the part of the ecclesiastical hierarchy against the Methodists] have not been wanting," and, in addition, that "these endeavours have caused some abatement in the pomp and grandeur with which these people for some time acted, yet they do not seem to have made any impression upon their leaders."[72]

Gibson, although a fierce opponent of the revival and its unorthodox use of canon law, had an enduring respect for the Methodists and their ability to evade criminal charges. He was also keen to use the Methodists to encourage the regular clergy to more active service. One of his earlier charges to the clergy of London in 1742 can be seen as embracing the idea of a competitive religious marketplace, much like Adam Smith would later describe in his *Wealth of Nations*. Gibson was simply applying the idea of a competitive religious marketplace to the London religious scene, placing Methodism and other forms of dissent as movements that should fire up the Church, and particularly its clergy, in the face of competition. In the letter, Gibson writes to his clergy colleagues:

---

[71]Edmund Gibson, *The Charge of the Right Reverend Father in God, Edmund Lord Bishop of London. At the Visitation of His Diocese in the Years 1746 and 1747*, 4.
[72]Ibid., 6.

> I need not tell you, what gross representations have been made both here and in the plantations, as if the generality of the clergy of the Church of England were shamefully remiss and negligent in the Pastoral Office. This slander upon our Church and clergy has been publickly spread and avow'd in a very unworthy and licentious manner; and has received a reprehension, though more gentle than it deserved, in a late pastoral letter against the enthusiasm of these days. But however, the reproaches of those men may be so far of use to us, as to be made a fresh incitement to care and diligence in the offices belonging to our function; that, after the example of St. Paul in a like case, we may cut off all occasion of slander, from them who desire occasion.[73]

Overall this 1742 letter was an attempt to call the clergy to the highest standards of clerical excellence. The letter was also a defense against what Gibson saw as rising opposition to the Church of England from diverse sources, including evangelical itinerants, reminiscent of "one hundred years ago," and those in Parliament who were calling for church reform. The Quaker Bill, a defeated attempt to alter the way in which church tithes were assessed, was seen by Gibson as a direct attack on the Church.[74] Gibson's purpose was to encourage what he saw as the best-found means of caring for the souls of his parishioners through the offices and liturgy of the established Church.

English evangelicals never experienced official persecution by Church or state authorities in the eighteenth century. Jeremy Gregory writes that this has as much to do with anti-Catholic sentiment, which remained strong in England. Gregory notes, "Persecution of dissent was contrasted as a hallmark of popery. Although evidence can be found of mobs stoning and harrying dissenters (including early Methodists), and pulling down their meeting houses, clergy were expected to work within a framework where they persuaded rather than persecuted non-conformists."[75] Impressions were being made, however, on the general

---

[73]Gibson, *Letter to the Clergy* (1742), 8-9.
[74]See Norman Sykes, *Edmund Gibson, Bishop of London 1669–1748* (New York: Oxford University Press, 1926), 148-75; and S. Taylor, "Sir Robert Walpole, the Church of England and the Quaker Tithe Bill of 1736," *Historical Journal* 28 (1985): 51-77.
[75]Jeremy Gregory, "The Long Eighteenth Century," in *The Cambridge Companion to John Wesley*, ed. Randy L. Maddox and Jason E. Vickers (New York: Cambridge University Press, 2010), 36.

population, who devoured anti-Methodist propaganda, and on the Evangelical clergy. The Evangelical clergy were most affected by episcopal censure. Only Evangelical clergy, or clergy with inclinations toward evangelicalism, were likely to have allowed the Wesleys and Whitefield to preach in their pulpits. Thus the censures from the bishops should be seen as censure of Methodism and warning to regular Evangelical clergy and to the general population.

To understand the ecclesiastical pressure that made disassociation from Wesley and all forms of Methodism essential to the regular Evangelical ministry within the prescribed structures of the Church of England, the censures of the bishops are vital. The same desire to group together the Wesleys, Whitefield and the Moravians in Bishop Gibson's *Charge* could have made Evangelical clergy wary of the ease with which guilt by association affected their ecclesiastical livelihood. The censures were part of a theologically charged political environment that created a context in which irregularity was all too easily connected to the practices and politics of earlier enthusiasts and parliamentarians of the previous century.

PRESSING ISSUES

The challenge for the historian is to see how the revival and its various offshoots, although perceived historically as a theological or religious movement, were seen in their own day as a political challenge. It was thought that the evangelicals were testing much more than the theology of conversion. Although much ink was used to argue for and against instantaneous or progressive paradigms of conversion, the theological debate was but an opening act to the larger challenge. The revival was seen to mount an offense against the ecclesiastical, political and social fabric of a nation with a long historical memory and one in which the Church and the state were intrinsically connected. A challenge to the Church could easily be seen as a challenge to the state and thus to the Crown itself. The Jacobite rebellions of both 1715 and 1745 justified the alarm caused by Methodist sectarianism and revived the historical memory of the English people. The appearance of armed soldiers marching into England from Scotland waving the Stuart banner looked all too familiar. Memories of the civil wars had not abated, and the political environment of the eighteenth century, with its connectedness to the seventeenth, created a context in which evangelicals passionately preaching the New Birth met opposition equally passionate to challenge them in order to maintain the delicate social fabric of post-Restoration society.

Gregory describes this interrelated social context, reiterating the work of J. C. D. Clark when he writes, "Many Churchmen believed that the interests of Church and State were in fact inseparable and interdependent, and that enemies of the Church were also enemies of the State."[76] Hempton, writing on the Church of England and its role within the political context, observes that "far from being regarded as a protected subsidiary of the State, the Church of England was an integral and indispensable part of the theory and practice of governing."[77] This interrelated social context was the context in which Methodists faced together the challenges and fears of those who saw the revival as a threat to English cultural norms.

---

[76]Ibid., 19.
[77]Hempton, *Religion and Political Culture in Britain and Ireland*, 3.

4

POLITICS AND POLITY

Methodist Structure and the
Question of Dissent

T. MORTIMER DESPISED THE METHODISTS. The advertisement in his *Die and Be Damned* makes this clear. Mortimer intended "to promote an extensive knowledge of the real principles and practices of the Methodists," not to understand better the growing movement but "in order to put some stop to the prevailing errors of this growing sect."[1] These "religious politicians" were a danger to the welfare of the English people, and on the ground, in the fields, on the street corner, these Methodists were setting up a competing structure in plain view of the establishment and its Church.

John Wesley's intentions when he set up the United Societies were obviously different from Mortimer's interpretation of the situation. Mortimer, however, was not the only person to come to the conclusion that Wesley's creation of a network of Methodist societies was more than a new form of Anglican revivalism—to these critics, Wesley created an ecclesiastical substructure that would challenge the hegemonic standing of the Church of England.[2] As such, this substructure was seen as a

---

[1]T. Mortimer, *Die and Be Damned: Or an Anecdote Against Every Species of Methodist; and Enthusiasm*, 2nd ed. (London: Printed for S. Hooper and A. Morley, at Gay's-Head near Beauforts-Buildings, in the Strand, 1758), advertisement.

[2]See Clive D. Field, *Anti-Methodist Publications of the Eighteenth Century: A Revised Bibliography* (Manchester, UK: John Rylands Library, 1991).

political statement, a challenge to the Church. J. R. H. Moorman in his history of the English Church quotes J. H. Overton and F. Relton, who state, "It is purely a modern notion that the Wesleyan movement ever was, or ever was intended to be, except by Wesley, a Church movement."[3] While the idea that Anglican Methodism, or Church Methodism, is a modern notion can easily be challenged, the idea that Methodism was a challenge to a Church prone to dissent was widely held.

Gibson was keen to observe the expanding challenge posed by Methodism in all of its various forms as it began to engage in ecclesiastical irregularity. These Methodists "began with Evening-Meetings at private Houses" and have "for some Time, to open and appoint *publick Places* of Religious Worship, with the same Freedom, as if they were warranted by the Act of *Toleration*."[4]

> And, not content with that, they have had the Boldness to preach in the *Fields* and other open Places, and by publick Advertisements to invite the *Rabble* to be their Hearers; notwithstanding an express Declaration in a Statute (*22 Car.* II. c. I.) against assembling in a FIELD, by Name. And how big with Mischief that Practice in particular is, may be abundantly seen in the past and present Accounts of it . . . and may be sensibly felt in our own, when it will be too late to remedy it, if not attended-to *in Time*.[5]

Gibson's observations, similar to those heard by Charles Wesley in Newcastle from a clergyman who railed against the Methodists as "enemies to the Church, seducers, troublers, scribes and Pharisees, hypocrites, etc,"[6] were principally concerned with two practices of irregular evangelicalism: societies and field preaching. The gathering of nonclergy-led societies and the unauthorized gatherings in fields and town squares touched a nerve in post-Restoration England that went far beyond theo-

---

[3]J. H. Overton and F. Relton, *The English Church from the Accession of George I to the End of the Eighteenth Century* (New York: Macmillan, 1906), 75, as quoted in J. R. H. Moorman, *A History of the Church in England*, 3rd ed. (London: A&C Black, 1980), 307.
[4]Edmund Gibson, *Observations Upon the Conduct and Behaviour of a Certain Sect, Usually Distinguished by the Name of Methodists* (London: Printed by Edward Owen, 1743 or 1744), 4.
[5]Ibid.
[6]S. T. Kimbrough Jr. and Kenneth G. C. Newport, *The Manuscript Journal of the Reverend Charles Wesley, M. A.* (Nashville: Kingswood Books, 2007), 1:358 (July 17, 1743).

logical dispute.[7] This chapter will look at the societies and social order. I will give particular attention to Wesley's societies and the question of dissent, the use of societies by regular Evangelicals, and the reaction both Evangelical and non-Evangelical within the Church to Wesley's burgeoning ecclesiastical subculture.

David Hempton writes, "in truth, Wesley's support of the Church of England was always more impressive in thought than in deed, and was neither static nor entirely unconditional."[8] Wesley's approach, seen by Methodists then and now as pragmatic and by others as schismatic, was not meant to be as radical as his opponents made it out to be. His approach was fueled by a desire to create a communal context within which his soteriological vision could be carried out.[9] Yet it was the creation of this soteriological laboratory and competing liturgical context that raised the ire of Wesley's opponents and many of the Evangelicals.

Wesley's structure of society, class and band within the Church is well known.[10] His societies were generally visited by himself, his brother or his army of lay preachers on rotation for preaching and hymn singing. Each society was divided into classes for more direct accountability, and in many cases into bands, an even smaller and more intimate gathering sometimes designated for particular purposes such as the "penitential bands" for those who had backslid in their faith. The evolution of Wesley's

---

[7]I use the term *nonclergy* rather than *lay* to highlight that Wesley's societies were not run by religious leaders of any kind but distinctly, regardless of issues of apostolic succession and valid ordination, by religious laypersons who did not fit into the categories of ecclesiastical leadership in eighteenth-century England. The radical nature of Wesley's experiment can be lost on the modern pluralist mind. The Evangelical societies were overwhelmingly led by clergymen of the Church. This is a radical distinction between the two groups. Within dissenting congregations, it must be remembered that religious leaders within their structures were ordained by their respective groups. Wesleyan ordination was not an issue in the 1740s when the revival began in full swing.

[8]David Hempton, "Wesley in Context," in *The Cambridge Companion to John Wesley*, Randy L. Maddox and Jason E. Vickers, eds. (New York: Cambridge University Press, 2009), 63.

[9]Henry Knight III goes so far as to state that Wesley's theological vision cannot be understood apart from the context of the Methodist bands, classes and societies within the Church of England. See his *The Presence of God in the Christian Life: John Wesley and the Means of Grace*, Pietist and Wesleyan Studies 3 (Lanham, MD: Scarecrow, 1992).

[10]See David Lowes Watson's *The Early Methodist Class Meeting* (Nashville: Discipleship Resources, 1985); and Kevin M. Watson's *Pursuing Social Holiness: The Band Meeting in Wesley's Thought and Popular Methodist Practice* (New York: Oxford University Press, 2014).

structure was gradual and arose from precedents already seen in English church history such as the religious societies that came to prominence during the Restoration on Josiah Woodward's model.[11] John Walsh aptly notes that "Wesley's genius came out less in originality than in the ability to snap up useful ideas and adapt them swiftly to his own purpose."[12] Unfortunately for Wesley and certain Evangelicals who founded similar societies within their own parishes, some of this borrowing of "useful ideas" created suspicion in the post-Restoration era because of the history of rebellion attached to these appropriated practices.

The extent to which Wesley founded and or swallowed up these small revivalistic groups continued throughout the period to complicate his relationship with Evangelical clergymen.[13] No attempt on the part of Evangelicals within the Church created anything near as complicated a schema as Wesley's United Societies, and some of Wesley's societies were found in Evangelical parishes, causing friction between the parties.[14]

What Wesley did not seem to foresee with the creation of a Methodist structure was the extent to which his societies would gain their own ethos separate from the Church. Charles Wesley was quick to remind his brother of the importance of maintaining distinct connections and remaining "only a sound part of that Church."[15] He was aware of the power of words to the formation of a distinct Methodist ethos and reminded his brother as early as 1744 to "guard against this; and in the name of the Lord, address tomorrow!"[16]

---

[11]See Watson, *Early Methodist Class Meeting*, 67-92; also Richard P. Heitzenrater, *Wesley and the People Called Methodists*, 2nd ed. (Nashville: Abingdon, 2013), 129-31, for the practical nature of the rise of the societies, classes and bands of Wesley's Methodism.

[12]John Walsh, *John Wesley 1703–1791: A Bicentennial Tribute* (London: Friends of Dr. William's Library, 1993), 6.

[13]See Henry D. Rack, *Reasonable Enthusiast: John Wesley and the Rise of Methodism*, 3rd ed. (Philadelphia: Trinity Press International, 2002), 177.

[14]Among Evangelicals it was as common to start clerical clubs, such as those started by John Fletcher and Samuel Walker, as it was to start small groups for laypersons. This emphasis on clerical clubs should be seen as a distinct difference between Wesleyans and Evangelicals, as the emphasis on clergy among the Evangelicals indicated a stronger commitment to the regular ministry of the Church of England.

[15]Kimbrough and Newport, *Manuscript Journal of the Reverend Charles Wesley*, 1:392 (March 6, 1744).

[16]Ibid.

Wesley may have been raised and trained within the Church and his faith given voice through the Prayer Book, but his followers would soon be formed within a dissenting system that had been created by an Anglican. Walsh writes that Wesley "saw his societies as an evangelical order within a Church whose surrounding environment of catholicity—apostolic order, liturgy, sacramental life—he took largely for granted and assumed to be readily available."[17] Wesley's assumption that his society members would participate within this catholicity did not prove realistic. The independent ethos of Methodism grew to become a stronger influence on the Methodist people than their founder's pronounced attachment to the Church.[18] Misty Anderson captures this well when she describes Methodists as "technically Anglicans."[19] Detached from the English Church's liturgical and social context, the ultimate separation of Wesleyan Methodism from its Anglican foundation was almost inevitable. Wesley's societies and the ever-increasing ethos of Methodist separatism within which they existed gave birth to a context of liturgical detachment.

Wesley assumed that the liturgical culture created by the parish structure of the Church of England was more durable than it was. His assumption was that the people under his care would retain a love for the Church that mimicked his own, although they would ultimately find meaning in his irregular practices. Wesley also underestimated the extent to which close-knit parishes would react to the incursion of Methodist preachers. The geographical landscape of early Wesleyan Methodism and its inability to flourish within the dense parish structures of southeast England is indicative of Methodism's independence. Had it been a movement within the Church, it is likely that its geography would have better reflected the geography of the Church. The opposition Wesley

---

[17]Walsh, *John Wesley 1703–1791*, 13.

[18]In fact, Ward writes that as "Wesley became embroiled with the hierarchy on matters doctrinal and practical . . . a certain desperation began to colour his pledges of loyalty." See Ward, "The Legacy of John Wesley: The Pastoral Office in Britain and America," in his *Faith and Faction* (London: Epworth, 1993), 227.

[19]Misty G. Anderson, *Imagining Methodism in Eighteenth-Century Britain: Enthusiasm, Belief, and the Borders of the Self* (Baltimore: Johns Hopkins University Press, 2012), 35.

received from Evangelical clergymen for supplanting the life of their parishes and disregarding parish boundaries becomes integral to understanding the separation of Wesleyan Methodism and Evangelical Anglicanism within this context of liturgical and social detachment.

What Evangelicals foresaw in their arguments with Wesley over the societies was the long-term effects of separation from the Church. Evangelical Thomas Adam wrote to Wesley during the turmoil of 1755 over the possibility of Methodist separation. Adam's larger concern was the sending of lay preachers and the founding of societies. He was already convinced that the irregularities of Wesleyan Methodism represented a form of separation from the Church but implored Wesley to pull back from these practices in order to retain an evangelical presence within the Church. He writes:

> Upon the whole, therefore, it is humbly submitted to your most serious consideration, whether the separation is not wide enough already, particularly in the instance of unordained persons preaching and gathering societies to themselves wherever they can; and whether all Methodists might not serve the interests of Christ better as witnesses and examples of a living faith, and expect a greater blessing from the God of order upon their talents, gifts, and graces, whatever they are, by returning to a closer union with the Church, and repairing the breach they have made, than by making it still wider, and separating what they think the gospel-leven from the lump.[20]

Wesley's desire to save souls without delay often clashed with the long-term project of creating an Evangelical presence within the Church of England. Newton, never an explicit opponent of dissent but still a proponent of the Church and of an evangelical presence within it, warned an eager young evangelical interested in holy orders in 1765 to refrain from the appearance of irregularities if he wanted to find a place within the Church.[21] Extemporaneous prayer, lay preaching and societies under

---

[20]*Works* 26:604 (from the Revd. Thomas Adam, Oct. 10, 1755).

[21]John Newton, *Cardiphonia: Or, the Utterance of the Heart; in the Course of A Real Correspondence in Two Volumes* (London: 1798), 2:51. Newton encouraged the young evangelical to "keep your zeal within moderate bounds."

lay control were seen as a rejection of the establishment. And these practices were considered fundamental by Wesley in his attempt to revive that very establishment.[22]

Wesley had little patience for canons that appeared to hinder the work of evangelism, and neither did he share the firm conviction of others that these irregular practices signified a separation. He appears to have been more concerned with the short-term effects of his decisions on those who had not heard the gospel, and he was little interested in the creation of a long-term "party" within the Church of England—a fundamental distinction between the Wesleyans and the Evangelicals.

For Wesley, separation from the Church meant the active and intentional negation of Church canons. He had ample reason to take this position. Subscription and eucharistic participation signaled an acceptance of the Church's authority. Wesley never encouraged his followers to subscribe to anything contrary to the Thirty-Nine Articles or the Homilies and was adamant that his preachers must have an "invariable attachment to the Church."[23] He continuously encouraged his followers to partake of communion whenever it was available.[24] In a letter to Samuel Walker, Wesley writes that "at present I apprehend those, and those only, to separate from the Church who either renounce her fundamental doctrines, or refuse to join in her public worship," arguing further that "as yet we have done neither, nor have we taken one step further than we were convinced was our bounden duty."[25] This "bounden duty" he at other times referred to as conscience. In another letter, "to a Clerical Friend," Wesley asks, "Do you desire us . . . to desist from advising those who now meet together . . . or in other words, to dissolve our societies?" to which he responds, "We cannot do this with a safe conscience; for we

---

[22]See *Works* 26:595 (Wesley to the Revd. Samuel Walker, Sept. 24, 1755).

[23]*Works* 26:470 (John Wesley to the Revd. Charles Wesley, July 17, 1751). Curiously, another letter to Charles Wesley (see *Works* 26:471) written by John three days later includes: "The Church, that is the Societies, both *must* and *shall* maintain the preachers *we send* among them," indicating at least in that particular letter that Wesley equated "Church" and "the Societies." In the summer of 1751, Charles Wesley was on a tour of the northern societies examining the Methodist lay preachers. John's language is an oddity at this point.

[24]See "The Duty of Constant Communion," *Works* 3.

[25]*Works* 26:595 (Wesley to the Revd. Samuel Walker, Sept. 24, 1755).

apprehend many souls would be lost thereby, and that God would require their blood at our hands."[26]

Representing the mature Evangelicalism that would mark the latter part of the eighteenth century into the nineteenth, Henry Venn, a friend of the Wesleys, wrote to his son in 1792 a letter titled "The Mistakes into Which Young Ministers are Apt to Fall." In the letter he outlines many of the mistakes that he had made as a young clergyman.

> I neglected to be large and full in describing the lamentable consequences of division and separation, amongst a people awakened, and called to the knowledge of Christ, by His minister—how separation and division lead men to conclude no one can certainly determine what the faith of Christ is; and that they serve no better purpose than to perplex and stumble the weak in faith—and give the ungodly occasion to boast, that passions and prejudices are nowhere less subdued than among the most religious.[27]

Having been close to Wesleyan Methodism throughout much of his ministry, Venn would have seen the continued movement that it had made and was speedily making after Wesley's death toward full separation from the Church.

METHODIST CONVENTICLES

The accusation that Methodists around the country were founding conventicles was a serious one laden with historical complexities. Archbishop William Laud described a conventicle as "when ten or twelve or more or lesse meet together to pray, reade, preach, expound, this is a conventicle."[28] Such a definition would have left Wesleyan Methodists with little room to object. Wesley's societies would have been seen as explicitly contrary to the parish structure of the Church of England.

---

[26]*Works* 26:126 (Wesley to a Clerical Friend, March 11, 1745). This particular letter is noteworthy. Frank Baker notes that this letter to an anonymous clergyman was definitely sent to a specific clergyman in Newcastle but that it was likely used as a template to send to numerous clergymen with criticism of Wesleyan Methodism. See *Works* 26:126n6.

[27]*The Letters of Henry Venn, with a Memoir by John Venn* (Carlisle, UK: Banner of Truth Trust, 1835, 1999), 591.

[28]Patrick Collinson, *From Cranmer to Sancroft* (New York: Hambledon Continuum, 2006), 145. For a helpful description of the "English Conventicle" as it arose during the 1640s, see 145-72.

In his 1742 letter to the clergymen of the diocese of London, Gibson made it clear that he was convinced that the parish structure of the Church of England was essential to the spiritual well-being of England. Gibson sounded a "sufficient warning to all who have a serious concern for religion, and a just regard to publick peace and order in Church and State" against those who would work apart from the parochial system as did the Puritans. Gibson argued that the Church's system, if promoted by the best endeavors of its clergymen, could

> oppose and suppress that spirit of enthusiasm, which is gone out; and which cannot be opposed and suppressed more effectually, than by preserving the bounds of parochial communion, and by every minister's satisfying his people, in the course of a regular life and a diligent discharge of pastoral duties and offices of all kinds, that they need no other instructions, nor any other means and helps for the saving of their souls, than those which the Church has provided for them.[29]

Regularity in ecclesiastical practice meant peace in England and in the hearts of its Christian people. The formation of conventicles, as illicit meetings that undermined the community, was an affront to the Church, the peace and the spiritual care of souls.

The Conventicle Act, passed in 1670 under Charles II and well known by Gibson, was a direct outgrowth of the religious turmoil of the English Civil War, as described so aptly by Christopher Hill in *The World Turned Upside Down*. Hill describes the religious and social extremism that was unleashed in the seventeenth century under the Commonwealth, calling the period after the execution of Charles I one of "glorious flux and intellectual excitement."[30] Written from Hill's distinctly revolutionary perspective, the book provides a clear picture of the radical elements, the Quakers, Baptists, Rankers, Diggers and Levellers, who appeared in this period. These radicals, some of whom questioned the legitimacy of Christ or promoted the idea that one could be divine as Christ was divine, would have horrified the moderate churchmen of the post-Restoration

---

[29]Edmund Gibson, *Letter to the Clergy* (1742), 11.
[30]Christopher Hill, *The World Turned Upside Down: Radical Ideas During the English Revolution* (London: Temple Smith, 1972), 12.

period.[31] These religious radicals would have contributed to an already unsettling picture of an executed monarch, a radically Protestant church and what Hill calls "the greatest upheaval that has yet occurred in Britain."[32] Hempton notes that it was "with Puritanism in mind and with Civil War memories to the forefront that Restoration lawyers and churchmen drew up the Conventicles Act." He describes that act as one "with draconian penalties, which magistrates were understandably reluctant to enforce."[33]

The Conventicle Act was implemented "to further and more speedy Remedies against the growing and dangerous practices of Seditious Sectaries and other disloyall Persons who under pretence of tender Consciences have or may at their Meetings contrive Insurrections (as late experience hath shewen)." These meetings included any indoor gathering that included five or more persons and met "under colour or pretence of any Exercise of Religion in other manner then according to the Liturgy and practice of the Church of England."[34] The authors, according to J. S. Simon, "must have thought that its stern provisions would crush out all religious meetings and private assemblies held 'in other manner than is allowed by the liturgy or practice of the Church of England.'"[35] Under this act, an outgrowth of the Act of Uniformity, participants could be fined five shillings for a first offense, with larger penalties following.[36] Methodists risked more than just their social and family connections when they attended society meetings potentially seen as conventicles.[37]

---

[31]Ibid., 151-52.

[32]Ibid., 11.

[33]David Hempton, *The Religion of the People: Methodism and Popular Religion, c. 1750–1900* (London: Routledge, 1996), 146.

[34]"Charles II, *1670: An Act to Prevent and Suppresse Seditious Conventicles. Statutes of the Realm: Volume 5: 1628–80* (1819), 648-51.

[35]J. S. Simon, "The Conventicle Act and Its Relation to the Early Methodists," *Proceedings of the Wesley Historical Society* 11 (1918): 88.

[36]Simon writes, "It is interesting to note that fines on married women convicted of being present at a conventicle had to be paid by their husbands, an arrangement which, in some cases, would not promote domestic felicity" (ibid., 89).

[37]Richard Heitzenrater describes the founding of the Methodist classes and the duty of the class leader to supplement the dues of its members who could not afford the penny a week necessary to participate. Many Methodists could not afford the class dues. Their participation in something that could be seen as a conventicle with fines beginning at five shillings should be taken into consideration. See Heitzenrater's *Wesley and the People Called Methodists*, 129-31. Obviously the

Hempton notes, however, that there were not only disparities in the application of the act but also various interpretations of it. He notes that one interpretation of the act, and the one that Wesley held, "was that for a conventicle to be unlawful it had to have a conspiratorial purpose."[38]

Gibson was clear that "in a Christian Nation, where the Instruction and Edification of the People is provided-for, by placing Ministers in *certain Districts*, to whom the Care of the Souls within those Districts is regularly committed," the gathering of "confused Multitudes of People" could only serve to "a Disesteem of their own Pastors, as less willing or less able to instruct them in the Way of Salvation."[39]

Methodist leaders did not always help their case when they publicly challenged the character of Anglican clergymen, the stewards of the parochial system, in print.[40] Walsh notes that at its very core the evangelical message of conversion was liable to be heard as criticism by the clergyman of the established Church. He writes that "the evangelical doctrine of conversion carried with it many ecclesiastical consequences, not least the imputation that those ministers of religion who did not preach the doctrines of grace, and had not themselves experienced the forgiveness of sins, were blind guides, false prophets or dumb dogs that would not bark."[41] Both Wesley and Whitefield published comments against the clergy early in the revival that were well known by Gibson and others in authority. Gibson quoted Whitefield, using his *Journal*, as proof that the revival was anticlerical:

> O my dear Brethren, have Compassion on our dear Lord's Church, which he has purchased with his own Blood. Suffer none of them to be as Sheep

---

implementation of the law was scattered and its interpretation varied. Otherwise this law could have put a stop to the United Societies at a very early stage of the revival. For a description of the social and communal connections that individual Methodists risked by membership in a society, see David Hempton, *Methodism: Empire of the Spirit* (New Haven, CT: Yale University Press, 2005), 87-90.

[38]Hempton, *Religion of the People*, 147.

[39]Gibson, *Letter to the Clergy*, 11.

[40]See Wesley's "An Address to the Clergy," in *Works* (Jackson) 10:480. Wesley, even as an Anglican, held the Puritan Baxter's description of the parish ministry in high esteem and recommended it widely.

[41]John Walsh, "Methodism and the Mob in the Eighteenth Century," *Studies in Church History* 8 (1972): 219.

having no Shepherd, or worse than none, those blind Leaders of the Blind, who let them perish for lack of Knowledge, and are no better than Wolves in Sheeps-cloathing.[42]

And again in another journal entry:

Though we are but few, and stand as it were alone, like *Elijah*; and though they, like the Priests of *Baal*, are many in Number; yet I doubt not but the Lord will appear for us as he did for that Prophet, and make us more than Conquerors.[43]

These attacks on the clerical authorities, least of all a biblical citation that implied that God should consume Methodism's opponents with fire, did little to further the interests of the revival among supporter or detractor.

There was a distinction, at times explicit, between the anti-Methodist propaganda aimed at Wesleyan Methodists and the other arms of the revival, be they under Whitefield's charge or within the established norms of the Church.[44] At the same time, the charge of schism was not reserved simply for the Wesleyans and Whitefieldites, nor should the criticism of one particular arm of the revival be seen as an indication that the revival was viewed in this early period as segregated into officially designated parts.

The charge of schism or social disruption was not simply a charge leveled against Methodism early on. As late as 1805, the archdeacon of Leicester publicly declared his fear that Methodism and dissent would bring about a rejection of the monarchy in favor of a democracy and revolution among the lower classes.[45] His explicit fear was "the dissolution

---

[42]As quoted in Gibson, *Observations*, 11. See *George Whitefield's Journals: A New Edition Containing Fuller Material Than Any Hitherto Published* (London: The Banner of Truth Trust, 1960), 317 (Aug. 3, 1739).

[43]Ibid. See *George Whitefield's Journals*, 344-45 (November 10, 1739).

[44]From a historiographical perspective, the separation of anti-Wesleyan Methodist propaganda from the larger antievangelical umbrella is a hindrance to the historical reconstruction of the period and places on the historical record a clear-cut system that resembles later divisions. The term *Methodist* was not the sole property of any one segment of the Evangelical Revival, although it would in time be associated with the Wesleyan arm. That present-day historians classify anti-Methodist propaganda from the eighteenth century using later nineteenth- and twentieth-century assumptions is problematic and represents the insular perspectives of many denominational histories.

[45]Robert Acklom Ingram, *The Causes of the Increase of Methodism and Dissension, and other Popu-*

of social order," a charge leveled against Methodism that appears to be consistent throughout the eighteenth century and even into the next.

While the establishment of societies had been a commonplace within the Church of England in the previous century under such organizations as the Society for the Reformation of Manners and the Society for the Promotion of Christian Knowledge, the structure that was being created under John Wesley was distinctly disconnected from local clerical oversight. The Wesleys' father had set up a society of the older model in his own Epworth parish as the parish priest. Wesley's model, while not opposed to clerical oversight, did not require it.

The Wesley brothers were not ignored by the church authorities of this period (as I discussed in the previous chapter). The brothers were brought before Bishop Gibson to discuss whether their societies were conventicles. Both brothers commented on their encounter with the bishop in their journals, with Charles claiming a certain sense of ambiguity on the bishop's part.[46] It is hard to juxtapose Charles's version of Gibson with Gibson's own writings, although the specific issue discussed was the simple act of reading in a society, not the creation of a system of societies throughout England. Charles describes the meeting this way:

> Next my brother enquired whether his reading in a religious society made it a conventicler. His Lordship warily referred us to the laws. But upon your urging the question, "Are the religious societies conventicles?" he answered, "No, I think not. However, you can read the acts and laws as well as I. I determined nothing." We hoped his Lordship would not henceforth receive an accusation against a presbyter, but at the mouth of two or three witnesses. He said, "No, by no means. And you may have free access to me at all times." We thanked him, and took our leave.[47]

---

larity of what is called *Evangelical Preaching, and the Means of Obviating Them, considered in a Sermon, preached at the Visitation of the Rev. the Archdeacon of Leicester, held at Melton Mowbray, June 20, 1805* (London: Stanhope and Tilling, 1807). It is fascinating to compare quotations such as the archdeacon's to the later work of the Marxist historian E. P. Thompson, who so famously argued for an entirely different understanding of Methodism—as a manipulation of the working classes and maintainer of the status quo. See E. P. Thompson's *The Making of the English Working Class* (New York: Pantheon, 1963), especially his chapter "The Transforming Power of the Cross."

[46] *Works* 19:359 (Oct. 20, 1738).

[47] Kimbrough and Newport, *Manuscript Journal of the Reverend Charles Wesley*, 1:151.

Charles Wesley's description highlights the bishop's mixture of support and caution. Bishops were keen to support loyal priests of the Church of England. They had no reason to suppress valid Anglican expressions. They cautioned the brothers, however, on their methods.

In a meeting with the Archbishop of Canterbury in 1739, Charles afterward records that the primate encouraged the brothers to "give no more umbrage than was necessary," to "forbear exceptionable phrases" and "to keep to the doctrines of the Church." They assured Archbishop Potter, the same man who had ordained them at Oxford, that they would keep to the Church "till her Articles and Homilies were repealed." He knew of no effort to repeal any of them, and neither would he support such efforts.[48]

Dissent and the creation of conventicles questioned the Church of England's hegemonic standing as *the* established Church. As such, the issues surrounding them were of both political and social importance. The creation of Wesley's ecclesiastical substructure produced political repercussions that Wesley was never fully aware of nor cared to address. He felt propelled to proclaim the New Birth by almost any means.

WESLEY AND THE QUESTION OF DISSENT

Wesley's relationship to Evangelical Anglican clergy must be seen within the larger picture of Wesley's relationship with the general clergy and the thorny issue of Methodism's relationship to the Church of England. From the beginning of the Methodist revival the accusation had been made that Wesley and those associated with him were dissenters. These accusations had little to do with the message of the Wesleys and much to do with their methods. Frank Baker notes that on Wesley's part, "Whatever deliberate separation from the Church of England took place during Wesley's ministry was primarily in the realm of deeds rather than of thought."[49] And yet Baker's less critical remarks need to be balanced by those like Hempton's, who reminds the student of the period: "The fact that an erstwhile Oxford high churchman like Wesley could bring himself, as a mere priest, to ordain preachers for America and Scotland

[48]Ibid., 1:162-63 (Feb. 21, 1739).
[49]Frank Baker, *John Wesley and the Church of England* (Nashville: Abingdon, 1970), 3.

in 1784–85 (much to the chagrin of his brother Charles) shows how far he was prepared to break the rule of the Church to fulfil his mission."[50] Wesley's allegiance to Anglicanism was questioned by family, friends and opponents. In a letter from his older brother Samuel Wesley Jr., written in April 1739, Samuel writes: "My mother tells me she fears a formal schism is already begun among you, though you and Charles are ignorant of it. For God's sake take care of that, and banish extemporary expositions and extemporary prayers."[51]

In a 1745 tract titled *The Question Whether It Be Right to Turn Methodist*, the author of the tract creates a dialogue "between two members of the Church of England" in which the question of whether to become a Methodist was never in doubt. The tract had been written to provide "as seasonable, as well as more reasonable, Appeal to Men of Reason and Religion, than what we have lately seen under that Title."[52] Wesley had published his *Appeal* in 1743 and would publish a further appeal in 1745. Outler describes these appeals as "Wesley's most important apologia for his own doctrine and for his movement as an evangelical order within the national church—beset as it was by the apathy of nominal Christianity and by the rising tides of rationalism and unbelief."[53]

Although, as Outler notes, these appeals bore "the tags of his Oxford education"[54] and according to Wesley's *Journal* made noticeable impact on many of his detractors,[55] the author of the *Question* saw the creation of Methodism's structure as a "great Danger of further Apostasy from the best-constituted Church in the World."[56] Methodism was a "sect" that had separated from the established Church.

The point of the author's Anglican hero is that the unity of the Church is shattered by Methodism and any other sect in England that would attempt to remove members from the Church. Regardless of the doctrines

---

[50]Hempton, "Wesley in Context," 64.
[51]*Works* 25:634 (a letter from the Revd. Samuel Wesley, Jr.).
[52]*The Question Whether It Be Right to Turn Methodist Considered: In a Dialogue Between Two Members of the Church of England* (London: 1745), 1.
[53]Albert Outler, ed., *John Wesley* (New York: Oxford University Press, 1964), 384.
[54]Ibid., 385.
[55]See *Works* 20:106, 112, 202, 249.
[56]*The Question Whether It Be Right to Turn Methodist*, 7.

in question, ultimately the question posed by the publication hinged on the definition of "Church" and subsequently whether the Church of England was a true expression of this larger Catholic vision. Sounding much like a precursor to the Tractarians, the author claims:

> One Member of this universal Kingdom of Christ is the *Church of England*; for no one will say, but that she is a *National*, yea the *only* National Church in this *Realm*; because she, and she alone, is the Church *Establish'd* here *by the Laws of the Land.* And herein she is not only a member of, but she bears the exact Image of, the Catholick Church: For as that, tho' consisting of many *National* Churches, is but One in the World; so our Church, tho' partitioned into sundry particular *Diocesan* and *Parochial* Churches, as members of the same Body, is but One Church in this Kingdom.[57]

Ironically, this description of the Church was very similar to the words of the Wesleys themselves. The issue was whether the creation of societies separate from parish structures constituted schism.

Throughout England the scars of past ecclesiastical skirmishes were visible on the buildings in which the Church worshiped. Among the remains of the iconoclasts were missing appendages on statues, carvings and roods, and plain windows where stained glass had once been. The English people could see these ecclesiastical and political skirmishes whenever they entered their parish church. Not only were Puritans of the time fearful of a resurrected Bishop Laud, but many within the established Church were keenly aware of any tendency within their ranks toward Cromwellianism.[58] Rack writes, "One can hardly over-emphasize the extent to which the seventeenth-century horrors haunted the inherited memories and fed the fears of eighteenth-century people," noting that as late as the end of the eighteenth century the "old war-cries of

---

[57]Ibid.

[58]During the American Revolution of the 1770s, many Loyalist Anglicans in the colonies saw the American patriots as "the descendents of Oliver Cromwell's army." See Margaret Wheeler Willard, ed., *Letters on the American Revolution, 1774–1776* (Boston: Houghton Mifflin, 1925), 120; and William H. Nelson, *The American Tory* (Oxford: Clarendon, 1961), 85-91. Many colonial Anglicans feared that the patriots' goal was to outlaw Anglicanism, much as the Puritans did during the Commonwealth. See David Hain and Gardiner H. Shattuck, *The Episcopalians* (New York: Church Publishing, 2004), 40.

'Church and King' and 'Down with the Rump' current in the 1650s could be repeated against Dissenters."[59]

Seen within the context of this heightened historical memory, the mobs who attacked and intimidated many of the early Methodist preachers and Wesley himself, regardless of later Methodist hagiography, were actually means by which a largely defunct legal system could maintain public order against a possible menace. Describing the violence used by these mobs, Walsh writes:

> Of the violence actually inflicted, a considerable portion was aimed at psychological humiliation rather than corporeal injury: this as the purpose of the stripping of clothes, the rolling of dungheaps and kennels. Its object was often a show of collective strength which would strike such terror into a preacher that he would pledge himself never to return to the parish. It says much for the fervour of the preachers that it very seldom worked.[60]

Walsh describes the participants of these mobs as "moved by ideas as well as irrational drives." These same participants, however, "not infrequently felt their actions justified in terms of social necessity or religious duty. There were villagers who felt that the Church Militant had the right to use a certain amount of deterrent force against those who threatened it."[61] Such mobs could be a means to prevent civil strife of a larger and more serious kind, whether dissenting or Jacobite. G. C. B. Davies notes that "the rioting which John Wesley encountered at Falmouth, for example, was directly attributed to fear of the young Prince Charles."[62] Davies writes that "it should be borne in mind, when considering this question, that many clergy were also magistrates, and their hostile attitude was not only on doctrinal and personal grounds, but also on grounds of maintaining the public peace in face of possible rioting and disturbance."[63] This is precisely why Gregory notes in his work on Anglicanism and the

---

[59]Rack, *Reasonable Enthusiast*, 29.
[60]Walsh, "Methodism and the Mob," 215.
[61]Ibid., 221.
[62]G. C. B. Davies, *The Early Cornish Evangelicals 1735–60: A Study of Walker of Truro and Others* (London: SPCK, 1951), 27.
[63]Ibid., 28.

continued task of reformation in this period that "there was . . . a tension between the clergy's role as ordained ministers of a comprehensive Church and as leaders of a religious community."[64] Clergymen could hold any number of roles within sprawling parishes, and in order to maintain a decent living wage many had to take on multiple charges.[65]

However ironic it may seem, the same structure that allowed for mob policing allowed for the growth of Methodism. It is certain that Methodism would not have been able to flourish within a church with strictly enforced ecclesiastical discipline. Even enforcing the canons, however, was not an easy task. Baker writes that "the 141 *Constitutions and Canons Ecclesiastical* of 1603 formed a body of law which could in dire need be invoked against miscreants or annoying innovation, but they were neither devoid of ambiguity nor easy to enforce."[66] Wesley's maverick use of Anglican polity and his tightrope interpretations of canon law, parish structures and laws meant to govern dissent were argued based on a benevolent interpretation of Methodist actions and a specific reading of the law's original intent. Hempton describes the debate over Methodism's legal standing as "one of the most controversial legal problems of the period between 1740 and 1820."[67] He argues that Wesley's legal perspective can be summarized as: "Methodists were not dissenters, therefore the Toleration Act was irrelevant to them."[68] Of course, the argument was much more nuanced, and Hempton writes that Wesley's argument pivoted on key interpretations of the law and Methodist practice, including the idea that "the Conventicles Act was designed to 'provide remedies against sedition.' Methodists were not seditious, quite the reverse." Additionally:

> Field preaching was legal in theory and safe in practice because it was
> conducted in daylight to known crowds which were much smaller than

---

[64]Jeremy Gregory, "The Eighteenth-Century Reformation: The Pastoral Task of Anglican Clergy After 1689," in John Walsh, Colin Haydon and Stephen Taylor, eds., *The Church of England c. 1689–1833: From Toleration to Tractarianism* (New York: Cambridge University Press, 1993), 81.

[65]Davies, *Early Cornish Evangelicals*, 24.

[66]Baker, *John Wesley and the Church of England*, 14.

[67]Hempton, *Religion of the People*, 146.

[68]Ibid., 148.

both Methodists and Anglicans alleged. If ordination was properly understood to be for a gospel ministry, not a specific territorial location, then
itinerant preaching was not an offence against the Church.[69]

It is unclear whether the original authors intended for the Conventicle
Act and the Act of Uniformity to be applied to field preaching, although
J. S. Simon claims that "it is evident that conventicles held in the open air
were unlawful assemblies. Every one acquainted with the religious history
of the seventeenth century is aware that such was the opinion of those
who administered the Act."[70] This distinction between the intention of the
act and its administration was pivotal to Wesley's legal argument.

Conflict between the law's intention and its administration can be
seen in a letter written by Bishop Edward Chandler of Durham in 1747.
Chandler was no friend to Methodism. He once described the preachers
as "insolent boys."[71] He wrote that Methodist crowds should be treated
with due caution to safety for the sake of calm, evidence of the legal latitude that allowed Methodism to continue. In a letter to the Rev. Sharpe,
also of Durham, he writes:

> I have indeed one doubt, whether a number of people gathered without
> arms and attempting no injury to any person can be treated as riotous;
> any more than a mob about a Ballad singer, or a crowd about a moun-
> teback, and therefore I cannot advise it absolutely, but if the Church-
> wardens or others will make the tryal, they may, but in case the people
> will not disperse upon the reading, it will not be advisable to go further.[72]

This admiration for the law, its application relative to the situation and
for civil order was keenly observed within the volatile social context of
the period, and most ecclesiastical figures of the time did likewise. The
complex situation in which these laws were interpreted, though, added
to the confusion related to their implementation. According to Hempton:

---

[69]Ibid.

[70]Simon, "Conventicle Act," 82-83.

[71]See Walsh, "Methodism and the Mob," 219; and Wesley F. Swift, "Headingley Papers," *Proceedings of the Wesley Historical Society* 28 (1951–1952): 49.

[72]Edward Chandler, written July 15, 1747, to the Revd. Sharpe, prebendary of and at Durham. See Swift, "Headingley Papers."

The issue was further complicated by legal ignorance in the localities,
genuine confusion about the precise limits of toleration afforded by post-
Restoration statutes, uncertainties about the respective responsibilities of
church courts and quarter sessions in controlling religious deviance and,
more prosaically, about who should bear the burden of legal costs.[73]

Hempton notes that Wesley's principles were "easier to defend in learned
debate than they were in English localities." This defense was made difficult at a time of "foreign warfare and domestic instability when tol-
erance had to accept the inconveniences of Methodism's uncertain legal
position" and while Methodists applied for certificates under the Act of
Toleration to "guard against intimidation."[74] Additionally, Wesley's irregular ministry should be seen in light of the decline of church courts
and the rising acceptance of dissent throughout the eighteenth century.

Often Methodism arose when and where ecclesiastical control was
weak, especially in large parishes. It did not take root in the southeastern
portion of the country, for instance, where parishes were more prevalent
and there was greater clerical oversight. In fact, Hempton and Walsh
have shown that Methodists lived often on the outskirts of parishes'
boundaries.[75] The lack of ecclesiastical coordination and the structuring
of parish lines were both important aspects in Methodist growth. What
this "Methodist geography" indicates is that Methodists were a marginal
people even geographically speaking.[76]

Given this context, Methodist irregularities may have been allowed,
but their effects on Methodism's relationship with the Church of
England and Wesley's relationship with the Evangelical clergy were detrimental. At issue is the definition of dissent. Was a dissenter one who
had to be in explicit secession from the established Church, as Wesley
contended, or was a dissenter anyone who practiced any form of

---

[73]Hempton, *Religion of the People*, 146.
[74]Ibid., 148.
[75]Hempton, *Methodism*, especially 18-23.
[76]Hempton has also pointed out that Methodist growth outside England was principally in areas
where Anglicanism had already taken root. In this way Methodism was able to grow in parts of
the American colonies where Anglicanism was strong, but it had little or no affect in Roman
Catholic parts of the world like France.

unauthorized ministry? This elusively defined term was used to argue Methodism's rightful designation.

Davies notes that in Cornwall, the Methodists were known as dissenters by some of the Anglican clergymen in reports from the 1740s.[77] The question is what gave the clergy this impression. Davies states that what is "noteworthy in these and other replies is the tendency for the Methodists to be accounted Dissenters," and that "this feeling was already hardening in other parts of the country, though some remain dubious."[78] Ironically, the Methodists debated among themselves how the public impression of Methodism should be managed. In conversation with his brother Charles and Samuel Walker, Wesley was faced with the question of how to manage the public impression of Methodism very early in the revival. Often overlooked in terms of Wesley's relationship to Evangelical clergy is the effect of the public impression of Methodism. Both parties, however, were well aware of it. In order to stem the impression that Methodism was distinct from Anglicanism, attention was given to the way in which Methodist leaders spoke of the movement.

Wesley's own acceptance of dissenters into the Methodist fold did nothing to help public impression. Despite his own Anglican status, he did not require members of his society to be active in the Church of England. This reinforced fears of Methodist dissent among many. Ironically, the Fetter Lane Society, from which Wesley broke in 1739 and which was thought to be run by Moravians, required that its members be in communion with the Church. Once Wesley broke from the Fetter Lane Society and founded his London headquarters at the Foundry, the requirement was dropped.[79]

Methodist lay preacher John Bennet represents well the fluidity of evangelicalism, dissent and Methodism and the challenges this fluidity

---

[77]Davies, *Early Cornish Evangelicals*, 25.

[78]Ibid., 26.

[79]Baker, *John Wesley and the Church of England*, 78. Kevin Watson argues that there was no requirement that Fetter Lane members be Anglican, although all of them, save Peter Böhler, were. Watson shows that Fetter Lane was not an "Anglican Religious Society," ultimately agreeing with Martin Schmidt that it was a combination of influences, including Herrnhut Moravianism, the Anglican Religious Societies and Wesley's own "ideas and experiences." See *Pursuing Social Holiness*, 34-38.

produced. His societies were taken into Wesleyan Methodism around 1744, but after Bennet's marriage in 1750 to Grace Murray, whom Wesley had intended to marry, there was a break between the two men. Subsequently, Bennet attempted to recreate his old northern connection of societies. This attempt met with varied success, largely because of Wesley's control of much of the property. Nonetheless, in Bolton Bennet "captured 107 out of the 126 members."[80] Not only was the revival fluid as a movement, but also personal connections and loyalties were vital within it. Many were more committed to personalities than structures, thus revealing one of the implications of voluntary associations.

FLETCHER AND WALKER: EVANGELICAL SOCIETIES

Evangelical clergy were not, as a group, against the notion of societies within their parishes. Thomas Haweis was very explicit in his writings that Christian fellowship was essential to the Christian life. He writes:

> Let me therefore recommend it to you to seek the company of those, whose course and conduct is most holy, heavenly, and zealous; to be free one with another; to open your hearts, as Christians, in that mutual confidence, which none but real Christians have any experience of, to delight in social prayer, and be desirous to join in it whenever you have opportunity. A conduct indeed, which, to those who know nothing of heart-religion, is always offensive and disliked; but which all, who have seriously set their souls to seek the kingdom of God in the first place, have found both most necessary to keep alive their holy purposes, and most conducive to their comfort as well as edification of their souls.[81]

Walsh writes, "Evangelical parish clergy were well aware that the piety they aroused could not easily be contained within the liturgical

---

[80]Henry D. Rack, "Survival and Revival: John Bennet, Methodism, and the Old Dissent," in *Protestant Evangelicalism: Britain, Ireland, Germany and America c. 1750–c. 1950, Essays in Honour of W. R. Ward*, ed. Keith Robbins (New York: Basil Blackwell, 1990), 14.

[81]Thomas Haweis, *The Communicant's Spiritual Companion. Or, an Evangelical Preparation for the Lord's Supper. In which I. The Nature of the Ordinance is Shewn. II. The Dispositions Requisite for a Profitable Participation Thereof. Wherein, The Careless Sinner is Admonished, The Formalist Detected and Reproved, The Feeble-Minded Comforted, The Doubting Relieved, The Sincere Assisted, and The Faithful Confirmed. With Meditations and Helps for Prayer, Suitable to the Subject. By the Reverend Thomas, Haweis, Rector of Aldwinckle, Northamptonshire; And Chaplain to the Right Hon. the Earl of Peterborow*, 6th ed. (London: 1770), 90-91.

framework of the Church, even when its Sunday services were enlivened by sermons and augmented by family prayers."[82] For this very reason, Charles Simeon later promoted Evangelical societies. The concern that most Evangelicals showed for Wesley's system was its independence from established structures and the oversight of local clergy, including Evangelical incumbents. Some, like Fletcher, William Grimshaw and Charles Perronet, encouraged the founding of Wesleyan societies, although Fletcher was more cautious in his support than were the latter two. Perronet had a Methodist society led by his daughter that met in his kitchen.[83]

Newton, ever the moderate, in a letter to a postulant for holy orders in the Church, conveyed his concern about speaking to societies. He did not forbid the practice, nor even discourage it. Newton writes, as late as 1770, even after the expulsions from Oxford two years before:

> And therefore as your years and time are advancing, and you have been for a tolerable space under probation of silence, I can make no objection to your attempting sometimes to speak in select societies; but let your attempts be confined to such, I mean where you are acquainted with the people, or the leading part of them, and be upon your guard against opening yourself too much amongst strangers;—and again, I earnestly desire you would not attempt any thing of this sort in a very public way, which may perhaps bring you under inconveniencies, and will be inconsistent with the part you ought to act (in my judgment) from the time you receive Episcopal ordination.[84]

This moderate stance was not uncommon for Newton. He was distinctly ecumenical in his engagement with and encouragement of all Christians. Yet he was well aware of the dangers of acting the part of a dissenter while attempting to remain within the establishment.[85] Newton

---

[82]John Walsh, "Religious Societies, Methodist and Evangelical: 1738–1800," in *Voluntary Religion: Papers Read at the 1985 Summer Meeting and the 1986 Winter Meeting of the Ecclesiastical Historical Society*, ed. W. J. Shields and Diana Wood (London: 1986), 295.

[83]*Works* 20:35n74 (Aug. 14, 1744).

[84]Newton, Letter IV (Aug. 30, 1770), in *Cardiphonia* 2:60.

[85]In another letter in the *Cardiphonia* collection, Newton counsels an anonymous "Methodist" who was apparently becoming or had become an independent. See his letter of Aug. 31, 1757, 2:68-70.

himself had faced problems attaining ordination on account of his evangelical connections.[86]

Walker, ever the ecclesiastical conservative, was one of the leading Evangelicals who started societies in his Cornwall parish. His society was founded in 1754, well after many of Wesley's societies in the previous decade.[87] Walsh describes Walker's society as "an Anglican alternative to the irregular societies of John Wesley."[88] Fletcher seems to have discovered societies springing up within his parish without his direct involvement. He notes in his correspondence that "a little society of about 20 or 30 people has come together of its own accord" in Madeley Wood, and "another of some 20" in Coalbrookdale, also known as the "the dale."[89] Societies for both laity and clergy were not uncommon in Evangelical parishes. They were uncommon, however, in the generality of parishes.

Fundamentally, what distinguished the Evangelical societies from Wesley's societies was Evangelical insistence on maintaining direct oversight of the societies within their parishes and the common use of established rules and patterns for running them. Rack describes Evangelical societies as "parochially-based societies, usually under close clerical supervision."[90] Walker, for instance, based his societies directly on those popularized in the early part of the century by Josiah Woodward.[91] Woodward's model was used by Samuel Wesley and may have inspired

---

[86]D. Bruce Hindmarsh, *John Newton and the English Evangelical Tradition: Between the Conversions of Wesley and Wilberforce* (Grand Rapids: Eerdmans, 2001), 83-118.

[87]Wesley visited some members of Walker's society briefly in August 1755. He records in his *Journal*: "As I was riding through Truro, one stopped my horse and insisted on my alighting. Presently two or three more of Mr. Walker's society came in, and we seemed to have been acquainted with each other for many years" (*Works* 21:25).

[88]Walsh, "Religious Societies," 297.

[89]Peter Forsaith, ed., *Unexampled Labours: Letters of the Revd John Fletcher to Leaders in the Evangelical Revival* (London: Epworth, 2008), 130 (letter from Fletcher to Charles Wesley, April 27, 1761).

[90]Henry D. Rack, "Religious Societies and the Origins of Methodism," *Journal of Ecclesiastical History* 38 (1987): 583.

[91]See Josiah Woodward, *An Account of the Societies for the Reformation of Manners, in London and Westminster, and other Parts of the Kingdom. With a Persuasive to Persons of all Ranks, to be Zealous and Diligent in Promoting the Execution of the Laws against Prophaness and Debauchery, for the Effecting A National Reformation, Published with the Approbation of a Considerable Number of the Lords Spiritual and Temporal* (London: Printed for B. Aylmer, at Three Pigeons in Cornhill, 1699).

the use later by his sons. The Woodward model assumed clerical over-sight, although the Wesleyan use of laypeople became a hallmark of the Methodist movement. It was rare for an Evangelical to allow lay oversight of his societies, although John Baddeley, rector of Hayfield in Derbyshire, appointed laymen to assist him, and Henry Venn was only able to visit his societies monthly because of the size of his parish.[92] Davies notes that Evangelical James Hervey left behind a society at Bideford, and Thomas Vivian at Cornwood maintained a "class" of his own parish-ioners for many years.[93]

Walker's society had a distinctly Anglican flavor. The rules of the so-ciety indicate a desire to evade the negative assumptions of Wesley's so-cieties and their dissenting counterparts. Walker formed his society with the full support of Whitefield and Berridge, whom he consulted before founding it.[94] He was convinced that the formation of a new society could be done for the edification of souls within the structures and ac-cording to the expectations of the established Church. This balance be-tween Evangelical practice and established norms characterized Walker's ministry. His letters to Wesley throughout the 1750s not only highlight this fact but were part of Walker's attempts to convince Wesley of the necessity of a similar approach.[95] Walker's approach to reform and evan-gelism was similar in temperament to that of his archbishop, who writes: "Hoping for perfection in any human thing, is visionary; and murmuring for want of it, is resolving never to be happy; and taking irregular methods to obtain it, is the sure way to be wretched."[96]

---

[92]Davies, *Early Cornish Evangelicals*, 66; Walsh, "Religious Societies," 296.

[93]Davies, *Early Cornish Evangelicals*, 66.

[94]Ibid., 70-71.

[95]Walker and Wesley's correspondence began in the fall of 1755. See Sept. 5, 1755, from the Revd. Samuel Walker, *Works* 26:582. The correspondence continued until the year of Walker's death, 1761. Davies writes concerning the correspondence: "The Walker-Wesley correspondence made clear the line on which the two parties, Methodists and Evangelicals, were to proceed: the Methodists into formal separation due to administration of the Sacraments by the former lay preachers; and the Evangelicals in loyal adherence to the parochial system, seeking to quicken their parishioners and united when possible with their clerical brethren" (Davies, *Early Cornish Evangelicals*, 220).

[96]Archbishop Thomas Secker, as quoted in Robert G. Ingram, *Religion, Reform and Modernity in the Eighteenth Century: Thomas Secker and the Church of England*, Studies in Modern British Religious History 17 (Woodbridge, UK: Boydell, 2007), 9.

The rules of Walker's society offer an insider look at the workings of this particular Evangelical society. Walker founded the society by issuing a letter to potential participants with a detailed list of the society's polity. His letter provides a three-part structure: "I lay before you the design of this Society, and give you some cautions concerning it. The design is threefold: 1. To glorify God. 2. To be quickened and confirmed ourselves. 3. To render us more useful among our neighbours."[97]

The society was not unlike others in that the members were encouraged to "watch over one another in love," "be willing to hear your faults" and "desire the prayers" of others.[98] In classic evangelical style the members were explicitly to "discountenance all such things as you see prejudicial to others, such as taverns, alehouses, gaming, and many sports which are destructive of souls."[99] The evangelical tendency to eschew certain popular vices was common throughout the period and did not add to evangelicals' popularity among an already suspicious public.

The rules concerning the membership of the society and its oversight distinguish it from Wesley's societies. This was a society for members of the Church of England in good standing with their parish priest and under his direct oversight. Walker's concern that his society be strictly connected to the established Church was twofold. He insisted that connection to the Church would better support the spiritual welfare of the society's participants and guard it against opposition and suspicion. The second rule of the society makes this point plain:

> That in order to the being of one heart, and one mind, and to prevent all things which gender strifes, as well as to remove all occasion of offence from being taken against this Society, no person is to be admitted a Member or allowed to continue such, who is a member of any other meeting, or follows any other preaching than that of the established min-

---

[97]Samuel Walker, *Fifty Two Sermons, on the Baptismal Covenant, the Creed, the Ten Commandments, and Other Important Subjects . . . To Which Is Prefixed a Preface* (London: 1763), 1:xxx.
[98]Ibid., xxxii.
[99]Ibid., xxxiii.

istry of the Church of *England*—That none be Members but such as attend the Sacrament every month, and that no person be at any time introduced except by request of the Director.[100]

And the society's third rule makes it plain that "the Director be the Reverend Mr WALKER."[101]

Walker also founded a society for Evangelical clergy that would ultimately solidify his status as a leading voice of the Evangelical Revival *within* the Church of England. Davies describes Walker as "the leader of the 'awakened' clergy" in Cornwall, one of the two major centers of Evangelical influence during the early period of the Revival.[102] The clerical society that Walker founded was "composed of the neighbouring Clergy," and like his other society, the clerical "club" was conducted with "proper regulations." One of the participants of the club writes in a letter:

> Mr WALKER was the person who first proposed a friendly meeting of neighbouring Clergymen, with a view to improve one another in Christian knowledge, for the better edification of the people committed to their care, and to encourage each other if, as it was likely, any difficulty or opposition should arise to either of them in the more vigorous discharge of the ministerial duty.[103]

The society, like his lay society, soon gained the negative attention of clergy and laity "as if the whole Society was methodistically inclined." Members of the clergy society were required by its own regulations to be members "zealously attached" to the Church of England.[104] The social stigma of small groups was simply stronger than the good intentions of those who established them for reasons of religious edification. These religious intentions could not assuage the political and social fears of their opponents. And soon enough after Walker's death the majority of his parish did leave the Church of England for dissent, fulfilling the prophecies of the opponents of this distinctly establishmentarian Evangelical.

---

[100]Ibid., xxxiv-v.
[101]Ibid., xxxv.
[102]Davies, *Early Cornish Evangelicals*, 53.
[103]Walker, *Fifty Two Sermons*, xviii-xix.
[104]Ibid.

John Fletcher's letters to Evangelical colleagues paint a different picture of the societies in his parish. Fletcher, as has already been noted, experienced the random nature of the revival, with societies springing up within his parish without his initiative. These letters, mainly to Charles Wesley, describe a parish at odds with a new Evangelical incumbent. Fletcher, appointed vicar of Madeley in 1760 much to the vexation of John Wesley, faced opposition to his preaching and his acceptance of religious societies. In a 1767 letter to George Whitefield, he writes that he wanted to see Whitefield in London but that opposition in his parish, and some outside it, kept him from traveling. He writes, "Tho' I want to see you, Yet I do not want to be seen; And I am best hid, I think, in my hole."[105]

Madeley parish in the heart of Shropshire ultimately became a stronghold of Church Methodism during Fletcher's incumbency and later after his death under the influence of his wife, Mary Bosanquet Fletcher.[106] The opposition that the revival encountered on a national level, Fletcher encountered at the parish level. This opposition included accusations that Fletcher was a Jesuit in disguise, a schismatic and an enthusiast. He was opposed by ecclesiastical authorities and also dragged before civil authorities. Within two years of his coming to Madeley, Fletcher was threatened with prison by the magistrate for allowing a cottage meeting to take place within the bounds of his parish.[107]

Although Fletcher practiced a regular Anglican ministry within the parish structure of the established Church, his ties to Methodism and to the Wesley brothers made him an easy target for anti-Methodist sentiment. The words of an anonymous author who warned a colleague

---

[105]Forsaith, *Unexampled Labours*, 229 (Fletcher to George Whitefield, July 3, 1767).

[106]Forsaith claims that "Madeley was one of the last parishes where Methodism remained within the Church of England" (Forsaith, *Unexampled Labours*, 20). The longevity of Church Methodism in Madeley was a direct outgrowth of the ministry of Mary Bosanquet Fletcher. For an analysis of the broader phenomenon of Church Methodism, see Gareth Lloyd, "'Croakers and Busybodies': The Extent and Influence of Church Methodists in the Late 18th and Early 19th Centuries," in *Methodist History* 42 (2003): 20-32; and John Lenton, *John Wesley's Preachers: A Social and Statistical Analysis of the British and Irish Preachers Who Entered the Methodist Itinerancy Before 1791*, Studies in Evangelical History and Thought (Eugene, OR: Wipf and Stock, 2011), 37.

[107]Forsaith, *Unexampled Labours*, 143 (Fletcher to Charles Wesley, May 16, 1762).

about even being associated with Methodism can be easily applied to the experience of Fletcher. The author of the tract writes, "The tenacity which the Methodists practice has to revive all those mad and mischievous proceedings [of an irregular ministry like the Commonwealth Period] and the countenance it has given to the revival of them in many parts of the kingdom, create a very strong prejudice against their advocates."[108] Fletcher was an advocate of Methodism. And yet he was an advocate firmly ensconced within the regular ministry of the establishment.

Peter Forsaith shows that once Fletcher was assigned to Madeley, he was firmly established as a regular member of the Church's ministry. John Wesley's desire that Fletcher would become the leader of the United Societies after Wesley's and his brother's deaths, and his interpretation of Fletcher's ministry in his sermon at Fletcher's funeral, has created a picture of Fletcher that Forsaith argues is not historically accurate.[109] In blunt terms, Forsaith writes, "Wesley's Short Account [of Fletcher's life] might be dismissed as the work of an idiosyncratic and egocentric octogenarian with mild amnesia."[110]

Fletcher wrote to Charles Wesley in June of 1762 that a "Young clergyman," whom Forsaith believes to be a "Mr. Hinton," has "openly declared war on me."[111] The young clergyman had with Lutheran finesse attached accusations against Fletcher to the door of St. Michael's Church. The accusations he made against Fletcher included "Rebellion of Schism" and "being a disturber of the public peace." The young clergyman lived in Madeley Wood, the same area of the parish where a society had sprung up and gained Fletcher's blessing. Soon this young clergyman and others in the parish wanted to charge Fletcher with breaking the Conventicle Act and had a layman arrested "who read and prayed one day that I was not able to be at the meeting."[112] Martin Madan, an Evangelical cler-

---

[108] *An Address to the Right Honourable —: with Several Letters to the D— of—, from the L—, in Vindication of Her Conduct, on Being Charged with Methodism* (London: Printed for W. Sandby, in Fleet-Street, 1761), 7.

[109] See Wesley, sermon 114, "On the Death of John Fletcher," *Works* 3:610-30.

[110] Forsaith, *Unexampled Labours*, 5.

[111] Ibid., 143, 147 (Fletcher to Charles Wesley, May 16, 1762, and June 8, 1762).

[112] Ibid., 147 (Fletcher to Charles Wesley, June 8, 1762).

gyman in London, cautioned Fletcher that the Conventicle Act could be used against those laypersons who had gathered without Fletcher.[113] Soon after, Fletcher attempted to form a society distinctly under his oversight. Yet the climate in Madeley was firmly set against a society, even under Fletcher's oversight. Fletcher's bishop was silent on the matter, which Fletcher interpreted to mean that the bishop did not know "how to disapprove; & dares not to approve this Methodist way of proceeding."[114]

Fletcher continued to preach throughout his parish, leaving Madeley on Easter Day in 1765 to "sacrifice the last remnant of my reputation" and preach outdoors at the Coal-pit Bank, about five miles from St. Michael's. As depicted in so many of Wesley's accounts, there were too many people to fit into a local house, and so Fletcher preached outdoors. He later wrote to Charles Wesley, "Our timorous people think all is over now, & I shall be turned out of my Living," the thought of which he claimed left him "without Anxiety."[115]

STAYING THE COURSE

John Wesley would never give up the use of his societies, classes and bands. Neither would he back down in the face of accusations that he was planting conventicles throughout the kingdom. Wesley strongly felt that the use of the societies was essential to the spread of the gospel. His criticism of Whitefield for not creating a structure of societies to gather up those who had heard him preach is well known.[116] Neither did Wesley ever seem to accept that his promotion of these means could be understood to be seditious or politically volatile.[117] The ghost of the Cromwellian Commonwealth was never a spirit Wesley seems to have taken

---

[113]Ibid.

[114]Ibid, 166 (Fletcher to John Wesley, Nov. 22, 1762).

[115]Ibid., 206.

[116]Rack argues that Whitefield did not want a connexion, although one formed without the hierarchy and structure of Wesley's; see *Reasonable Enthusiast*, 282.

[117]See Wesley's sermons "On the Laying the Foundation of the New Chapel," *Works* 3:577-93; "Earnest Appeal to Men of Reason and Religion," *Works* 11:37-94; and "Farther Appeal to Men of Reason and Religion, Part I," *Works* 11:95-202. On his adamant insistence that he was not a schismatic and intended his followers to remain within the Church, see his sermon "Of the Church," *Works* 3:45-57; and his tract "Ought We to Separate from the Church of England," in Baker, *John Wesley and the Church of England*, appendix, 326-40.

seriously. Within the context of eighteenth-century moderation in the post-Restoration period, the use of societies by both Wesley and the Evangelicals continued to cause many to question their allegiances. As Wesley's societies spread, however, he began to not merely raise the ire of his opponents; with the incursion of Wesleyan Methodist societies and lay preachers in Evangelical parishes, a whole new level of tension and opposition was created. Wesley now had to attend to the complaints of his Evangelical colleagues, who were losing their patience with Wesley's cavalier disregard for ecclesiastical protocol.

Wesley was cautioned by numerous Evangelicals. Samuel Walker continued to caution him, but Walker's early death left ecclesiastical conservatism with one less voice in the inner circles of Methodism. Charles Wesley would continue to caution his brother and was a persistent voice for restraint. Even the Methodist-friendly Fletcher would begin to question Wesley's use of lay preachers when they began to cause him trouble in his Madeley parish. Fletcher was not the only Evangelical to be concerned with these Wesleyan Methodist incursions, and the strain that these incursions placed on Wesley's relationship to the Evangelical clergy is the topic to which we now turn.

5

ENCLAVES AND INCURSIONS

The Geography of Evangelicalism

JOHN WESLEY'S RELATIONSHIP to Evangelical clergy was greatly challenged by the army of lay preachers that gave allegiance to Wesley. This group of men, vital to early Methodism, acted as Wesley's "helpers" and created tension between Wesley and the majority of his Evangelical colleagues. The lay preachers of Wesley's Methodism were a key dynamic in the unhurried divide that would take place between Wesley and the Church of England. It was their ordination at his hands in 1784 that many see as the end of Wesley's mission within the Church. Yet the events of 1784 did not appear out of thin air. Arguments over the place or status of Wesley's assistants raged from the 1740s onward. These arguments over the status and function of lay preachers fueled the continued separation between Wesley and the Church, but especially his connection to the Evangelicals.

Wesley did not necessarily control the lay preachers under his charge. These "sons in the gospel" and "helpers" in the cause became throughout the century an increasingly independent subclerical class. Walsh writes that Wesley "persisted in regarding Methodism as no more than his own private army; the mere aggregate of those he had permitted as an act of grace to join him, on his own terms. This was a view which became rapidly at odds with reality as his movement took on a life of its own."[1]

---

[1]John Walsh, *John Wesley 1703–1791: A Bicentennial Tribute* (London: Friends of Dr. William's Library, 1993), 8. See *Letters* (Telford) 4:375-76 (Wesley to Dr. Warburton, bishop of Gloucester, Nov. 26, 1762).

The preachers were neither clergy nor laymen within Methodism. They were in ecclesiastical limbo, an indeterminate state that Wesley helped to create. He often treated them like clergy. Wesley's *Address to the Clergy*, written in 1756, is roughly the same instruction he gave to his preachers.[2] And the role model he held up for his preachers was none other than a seventeenth-century dissenting clergyman, Richard Baxter.[3] This limbo helped to create a context in which some of Wesley's helpers thought of themselves more as his colleagues, and as his colleagues they were willing to clash with both Wesley brothers as though they had clerical orders themselves.

The conference that Wesley founded in 1744 continued to evolve. It was meant to be a body of advisors and a means to direct the lay preachers. By the end of his life, Wesley had structured the conference to become a legal body with full control of the connexion. Wesley may have run his conferences with an iron fist, and used his personality and status as father of the movement to contain the lay preachers, but the preachers should not be seen as passive agents of the Wesley brothers. The preachers displayed an independent streak that only gained traction as the Wesley brothers aged and the Wesleyan movement attained a distinct ethos.

In terms of John Wesley's relationship to his Evangelical colleagues, these increasingly independent lay preachers introduce a new level of

---

[2] *Works* (Jackson) 10:480-500. This particular tract produced significant backlash. William Law called it "empty babble, fitter for an old grammarian who has grown blear-eyed in mending dictionaries" (*Letters* [Telford] 4:184). Others publicly denounced the letter. See, for example, Anonymous, *A Letter to the Revd. Mr. John Wesley; Occasioned by His Address to the Clergy, February 6, 1756. By One of That Clergy* (London: Printed for M. Cooper, 1756); James Buller, *A Reply, to the Rev. Mr. Wesley's Address to the Clergy* (Bristol: Printed by S. Farley, 1756); and Richard Fawcett, *An Expostulatory Letter to the Rev. Mr. Wesley: Occasioned by His Address to the Clergy* (London: Printed for J. Wilkie, 1757).

[3] Wesley often recommended Richard Baxter's *Reformed Pastor*. Rack notes that Baxter's *Call to the Unconverted* was frequently mentioned in the conversion stories of Evangelicals and may help to explain the Calvinism of most Evangelicals; see Henry D. Rack, *Reasonable Enthusiast: John Wesley and the Rise of Methodism*, 3rd ed. (Philadelphia: Trinity Press International, 2002), 176. Dewey Wallace describes Baxter as one who "wanted a 'reduced episcopacy'; or 'primitive episcopacy' such as had been proposed by Archbishop James Ussher of Armagh in Ireland, an episcopacy without dictatorial bishops lording it over the general body of clergy, and which allowed for ministerial associations with which bishops would consult. Baxter and those of his party also had no objection in principle to a liturgy or set form of prayer" (see *Shapers of English Calvinism 1660-1714: Variety, Persistence, and Transformation* [New York: Oxford University Press, 2011], 22). This description of Baxter could easily be used to describe Wesley later in life.

complexity. As Wesley's helpers, these lay preachers were in a certain sense an extension of Wesley himself. Wesley created a system much like the system of the early church, where a bishop would ordain others to represent him within a community where he could not always be present. He sent them out on circuits that he approved. Wesley acted as though he was an episcopal agent, and the preachers soon began to act as though he had ordained them to clerical orders. If there was confusion about ecclesiastical status on the part of the Methodist preachers, it was not entirely their fault.

In a letter to Robert Marsden written in summer 1756, Wesley argued that the lay preachers were not *"ministers"* because "none of them undertakes *single* the care of an whole flock, but ten, twenty, or thirty, one following and helping another."[4] This argument, however, based on numbers and movement, did not address the concerns of parish priests, nor did it address the actual status of the lay preachers. In keeping with the ever-changing dynamics of the revival, Wesley left the status and location of his preachers in a continual state of flux. When later he added a small, but noticeable, number of women to assist him on the basis of the "exceptional" nature of the movement, Wesley added another layer of complexity to the situation and faced opposition from the Church and his "sons."[5]

Within the structures of the Church of England these Methodist preachers were laypersons. They had no ecclesiastical standing. Yet their influence within the culture was much greater than their status or title. With not only Wesley's imprimatur but also the rise of populist forms of religion in the English-speaking world, these lay preachers could attract

---

[4]To Robert Marsden, Aug. 31, 1756. In the same letter Wesley also indicates that the preachers only needed knowledge of Scripture and not a further education to do the work of the itinerancy. This is in stark contrast to his intentions for publishing the Christian Library.

[5]See David Hempton, *Methodism: Empire of the Spirit* (New Haven, CT: Yale University Press, 2005), 138; and Paul Wesley Chilcote, *John Wesley and the Women Preachers of Early Methodism* (Metuchen, NJ: Scarecrow, 1991). This chapter deals with issues around the use of lay preachers in general and their impact on Evangelical relations, but Wesley's sporadic use of female preachers adds an additional layer of complexity to the overall situation of Wesleyan Methodism's place within the Church of England and would create heated debate in the next century as Methodism moved from movement to church.

a following regardless of their status, profession or education. These preachers had the admiration of the Methodist people, and the capitalist structures outlined in Adam Smith's *Wealth of Nations* were at work in the religious marketplace to create a context in which they could thrive.[6] A popular lay preacher could challenge the authority of the most austere clergyman in the very confines of his own parish, and do so in the name of Wesley. Ever the witty critic, T. Mortimer writes:

> Strange effect of credulity in a Christian country, and under the eye of the best disciplined church on earth, that a man should be deemed an inspired preacher, and followed from one end of the town to the other, that cannot speak good English, and does not understand the first rudiments of his native tongue![7]

Unlike the eloquent Dinah Morris of George Elliot's *Adam Bede*, the Wesleys' assistants were not known for their rhetorical skills but for their ability to persuade. The university-trained clergy of the Church, including its Evangelical incumbents, were a sharp contrast to these artisan preachers.

The parish system of England had been created for the spiritual benefit of its people. Field preaching, a rejection of that system, was the arena of rabble-rousers and enthusiasts. And yet here the Oxford don after being expelled from pulpit after pulpit was found preaching to anyone within earshot. What complicates the relationship of Wesley to the Evangelicals is his remedy for a dearth of clergy willing to follow his footsteps. He insisted that he must send his lay preachers into every parish in England, including those overseen by Evangelical incumbents. This created tension between the two parties, which eventually came to a head at the 1764 conference. Ultimately Wesley's use of lay preachers proved to further erode his connection to the parish ministry of the Church. Ironically, both parties were attempting to secure a future for evangelicalism. The difference was that the Evangelicals aimed to make room for an

---

[6]Hempton, *Methodism*, 43-46.

[7]T. Mortimer, *Die and Be Damned: Or an Anecdote Against Every Species of Methodist; and Enthusiasm*, 2nd ed. (London: Printed for S. Hooper and A. Morley, at Gay's-Head near Beauforts-Buildings, in the Strand, 1758), 35.

evangelical witness within the Church; Wesley wanted an evangelical witness in England whether in the Church or outside it.

GEOGRAPHY AND A MATURING MOVEMENT
WITHIN THE CHURCH

David Bebbington has convincingly argued that evangelicals found themselves competing with one another on the same soil, in the same geography, because they attracted similar occupations and classes within English society.[8] Wesley's preachers found their greatest success in areas where the Evangelical clergy had found theirs. Evangelicalism's initial success created an "evangelical belt" that existed sporadically from Yorkshire to Cornwall, creating something of an arc on the out-skirts of the Church's most concentrated area of parishes in the southeast. A simple charting of Evangelicals in parishes in 1750 reveals this distinctive geography. Wesleyanism's London-Bristol axis, highlighted in the early rise of Wesley's Methodism, does not represent the mass of Wesleyan Methodism beyond its earliest years. The strength of the movement was to be found in this sweeping arc, where the Industrial Revolution was changing the social fabric of rural England and thin parish coverage made it near impossible to keep an eye on every corner of expansive parishes. Evangelical Anglicanism saw its greatest strength in these same areas, and would expand from it, making inroads after the early decades in places such as Cambridge, parts of Essex and very near London in Clapham.

Yorkshire and Cornwall were the strongholds of Evangelicalism in the eighteenth century. The revival seems to have "struck deepest root," according to Bebbington and Hempton, in areas of the country populated heavily by artisans and small farmers.[9] Bebbington writes, "Therefore, areas springing into life with proto-industrial employment for the skilled

---

[8]David Bebbington, *Evangelicalism in Modern Britain: A History from the 1730s to the 1980s* (London: Unwin Hyman, 1989), 26.

[9]For small farmers, the social, geographical and economic disruption caused during this period as large swaths of land were being taken out of common use to create large farms owned by the wealthy must be kept in mind. This social shift created a context of flux similar to the religious flux of the revival itself.

worker, townships like Paddiford Common in 'Janet's Repentance' with weaving and mining as the chief occupations, were ideal territory. Methodism and Calvinistic Dissent as well as the Evangelical Anglicanism that George Eliot depicts thrived there."[10] The Yorkshire parish of Henry Crooke is a good example of this Evangelical growth. Crooke's diary describes a lively evangelical parish where not only did the pipe-smoking Crooke oversee his flock, but also Evangelical luminaries such as Wesley, Whitefield, Grimshaw, Stillingfleet, Romaine and Venn made regular appearances, with the parish seeming to be a crossroads of the movement. Crooke oversaw the parish church but also a chapel where he allowed lay preachers—some of them Wesley's—to preach on Saturday evenings.[11]

What this shared geography created was direct competition between already marginalized groups. Given Wesley's insistence that his intention was never to be in competition with the established Church but rather to enliven it, these areas of geographical overlap created opportunities and opposition. In Haworth, Grimshaw was open to Wesley's preachers, and a Methodist circuit was established.[12] In Madeley, Fletcher was supportive but had to moderate his connections to Methodism for political reasons. In Venn's parish of Huddersfield, Venn asked Wesley personally not to appoint his preachers.[13] The majority of the Evangelicals were more in line with Venn than they were with either Grimshaw or Fletcher.

What complicated this overlap was the parish system itself. Those clergy appointed to a parish were legally charged to care for the souls within their parish boundaries. This system, sponsored by the state and upheld by the Crown, was the appointed means by which the spiritual health of the nation was to be maintained. Roving pseudoclergy did not

---

[10]Bebbington, *Evangelicalism in Modern Britain*, 26.

[11]Henry Crooke, *Extracts from the Diary of the Reverend Henry Crooke: Curate of Hunslet and Vicar of Kippax*, The Frank Baker Collection of Wesleyana and British Methodism, box 22, David M. Rubenstein Rare Book & Manuscript Library, Duke University, 98.

[12]It appears that as early as 1753 there was a society visited by Wesley's preachers in Haworth that was producing lay preachers for the Methodist Conference. "John Greenswood" is listed as a preacher in the 1753 conference minutes. Rack indicates that he was earlier listed in the Todmoreden Society Accounts of 1750–1752, a society in Haworth. See *Works* 10:260.

[13]It is likely that Venn discussed the issue of Methodist preachers in his parish with Wesley on March 25, 1761, when they "breakfasted." See *Works* 21:313. See also 21:336n96.

fit within the official geography of English ecclesiastical life. These lay preachers presented a challenge to the system, not simply as competition but as a challenge to the established order. The parish priests were not interested in participating on a neutral playing field, nor did they have to be. And their primary concern was the parish under their legal charge. Evangelical clergyman John Milner, writing to Wesley in 1750, indicates his strong attachment to Wesley on a personal level and praises his writings but notes kindly that his primary duty is the care of his parish.[14] Walsh writes that "for many clergymen of the decentralised Church of England the parish was their world" and contrasts this parish-centered perspective with Wesley's bold pronouncement that "I look upon all the world as my parish."[15]

The evangelical impulse was not always strong enough to overcome the clerical attachment to localized parishes. Comparing Wesley's efforts to the monastic renewal efforts of medieval Europe, Walsh claims: "Wesley had formed what was in part a new preaching order—like that of the Friars—and in part a lay devotional confraternity. His itinerant preaching force embraced that principle of mobility which the Roman Church welcomed, but which the Hanoverian Establishment as yet refused to entertain."[16] Evangelical clergy also felt this lack of an evangelical clerical witness. Early in the revival in Cornwall, Wesley encountered a

---

[14] *Works* 26:397. Another letter dated the following year indicates that Milner itinerated with Wesley "into the north" and was reproved by the bishop of Chester, Samuel Peploe. See ibid., 26:467.
[15] Walsh, *John Wesley 1703–1791*, 5. Walsh argues that later biographers of Wesley had to look to the Roman Catholic tradition to find appropriate parallels. "By the time of Wesley's death, when his system had evolved in its fullness, his memorialists were driven to the Roman Church to find informative parallels for Wesley and his movement. Macaulay later embroidered this theme in a brilliant passage of his essay on Ranke's Popes. Rome, he suggested, would have known just what to do with the early Methodists. It would have made rapid use of Wesley's plebeian preachers. 'The ignorant enthusiast of whom the Anglican Church makes an enemy . . . the Catholic Church makes a champion. She bids him nurse his beard, covers him with a gown and hood of coarse dark stuff, ties a rope around his waist and sends him forth to teach in her name. He costs her nothing.' So too of the genteel leaders of Methodism: Macaulay suggested that 'at Rome, the Countess of Huntingdon would have a place in the calendar as St Selina. . . . Place Ignatius Loyola at Oxford. He is certain to become the head of a formidable secession. Place John Wesley at Rome. He is certain to be the first General of a new Society devoted to the interests and honour of the Church'" (4). See Thomas Babington Macaulay, *The Complete Works of Lord Macaulay, in Twelve Volumes* (New York: P. G. Putnam's Sons, 1898), 9:320.
[16] Walsh, *John Wesley 1703–1791*, 5.

number of Evangelicals willing to itinerate throughout the area to fill the
need for evangelical preaching. These Evangelicals, however, would
never become like Wesley's new preaching order.

Wesley's relationship to Evangelicals in Cornwall early on is a picture
of cooperation. In his *Journal* Wesley recounts numerous invitations to
Evangelical parish churches. He also indicates that Evangelicals in
Cornwall, for the most part, encouraged his itinerating practices and
joined with him. Three Evangelical clergy are known to have itinerated
during the early 1740s in Cornwall: John Bennet,[17] John Meriton[18] and
George Thomson.[19] All three of these clergy itinerated with Wesley.
Thomson even joined Wesley in an attempt to save one of the lay
preachers from being shipped out for naval service.[20]

In April 1744 Wesley describes visiting Bennet and being invited to
preach in his church. Wesley's reputation had apparently preceded his
visit, and he was expected to preach at the Laneast Church when he arrived. He writes in his *Journal*:

> In the afternoon we came again to Trewint. Here I learned that notice had
> been given of my preaching that evening in Laneast Church, which was
> crowded exceedingly. Mr. Bennet (the minister of Laneast) carried me

---

[17]Rev. John Bennet (c. 1670–1750) was admitted at Queen's College, Cambridge, September 7,
1693, and earned a BA in 1697 and an MA in 1726. He was apparently a contemporary and ac-
quaintance of the elder Samuel Wesley; see S. T. Kimbrough Jr. and Kenneth G. C. Newport, *The
Manuscript Journal of the Reverend Charles Wesley, M. A.* (Nashville: Kingswood Books, 2007),
2:408 (July 13, 1744). He was perpetual curate of North Tamerton, 1705; curate of Tresmeer
(where he resided), 1720; and curate of Laneast, 1731. "Not merely a pluralist but a hunting
parson, Bennet was converted in 1742" (G. C. B. Davies, *The Early Cornish Evangelicals 1735-60:
A Study of Walker of Truro and Others* [London: SPCK, 1951], 34–45).

[18]See Kimbrough and Newport, *Manuscript Journal of the Reverend Charles Wesley*, 2:356 (July 3,
1743); and Charles Wesley's *Funeral Hymns* (1759), 28-29. Meriton died in 1753.

[19]It was in 1745 through George Whitefield that John Wesley met George Thomson (1698/99–
1782). Thomson, sometimes spelled Thompson, was the rector of St. Gennys, Cornwall. He invited Wesley to preach at his church in June 1745. Wesley records in his journal, "We left Bristol
early on Friday 14, and on Sunday morning reached St. Gennys. The church was moderately
filled with serious hearers, but few of them appeared to feel what they heard. I preached both
morning and afternoon, and on Monday evening. And many assented to and approved of the
truth." See *Works* 20:69 (June 14, 1745).

[20]They were not successful. John Downes was shipped out in order to remove him from the area.
Local magistrates found this unique way to rid themselves of his influence by conscripting him
for idleness. See May 11, 1744, in *Works* 20:28 and n. 46. See also Theodore R. Weber, *Politics in
the Order of Salvation: Transforming Wesleyan Political Ethics* (Nashville: Kingswood Books,
2001), 432n24.

afterwards to his house and (though above seventy years old) came with me in the morning to Trewint, where I had promised to preach at five.[21]

Wesley was warmly welcomed in Cornwall by Evangelicals who held theological views similar to his own and whose irregularities matched those that were making him famous. They also experienced persecution for their irregularity.

By 1747, Bishop Lavington, then bishop of Exeter, officially reproved Evangelical clergy for itinerating outside the bounds of their parishes. His tombstone would rightly describe him as "the successful Exposer of Enthusiasm & Pretence."[22] Yet well before this episcopal injunction Wesley sent lay preachers into Cornwall to create a Wesleyan structure among the Evangelical parishes that occupied much of Cornwall. If there were three itinerating clergymen traversing Cornwall in the early 1740s, before the censure, it is not clear why Wesley still thought it necessary to send lay preachers.

Of the three Evangelical itinerants, only Thomson lived well beyond Bishop Lavington's censure in 1747. Thomson and Wesley, however, appear to have ceased communicating in the 1750s. Thomson received episcopal censure for his irregularities and was caught up by association with Wesley in concerns over Jacobitism and a sexual scandal involving a tavern maid who accused Wesley of trying to seduce her. It is not clear exactly why the two men lost contact with each other, but it is evident that Thomson paid dearly for his association with Wesley. According to H. Miles Brown, "the vicar of Marham-Church complained in 1744 to the bishop about Thomson's 'circumforaneous vociferations,' and the worthy itinerant was admonished to confine his preaching henceforth to his own parish."[23] By the end of the 1750s there was no clerical cooperation with Wesleyan Methodist lay preachers or societies in Cornwall. The Cornish Evangelicals dedicated themselves to the maintenance of the evangelical message within the Church and its structures.

---

[21] *Works* 20:25 (April 25, 1744).
[22] Bishop George Lavington is buried in Exeter Cathedral, Devon, UK.
[23] H. Miles Brown, *The Church in Cornwall* (Truro, UK: Oscar Blackford, 1964), 68.

Bennet and Meriton were of an older generation than the leading figures of the Evangelical Revival, which began in earnest in the late 1730s. Both clergymen had died by 1753. They were of the generation of George Conon, the influential headmaster of the Truro Grammar School, who was instrumental in the conversion of Samuel Walker. Walker would become archetypical of the later Evangelicals, although he died in mid-life in 1761. The next generation, the generation who had experienced the episcopal backlash of the 1740s and the scandals surrounding itinerancy, lay preaching and supposed schism in the 1750s, was more conservative in their practices than were their predecessors. George Whitefield, rarely the moderate, was actually an example of what can be called a maturing of the revival in this period.

Whitefield published over six hundred pages of autobiographical narrative by his early twenties and later regretted aspects of it, including comments on persons and portions of the text that appeared to promote enthusiasm. By 1756 he reprinted an edited and abridged edition of these works. Hindmarsh notes:

> He finally made good on all this contrition in 1756, at 41 years of age, when he republished his whole autobiographical corpus (the two-part autobiography and the Journals) in a corrected and abridged version. Many passages that were "justly exceptionable" were silently omitted. By comparing the originals with the 1756 edition, we can thus see two narrative identities for Whitefield: an ebullient and obstreperous young evangelist in the late 1730s and early 1740s, and a chastened and experienced evangelical minister in 1756.[24]

This revisionism reflects the maturing that took place in the 1750s as Evangelical clergymen began to assert their place in the Church and differentiate their work from the roving evangelists, both Anglican and dissenting. Whitefield's maturation and the maturation of the Evangelical clergy correspond. The 1755 conference of the Wesleyan Methodists was dominated by the clash of these two evangelical forces within the

---

[24]D. Bruce Hindmarsh, *The Evangelical Conversion Narrative: Spiritual Autobiography in Early Modern England* (New York: Oxford University Press, 2005), 109.

Wesleyan fold: one settling into the rhythms of ecclesiastical structures and the other intent on the use of irregular methods. The continued clash, evidenced throughout the 1750s and '60s, simply reinforced the differing trajectories of these two branches. What it did not indicate, however, was a shift in geography. The same evangelical branches were still to be found in the same "evangelical belt" as before. Yet in fewer cases would Wesley find clergy willing to itinerate with him, and even fewer Evangelicals who were open to the idea of unlicensed laymen let loose to preach within their parish boundaries.

EVANGELICAL ATTEMPTS TO CURTAIL THE PREACHERS

As the revival within the Church matured, one principal effect was the declining participation of regular clergymen in the activities of the Wesley brothers.[25] The number of regular clergy associated with Methodism was never high, yet it became increasingly difficult to associate with Wesleyan Methodism as Wesley continued to look for a replacement for these clerical colleagues in the ranks of his "awakened" followers. Including the Wesley brothers themselves, only six clergy were present at the first conference.[26] The highest number of clergy at a conference during Wesley's lifetime was twelve, and they attended in 1764 to share their concerns about lay preachers in Evangelical parishes.[27] Wesley's solution to a lack of clerical assistance created a context in which clerical assistance became less likely. The difficulties created by Wesley's use of the lay preachers occupied Thomas Adam, Samuel Walker, Charles Wesley and John Fletcher from the 1750s until their deaths. Each saw the continued use of the lay preachers as a stumbling block to future relations with the Church.

Wesley did not relinquish his vision of a cooperative evangelical effort until late in the 1760s. Baker writes that Wesley dreamed of "a national union of evangelical clergy who might keep in touch with each other by

---

[25]Even Charles Wesley began to itinerate less and less as he entered married life and he and his wife began to have children.

[26]*Works* 10:123-24.

[27]Ibid., 10:298.

correspondence and occasional itinerancy, and who could both serve Methodism and be served by it in ensuring a continuing evangelical witness within the Established Church."[28] Such a system would have intertwined the Evangelicals under their bishops with the Wesleyan Conference under Wesley. Baker believes that this plan was first adumbrated at the 1757 conference. In a letter to Samuel Walker outlining that year's conference, Wesley writes:

> I proposed that question to all who met at our late Conference, "What can be done in order to a closer union with the clergy who preach the truth?" We all agreed that nothing could be more desirable. I in particular have long desired it: not from any view to my own ease or honour or temporal convenience in any kind, but because I was deeply convinced it might be a blessing to my own soul and a means of promoting the general work of God.[29]

Baker provides a detached comment, simply stating: "This project Wesley discussed with others of the Cornish clergy, but apparently with little success."[30]

Evangelical clergy sought to work with Wesley but were convinced that his helpers should either be settled as active laymen or begin the process for holy orders within the Church. Some proposals, such as Fletcher and Benson's in the 1770s, would have created a "Methodist Church of England" much like the English Huguenot structure under Anglican episcopal oversight that Fletcher knew himself.[31] Wesley did not agree to any of these proposals, nor is it clear that episcopal leaders would have been open to these proposals either. William Law had told Charles Wesley in the 1740s that he had hoped the lay preachers of Wesleyan Methodism would have entered holy orders. Charles noted in his journal that Law "had had great hopes that the Methodists would have been dispersed by little and little into livings, and have leavened the

---

[28]Frank Baker, *John Wesley and the Church of England* (Nashville: Abingdon, 1970), 183.

[29]*Works* 27:93-97 (Wesley to Samuel Walker, Sept. 19, 1757).

[30]Baker, *John Wesley and the Church of England*, 184.

[31]Richard P. Heitzenrater, *Wesley and the People Called Methodists*, 2nd ed. (Nashville: Abingdon, 2013), 317. Heitzenrater compares the Fletcher-Benson plan to what Wesley ultimately carried out with the ordinations of 1784.

whole lump." He was entirely against laymen serving as preachers "as the very worst thing, both for themselves and others."[32]

Pressure was mounting, however, from Evangelicals close to Wesley and from bishops of the Church who saw these itinerating lay preachers as dangerous. In a letter to his brother Charles, John wrote from London in summer 1755: "The good Bishop of London has excommunicated Mr. Gardiner for preaching without a license. It is probable the point will now speedily be determined concerning the Church: for if we must either *dissent or be silent, actum est.* [[Adieu.]] We have no time to trifle!"[33] This letter indicates the seriousness with which Wesley felt compelled to mitigate the legal structures of the Church in order to promote his evangelical message. His "*actum est,*" or "it is all over," to the Church seems a radical departure for the Tory Wesley but indicates the extent to which he would protect the structures that he had created to promote the revival.

Telford, with all the prejudice of nineteenth-century Methodism, wrote that this letter was "one of the most momentous of Wesley's letters." He argued that Wesley "could not consent to give up his lay preachers, who had been so greatly blessed; and he clearly saw that to do so would be an end to the Evangelical Revival. He was awake to the situation, deeply anxious to do nothing inconsistent with his position as a clergyman, yet utterly unable to take any step that would destroy his work."[34] It is not hard to imagine that Wesley felt much as Telford describes. Wesley's connection to his lay preachers at times even in the 1750s seems to have been stronger than his connection to the Church. Wesley's response to the bishop's verdict indicates growing dissonance between the brothers on the issue of lay preachers. As early as 1752, Charles, in a letter to Lady Huntingdon, writes: "Unless a sudden remedy be found, the preachers will destroy the work of God."[35] While John was ever ready to defend

---

[32]Kimbrough and Newport, *Manuscript Journal of the Reverend Charles Wesley*, 1:184.

[33]*Works* 26:563 (John Wesley to the Revd. Charles Wesley, June 23, 1755). In the bicentennial edition of the *Works*, text written in the Wesley brothers' shorthand is enclosed in double brackets.

[34]*Letters* (Telford) 3:143 (Sept. 24, 1755).

[35]Baker, *John Wesley and the Church of England*, 160 (Charles Wesley to Lady Huntingdon, Aug. 4, 1752).

the preachers, Charles was eager to jettison them if they threatened to divide the revival from the Church.

In addition to his brother Charles, Wesley consulted Walker on the situation. The correspondence of Wesley and Walker during this period encompasses nearly every issue that stood between Wesley and a continued connection to Evangelicals within the Church.[36] The correspondence, which covers 1755–1761, was not simply between Walker and Wesley but included additional insights from both Charles Wesley and Thomas Adam.[37] Charles, however, appears to have been the pivotal player. It was his working relationship with both Walker and his brother that kept the parties in conversation. Without Charles's input, the words of Walker would have fallen on the deaf ears of an increasingly independent-minded Wesley.

Charles was essential to the maintenance of Evangelical communication during the crises of the 1750s, but he continued to push his brother with increasing severity to declare once and for all his allegiance to the Church. Baker notes, "It seems likely that C[harles] W[esley] pressed his brother to sign a declaration binding himself and the societies never to separate from the Church of England."[38] John was not willing to sign. His response to Charles's increasing pressure was to write his brother in the summer of 1755: "I do not myself, and dare not give *that* under my hand, to you or any man living. And I should count anyone either a fool or a knave that would give it under his hand to *me*."[39] His parting shot at his brother was to tell him that his "gross bigotry lies here, in putting a man on a level with an adulterer because he differs from you as to church government."[40] Charles was becoming the voice of regular Evangelical Anglicanism within the confines of Wesleyan Methodism.

---

[36] *Works* 26:583 (Wesley to Samuel Walker, Sept. 5, 1755).

[37] Adam was by far the most conservative voice in this quadrangle of Evangelicals. Davies notes that Adam "could not approve of the ordination of lay preachers, or of those not ordained being retained as inspectors of societies, which were themselves irregular, as setting up 'a Church within a Church.' He felt on the whole that they had embarrassed themselves past recovery; and that it would be wiser for them to separate completely and openly" (*Early Cornish Evangelicals*, 119).

[38] *Works* 26:572n15.

[39] *Works* 26:572 (John Wesley to Charles Wesley, July 16, 1755).

[40] Ibid., 573.

Walker was convinced that Methodists' "present very critical circumstances" were founded on a debate over opinions and thus incapable of providing a lasting standard. Leaving the Church was never an option for Walker, and he encouraged Wesley not to publish his *Ought We to Separate* (1758) for fear that it would cause dissent among Methodists, encourage their opponents and make "friends who are not Methodists to fear."[41] Walker insisted that the Methodists had in practice become separate from the Church, causing their discussion of separation to become unintelligible. He encouraged Wesley to come back to the fold.

In characteristic evangelical fashion, Walker challenged Wesley to look to the Scriptures for the answer to whether it was "lawful" for the Methodists to separate from the Church. He was deferential toward Wesley and kind, but he laid out for the Oxford logician a very consistent formula whereby Wesley would have to prove from Scripture the need to separate from the Church. Implied in Walker's formula is the scriptural concept of the unity of the faithful. Walker wrote, "I know you will search the Scriptures, which no doubt are clear enough to determine any meek inquirer whether it be lawful for him or not to abide in the communion of that Church to which he belongs."[42] It was from the argument for unity that Walker addressed the issue of lay preachers.

> If the laws of the Church of England admit not such preachers, then herein is a step made in separation and that whatever necessity there may be of them. Put this together, and may you not have cause to think that *either you will not be able to stop a separation, or must somehow or other stop these preachers?* As long as they remain there is a beginning of separation; and that also which will keep the people in mind of it.[43]

Walker was certain that the very structure of Wesley's Methodism was itself a form of separation. The Church already had a structure, and in Walker's view that structure was the essence of the Church of England.

---

[41] *Works* 26:583 (Sept. 5, 1755). Walker was a churchman throughout his life. He was instrumental in keeping William Romaine within the Church of England in 1759. See Davies, *Early Cornish Evangelicals*, 177.

[42] *Works* 26:583.

[43] Ibid.

He wrote in the same letter that the "permission or appointment" of the preachers was "a form of separation from the Church of England, the essence of which, considered as such, consists in her orders and laws rather than in her doctrines and worship, which constitutes her a Church of Christ."[44]

Walker was not the only Evangelical to take this view. In a sermon preached that same year, Henry Crooke declared, "If the *Constitution* of our *Church* answers to the Scriptures (and I am thoroughly satisfied it does) then doubtless, the *Constitution*, not the *mere Mode* or *Manner* of Worship, is the good unchangeable *Way*; and, whatever Doctrine is contrary to it, is no better than *Novelty*, and *Innovation*, be the Person who he will, that maintains it."[45] Crooke was quick to add, "He who does (whether *Priest* or *Layman*) is himself (in *Fact*) a *Separatist* from the *Church* in *Sentiments*, not withstanding his *loud* and *pretended* Friendship for her." Cooke's sermon was directed to "Separatists in *Mask*."[46] It was separatism, or sectarianism, that most alarmed Crooke, and in particular that which he saw in Wesley's Methodism. Although a friendly critic, Crooke complained in his diary about "the Bigotry of Christians, especially of the Methodists."[47]

Here, then, the issues between Wesley and Walker and other Evangelicals of similar mind were laid bare. Wesley never accepted the idea that the essence of the Church was in its "forms." He believed that the essence of the Church was found in its faithful proclamation of the Christian gospel. Thus while Evangelicals wanted to maintain the Wesleyan message within the Church, understood by its hierarchy and structure, Wesley saw all practical impediments to the spread of the gospel as a hindrance to the faith, and thus of the Church. Only with the continued evolution of the revival would Wesley act on his ideals, but

---

[44]Ibid., 584. Baker describes this differentiation simply in that Walker was arguing that doctrine belongs to all Christians, polity to the Church of England. See *John Wesley and the Church of England*, 170.

[45]Henry Crooke, *The Church of England a Pure and True Church: Attempted in a Sermon, Preached at the Parish Church of Leeds, in Yorkshire, on Wednesday the 12th Day of March, Being the 5th Wednesday in Lent* (London: 1755), 8.

[46]Ibid.

[47]Crooke, *Extracts from the Diary of the Reverend Henry Crooke*, 85.

they were evident from the 1750s onward and would continue to create a fissure between him and the Evangelicals within the Church.

Wesley was able both to maintain an irregular ministry and to insist that he was a faithful member of the Church of England precisely because of his insistence that the essence of the Church of England was to be found in its teachings and not in its practices. Such a bifurcation of the English Church made it possible for him to see his proclamation of an Anglican gospel as participation in the English Church, structures and all. This bifurcation also made room for the arguments Wesley outlined in his Korah sermon, now known as "Prophets and Priests." Wesley, in good Anglican fashion, argued in this sermon for a differentiation between prophets sent to preach the word of God and priests authorized to administer the sacraments. This functional reading provided Wesley with a lens through which to justify his sending of prophets (i.e., lay preachers) to preach to the masses, while dodging the question of sacramental authority, validity and ordination.[48] For Walker, Adam and Crooke, this analysis of English Church life did not hold up to scrutiny. They were convinced that to be within the Church of England one must abide by its practices and its form of governance. Neither does it appear from their sermons or from Adam's popular catechism that they would have denied the importance of Anglican teachings. Yet, they would have insisted that the standards of the Church, such as the Thirty-Nine Articles, the Book of Homilies and the Book of Common Prayer, were to be understood and used within the community that had created and maintained them.[49] Wesley was preaching an Anglican gospel but not within what could reasonably be called the Church of England.

Wesley's second letter to Walker outlined the objections of the lay

---

[48]See "Prophets and Priests," *Works* 4. Also see W. R. Ward, *Faith and Faction* (London: Epworth, 1993), 225-48, for a description of the legacy Wesley left to Methodists. This legacy included various battles that would erupt in the nineteenth century as Methodism moved from movement to church.

[49]See Thomas Adam, *Practical Lectures on the Church-Catechism. By Thomas Adam, The Fifth Edition. To Which Is Now Added, an Exercise, by Way of Question and Answer, Preparatory to Confirmation* (London: 1767); and Samuel Walker, *Fifty Two Sermons on The Baptismal Covenant, The Creed, The Ten Commandments, and other Important Subjects of Practical Religion . . . New Edition* (London: 1810).

preachers and other members of the Wesleyan Conference.[50] These objections were not new to English Church life; precedents for them were known, mostly in dissenting circles. Members of the conference objected to the confusion caused by Calvinism, but they also objected to the strictures of the Prayer Book and laws of the Church "if they include the Canons and Decretals" that were thought to be "the very dregs of Popery."[51]

Wesley's third and fourth reasons were based on the assumption that the majority of the English clergy had not been called of God nor preached the faith. To these Walker responded critically, challenging Wesley that he could see "at the bottom of this a factious unsubmissive spirit," evident specifically "in their third and fourth reasons for a separation."[52] These arguments "would never have got into their heads, [had] not a conceit of themselves, and an ambition of being ministers, first got into their hearts."[53] Edwin Sidney, Walker's early biographer, claims that Walker sent a copy of this letter to Adam with the comment, "Will he be able to stand his ground? For my part I think not. I fear he hath too high an opinion of Methodism, and imagines it will be lost if the preachers leave him, which I am fully confirmed they will do, if he will not go with them."[54]

Walker outlined much the same argument for Charles Wesley. In a letter from 1756 he wrote that lay preachers were "contrary to the constitution of the Church of England" and therefore signified separation from it. For Walker, the practice was "plainly inconsistent with the discipline of the Church of England; and so in one essential point setting up a church within her, which cannot be of her."[55] Walker's frankness with

---

[50]Baker believes that Wesley was seeking support for the ordination of the lay preachers in this second letter, although implicitly. Baker, *John Wesley and the Church of England*, 171.

[51]*Works* 26:582 (Wesley to Samuel Walker, Sept. 24, 1755). Interestingly, the Methodists would only remove manual acts from their communion ritual in the political aftermath of the Worship Regulation Act of 1874.

[52]Davies, *Early Cornish Evangelicals*, 101; *Works* 26:606-8 (Samuel Walker to John Wesley, Oct. 20, 1755).

[53]Davies, *Early Cornish Evangelicals*, 101.

[54]Quoted in Davies, *Early Cornish Evangelicals*, 102. See Edwin Sidney, *The Life and Ministry of the Rev. Samuel Walker, Formerly of Truro, Cornwall* (London: 1838), 182.

[55]Davies, *Early Cornish Evangelicals*, 111.

Charles is evident in this letter. While Walker was a friend of Methodism, he was concerned about the long-term relationship of Methodism to the Church and its Evangelical clergy. Walker had the ability to see plainly the consequences of Wesleyan Methodism's maverick practices. He wrote to Charles that the use of lay preachers would put Methodist and Evangelical cooperation at a standstill.

> Meantime, there is a continual bar kept up between you and any regular clergyman, who cannot in conscience fall in with this measure. The most he can do is not to forbid them. He cannot take them by the hand. And so there must be two disunited ministrations of the word in the same place, by people who yet do call themselves of the Church of England. You cannot but observe there shall never be a nearer connection between the most zealous clergy of the Church of England and the Methodists than now subsists, until this block be taken out of the way.[56]

The Huddersfield Compromise and the Conference of 1764

Most Evangelical clergy either ignored Wesleyan Methodists or encouraged Wesley to regularize the movement within the structures of the Church. Henry Venn of Huddersfield, a close friend of the Wesleys, however, sought a unique compromise. He was not the first Evangelical to approach Wesley with the idea, but he asked whether Wesley would allow him oversight of Methodist societies in his parish. Samuel Walker was surprised when Wesley refused to place the local Methodist society under the care of Evangelical James Vowler in Cornwall. Walker wrote to Adam in 1758, a letter describing Vowler's work. He writes that "Christ rides prosperously at St. Agnes" and indicates that "Brother Vowler" had organized societies "who meet among themselves in little parties weekly for free conversation." All this was in spite of the "strange opposition

---

[56]Ibid. John Munsey Turner's description of Wesley's argument with Walker is apt. He writes, "We can only conclude that Wesley was endeavouring to have the best of the church-world and the Methodist-world, his actions being justified only on his own principle of the primacy of the gospel—and of the nature of separation" (*Conflict and Reconciliation: Studies in Methodism and Ecumenism in England, 1740–1982* [London: Epworth, 1985], 12-13).

made against him by the Methodists." Walker was convinced—after Wesley's refusals to turn over the Methodist societies in Evangelical parishes, and his and Wesley's correspondence—that in the eyes of Methodists both he and Vowler were "well-meaning legalists."[57]

The Huddersfield Compromise, which somewhat ceded the society in Huddersfield to Venn's oversight, lasted a few years and may or may not have worked as either Wesley or Venn had intended. But the compromise created the possibility that Evangelical parishes could be free from the wandering itinerants of Wesley's Methodism. Deliberation over the society revealed the relational nature of the revival. Not only were Wesley and Venn friends, and Methodists in Huddersfield fond of Venn, but the Huddersfield Compromise highlighted the connectional layers of Methodism. Local Methodists felt connected to Wesley. They also cherished connection to his lay itinerants.

Venn went to the parish of Huddersfield to St. Peter's Church in the evangelical stronghold of Yorkshire in 1759, having served as a curate in Clapham just south of London. Clapham would become a center of evangelical activism in the next century. Venn's son and biographer called Huddersfield "the grand scene" of his father's work in the Church.[58] Methodists had founded a society in the parish prior to Venn's arrival, and the situation created by this confluence of Evangelicalism and Methodism, according to Baker, caused Wesley a bit of embarrassment. He could not claim, as he had in the case of Vowler, that he was unsure of Venn's pastoral experience.[59] The entire compromise was built on the basis of longtime friendship and camaraderie.

Venn's curate, Evangelical George Burnett, had also come to Huddersfield in 1759 and had been warned by Walker that same year of a Methodist society in the parish. Walker wrote a letter to Adam describing Burnett's work, adding that the parish included "an old society of John Wesley's." His advice

---

[57]Sidney, *Life and Ministry of the Rev. Samuel Walker*, 436 (dated June 7, 1758).

[58]*The Letters of Henry Venn, with a Memoir by John Venn* (Carlisle, UK: Banner of Truth Trust, 1835, 1999), 26.

[59]See Walker to Adam, June 7, 1758, in Sidney, *Life and Ministry of the Rev. Samuel Walker*, 436. For more on Vowler, see John Gillies, *Historical Collections Relating to Remarkable Periods of the Success of the Gospel* (Kelso, UK: John Rutherford, 1845), 532. Wesley mentions Vowler twice in his journal. On September 3, 1757, he wrote that Vowler "both preaches and lives the gospel." See *Works* 21:122. See also *Works* 21:389 (Sept. 17, 1762) for a very similar remark.

was that "it will be a nice matter neither to quarrel nor join with them." The Methodists "are in our parts hot, and must be treated with much forbearance."[60] Burnett, with closer connections to the regular ministries of the revival, does not figure in descriptions of Wesley's compromise with Venn.

Two years into Venn's incumbency at Huddersfield a compromise was reached. Wesley wrote in his *Journal*: "I came to a full explanation with that good man, Mr. V[enn]. Lord, if I *must* dispute, let it be with the children of the devil. Let me be at peace with *thy* children!"[61] He had brokered a compromise with Venn, the 1761 conference and the local society in the parish. Explaining the situation later, Wesley wrote:

> Several years before [Venn] came to Huddersfield some of our preachers went thither, carrying their lives in their hands, and with great difficulty established a little earnest Society. These eagerly desire them to preach there still; not in opposition to Mr. Venn (whom they love, esteem, and constantly attend), but to supply what they do not find in his preaching. It is a tender point. Where there is a gospel ministry already, we do not desire to preach; but whether we can leave off preaching because such an one comes after, is another question, especially when those who are awakened and convinced by us beg and require the continuance of our assistance.[62]

The immediate outcome of the present discussion was satisfactory: "We have amicably compromised the affair of preaching. He is well pleased that the preachers should come once a month."[63] While the focus of this work is the political situation caused by evangelical competition, the concerns of the participants centered on the spiritual welfare of those under their care. Given the voluntary nature of the societies, both Venn and Wesley had to gain the support of the local Methodists themselves.

Within a year Wesley had withdrawn his preachers from Huddersfield.[64] Venn built chapels in the parish to continue the Evangelical work.

---

[60]Davies, *Early Cornish Evangelicals*, 183 (Samuel Walker to Thomas Adam, Oct. 22, 1759).

[61]*Works* 21:336 (July 20, 1761).

[62]*Works* 27:268-69 (Wesley to Ebenezer Blackwell, July 16, 1761). In this same letter Wesley mentions Walker's impending death and also describes Grimshaw saying that "a few such as him would make a nation tremble. He carried fire wherever he goes."

[63]*Works* 27:271 (Wesley to Ebenezer Blackwell, August 15, 1761).

[64]*Works* 27:335-39 (Wesley to Venn, June 22, 1763); Thomas Jackson, *Early Methodist Preachers* (London: Wesleyan Conference Office, 1865), 4:34.

It is not clear whether these chapels should be categorized as "Methodist preaching-houses free of Anglican control," as Baker describes them, or "non-episcopal chapels," as Telford describes them.[65]

The Huddersfield Compromise was one of cooperation between friends. But at its core, at least for Venn, was Evangelical concern for the maintenance and good ordering of parishes. Venn's case is a prime example of a cooperative effort between regular and irregular, both of whom were answerable to larger constituencies.

Just a year before the compromise, Venn had preached a visitation sermon widely published entitled *The Duty of a Parish Priest: His Obligations to Perform It; and the Incomparable Pleasure of a Life Devoted to the Cure of Souls.* He praised the work of the parish priest and his ability to affect transformation in the lives of the parishioners under his care. Like Bishop Gibson, Venn was convinced that the parish system offered the best means of promoting the Christian faith throughout the nation. Venn wrote:

> A more popular Way is continually wanted for the Multitude; and such a one as Men of common Parts may walk in. Now, such a Way, every faithful, conscientious Pastor is enabled to take with his Flock. He can display before their Eyes those all-sufficient Assistances, and mighty Privileges; that Grace, Mercy, and Peace from GOD the Father, and from the Lord JESUS CHRIST, which the Gospel promises, and when truly believed, gives Men now to possess. This, from an experiential Acquaintance with them, he can do in such a Manner, that Deism shall appear that worthless, impotent, forlorn Thing it really is; and, put in Comparison with the glorious Gospel, shall share the ignominious Fate of its Fellow-Idol of old; like the Dagon of the uncircumcised Philistines, it shall fall to the Ground before the Ark of the GOD of Israel.[66]

---

[65]See Baker, *John Wesley and the Church of England,* 186; and *Letters* (Telford) 4:215-18 (Wesley to Venn, June 22, 1763). Grimshaw built chapels in his parish. The description of a "Methodist" chapel seems to fit better in Grimshaw's case. His cooperation with Wesleyan Methodism makes it more likely than in the case of Venn. See Frank Baker, *William Grimshaw, 1708–1763* (London: Epworth, 1963), 223, 252-53.

[66]Henry Venn, *The Duty of a Parish Priest: His Obligations to Perform It; and the Incomparable Pleasure of a Life Devoted to the Cure of Souls. A Visitation Sermon at Wakefield on Col. 4.17. July 2, 1760* (Leeds, UK: Printed by G. Wright, 1760), 19.

Venn's request that Wesley stop the flow of itinerant lay preachers into his parish fits well within the ideological slant of this popular sermon. Unlike other Evangelicals who settled into parishes, such as Newton, Venn did not intend to separate himself from Wesley but simply to fulfill the duties of his ministry as he understood them.[67]

The year 1761 can be seen as one of cooperation between Wesley and the Evangelicals, but only as Wesley compromised his irregular ministry. At Kippax a confluence of the revival was seen that year when Venn, Wesley and Romaine all converged there at the same time. Wesley wrote in his *Journal*: "From Branley I rode to Kippax. Mr. Venn came a little after we were gone into the church. Mr. Romaine read prayers. I preached on 'Christ crucified, to the Jews a stumbling-block, and to the Greeks foolishness.' O why should they who agree in this great point fall out about smaller things!"[68] Ward notes that Kippax, a substantial parish in Yorkshire and a mining community, had become this "constellation of evangelical clergy" due to Lady Huntingdon's niece, Mrs. Medhurst, who lived in the parish. Evangelical Samuel Furley was acting curate in the parish and had been a friend of Venn's at Cambridge and curate to Romaine in London.[69] This cooperation, the compromise and even the friendship with Venn all came to an end within a few short years. The Huddersfield Compromise ended in 1764.

Wesley continued to recruit lay preachers, and the conference of 1764 sealed the practice in Methodism. After 1764 the use of lay preachers was assumed by both groups, and their separation further ensured. At a very basic level the Wesleyan conferences were simply the meetings where it was determined what Wesleyan Methodists would teach, who would teach and where they would promulgate their message.[70] The conferences were small meetings attended by few and should not be seen as the headline-making events that later Methodist propagandists would have them be.

---

[67]Hindmarsh notes, "Charged with the cure of souls, Newton did not in any case want to appear to condone Wesley's teaching through continued co-operation, since there would not be wider pastoral implications of his friendship with Wesley" (D. Bruce Hindmarsh, *John Newton and the English Evangelical Tradition: Between the Conversions of Wesley and Wilberforce* [Grand Rapids: Eerdmans, 2001], 135).

[68]*Works* 21:338.

[69]Ibid., n. 99.

[70]*Works* 10:122-23.

Wesley's intention for the August 1764 meeting in Bristol was for "a good understanding with all our brethren of the clergy who are heartily engaged in propagating vital religion."[71] His intentions met what Baker describes as his "readiness to go only so far in sacrificing Methodism to the Church."[72] Wesley would not, for instance, settle his itinerants, and Baker further notes that this willingness only to go so far "would not endear him to those who (like his brother Charles) did not acknowledge the same scale of values."[73]

This different scale of values developed in the course of the conference. Rack notes from manuscript evidence of the conference that the twelve clergy who attended that year "came to oppose, not to cooperate," although it is not exactly clear how accurately this description fit the intentions of the gathered clergy.[74] The outcome of the conference would give credence to this evidence, although both Wesley's and John Pawson's accounts describe the clergy's attendance more in terms of concern than of opposition.

Pawson notes in his *Short Account* that "twelve clergymen attended that conference, whose principal business was to convince us that we ought not to preach in any parish where there was a gospel minister," adding that some of the clergy "were much more moderate than others."[75] Pawson's definition of *moderate* corresponds to irregularity. Pawson writes, "One of them said 'if a layman was called of God to preach the gospel, then he had as good a right to do it as any clergyman whatever.' Mr. Madan could not agree to this, but said he would not dare to forbid such a person."[76] These ideologically "moderate" Evangelicals, along with their more conservative colleagues, were at the conference, however, to address lay preaching incursions in the confines of their legal parishes.

Charles Wesley provided the greatest fireworks at the conference when he and John Hampson Sr. broke out in an angry display. According

---

[71] *Works* 21:485 (Aug. 6, 1764); 10:298.

[72] Baker, *John Wesley and the Church of England*, 186.

[73] Ibid.

[74] *Works* 10:298n1026: "Sutcliffe's MS 'History' (fol. 641) says that the clergy came to oppose, not to cooperate."

[75] *Works* 10:298.

[76] Ibid.

to Pawson's *Short Account*, Charles claimed that "if he was a settled minister in any particular parish, the preachers should not preach there." Hampson, a lay preacher ever ready to challenge the high church Charles, replied, "I would preach there and never ask you leave, and should think I had as good a right for doing so as you had." To this, Charles is said to have retorted: "I know you are a grievous wolf, and you will tear the flock when once mine and my brother's heads are laid, if God do not give you repentance."[77] This episode was later left out of the official documents of conference[78] but explains why Charles later wrote to his brother: "The short remains of my life are devoted to this very thing, to follow your sons . . . with buckets of water, and quench the flame of strife and division which they have or may kindle."[79] Ironically, perhaps, the episode mirrors another where Charles played the role of young rebel. Early in the revival, John Bray, in whose home Charles had his evangelical conversion, tried to persuade Charles not to preach without episcopal approval. Charles recorded in his journal for July 8, 1743, his response: "[The bishops] have not yet forbid me; but, by the grace of God, I shall preach the word in season, out of season, though they and all men forbade me."[80] Despite his later stance, Charles was not always such a strict churchman until, as Gareth Lloyd points out, beginning between 1750 and 1756, when he would gain the reputation of "the ultimate Church Methodist."[81]

---

[77]Ibid. For further descriptions of the interplay between Charles Wesley and Hampson, see Ward's footnote in *Works* 21:485, as well as John Pawson, *An Affectionate Address to the Members of the Methodist Societies, Containing an Account of the State of their Temporal Affairs, Namely, the Preachers Fund, the Yearly Collection, Kingswood Collection, and the Back-Room. In Which Some Notice Is Taken of the False Accusations of Alexander Kilham* (London: 1795), 11; and William Myles, *A Chronological History of the People Called Methodists, Of the Connexion of the Late Rev. John Wesley; From Their Rise, in the Year 1729, to Their Last Conference, in 1812* (London: Printed at the Conference Office, 1813), 104-5.

[78]Rack notes, "The closing interplay between Charles Wesley and Hampson was omitted from the revision in *MM* (1806): 845, and Jackson, *Early Methodist Preachers*, 4:28-29." See *Works* 10:298. See n. 1027. Continuing this revisionism, Telford does not even mention the conference of 1764 in his *Life of the Rev. Charles Wesley*, rev. and enlarged (London: 1900).

[79]Frank Baker, "Charles Wesley's Letters," in *Charles Wesley: Poet and Theologian*, ed. S. T. Kimbrough Jr. (Nashville: Kingswood Books, 1992), 72-84. See also 96-97.

[80]Kimbrough and Newport, *Manuscript Journal of the Reverend Charles Wesley*, 2:356.

[81]Gareth Lloyd, *Charles Wesley and the Struggle for Methodist Identity* (New York: Oxford University Press, 2007), 121.

John Hampson Sr. had an uncomfortable relationship with authority. There is reason to doubt that he was ever officially appointed by Wesley until 1777, although he itinerated among the Methodists as early as the 1750s.[82] At the 1760 conference he promoted the idea that laymen could administer the sacraments. In 1765 he was found to be negligent of the care of the Kingswood School children,[83] and by 1784 he and his son left the Wesleyan Connexion altogether over the Deed of Declaration. Their departure was not quiet. Hampson Sr. published *Appeal to the Reverend John and Charles Wesley*, which caused an eruption in the conference. Wesley demanded that those who had written or supported the *Appeal* should "acknowledge their fault and be sorry for it, or he should have no further connection with them."[84] The two Hampsons, along with Joseph Pilmore, William Eells and John Atlay, left the conference, although it appears that Eells and Atlay may have recanted in time to leave again in 1788.[85] Ironically, given his father's dissenting slant, John Hampson Jr. was ordained a priest in the Church of England the year after Wesley's death.[86]

The conference of 1764 put on display the strong feelings of both clergy and lay participants. The concerns of the Evangelical clergy were not addressed. By 1766 the conference agreed that "field preaching should not be omitted to please anyone" and lessened the requirements on Methodist itinerants attending Church of England services on Sundays.[87] The Evangelicals departed the Wesleyan Methodist conference and along with Charles Wesley met soon after under the auspices of Lady Huntingdon. On August 28, 1764, Charles wrote to Samuel Lloyd in London: "We have had a Conference of the gospel clergy at Lady H[untingdon]'s. Good, I think, will come out of it. I had much conversation with your friend Mr. Jesse. Her Ladyship has invited more than an hundred to the opening of her chapel at Bath."[88] Rack notes that "it

---

[82]See C. J. Spittal's entry on Hampson, *DEB* 512.
[83]*Works* 10:311n42.
[84]*DEB* 547.
[85]Ibid., 548.
[86]Ibid., 512.
[87]*Works* 10:324-25.
[88]Ibid., 298.

seems likely that this otherwise unknown Conference was supplementary to and later" than John Wesley's conference, and it appears that John had attempted to organize such a meeting with Lady Huntingdon for that time as early as May. What is clear is that John Wesley was not in attendance at that meeting.[89] The trajectory of the Wesleyans and the Evangelicals continued to go in ever-increasingly separate directions.

---

[89] *Works* 21:338-39. According to his *Journal*, Wesley was in Derbyshire.

6

EUCHARIST AND ETHOS

The Formation of Methodist Identity

I_F Methodist incursions into_ Evangelical parishes and the use of
lay preachers were detrimental to Evangelical/Methodist relations and
continued the slow divide between the two, the issue of eucharistic administration was equally damaging. Attempts by Wesley's lay preachers
to administer communion or gain the right to administer it, either as
laymen or after ordination at Wesley's hands, were seen by many within
the Evangelical "party" as the end of their association. William Grimshaw,
Wesley's close associate and head of the Methodist work in the north of
England, warned Wesley that any attempt by the lay preachers to administer the sacraments would drive him from Methodism. Many saw eucharistic practice, a theological issue and an issue of church polity, as
determinative of Wesleyan Methodism's trajectory.

Grimshaw was one of Wesley's most supportive Evangelical colleagues,
yet he grew uncomfortable with Methodism's association with dissent.[1]
He was a leading supporter of the itinerant practices of Methodism, the
formation of societies and of the use of lay preachers, but unwilling to
remain connected to Methodism if it advocated outright dissent from
the Church.[2] Grimshaw's commitment to the Church was nuanced,
however. Like so many Evangelical Anglicans he was concerned for the

---

[1]Frank Baker, *John Wesley and the Church of England* (Nashville: Abingdon, 1970), 175-77.
[2]See Frank Baker, *William Grimshaw, 1708–1763* (London: Epworth, 1963).

maintenance of an evangelical ministry after his departure, and so he built a chapel in his parish for "the purer part of the Church of England" should his successor be averse to evangelicalism.[3] His oversight of the large and ever-expanding Haworth Round, a string of Methodist societies, was jeopardized by efforts made by Wesley's itinerants to align themselves with outright defiance of the Church. Charles Wesley was instrumental in igniting Grimshaw's reaction. Before the issues of licensing, ordination and sacramental administration were discussed at the 1760 conference, Charles sent Grimshaw a letter:

> Our preaching-houses are mostly licensed, and therefore proper [dissenting] meeting-houses. Our preachers are mostly licensed, and so dissenting ministers. They took out their licences as Protestant Dissenters. Three of our steadiest preachers give the Sacrament at Norwich with no other ordination or authority than their sixpenny licence. My brother approves of it. All the rest will most probably follow their example.[4]

The Methodists under Wesley had moved further from the Church than Grimshaw had imagined. Or at least this was Charles Wesley's interpretation. John Wesley, in order to mitigate the effects of the Conventicle Act, allowed the registration of Methodist preaching houses but remained defiant that he had not left the Church.[5] Whether or not Wesley's interpretive lens was correct, Baker notes that Grimshaw had complained about the licensing of preaching houses in the north.[6] His response to Charles's letter ignited a firestorm in the London society that Charles used to keep Methodism within the Church. Grimshaw's letter made it plain that he would not countenance any connection to Methodism as a dissenting body. "It's time for me to shift for myself—to disown all connection with the Methodists, to stay at home and take care

---

[3]Ralph Lowery, "William Grimshaw," in *Proceedings of the Wesley Historical Society* 34 (March 1963): 3.
[4]Baker, *John Wesley and the Church of England*, 176.
[5]See David Hempton, *The Religion of the People: Methodism and Popular Religion, c. 1750–1900* (London: Routledge, 1996), 148. Hempton notes that Wesley refused to accept registration of Methodist preaching houses as a form of separation but "a device to protect life and property from the license of the crowd."
[6]Ibid., 177.

of my parish, or to preach abroad in such places as are unlicensed and to such people as are in no connection with us. I hereby therefore assure you that I disclaim all further and future connection with the Methodists."[7] As a priest within the Church, connection to a dissenting group under his care and the administration of communion by laymen within it called into question his loyalty and his ordination.

Likely because of his friendship with Grimshaw, Wesley never challenged Grimshaw's squeamishness for Methodist use of the Act of Toleration. Charles used Grimshaw's concerns to bolster his war against Methodist schism. Wesley was not close to Thomas Adam, however, and was quick to respond to his criticism. Toward the end of any meaningful cooperation between Evangelicals and Methodists in 1768, he wrote to Adam that the Methodists had little or no choice in the matter. "One of Wintringham informed me yesterday that you said no sensible and well-meaning man could hear and much less join the Methodists; because they all acted under a lie, professing themselves members of the Church of England while they licensed themselves as Dissenters." Wesley was quick to add, "You are little misinformed."[8] Wesleyan Methodist lay preachers had attempted for some time to gain the protection of the Toleration Act without the dissenting label. The issue was not dissent but protection. Deryck Lovegrove writes, "Behind the smiling façade of the 1689 act lurked the spectre of penal legislation enacted in the Stuart era."[9] The Methodist balancing act between establishment and dissent placed them in legal jeopardy regardless of their actual ecclesiastical loyalties. Wesley's arguments on the matter, however, held little sway with the orthodox Adam. Wesley insisted that Adam needed the Methodists more than they needed him and arrogantly concluded his rebuttal by challenging the usefulness of Adam's work within the parish structure of the Church.

> O sir, what art of men or devils is this which makes you so studiously stand aloof from those who are thus minded I cannot but say to you, as I

---

[7]Baker, *Grimshaw*, 255-57.

[8]*Letters* (Telford) 5:98 (John Wesley to Thomas Adam, July 19, 1768).

[9]Deryck Lovegrove, *Established Church, Sectarian People: Itinerancy and the Transformation of English Dissent, 1780–1830* (New York: Cambridge University Press, 1988), 6.

did to Mr. Walker (and I say it the more freely because *Quid mea refert* I
am neither better nor worse, whether you hear or forbear), "The Methodists do not want you; but you want them." You want the life, the spirit,
the power which they have, not of themselves, but by the free grace of
God; else how could it be (let me speak without reserve) that so good a
man and so good a preacher should have so little fruit of his labour—his
unwearied labour—for so many years. Have your parishioners the life of
religion in their souls? Have they so much as the form of it? Are the people
of Wintringham in general any better than those of Winterton or Horton?
Alas! sir, what is it that hinders your reaping the fruit of so much pains
and so many prayers?[10]

Writing on the pastoral office, Adam once noted that "to relinquish, or
intermit parochial labour, because it is not attended with success, would
be terribly inexcusable." His advice in such a situation was to "labour on;
commit the matter to God; wait patiently; get a feeling of the bowels of
Christ; and die praying, 'Lord, pity the people!'"[11] Wesley had a distinctly different vision.

Wesley's disdain for a settled ministry was, in part, behind his licensing of Methodist buildings under the Toleration Act. He was consis-
tently cynical of the efficacy of parish-based evangelical efforts. At one
point he claimed that the only successful parish-based Evangelical was
Samuel Walker.[12] Wesley was greatly concerned that Fletcher's gifts
would be wasted when he went into parish ministry. He made efforts in
spring 1758 to help Samuel Furly, an Evangelical later of Kippax, to attain
holy orders without the required "title" of a parish appointment.[13] He
wrote Furly that he was in conversation with the bishop of Derry, William
Barnard, who "loves the Methodists from his heart," about ordaining
him, attempting to gain a nonparochial priest for Wesleyan Methodism,

---

[10]*Letters* (Telford) 5:99.

[11]Thomas Adam, *Posthumous Works of the Rev. Thomas Adam, Late Rector of Wintringham. In Three
Volumes. Containing His Private Thoughts on Religion, and Sermons on Different Subjects. To Which
Is Prefixed a Short Sketch of His Life and Character* (York: 1786), 1:245.

[12]See *Works* 26:149-52. Ironically, perhaps, Walker's parishioners wanted little or nothing to do
with Wesley.

[13]Anglican polity required that a candidate for ordination hold a "title" to a specific position
within the church. See Edmund Gibson's *Codex Juris Ecclesiastici Anglicani* (1713), 1:168-78.

much as he had at the time in Thomas Maxfield.[14] The plan never came to anything. Furly was ordained in London and worked with Romaine, as has already been noted, and had a successful parochial career.

Wesley's plan indicated his low estimation of the potential success of parish ministry. This perspective was evident in the late 1780s when he told Francis Asbury to make certain that Methodist preachers in America were not settled in parochial appointments.[15] Such a perspective would naturally produce an irregular ministry, one in which Evangelicals refused to participate, and where Methodist chapels would teeter tenuously on the border of dissent. Regardless of Wesley's claims to Adam and others, the number of licensed Methodist preachers and preaching houses had been rising throughout the early period of the revival. In fact, the first preaching house ever built, the New Room in Bristol, was registered under the act.[16]

The issues that concerned Grimshaw, Adam and Walker in the 1750s were public knowledge. Methodists debated them openly, including the Wesley brothers themselves. It was this public debate that most likely instigated Walker and Wesley's correspondence. If there can be said to be one reason why Wesley and George Thomson, for example, and many of the Evangelical clergy no longer worked together, the conference at Leeds in 1755 and public debates about separation and the ordination of lay preachers were reason enough. Similar to the conferences of 1760 and 1764, where the use of itinerant lay preachers was hotly debated, the conference of 1755 focused on the issues of ordination and sacramental administration.

METHODIST IDENTITY AND THE 1755 CONFERENCE

Wesley described the 1755 conference in his *Journal* in terms of the legality of Methodist separation when he wrote:

---

[14]*Works* 27:126-27 (Wesley to Samuel Furly, May 1, 1758). In terms of Maxfield, he and Wesley worked together in London until 1763, when both men separated over the Christian perfection controversies of the early 1760s.

[15]John A. Vickers, *Thomas Coke: Apostle of Methodism* (Eugene, OR: Wipf and Stock, 2013), 74-75.

[16]Richard P. Heitzenrater, *Wesley and the People Called Methodists*, 2nd ed. (Nashville: Abingdon, 2013), 190. Heitzenrater notes that on the back of the document registering the building under the act someone has written, "Needless, useless, senseless," and that the very registering of Methodist buildings under the act conflicts with Wesley's *Farther Appeal* (1745); see *Works* 11:183.

Tue. [May] 6 [, 1755]. Our Conference began at Leeds. The point on which we desired all the preachers to speak their minds at large was, whether we ought to separate from the Church. Whatever was advanced on one side or the other was seriously and calmly considered. And on the third day we were all fully agreed in that general conclusion, that (whether it was lawful or not) it was no ways expedient.[17]

Ward notes that Wesley's "minutes of the Leeds Conference are even more terse than this laconic account," adding that "the issue was the more painful, not merely because of the conflict it generated between the stiff churchmanship of Charles Wesley and the desire of experienced preachers like [John] Cownley and [Thomas] Walsh to administer the sacraments, but because of the almost desperate indecision in [John Wesley] himself."[18] He describes the arguments for separation as "a curious mixture of rationalism, Protestantism, and pietism in that order, with [Wesley] admitting [to Walker in a subsequent letter] 'I will freely acknowledge that I cannot answer these arguments to my own satisfaction. So that my conclusion (which I cannot yet give up) that it is lawful to continue in the Church, stands, I know not how, almost without any premises that are able to bear its weight.'"[19]

The question is what Wesley meant by "lawful." It was lawful to become a dissenting body in 1755. The term could have been used in reference to conscience. Was separation "lawful" in terms of not violating one's conscience, based on the "law of conscience" in works such as Bishop Robert Sanderson's *Lectures on Conscience and Human Law*, published in 1615? Sanderson's work dealt with the conflict between what he termed "human laws" and "conscience" and the obligations that such a conflict demands.[20] It called for giving a place to conscience when one felt conflicted by human laws. Such an assertion would call into question the epistemological underpinnings of ecclesiastical structures based on the idea of an apostolic succession. Thus Methodist com-

---

[17] *Works* 21:10-11 (May 6, 1755).

[18] *Works* 21:11n.

[19] Ibid.; for Wesley's letter to Walker, See *Works* 26:594.

[20] Robert Sanderson, *Lectures on Conscience and Human Law: Delivered in the Divinity School at Oxford* (Lincoln, UK: James Williamson, 1615, 1877).

plaints came from a different epistemological understanding of church, and one that could not have either sustained itself within the Church of England as a party or, as Wesley envisioned it, practiced his fourfold structure of church, society, class and band. These Methodists wanted to make the Church like the Wesleyan society. But essentially they were following what had commonly been called by this time the "law of conscience," an idea that applied Enlightenment values and reason to seemingly contradictory principles.

The crisis of 1755 was the first major battle for Methodist ecclesiastical identity. It would include skirmishes at the conferences of 1760 and 1764, culminating in the ordinations of 1784. This string of conflicts represents the blossoming of Methodist identity. After both John and Charles Wesley had died, these same battles raged for years, especially in the 1790s, when Church Methodists, trustees, preachers and populists clashed with a vengeance.[21] Issues that had arisen during the time of the Wesleys only became more divisive after their deaths. The crisis of 1755 represents the first shots of a much longer battle.[22]

The issue in 1755 stemmed from concerns brought by Wesley's preachers about the spiritual welfare of their people. Already by this time, the lay preachers had begun to look on the Methodist people as their pastoral charge. Acting the part of the dissenter, the lay itinerants saw their work as separate from the work of the Church, as can easily be seen in Methodism's widening detachment from the liturgical and structural patterns of local parishes.[23] The preachers were not the only ones clamoring for Methodist sacramental administration. Members of the societies were often loath to take the sacrament from the hand of a clergyman who berated Methodism or whose morality was under suspicion by the tight-lipped Wesleyans. John Wesley described a scene in the 1780s that

---

[21]See especially Gareth Lloyd, *Charles Wesley and the Struggle for Methodist Identity* (New York: Oxford University Press, 2007), 219-33.

[22]See especially David Hempton, *Methodism and Politics in British Society 1750–1850* (London: Hutchinson, 1984), 55-84.

[23]See the minutes for the 1755 conference. The minutes, beginning that year, show increasing detachment from the church on the part of the preachers. In 1755, this can be seen in the preachers' surprised reaction to the Wesleys' opposition to their administration of Holy Communion. See *Works* 10:271-72.

is a perfect picture of this Methodist aversion. In a journal entry describing a Sunday service in Epworth, Wesley wrote:

> I fain *would* prevent the members here from leaving the church, but I
> cannot do it. As Mr. G[ibson] is not a pious man, but rather an enemy to
> piety, who frequently preaches against the truth and those that hold and
> love it, I cannot with all my influence persuade them either to hear him
> or to attend the Sacrament administered by him. If I cannot carry this
> point even while I live, who then can do it when I die? And the case of
> Epworth is the case of every church where the minister neither loves nor
> preaches the gospel. The Methodists *will not* attend his ministrations.
> What then is to be done?[24]

The preachers were not alone in their desire to celebrate the Lord's Supper within the warm embrace of Methodism. Such a pursuit, however, would lead the Methodists to dissent. In a sense, 1755 can be seen as the beginning of that journey. The subsequent conferences, deeds and ordinations can be seen as the growing pains of a movement coming to maturity and leaving the nest.

In his biography of Wesley, Tyerman writes: "The year 1755 was a crisis. It was an infinite mercy that Methodism was not dashed to pieces."[25] Tyerman's description is anything but balanced, however.[26] He leaps into prosectarian Methodist propaganda to describe the arguments of the 1755 Leeds Conference. His argument hinges on the "right" of Methodist sacramental activity and the entitlement of the Methodist preachers to administer the sacraments. He claims that the men arguing for sacramental rights "were as capable of forming correct opinions as the two Wesleys were."[27] Tyerman's statement is based on

---

[24]*Works* 24:100-101.

[25]Luke Tyerman, *Life and Times of the Rev. John Wesley, M.A., Founder of the Methodists* (New York: Harper and Brothers, 1872), 2:200.

[26]See ibid., 200-211. In spite of this propagandistic hue, Heitzenrater and Ward refer to Tyerman's account as the fullest account we have in notes in Wesley's journal in the bicentennial edition of the *Works* of John Wesley. Their footnote, however, was written before the publication of volume 10 of the *Works* by Henry Rack. What their footnote may indicate more than anything else is the critical need for the bicentennial works project in face of the propaganda, myth and sectarianism still inhibiting modern Wesley scholarship without a complete critical edition of the necessary primary sources.

[27]Ibid., 200.

nineteenth-century comparisons of Oxford- and Cambridge-trained clergy of the established Church and their Methodist revivalist counterparts. His historiographical slant is based on the arguments of the lay preachers in the 1750s and 1760s. Tyerman writes that "Cownley, Walsh, and the Perronets were right, but the time was scarcely come for this to be acknowledged."[28]

As he would in 1760, Charles Wesley did not wait for the conference of 1755 to begin before writing letters to Evangelicals. He believed that their accumulated influence could sway the conference. Baker describes this as Charles's continued effort to "undermine John's apparent drift away from the Church of England by fiery letters to clergy otherwise friendly to Methodism."[29] In particular, Charles wrote several letters to the Evangelical Walter Sellon of Leicestershire, beginning a correspondence in 1754.[30] He wrote to Sellon:

> I have always loved you, but never so much as now. How unlike the spirit of poor Perronet and his associates! What a pity, that such spirits should have any influence over my brother! They are continually urging him to a separation; that is, to pull down all he has built, to put a sword in our enemies' hands, to destroy the work, scatter the flock, disgrace himself, and go out—like the snuff of a candle.[31]

Charles added a reminder of the "debt you owe the Methodists and me, and the Church," as well as Wesley, to write "a full, close, plain transcript of your heart on this occasion."[32]

---

[28]Ibid.

[29]Frank Baker, "Charles Wesley's Letters," in *Charles Wesley: Poet and Theologian*, ed. S. T. Kimbrough Jr. (Nashville: Kingswood Books, 1992), 79.

[30]A. S. Wood lists both Walter Sellon and John Meriton as Evangelical clergy who traveled with John Wesley. See A. S. Wood, *Brothers in Arms: John Wesley's Early Clerical Associates* (Wesley Historical Society Publishing Office, 1992), 18-22. See also *Works* 20:473n13.

[31]Tyerman, *Life and Times of the Rev. John Wesley*, 201-2, Charles Wesley to Rev. Walter Sellon, settled at Smithsby, near Ashby-de-la-Zouch, probably ca. 1754. Baker notes in *John Wesley and the Church of England* that the manuscript letter is located at Drew University. He provides a date of November 29, 1754. See 374n15.

[32]Tyerman, *Life and Times of the Rev. John Wesley*, 201-2. Sellon, who had been a baker, was converted by Whitefield and became one of Wesley's itinerants. Later, by the influence of Lady Huntingdon, he was given holy orders in the Church. Sellon became instrumental in the later Calvinist controversies of the 1770s.

Charles's letters to Sellon continued. He was not convinced that his brother was committed to the Church. He asked Sellon in late 1754 to write again and "spare not" because "the Melchisedechians have been taken in" and apparently Charles was excluded from conversations related to the Methodists and the Church. Charles continued to "stand in doubt" of his brother, something of which he wanted Sellon to be aware but not the general public. He wanted to end debates over Methodism's place in the Church by finding a way to qualify the lay preachers for holy orders. He was convinced that Sellon could be of assistance in the effort and wrote, "I know none fitter for training up the young men in learning than yourself or J. Jones. We must, among us, get the sound preachers qualified for orders."[33]

During this period Charles continued to hear reports from various supporters. In his shorthand diary he outlined reports he had gathered from October 1754. On two consecutive days, three different Methodist women reported that the lay preachers were administering communion. Charles was informed by "Sister Macdonald" and then "Sister Clay" that Charles Perronet had given communion to the lay preachers "Walsh and Deavens, and then to twelve at Sister Gardner's, in the Minories." The next day "Sister Meredith" reported hearing that "Walsh had administered the sacrament at Reading."[34] According to the diary, Charles was with his brother the day after he had received these reports. He records his brother's response to them, "We have in effect ordained already." Wesley was, according to his brother, "inclined to lay on hands; and to let the preachers administer." Five days later, Wesley was supposedly still wavering, but apparently willing to wait before proceeding with any ordinations.[35]

---

[33]Tyerman, *Life and Times of the Rev. John Wesley*, 202. "J. Jones" is likely John Jones, John Wesley's assistant in the mid-1740s. Jones was ordained in 1767. According to R. Davies, "He had been refused episcopal ordination several times in his early years, because, presumably, of his Methodism" (*DEB* 621).

[34]Tyerman, *Life and Times of the Rev. John Wesley*, 202n1. These particular references come from Charles Wesley's journal letters, which were distinct from his *Manuscript Journal*, recently published by Kingswood Books. See Richard Heitzenrater, "Purge the Preachers: The Wesleys and Quality Control," in *Charles Wesley: Life, Literature, and Legacy*, ed. Ted A. Campbell and Kenneth Newport (London: Epworth, 2008).

[35]Tyerman, *Life and Times of the Rev. John Wesley*, 202.

This back and forth on Wesley's part was particularly pronounced in the 1750s as he continued to struggle between a dichotomy that began to see Church tradition and authority in competition with the spiritual needs of the Methodist people. This wavering simply confirmed the worst fears of his brother and likely worked to solidify Charles's opposition to any irregularities on the part of the itinerants, and his continued letter writing. Gareth Lloyd insightfully writes that Wesley's "ambiguity was not new; what was different in the early 1750s was that Charles was no longer his brother's devoted partner."[36] This gradual division would be repeated as Evangelicals recoiled from Wesleyan Methodist irregularities that challenged common Anglican practice connected to identity and ethos.

Methodist practice confused the situation. John Lenton notes in his book on the early preachers, "From the early days preachers were admitted to the status of travelling preacher in a solemn service. Joseph Cownley in 1747 had the New Testament put in his hands with the words 'take thou authority to preach the Gospel.'"[37] Such a designation would have explicitly mirrored the Ordination of Deacons in the Book of Common Prayer.[38] Rack does not necessarily accept the historical validity of the Cownley account. The procedure for the acceptance of lay preachers was described in the 1749 Large Minutes. Rack does admit, "Two well-known incidents might suggest a quasi-ordination of preachers distinct from Wesley's acknowledged ordinations," although he also acknowledges that the historical record is not clear. The likelihood is that no formal procedure was in place in the early years of Wesleyan Methodism.[39]

In February 1755 Charles wrote to Sellon one more time about his efforts to sway Wesley away from the appearance of dissent. Apparently Sellon had sent multiple letters that along with "some others" and these

---

[36]Lloyd, *Charles Wesley*, 125.
[37]See John Lenton, *John Wesley's Preachers: A Social and Statistical Analysis of the British and Irish Preachers Who Entered the Methodist Itinerancy Before 1791*, Studies in Evangelical History and Thought (Eugene, OR: Wipf and Stock, 2011), 75.
[38]For the fuller story, see Thomas Jackson, *The Lives of the Early Methodist Preachers, Chiefly Written by Themselves* (London: Wesleyan Conference Office, 1865), 2:7.
[39]See *Works* 10:77.

efforts had made Wesley "forget he was ever inclined" to the ordination of the lay preachers or of lay administration of communion.[40] Charles wrote that Wesley "has spoken as strongly of late, in behalf of the Church of England, as I could wish," adding that Wesley now "never intends to leave her."[41] This certainty on Charles's part was short-lived. Wesley's wavering commitment to his brother's plan to settle many of the lay preachers and to demand statements of Church loyalty from them continued to unnerve his brother.[42] Charles never showed full confidence in the lay preachers until they were in holy orders, and few of them took that route. He was convinced that without ordination in the Church of England the lay preachers would continue to promote separation while the brothers were living and succeed at their attempts once they were both deceased. Charles ended his letter to Sellon by reporting on the efforts of Evangelicals around London. He pleaded to Sellon to "pray for them and for us."[43]

The conference of 1755 did not take place until May of that year. According to J. R. Tyson, the Leeds Conference was pivotal to Methodism's connection to the Church. He notes that "over sixty-three Methodist preachers arrived to debate the 'question of conservation'" and claims that such numbers represented the importance of the topics addressed.[44] By May 25 Charles published his public answer to the proceedings in *An Epistle to the Reverend Mr. John Wesley, by Charles Wesley, Presbyter of the Church of England*.[45] Charles published four thousand copies of this lyrical tract against the Methodist preachers and his brother. The question is whether this very public plea made the Evangelical Anglicans even more suspect of Methodism's dissenting tendencies.

Stanley Ayling writes that "there had never been a time when the Wesley brothers did not feel free to criticize one another," but this publi-

---

[40]Tyerman, *Life and Times of the Rev. John Wesley*, 203 (Charles Wesley to Sellon, Feb. 4, 1755).
[41]Ibid.
[42]Ibid. See the Feb. 4 letter for Charles Wesley's intention to divide the lay preachers "church or meeting."
[43]Tyerman, *Life and Times of the Rev. John Wesley*, 203.
[44]John R. Tyson, ed., *Charles Wesley: A Reader* (New York: Oxford University Press, 1989), 408. Rack doubts the numbers reported by the participants. See *Works* 10:270n949.
[45]Note that Charles describes himself as a "presbyter of the Church of England" in the title, and although John was also a presbyter, Charles does not mention it on the title page.

cation on Charles's part represents a particularly public condemnation of his brother.[46] His criticism of his brother would never again be so loud until the 1784 ordinations, although in 1760, Charles would republish ten thousand copies of his brother's *Reasons Against a Separation from the Church of England* (1758) accompanied by his own *Hymns for the Methodist Preachers*, clearly laying out his vision of Methodism within the Church and convinced that any move toward an independent Methodism was fueled by pride.[47] Charles wrote in his *Epistle to the Reverend Mr. John Wesley* that the Methodists do not comprise the Church, nor should they think of themselves as such.

> Yet still the Methodists *The Church* are not:
> A single Faculty is not the Soul,
> A Limb the Body, or a Part the Whole.

From Charles's perspective, Methodists were abandoning their calling to be a renewal movement within the Church and had thus misunderstood their place:

> But should the bold usurping Spirit dare
> Still higher climb, and sit in Moses's chair,
> Power o'er my Faith and Consience to maintain,
> Shall I submit, and suffer it to reign?
> Call it *the Church*, and Darkness put for Light,
> Falsehood with Truth confound, and Wrong with Right?
> No: I dispute the Evil's haughty Claim,
> The Spirit of the World be still its Name,
> Whatever call'd by Man it's purely Evil,
> 'Tis Babel, Antichrist, and Pope, and Devil![48]

For Charles, the assumptions of the lay preachers went beyond the rightful duty of laypersons with little or no education lacking episcopal

---

[46]Stanley Ayling, *John Wesley* (Nashville: Abingdon, 1979), 232.

[47]See especially hymn II. "Hymns for the Methodist Preachers," ed. Randy Maddox (last updated April 2, 2010), can be found at the Duke Center for Wesleyan Studies website: https://divinity .duke.edu/sites/divinity.duke.edu/files/documents/cswt/62_Hymns_for_the_Methodist_Preach ers_%281760%29.pdf.

[48]Tyson, *Charles Wesley*, 411.

ordination. He would publish this same tract in 1784 after John had ordained Coke, Whatcoat and Vasey for work in the United States. Charles's arguments remained the same. By 1750, he was securely positioned as Methodism's Churchman.[49] It was John's ecclesiology that was undergoing continued change. Charles's ecclesiology is summarized in a line of his tract when he claims that "The Church of Christ *and England*—is But One!"[50]

Charles's *Epistle* was printed by William Straham at a cost of eight guineas. In a letter to his wife, Sarah, he wrote: "On Thursday I read my Epistle a second time to a crowded audience and yesterday at the watch-night. Seven hundred are sent by this day's carrier."[51] Not convinced of the lay preachers' sincerity, Charles was determined to publicly shame them and his brother into conformity.

Charles's concerns with the integrity of the lay preachers had as much to do with John's continually evolving understanding of ordination.[52] By 1755 not only had Wesley told his brother that they had "in effect ordained already," as noted previously, but in terms of ordination he sounded much like the Puritans. Baker describes Wesley's evolving understanding of ordination, arguing that for Wesley in 1755 "true ordi-

---

[49]As noted earlier, Charles was not consistent in his churchmanship before the 1750s. Rack points to this discrepancy in Henry D. Rack, *Reasonable Enthusiast: John Wesley and the Rise of Methodism*, 3rd ed. (Philadelphia: Trinity Press International, 2002), 304. Neither was he ever as staunchly committed to the parish system of the church as were the majority of Evangelical Anglicans. Charles was consistent in his opposition to separation. As early as 1739 he was working diligently to stop a schism brewing in the Fetter Lane Society. He recorded in his journal for Feb. 28, 1739, that he "met the bands at John Bray's, and cautioned them against schism." In April of the same year he continued his efforts against the "wild ramblings" of John Shaw, a member of the society, whose ideas about the "Christian priesthood" were seen as heretical to Charles. See S. T. Kimbrough Jr. and Kenneth G. C. Newport, *The Manuscript Journal of the Reverend Charles Wesley, M. A.* (Nashville: Kingswood Books, 2007), 1:170.

[50]Tyson, *Charles Wesley*, 412.

[51]Thomas Jackson, *Life of the Rev. Charles Wesley, Revised and Enlarged* (London: The Wesleyan Methodist Book Room, 1900), 2:81.

[52]Throughout much of this period Charles looked for ways to have the preachers ordained within the regular ministry of the Church. In 1756 he and Walker presented a plan to Wesley to have many of the preachers ordained—a plan that the archbishop of Canterbury, Thomas Herring, was sympathetic toward. See Baker, *John Wesley and the Church of England*, 171; Frank Baker, *Charles Wesley as Revealed by His Letters* (London: Epworth, 1948), 95; and Edwin Sidney, *The Life and Ministry of the Rev. Samuel Walker, Formerly of Truro, Cornwall* (London: 1838), 201-3.

nation, the conferring of spiritual grace, was the work of God alone."[53] For Wesley, the role of the Church was simply "through its authorized officials to acknowledge the divine call and divine empowerment, adding the seal of its own commission so that the minister would generally be recognized as such."[54] This description of ordination almost negates the necessity of an episcopacy. It quite clearly disregards the catholic understanding of ordination as a sacramental action restricted to an episcopate in succession with the apostles. Three years later, in 1758, Wesley appears to have again adapted his understanding of ordination to support episcopal ordination in his *Treatise on Baptism*.[55]

John Wesley's letter to Charles after the publication of Charles's *Epistle* provides insight into the internal debate between the brothers. Charles was obviously not convinced by the promise of the lay preachers not to administer communion. Two sons of the vicar of Shoreham, the Perronets, had administered the sacrament, as had lay preachers Joseph Cownley and Thomas Walsh. The four of them were, according to Telford, "leaders of this movement" for lay administration. John wrote to his brother, "Do not you understand that they all promised by Thomas Walsh not to administer even among themselves? I think that an huge point given up—perhaps more than they could give up with a clear conscience . . . When I reflect on their answer I admired their spirit and was ashamed of my own."[56]

Wesley's willingness to believe that the lay preachers had given up a major point of contention is key. Within English ecclesiastical law, a tradition that Wesley begins to read with increasing leniency, there was no question of lay administration whatsoever. This may explain Charles's hostility to the very notion. Charles was unconvinced that a layman who had acted as a clergyman without ordination would simply desist from further acts of dissent. John appears confused by the continued controversy. He wrote to his brother in the same letter:

[53] Baker, *John Wesley and the Church of England*, 154.
[54] Ibid.
[55] *Works* (Jackson) 10:190.
[56] *Works* 26:561 (Wesley to Charles Wesley, June 20, 1755).

The practical conclusion was "Not to separate from the Church." Did we not all agree in this? Surely either you or I must have been asleep or we could not differ so widely in a matter of fact! Here is Charles Perronet raving "because his friends have given up *all*" and Charles Wesley "because they have given up *nothing*"; and I in the midst, staring and wondering both at one and the other. I do not want to do anything more, unless I could bring them over to my opinion; and I am not in haste for that.[57]

Wesley concludes this particular letter with a litany of practical concerns including tunes for Charles's hymns, but finally ends it with a clue to the lay preachers' concerns. He wrote: "Jos. Cowley says, 'For such and such reasons I dare not hear a drunkard preach or read prayers.' I answer, 'I dare.' But I can't answer his reasons."[58] The spiritual, or even practical, concerns were becoming tantamount to law within the experiential nature of the revival. What seems to be jettisoned with this shift is the legality of their actions and the political ramifications of acting as dissenters from the Church. The Wesley brothers were not oblivious to these concerns, although Charles was much more tuned in to them than was his brother, but the lay preachers appeared to be dominated by pastoral concerns exclusively. The issues of legality and the political ramifications only appeared at conference once the deed was done.

To partake of the sacrament in the state-sponsored church was a statement of conformity not simply to the Book of Common Prayer but to the national aspirations of the English people. In the context of war with France and Spain in the Seven Years' War (1754–1763), the first war that "was truly an Imperial war for Britain," political connections gained special importance. Before 1757 Britain was on the defensive "against an aggressive France which was testing the limits of the peace of 1748."[59] Only after William Pitt's calculated use of the British Navy in America, Europe and

---

[57]Ibid.

[58]Ibid. John includes a comment that he is working on his *Notes*, a project that he was coordinating with the assistance of John Fletcher.

[59]Bruce P. Lenman, "Colonial Wars and Imperial Instability," in P. J. Marshall, ed., *The Oxford History of the British Empire*, vol. 2, *The Eighteenth Century* (New York: Oxford University Press, 1998), 159.

India, and unified effort on the part of Anglo-American colonists, including George Washington, did Britain see a turn in their favor. Thus John Fox could preach in a sermon at the height of political tension: "Religion and Loyalty are the only true and certain Supports of any kind of Kingdom. The best Christian is always the best Patriot; his Schemes procure the Alliance and Favour of the King of Kings; he truly serves his Country by being a leading Example of Virtue, and by using his Power to discountenance and punish Vice and Immorality."[60] Fox argued in the sermon for a unified English response to national crisis built on religious uniformity.

One response to Charles's *Epistle* was written by a "Christophus," who although anonymous appears from his terminology to have been an Evangelical himself. The title of Christophus's work is *A Serious Inquiry Whether a Late Epistle from the Rev. Mr. Charles Wesley to the Rev. Mr. John Wesley Be Not an Evident Mark of Their Being Unhappily Fallen.* According to Christophus, all true members of the Church of England and the true Church of Christ cannot deny ecclesiastical authority:

> For such can never belie, revile and villify that Church or her ministers, for fear of weakening at least the interest of Christianity, and scattering the flock of Christ, that they may the easier fall a prey to every wolf in sheep's cloathing, and settle down contentedly in a causeless and avowed separation from the Established Church, notwithstanding the apostle warns us all so strenuously to beware of dogs, beware of evil workers, beware of the concision, Phil. iii.2.[61]

While liberally quoting the Book of Common Prayer, the author warns those who would administer communion as laypersons by referring to

---

[60]John Fox, *An Earnest Persuasive to the Manly Defense of Our Happy Constitution in Church and State; a Sermon, Preached in the Parish-Church of Kildwick-Piercy, in the County of York, on Friday, February 17, 1758* (York: 1758).

[61]Christophus, *A Serious Inquiry Whether a Late Epistle from the Rev. Mr. Charles Wesley to the Rev. Mr. John Wesley Be Not an Evident Mark of Their Being Unhappily Fallen into One of the Most Crafty and Most Dangerous Wiles of the Devil, for the Delusion of Many Innocent, Unthinking Christians; by Inducing Their Hearers to Have Too High an Opinion of Them, as the Peculiar Servants of God, and Apostles Sent by Him to Have an Apostate, Sinking Church, and Encouraging Them Utterly to Contemn Their Own Regular Pastors, Set over Them by the Providence of God, Whom They by Their False Insinuations Represent as Apostates from the Church of England, and the True Church of Christ* (England and Wales: Printed for the author, 1755), 10.

God's punishment of those who had challenged the authority of Moses and Aaron. He writes, "But how severely God punished this their usurpation of offices not belonging to them, and undervaluing those whom God had set over them, you may read at large in the 16th chapter of Numbers, for the earth opened her mouth and swallowed them up, and all that appertained unto them."[62] However, his warning was not simply meant for the lay preachers but also for the Wesley brothers themselves. Christophus explicitly warns the Methodists not to fall into schism, which he argues was a sign of being "more puffed up with spiritual pride and good opinions of themselves than with real and substantial holiness."[63]

The fact that any work was written in response to Charles's *Epistle* is proof that the debates within Methodism were no longer internal. These debates influenced public opinion of Methodism. In this case, the public perception of Methodism's place within the Church was being challenged by one of the Wesley brothers themselves.

John's response to Charles was not altogether positive. Of the lay preachers known to have fought for the right to administer communion, and who did administer it without permission, Thomas Mitchell and Paul Greenwood were both appointed to Cornwall at this time.[64] Whether they spoke openly about this issue is difficult to know. The historical record and Wesley's *Journal* just days after the conference prove that Charles Wesley's suspicions were accurate. Within a week of the conference, Wesley and his wife traveled to Newcastle, where he recorded, "I did not find things here in the order I expected. Many were on the point of leaving the Church, which some had done already—and as they supposed, on my authority!"[65] The confusion among the Methodist rank and file simply mirrored the confusion conveyed by the leadership. Conflict between the

---

[62]Ibid., 6.

[63]Ibid., 7.

[64]*Works* 10:272-75. Greenwood continued to promote lay administration. See John S. Pawlyn, *Bristol Methodism in John Wesley's Day: With Monographs of the Early Methodist Preachers* (Bristol: W. C. Hemmons, 1877): "Greenwood, several years later became somewhat conspicuous by persisting in his ecclesiastical right to administer the Sacrament in opposition to Charles Wesley's wish" (47).

[65]*Works* 21:11 (Tuesday, May 13, 1755).

message of the Wesleys as Anglican clergyman and the method exemplified in the irregular system they had created would continue
well into the next century.

In Norwich this conflict between message and method came to a head
when in 1758 Methodist preachers administered the sacrament alongside
dissenters. Norwich Methodism was unique in that the society at
Norwich met together with an evangelical dissenting group. Close association with dissent simply pulled the Methodists further from their
Anglican bearings.[66] The controversy that arose once again brought the
opposing factions of the 1755 conference together in the conference at
Bristol in 1760.

THE 1760 CONFERENCE AND SACRAMENTAL ADMINISTRATION

Wesley's Norwich Foundry and the Norwich Tabernacle, a chapel built
by Lady Huntingdon and led by William Cudworth, began meeting together in 1758. In a 1759 tour of the area Wesley implemented some distinctive Wesleyan practices in the society, including the introduction of
classes, separate seating for the sexes and class tickets.[67] His description
of the society is of a harmonious ecumenical effort, apparently capable
of blurring the lines of theological division that had marked aspects of
the revival. This ecumenical effort, however, ran aground with the increasing influence of dissent.

It is surprising that Wesley had such an optimistic view of the merger
of his society with Cudworth's. Ward notes that Cudworth was a leading
figure in a small Calvinistic Methodist connexion called "The hearers
and followers of the Apostles" and that he and Wesley had engaged each
other in polemical battles for almost twenty years.[68] Wesley and Cud-

---

[66] An analysis of the religious upbringing of the preachers also sheds light on Wesleyan Methodism's general loss of Anglican identity. John Lenton notes that among Wesley's preachers their
religious upbringing was 40 percent Church of England/Ireland, 25 percent Methodist, 23
percent Dissent; 6 percent Roman Catholic; 6 percent Religious. See Lenton, *John Wesley's
Preachers*, 45. The designation *Methodist* is telling in this period. That the preachers might self-
identify as Methodist rather than Church of England or Church of Ireland is indication of a
form of separation.

[67] *Works* 21:180.

[68] *Works* 21:180n12.

worth's divergent visions of the revival came to a head in the administration of communion. Baker notes that "from the outset the Tabernacle
worshipers had been accustomed to receive the Lord's Supper from their
own preacher, William Cudworth," and argues that it was "almost certainly upon their insistence that Wesley's preachers administered communion here in 1760, and thus almost precipitated a separation from the
Church of England."[69]

Rack describes the relationship between Methodist and other religious bodies as the major point of conversation in the 1760 conference.[70]
In February of that year, three of Wesley's itinerants, described by Lloyd
as "well-regarded preachers of long standing," had administered the
sacrament at the united Norwich society. Charles had been asked by
his brother to go to Norwich to calm the situation, but Charles refused
to go without his brother's firm commitment to reprimand the
preachers and put an end to the offending practice.[71] He also wrote
letters to his brother, sarcastic letters to his wife, pastoral letters to
societies in major cities, and, as was already mentioned, letters en-
listing Evangelical support for his vision of Methodism.[72] Grimshaw's
response, noted at the beginning of this chapter, was read by Charles
to the London society, and it "put them in a flame." Rack writes that
with all the preliminary events, "the Bristol conference was going to
prove a stormy gathering."[73]

Howell Harris was invited by Charles to come to the conference and
recorded that when the lay preachers proposed to Wesley to ordain
them, Wesley "said it was not clear to him that he had the power so to
do except they were wholly cut off from the Church by a public act," and
added that this would need to entail "a total renouncing of the bishops
and the Established Church, which he could not do, and stumbling
thousands."[74] Wesley was simply repeating what he had published two
years earlier in *Reasons against a Separation* when he wrote that the

---

[69]Baker, *John Wesley and the Church of England*, 129.
[70]*Works* 10:289.
[71]Lloyd, *Charles Wesley*, 164-65.
[72]See especially Baker, *Charles Wesley as Revealed by His Letters*, 97-103, 272-82.
[73]*Works* 10:289.
[74]*Works* 10:290.

Methodists could not separate from the Church "because it would hinder multitudes of those who neither love nor fear God for hearing us at all, and thereby leave them in the hands of the devil."[75] Likewise, a separation would "be throwing balls of wild-fire among them that are now quiet in the land."[76]

According to Harris, Wesley warned the preachers who still justified their administration of the sacrament that "he would renounce them in a quarter of an hour" and "that they were the most foolish and ignorant of the whole Conference."[77] Yet these same preachers appear in Harris's account to be dumbstruck by Wesley's high churchmanship and by the idea that the offices of prophet and priest were distinct.[78] Wesley would not write his sermon on the topic, now known as "Prophets and Priests," mentioned above, until the late 1780s.[79] Harris's account implies, however, that these preachers were ignorant of the Church's traditions and of the roles and responsibilities of the ordained priesthood. They appear detached both theologically and liturgically from the Church that the Wesley brothers so adamantly promoted. Commenting on the sermon, Outler notes that the concept of distinct roles for prophets and priests was common in the English Church and "went back to Richard Hooker and before."[80] While Charles described these "Melchezidekians" with acidic vitriol, Harris described a group of Wesley's helpers formed in and promoting a Methodism detached from its Anglican foundations.

Wesley published "Prophets and Priests" in 1790, and it was not well received by Methodists, who by that time were headed toward independence. Outler provides a detailed account of the sermon's publishing history.[81] The sermon represents Wesley's dying wish to

---

[75]Ibid., 9:334.

[76]Ibid.

[77]See *Works* 10:289-90.

[78]Ibid.

[79]Wesley wrote the sermon in 1789 as a response to a similar situation in the Irish Conference.

[80]*Works* 4:73. Outler footnotes Hooker's *Laws of Ecclesiastical Polity* (1:xxxviii.6) and also claims that it was a distinction "differently nuanced" among the Puritans. See *Works* 4:73n2.

[81]See *Works* 4:73-74. Outler writes, "Since the sermon's first publication, Methodists have left it largely in limbo. George Story deliberately excluded it from [*Sermons on Several Occasions*], IX, as did Joseph Benson from his edition of the *Works*. Thomas Jackson decided to include it in his

his followers, a last-ditch effort to leave them united to the Church of England.

> In 1744, all the Methodist preachers had their first Conference. But none of them dreamed that the being called to preach gave them any right to administer sacraments. And when that question was proposed, "In what light are we to consider ourselves?" it was answered, "As *extraordinary messengers*, raised up to provoke the *ordinary* ones to jealousy."[82]

In response to the question whether an appointment in the Methodist system entailed the right of sacramental administration, Wesley stated that "such a design never entered into our mind; it was the farthest from our thoughts."[83]

Wesley argued in the sermon that the Methodist preachers were essentially what Walsh has described as a preaching order.[84] Their sole purpose was to "preach the gospel." Wesley notes that in Norwich "it was several years after our society was formed" before any of the preachers attempted to administer the sacraments. His memory was not accurate. The preachers had administered communion in the previous decade. But Wesley describes the attempts at Norwich made by "one of our preachers" who had "yielded to the importunity of a few." He was insistent that "as soon as it was known, [the preacher] was informed it must not be, unless he designed to leave our connexion. He promised to do it no more—and I suppose he kept his promise."[85] Outler describes this as "a blurred memory of a much more complicated episode."[86]

1825 edition of the *Sermons* and the 1829–31 edition of the *Works*, but with Moore's disparaging comment quoted in full as an introductory note" (74). During the debates of the late nineteenth century over "rights" to John Wesley, the high church Anglican, R. Denny Urlin included a whole appendix on the sermon in his *The Churchman's Life of Wesley*.

[82] *Works* 4:79.

[83] Ibid.

[84] John Walsh, *John Wesley 1703–1791: A Bicentennial Tribute* (London: Friends of Dr. William's Library, 1993), 5.

[85] *Works* 4:80.

[86] Ibid., n. 21.

WESLEY'S HIGH CHURCHMANSHIP AND
METHODISM'S DISTINCTIVE ETHOS

John Wesley's sacramental theology is best summarized in his extract of Daniel Brevint's *Christian Sacrament and Sacrifice*, the *Hymns on the Lord's Supper* published by the two brothers and two sermons—"The Means of Grace" and "The Duty of Constant Communion."[87] Brevint, a Caroline divine, served as dean of Lincoln Cathedral after the restoration of the monarchy under Charles II. It is not surprising that Wesley, with his connections to Lincolnshire, would use Brevint's work. It was at Lincoln College, Oxford, in 1732 that Wesley rewrote the work of non-juror Robert Nelson to produce for his students what would become his sermon "The Duty of Constant Communion."[88] In these sources Wesley's high churchmanship is explicitly on display. In his extract of Brevint he claimed: "At the holy Table the people meet to worship God, and God is present to meet and bless the people. Here we are in a special manner invited to offer up to God our souls, our bodies, and whatever we can give: and God offers to us the Body and Blood of the Son, and all the other blessings which we have need to *receive*."[89] Here the Book of Common Prayer undergirds the theology of both men, as they reiterate the Eucharistic Prayer of the Prayer Book.

Henry Knight argues that the ecclesiastical context in which Wesley promoted the means of grace and thus communion is essential to understanding Wesley's theology. The very structure of the Methodist system was consistent as a movement of societies, classes and bands within the Church of England. Knight notes that Wesley "was not offering a vision of the Christian life which could be reasonably sought in any church and

---

[87]See J. Ernest Rattenbury, *The Eucharistic Hymns of John and Charles Wesley, to which is appended Wesley's Preface Extracted from Brevint's Christian Sacrament and Sacrifice together with Hymns on the Lord's Supper*, American ed., ed. Timothy J. Crouch (Cleveland: OSL Publications, 1990); and *Works* 1:376-97; 3:427-39. For the most comprehensive treatments of Wesley's sacramental theology, see Ole E. Borgen, *John Wesley on the Sacraments: A Definitive Study of John Wesley's Theology of Worship* (Grand Rapids: Francis Asbury, 1972, 1985), and John C. Bowmer's *The Sacrament of the Lord's Supper in Early Methodism* (Westminster, UK: Dacre, 1951).

[88]It should be noted that by the time of his death Robert Nelson had returned to the Church of England.

[89]Rattenbury, *Eucharistic Hymns*, 145.

under any conditions," but rather one that was lived out "within the structures and discipline of the Methodist movement in the Church of England."[90] Here, however, the consistency of Wesley's system was not always implemented or followed in the tumultuous context of the revival.

The clash between Wesley's high churchmanship, as exemplified in his understanding of the efficacy and necessity of the sacraments, and a system of societies and bands that became increasingly separate from the liturgical and social bearing of the Church, is evident in the controversy surrounding the lay preachers and ordination. While Rack notes that the root of the controversy was not communion but separation, the emphasis on the sacrament within the increasingly distinct ethos of an isolated Methodism created the context in which the lay preachers' requests and actions make sense.[91] The lay preachers of early Methodism were caught up in the confusing dichotomy that was John Wesley. The continual efforts on the part of the lay preachers either to administer communion as laymen or receive ordination at Wesley's hand exemplify Wesley's high churchmanship, and thus emphasis on eucharistic reception, within the context of Methodism's liturgical detachment.

Describing the issue of the lay preachers and ordination, J. Ernest Rattenbury writes that the issue caused "much trouble" to the Wesleys. Yet Rattenbury also emphasizes the almost confused reaction of the lay preachers to the Wesleys' strictures. He writes that "we may be assured that [the lay preachers'] own deep Sacramentalism and their sense of necessity of Holy Communion to the spiritual life of their people, was what made them so urgent."[92] Rattenbury is quick, however, to place blame more on the Church for its opposition to Methodism than on Wesley's creation of an awkward ecclesiology.

The promotion of a strong eucharistic theology was not simply the creation of the Wesleys. The Evangelicals of the early period of the revival were strong promoters of sacramental reception. Samuel Walker, in a

---

[90]Henry Knight III, *The Presence of God in the Christian Life: John Wesley and the Means of Grace*, Pietist and Wesleyan Studies 3 (Lanham, MD: Scarecrow, 1992), 2.

[91]See Rack, *Reasonable Enthusiast*, 419.

[92]Rattenbury, *Eucharist Hymns*, 5.

series of practical sermons, argued that a strong desire for the sacrament was a repercussion of a sincere conversion. Those who are "determined for the Feast, are in general Partakers of the new Nature, seeking Growth and Improvement in this wonderful Change."[93] Rattenbury argues that "nothing is more clear than the tremendous emphasis of the leading Evangelicals on the necessity of Eucharistic worship."[94] Even some later Evangelicals, such as Charles Simeon, would promote eucharistic reception. Not all Evangelicals held to the high sacramentalism of the Wesleys, but they emphasized the importance of reception. Hindmarsh notes that for John Newton, the Saturday evening before receiving communion "became an occasion for particular spiritual seriousness, though, viewing the Lord's Supper as a commemorative ordinance, Newton did not worry himself over questions of sacramental efficacy or the nature of the divine presence in the sacrament."[95]

Adam's *Catechism* is high church in its assessment of the centrality of the sacrament in the Christian life. The sacrament contained "the chief points of Christian knowledge"; "the Christian covenant, the Christian faith, the Christian obedience, the Christian prayer, are summed up and represented in it; enforced, or exercised by it."[96] Arguing for something similar to Wesley's "duty of constant communion," Adam asks, if the lack of reception "is not darkness in the midst of gospel light, ignorance of Christ, and spiritual darkness in a country, what is?"[97]

Ironically, the similar emphases of Adam and Wesley within their differing spheres may have promoted schism. The increasingly foreign

---

[93]Samuel Walker, *The Christian. Being a Course of Practical Sermons. Sermon I. The Sinfulness and Misery of Man. Sermon II. The Helplessness of Man. Sermon III. The Power and Love of Christ. Sermon IV. Faith in Christ. Sermon V. VI. Vii. Viii. IX. X. The Believer a New Creature; Wherein that Character is Largely Described—Opposed to that of a Careless Sinner—and Contradistinguished from that of a Formalist. Sermon XI. An Earnest Address to the Careless—the Formal—the New Creature. By Samuel Walker, A. B. Curate of Truro in Cornwall, and formerly of Exeter-College in Oxford* (London: 1755), 214.

[94]Rattenbury, *Eucharistic Hymns*, 5.

[95]D. Bruce Hindmarsh, *John Newton and the English Evangelical Tradition: Between the Conversions of Wesley and Wilberforce* (Grand Rapids: Eerdmans, 2001), 225.

[96]Thomas Adam, *Practical lectures on the Church-Catechism. By Thomas Adam, The Fifth Edition. To Which Is Now Added, an Exercise, by Way of Question and Answer, Preparatory to Confirmation* (London: 1767), 88.

[97]Ibid., 89.

sphere of the Anglican liturgy had to compete with the warmth of Methodist sacramental festivals such as those celebrated on a regular basis at the West Street Chapel in London, or even those later celebrated at City Road. Ironically, these celebrations were led by Evangelicals such as the Wesleys and Fletcher, all of whom intended to remain within the Church.

CONTINUING STRUGGLES

The 1760 conference dealt with the issue of lay administration, and with the issue supposedly settled, John and Charles continued to look for a union with Evangelicals and also with the Moravians.[98] In 1763, however, Wesley's preachers in Norwich were still administering the sacrament, and Wesley was willing to overlook the practice. His stance in 1760 that lay administration was just as illegal as was "murder" had changed. He thought it might be "legal" but that it was not "expedient."[99] This description seems to fit better with Wesley's descriptions of the situation in 1755.

As the battle over lay administration raged on in Methodism, key Evangelicals friendly to Methodism and yet staunchly attached to the Church began to die. Samuel Walker died in 1761, and in an ironic twist most of his congregation left for dissent. Walker retired from his living in 1760, and his successor, Charles Pye, is said to have declared that "my pulpit so stinks of Calvinism that not a century will purge it."[100] Ward notes that Pye "successfully purged his congregation, many of whom removed themselves to a disused cockpit for the fellowship to which they were accustomed."[101] By 1770 they had become Congregationalist. Wesley

---

[98]Harris described a proposed meeting with the Wesley brothers and Haweis, and from the 1763 conference "a motion was made to meet some of the clergy and two of the Moravian bishops for union. A meeting was settled next week with Madan, Haweis, and the two brothers—John and Charles Wesley" (*Works* 10:296). It is not clear from Wesley's journal account for the week following the conference that such a meeting took place, however. Harris had a particular gift for peacemaking. While controversial among some evangelicals in his native Wales, in England Harris "was able to act as the go-between among the warring factions," as David Ceri Jones writes in his history of Welsh Methodism. See Jones's *'A Glorious Work in the World': Welsh Methodism and the International Evangelical Revival, 1735–1750* (Cardiff: University of Wales Press, 2004), esp. 147-48, for a description of Harris's peacemaking roles.

[99]*Works* 10:295.

[100]*Works* 22:59n63 (Sept. 4, 1766).

[101]Ibid.

wrote in 1766 that he preached in Truro and was "in hopes, when Mr. Walker died, the enmity in those who were called 'his people' would have died also." This had not come to pass. According to his journal, "they still look upon *us* as rank heretics."[102] In the late 1780s these animosities seem to have waned.

Just before the conference where he was going to be named the successor to the Wesleys, and within two years of Walker's death, Grimshaw died, in April 1763. The loss of these Evangelicals cannot be underestimated, for their deaths left Methodism, and John Wesley, increasingly isolated from the Church. The loss of these two men in particular left Charles with fewer allies in his crusade. Death, it seems, was as much a factor in the gradual separation of Wesley and his Evangelical colleagues as was anything else. As new leaders began to emerge who were unfamiliar to one another, the divide between the two parties expanded almost naturally.

The ordination of lay preachers and their administration of the sacraments kept surfacing in Wesleyan Methodism and was discussed in conferences intermittently from 1755 through 1764. These issues challenged Wesleyan Methodism's relationship to the Church of England. In both 1755 and 1764 the Evangelical clergy were keenly aware of the debates of conference and even engaged in them. Whether the larger Church had any interest in these proceedings is hard to tell.[103] These were small meetings whose primary engagement was the placement of Methodist itinerants. Most of the time the only clergy presence in these meetings was that of the Wesley brothers, and after 1755 Charles took less and less interest in the meetings. Charles only stayed at the 1755 meeting until issues related to the Church had been discussed and settled. He left immediately afterward, having evaded the opportunity to participate in matters of Methodist mechanics.

As the years went by, Charles Wesley's venom toward any dissenting idea or would-be dissenter became more vitriolic. Ayling argues that this

---

[102]Ibid.

[103]It is important not to imagine that Methodist conferences were front-page news or that they made lasting impressions outside the organizational structures of Wesleyan Methodism. The tendency to make both John Wesley and his conference meetings larger than they really were is a historiographical error that Wesley scholarship is prone to encourage.

vitriolic high churchmanship, along with his attachment to Lady Huntingdon, Whitefield and other leading Evangelicals known for their moderate Calvinism, created a context in which the lay preachers began to doubt his attachments to Methodism and his commitment to an Arminian gospel.[104] Regardless of Charles's supposed affinity to Calvinism, his rising fury against the threat of Methodist dissent corresponded with a lessening degree of interest in the Wesleyan Methodist scheme among Evangelical Anglicans.[105]

Some Evangelicals continued to show interest in the Methodist conferences in the early 1760s. Wesley read a letter from Grimshaw at the 1760 meeting saying that the Methodist system as it had been set up was not dissenting but that ordination of the preachers and lay administration of communion were schismatic acts.[106] Not one Evangelical Anglican in regular ministry was in attendance at the conference, although Evangelical Anglicanism was alive and well in Bristol.[107]

The 1764 conference appears to have been one final effort on the part of the Evangelical clergy as a group to keep Wesleyan Methodism within the bounds of the Church. They showed little interest in conference after this date and, having been discouraged by the response of Wesley's lay preachers, held a meeting of their own to organize regular Evangelical efforts. This does not mean that the Evangelicals were disinterested in Wesley's Methodism or unaffected by its growing irregularity. That same year, a number of the lay preachers received ordination at the hand of Gerasimos Avlonites, also known as Erasmus, whom Heitzenrater describes as "a purported Orthodox heirarch" who had also ordained Wesley's assistant, John Jones. Heitzenrater claims that twelve lay preachers were ordained by Erasmus.[108]

---

[104]Ayling, *John Wesley*, 232.

[105]For a thorough description of Charles's anti-Calvinism, see Geoffrey Wainwright, "Charles Wesley and Calvinism," in *Charles Wesley: Life, Literature, and Legacy*, ed. Kenneth G. C. Newport and Ted A. Campbell (Peterborough, UK: Epworth, 2007).

[106]Baker, *John Wesley and the Church of England*, 165; *Works* 10:271n950.

[107]James Brown of the Bristol Grammar School, a leading Evangelical among the Bristol and Somerset clergy, as well as Richard Hart at St. George's, Kingswood, Bristol, were both in Bristol at this time. St. George's had been built by Evangelicals intent on reaching the coal miners of the area.

[108]Heitzenrater, *Wesley and the People Called Methodists*, 232. Ted Campbell has written the most

Telford writes that six of the names were "exposed in Lloyd's Evening Post" and that "the sentence [against the irregular ordinations] had been required by the Rev. Messrs. Madan, Romaine, and Shirley. 'Mr. Charles, Dr. Dodd, De Coetlogon (the colleague of Madan at the Lock Chapel)," were nonetheless wise enough to keep their names out of print.[109] This list of Evangelical clergy, mainly from London, where the ordinations took place, included many of the leading Evangelicals of the day. Rack notes that Wesley suffered "much embarrassment" for the actions of these preachers. A special conference in January 1765 agreed that the men had "acted contrary to the Word of God and the duty they owe to their ministers and their brethren."[110]

The implications of these irregular ordinations were felt throughout evangelicalism. Newton, in his attempts at the time to gain holy orders, was rejected in part because of them. Newton, however, was not entirely detached from the situation. In a letter to Wesley just over a week from his own ordination within the Church, Newton communicated that Lady Huntingdon "believes [Erasmus's] services would be of unestimable value in the creation of a new ministry."[111] The full implications are not clear, although it is clear that Wesley was not the only evangelical attracted to an orthodox option to English episcopal roadblocks. According to Hindmarsh, Archbishop Secker counseled against ordaining anyone associated with Methodism because of the ordinations that he performed among Wesley's preachers. Secker had advised John Gilbert, the archbishop of York, "to reject an application for priest's orders from the Moravian and former Methodist lay preacher Francis Okely, and he had been displeased that certain other Methodists were being ordained

---

comprehensive treatment of Erasmus in "The Transgressions of Gerasimon Avlonites," now available at the Southern Methodist University Digital Repository: http://digitalrepository.smu.edu/theology_research/3/.

[109]See *Works* 27:418-19 (to Six Preachers, Feb. 27, 1765). See also Wesley's letter to Charles on January 11, 1765, 27:413-14; and his two letters to the printer of the *St. James's Chronicle* (Feb. 5 and Feb. 10, 1765), 27:415-18.

[110]*Works* 10:302.

[111]John Newton to John Wesley, April 24, 1764. Manuscript in the United Methodist Archives at Drew University identified as "1647-3-2:144."

by a 'a pretended' Greek Bishop."[112] Ironically, Newton thought for a time
to become a Methodist itinerant, though he was later swayed to seek
orders again by Haweis and Crooke.[113]

About a month after the controversy, six lay preachers requested to
resume their work within Methodism. Wesley's reply, written from
Norwich, is short and to the point. Madan, Romaine and "the good-
natured" Shirley had continued to pressure Wesley about the irregularity
of these ordinations. Wesley responded that these clergy were "almost
out of patience with me for not disowning you on the house-top." London
Evangelicals were keeping Wesley in what he described as "good behaviour," and he was "obliged to move with all possible circumspection."
He ends his letter saying that if he were to allow them to preach in his
connexion so soon, he would be in "hotter fire than ever."[114] Heitzenrater
notes that during this controversy Wesley "was barely being kept in check
by political pressure from some of the clergy who were friendly to
Methodism."[115] Evangelical ability to keep Wesley in check would soon
come to an end, as political pressures forced them to distance themselves
from Wesley, and Wesley himself would finally relinquish his plan for an
evangelical union.

[112]Hindmarsh, John Newton and the English Evangelical Tradition, 91.

[113]Haweis may have also been affected by the controversy surrounding the "Greek Bishop." About
the same time, Secker ignored his appeals when Haweis was threatened with expulsion from
St. Mary Magdalene, Oxford. Crooke, it should be noted, may have placed Newton's earlier efforts to gain holy orders in jeopardy. See Hindmarsh, John Newton and the English Evangelical
Tradition, 90.

[114]Works 27:418-19 (to Six Preachers, Feb. 27, 1765).

[115]Heitzenrater, Wesley and the People Called Methodists, 260-61.

7

HEGEMONY AND CASUALTIES

The Oxford Expulsions of 1768

IN THE LATTER THIRD OF the eighteenth century the Church of England begrudgingly entered an era of ecclesiastical pluralism on account of the slow change in English's shifting religious marketplace.[1] With this adjustment, Anglican attitudes toward continued dissent from the Church's model of governance and theological breadth also changed. Dissent challenged the Church's hegemonic standing within the *ancien régime* of post-Restoration England. The Church's reaction during the reign of George III to the continuing existence of dissent, irregularity, Methodism and liberalism can be seen as akin to the western American frontier model of "circling the wagons." Anderson notes that within this larger context Methodism itself "was a challenge to the priority of the national church from within," a dangerous insider threat "in a democratized ecclesial landscape."[2] Continuing challenges to the Church's hegemony by others from within—those who wanted to end subscription requirements for the universities and holy orders; the Feather's Tavern

---

[1]See David Hempton, *Religion and Political Culture in Britain and Ireland: From Glorious Revolution to the Decline of Empire* (New York: Cambridge, 1996), especially chap. 1, "The Church of England: A Great English Consensus?" Hempton concludes the chapter by stating, "However vigourously Established Churchmen defended their interests, they were no match for the corrosive forces of religious pluralism, class conflict and state welfarism. The establishment principle miraculously survived, but its social foundations were swept away" (24).

[2]Misty G. Anderson, *Imagining Methodism in Eighteenth-Century Britain: Enthusiasm, Belief, and the Borders of the Self* (Baltimore: Johns Hopkins University Press, 2012), 35.

petition; the Bangorian controversy; and antitrinitarianism, especially coming out of Cambridge—shook the ecclesiastical landscape. The reaction of the newly ascended Tories and their Church allies was to turn the Anglican big-tent model of an all-inclusive national Church with an outward focus toward an inward one that advanced internal cohesion, strengthened orthodoxy and promoted high churchmanship.[3]

David Hempton, in his description of these changes, describes events that hinge on realities that grew to maturity later in the century. His arguments describe the larger political context in which the Church participated. Yet it is not difficult to see that the isolationism he describes began to be felt first by those on the fringes of the Church as it reacted to perceived threats and positioned itself to defend its place in English society. Hempton asserts that "by the end of the eighteenth century the popular basis for a consensual Anglicanism was under threat from a formidable range of pressures," and that, in response, the Church "increasingly turned its back on the national consensus it had worked so hard to create, and became more wedded to establishment values on the one hand and isolation from some of the major currents in European religion on the other." What was coming into being was "a more competitive and pluralistic religious environment" and one in which threats to Anglican hegemony were taken very seriously.[4] William Gibson highlights this same defensiveness: "By the second half of the century militant High Churchmanship had evolved into a movement for doctrinal orthodoxy that was mobilised to defend the State from Dissent and radicalism."[5] High churchmanship had come back to the mainstream.[6]

---

[3]See Hempton, *Religion and Political Culture in Britain and Ireland*, 14.
[4]Ibid.
[5]William Gibson, *The Church of England 1688–1832: Unity and Accord* (New York: Routledge, 2001), 2.
[6]For a good example of the newly re-risen Tory political viewpoint under George III, see George Horne, *The Christian King: A Sermon Preached Before the University of Oxford, at St Mary's on Friday, January 30, 1761*. See also Wesley's reply to Horne, "A Letter to the Rev. Mr. Horne," in *Works* 11:437-58. Horne had described the "Tabernacle" and the "Foundry" as sectarian and antinomian. His comment was meant to defend "the Catholic doctors of the ancient church." Horne saw the radical elements of the revival in stark contrast to the Catholic nature of the Church of England. Wesley, although friendly toward Horne, had to respond to his own inclusion in this blanket statement. Gerald R. Cragg notes, "Wesley's respect for Horne remained undiminished to the end" (ibid., 439).

Within this context of ecclesiastical shifts, the irregularities of Wesleyan Methodism—although ironically led by two Tories who applauded aspects of the Church's turn—became casualties of this political paradigm.[7] Irregular Methodism was not banished but gradually left more and more to its own devices and treated as other dissenting groups. With this, Evangelicals, their status under suspicion, began in the 1760s and early 1770s to find the irregularities of Wesley's ecclesial subculture threatening to their own survival. The expulsion of six Oxford evangelicals from St. Edmund Hall in 1768, the growth of Tory influence and Church exclusion, debates among Wesleyans and Evangelicals over parish boundaries, theological controversies that included debates over perfectionism, and finally the outright rejection of Wesley's overtures toward evangelical unity mark this decade as the end of what should be seen from 1740 to 1770 as a period of nonpartisan evangelical revival and cooperation in England.[8] The evangelical fraternity gave way to the pressures and social contexts in which the later formal structures of a Methodist Church, the Evangelical Party within the Church of England and a dissenting connexion under Lady Huntingdon would appear.[9]

The year 1770 was not significant in itself but rather a culmination of watershed moments, such as the 1768 St. Edmund expulsions and their aftermaths. It should not be viewed as a date after which Wesley had no contact with Evangelicals in the Church. It is a date after which the trajectories of these two evangelical groups can be seen distinctly to diverge. The reader should not think that politics alone made for this separation of evangelicals, but that, when taken together with theological and

---

[7]See *Works* 22:164 and n. 13.

[8]See especially Frank Baker, *John Wesley and the Church of England* (Nashville: Abingdon, 1970), and his chapter on Wesley and the Evangelicals.

[9]Lady Huntingdon would dissent following pressure over her chapels in 1779. See Alan Harding, *The Countess of Huntingdon's Connexion: A Sect in Action in Eighteenth-Century England* (New York: Oxford University Press, 2003), esp. 233-95. See also Henry D. Rack, *Reasonable Enthusiast: John Wesley and the Rise of Methodism*, 3rd ed. (Philadelphia: Trinity Press International, 2002), 285; and Mark Noll, *The Rise of Evangelicalism: The Age of Edwards, Whitefield and the Wesleys* (Downers Grove, IL: InterVarsity Press, 2003), 202. Rack notes: "Secession at once lost Lady Huntingdon the support of Evangelicals who had acted as her chaplains, and helped to precipitate a hardening of their feelings against 'irregularities' for fear of further schisms" (*Reasonable Enthusiast*, 285).

ecclesiastical challenges, it made the connection between these two groups too difficult to maintain.

I will give much attention in this chapter to the expulsion of six evangelicals from St. Edmund Hall for "methodistical behaviour," and the political and ecclesiastical fallout that ensued. Ironically, the six students were not connected to Wesley; they were theologically Calvinistic. Yet the expulsion of six Calvinists during the reign of George III further relegated John Wesley to the fringes of Anglican life. The intertwined nature of evangelicalism meant that the ramifications of popular opinion and ecclesiastical censure were felt by the movement as though it were homogenous. In the 1760s it was the fringe that most felt the repercussions of political turmoil.

The prevailing irregularity of Wesleyan Methodism, with its army of lay itinerant ministers, connected it to the same irregularities that triggered the Oxford expulsions. Since holy orders often, if not almost always, depended on the completion of a degree from either Oxford or Cambridge, evangelical expulsions from Oxford triggered fear among the regular Evangelicals. These expulsions can be seen as a part of a nearly two-decade-long move to relegate evangelical influence within the university. Lady Huntingdon, in response to the expulsions, created an academy at Trevecca where she required her pupils to participate in irregularity.[10] Many Evangelicals looked to Cambridge as the sole path to traditional orders after 1768, even if an evangelical presence would, again, be found in Oxford within a few years.[11]

The expulsions in spring 1768 were the result of official censure and personal politics. It was the culmination of efforts, like the removal of Thomas Haweis from St. Mary Magdalene, Oxford, just a decade earlier, to rein in fringe elements within the university—from enthusiasts on the one hand to deistic or unitarian impulses on the other. And while Oxford had been the cradle of Wesleyan Methodism, home of Evangelical lumi-

---

[10]Faith Cook, *Selina, Countess of Huntingdon* (Carlisle, UK: Banner of Trust, 2001), 243-53; and Alan Harding, *Selina: Countess of Huntingdon* (London: Epworth, 2008), 90.

[11]In 1767 Evangelical George Burnett founded the Elland Clerical Society to assist Evangelical ordinands. The society in its early years directed their students to Cambridge, where they knew some tutors who would share their views. See Harding, *Selina, Countess of Huntingdon*, 88-89.

naries such as the Wesleys, Whitefield and Walker, the late 1760s witnessed a change in the political climate that saw a move from toleration to exclusivism played out with the expulsion of these six students. S. L. Ollard provides the most comprehensive treatment of the personalities involved and attempts to follow the characters through their respective careers.[12] He succinctly summarizes the charges against the students when he writes that "the crux of the matter lay in the charge of being Methodists, and, therefore, by implication, enemies to the doctrine and discipline of the Church of England."[13]

Evangelical Entanglement

Most of the material available on the expulsions comes from polemical pieces written between 1768 and 1770. Richard Hill was by far the most prolific writer during the controversy. He staunchly defended a Reformed view of the Church of England and its doctrinal standards, especially against the high church view of Thomas Nowell. One anonymous piece, *Priestcraft Defended*, was a Baptist work published on both sides of the Atlantic well into the nineteenth century. The expulsions touched a nerve. Numerous authors used the controversy to engage in arguments over the Homilies or the role of subscription, and even the historic place of Calvinism within the Church.[14] Within each of them, however, is the lurking question of the place of evangelicalism within the establishment.

The expulsions were particularly felt in the evangelical world because of the evangelical fraternity. These six students, although not connected to Wesley, were distinctly connected to other Evangelical clergymen and Lady Huntingdon.[15] According to Hill, a letter was read

---

[12]S. L. Ollard, *The Six Students of St. Edmund Hall Expelled from the University of Oxford in 1768 with a Note on the Authorities for Their Story* (London: A. R. Mowbray, 1911). No scholarly book-length study of the trial has been written. W. Reginald Ward includes a section on the topic in his history of Oxford in the eighteenth century, and J. S. Reynolds includes a slightly larger section on the trial and its aftermath in his book on Evangelicals at Oxford.

[13]Ibid., 13-14.

[14]See especially Richard Hill, *Pietas Oxoniensis: or, A Full and Impartial Account of the Expulsion of Six Students from St. Edmund Hall, Oxford; With a Dedication to the Right Honourable the Earl of Litchfield, Chancellor of that University by a master of arts of the University of Oxford* (London: Printed for G. Keith, et. al., 1768).

[15]Harding, *Selina, Countess of Huntingdon*, 88-89.

at the trial from Evangelical Thomas Haweis, in which Erasmus Middleton, one of the six students, was described as "a dear child of God." According to Hill, this met with opprobrium.[16] Mention of Haweis, one familiar to Oxonians, simply added another Evangelical clergyman to the list of those associated with the trial, including John Newton, John Fletcher, Henry Venn, Joseph Townsend and William Davies. Hill believed that these Evangelicals were implicitly tried by the court alongside the six students.[17] One local Evangelical who was not mentioned was James Stillingfleet, although he was known to have filled in for Haweis at St. Mary Magdalene and served as an Evangelical presence within the university. One can only speculate as to why Stillingfleet was left out, but it was likely to do with his recent status as a fellow. This Evangelical entanglement, however, although not explicitly including the Wesley brothers or Stillingfleet, implicitly included all "Methodists." The focus of the trial and the naming of Evangelicals during it implicated anyone suspected of taking stances that challenged the polity and doctrine of the Church.[18]

The trial, as Ollard describes it, was a "strange tragedy."[19] The university would look back with reservations on the expulsions of the six, according to Ward, but in 1768 these students met the full fury of a public trial and the wrath of a seemingly spurned tutor able to tap into the uneasiness with which the establishment viewed evangelical piety. Reading the charges now, which included among others lay preaching, extemporaneous prayer and an insufficient knowledge of classical languages, the modern reader is struck by their seemingly benign nature. Personal issues cannot be disregarded within the politics of a small academic community, yet the larger politics of the day placed these charges in a malevolent light.

---

[16]Hill, *Pietas Oxoniensis*, 10-11.

[17]Ibid., 18. See also Hill's arguments about the legality of society meetings and opposition to evangelicals in Kent. See *Pietas Oxoniensis*, 20-22.

[18]See Richard Hill, *A Letter to the Rev. Dr. Adams of Shrewsbury: Occasioned by the Publication of His Sermon, Preached Against the Rev. Mr. Romaine: Entitled a Test of True and False Doctrines. To Which Is Now Added, a Dedication . . . As Also a Letter from Mr. Romaine to Dr. Adams. By the Author of Pietas Oxoniensis*, 2nd ed., rev. (London: 1770), especially 51-52.

[19]Ollard, *Six Students of St. Edmund Hall*, 30.

Lay preaching, a charge brought against four of the students, was a challenge not to the traditional Anglican designation of prophets and priests but to the structures of the Church and state. Within the political context of the trial, cries to bring about a breakdown in Anglican political hegemony were becoming louder. "In Georgian England, as much as in the seventeenth century, politics was a branch of theology."[20] The two cannot be separated. Political acts were theology, and vice versa. Although in the early part of the century lay preaching and itinerancy were easily connected to the actions of political radicalism akin to Cromwell and the parliamentarians, and thus a challenge to the entirety of the *ancien régime* of state, Church and aristocracy, the actions of ecclesiastical mavericks in the latter part of the century were seen as a direct challenge to the Church and its place within the structure of that three-part schema.[21]

This shift signified a distinct difference in the politics of dissent. Early in the century challenges to the Church were thought to test its right to exist as an episcopal structure with its Catholic heritage intact within the Anglican via media. The perceived challenge of dissent in the latter part of the century, especially under George III, was a perceived threat to the Church's right to claim to be a truly national church under which all subjects of the Crown would identify and thus an endorsement of ecclesiastical pluralism. Within this context, lay preaching and antisubscription efforts were seen similarly—as efforts to unseat the Church from its preferred pedestal.

THE CONTEXT

The accounts of the trial and what led up to it are distinctly biased and written within the context of a propaganda war. Ollard remains the most comprehensive source for information on the trial, although most of his information is drawn from Hill's polemical pieces, especially *Pietas*

---

[20]Gibson, *Church of England 1688–1832*, 5.

[21]For specific discussion of Wesley and the *ancien régime*, see David Hempton, *The Religion of the People: Methodism and Popular Religion, c. 1750–1900* (London: Routledge, 1996), especially his chapter "John Wesley and England's Ancien Régime," 77–90.

Oxoniensis. Hill's work is a sharply worded piece decrying the university and its leadership. It promotes an exclusively Calvinistic interpretation of the Thirty-Nine Articles and the English Reformation. He begins *Pietas Oxoniensis* with a disclaimer, "to acquaint the reader, that I am a member of the Established Church, into whose communion I was in my infancy baptized, and for whose doctrine and discipline I still profess the highest veneration."[22] The trial forced the question of ecclesial loyalty. Hill's polemical works would later become a cause of scandal, as the usual proponent of decorum came through in these writings as venomous and sectarian.[23]

The students came from various parts of England; five of them intended to go into holy orders. They were a part of a larger rebirth of Methodism among the students of the university after the initial student-led efforts of the 1720s and 1730s became dominated by town rather than gown. The Wesley brothers' initial efforts to start the Methodist revival among the students of Oxford did not survive long after their departure for colonial Georgia. Oxford Methodism after the 1730s was populated primarily by residents of Oxford. However, evangelicalism was not entirely bereft among the academic cloisters. Evangelical leaders would emerge from Oxford throughout the century. The new Methodists of Oxford in the 1760s, however, were not to be found under the tutelage of the Wesleys, but under the influence of Evangelicals such as Edward Stillingfleet and Thomas Haweis, regular clergymen.

Seymour notes that during the 1760s a shift had occurred and "considerable attention was paid to the subject of religion by many students in the University of Oxford."[24] Both Lady Huntingdon and Whitefield were aware of this evangelical impulse at Oxford, and Lady Huntingdon sent news of it in a letter to Stillingfleet. In the letter she mentions prayer meetings among the students: "I am really rejoiced that so many at the Universities are determined to be on the Lord's side. May they be kept

---

[22]Hill, *Pietas Oxoniensis*, 7-8. I use the second edition of the work because Hill greatly expanded his initial publication with the second edition published the same year.

[23]Edwin Sidney, *The Life of Sir Richard Hill* (Oxford: Oxford University Press, 1839), 112.

[24]Aaron C. Hobart Seymour, *The Life and Times of Selina, Countess of Huntingdon, By a Member of the Houses of Shirley and Hastings, Volume 2* (London: William Edward Painter, 1840), 226.

faithful and steady!"[25] Likewise, Whitefield described students as "awakened to the knowledge of the truth" and "earnestly learning Christ."[26] Other Evangelical leaders visited Oxford in the 1760s to find students who had embraced the evangelical message. Reynolds writes that "early in 1761, Samuel Walker again visited Oxford, where 'he met a group of promising young men preparing for orders, for whom he was at pains to draw up some instructions.'"[27]

Within this context it is easy to see that the six students expelled from St. Edmund Hall were part of a growing movement, although there is no record of other evangelical expulsions from the university in such a public manner.[28] The six were meant to be examples to others among their peers, some of whom had already been sent down from the university in more discreet fashion. One of those was Matthew Powley, who had gone up to Queen's College in 1760 and lost his academic preferment because of his association with Haweis, then a curate at St. Mary Magdalene.[29] The trial and expulsion of the St. Edmund students was anything but discreet. Gibson calls the episode "the highest expression of the universities' determination to defend orthodoxy."[30]

The expulsion of the six took place at a time when an ordained Evangelical presence was at a lull in Oxford, a distinct moment of Evangelical weakness in the university between two periods of relative strength. The later period would begin in the 1780s, ironically at St. Edmund Hall, as the hall would become Evangelical-friendly under the leadership of Isaac Crouch and Daniel Wilson. This lull was caused by the departures of Haweis, Stillingfeet and Joseph Jane from St. Timothy's in 1763.

---

[25]Ibid.

[26]Ibid.

[27]J. S. Reynolds, *The Evangelicals at Oxford 1735–1871: A Record of an Unchronicled Movement with the Record Extended to 1905* (Oxford: Marcham Manor, 1975), 30.

[28]Gibson notes in *Church of England 1688–1832*, "The colleges and universities regularly took formal action against the heterodox: in 1730 Magdalen College, Oxford expelled three students for Deism and in 1745 the Convocation of Oxford expelled Selwyn for blasphemy" (139-40). What was so exceptional about the expulsions of the students at St. Edmund's Hall was their publicity.

[29]Reynolds, *Evangelicals at Oxford*, 30.

[30]Gibson, *Church of England 1688–1832*, 140.

Haweis, who served at the center of Oxford, was a lightning rod during his short curacy. His ministry began like that of most other Evangelicals. His attempts to gain holy orders met episcopal concerns over his theology. Bishop Lavington, a staunch anti-Methodist, rejected the suitability of Haweis's three clerical signatories and refused to recommend Haweis to the bishop of Oxford, Thomas Secker, later archbishop of Canterbury. The three signatories were beneficed clergyman but were known Evangelicals, including Samuel Walker of Truro, John Penrose of Penryn and Thomas Michell of Veryan. Others signatories were found, and Haweis was ordained in October 1757, but his clashes with episcopal leadership were far from over. Secker, now archbishop, had been replaced as the bishop of Oxford by Dr. John Hume, who would take steps to have Haweis removed by 1762.

Haweis's removal took place after he had already earned the ire of Oxford. St. Mary Magdalene was thought notoriously evangelical and was declared out of bounds to undergraduates. Authorities from the university would sweep through the congregation and remove undergraduates who dared attend services. Haweis often lost his hat to pranksters on the streets, and rocks were thrown through the church windows during his sermons. His ministry was an embarrassment to many in Oxford, but his removal by the bishop was just a precursor to the challenges Evangelicals would face at Oxford throughout the rest of the decade. Charles Smyth, writing about Haweis's departure from St. Mary Magdalene, writes that "it was evident that there was a storm brewing over Oxford and in 1768 it broke."[31]

The relationship between Evangelicalism and the university both before and after 1768 needs further explanation. After the expulsions, Evangelicals at Oxford held a distinctly different ecclesiastical outlook. The irregularity of the earlier period was jettisoned. The Evangelical party that would hold a permanent place within the structures of the Church or the university turned to regularity under leaders such as Isaac Crouch. The *Christian Observer* described Crouch's "meekness of spirit,

---

[31]Charles Smyth, *Charles Simeon and Church Order: A Study of the Origins of the Evangelical Revival in Cambridge in the Eighteenth Century* (Cambridge: Cambridge University Press, 1940), 209.

his retired habits, his strict regard to discipline, his unwearied assiduity, his unimpeachable piety and holiness, his constant enforcement of Church doctrine and principles in all their spiritual savour."[32] J. S. Reynolds's description of Crouch is key to the pre- and post-1768 difference. He describes Crouch as a reserved academic. According to Reynolds, it was Crouch's conservatism that "by slow degrees" earned the respect of Oxonians.[33] The concept of "slow degrees" was markedly different from the passionate and erratic nature of the earlier evangelists.

Not all Evangelicals connected to Oxford were irregular before the expulsions, and the lull in Evangelical leadership by 1768 was not caused by any effort to rid the university of irregularity. Between the 1730s, when Whitefield and Wesley were active as members of the "Holy Club," and the late 1760s, Haweis, Jane and Stillingfleet had regular ministries within the confines of Oxford. Their absence in 1768, however, left the six St. Edmund students without the benefit of Evangelical leaders in Oxford to aid their defense.

THE TRIAL

The Shaver, or barber, as he was known in *Priestcraft Defended*, began his text with a description of the trial and expulsion of the six students as it was said to appear in a local newspaper.

> On Friday last six students belonging to Edmund-Hall were expelled the university, after an hearing of several hours, before Mr. Vice-Chancellor, and some of the Heads of Houses for holding Methodistical tenets, and taking upon them to pray, read, and expound the scriptures, and sing hymns in a private house. The [Head] of the [Hall] defended their doctrines from the thirty-nine articles of the established church, and spoke in the highest terms of the piety, and exemplariness of their lives; but his motion was overruled, and sentence pronounced against them.[34]

---

[32] Reynolds, *Evangelicals at Oxford*, 60.
[33] Ibid.
[34] A Shaver, *Priestcraft Defended: A Sermon Occassioned by the Expulsion of Six Young Gentlemen from the University of Oxford, for Praying, Reading, and Expounding the Scriptures* (London and Boston: 1771), 5-6, where the author has taken the quotation "from St. James's Chronicle, for Thursday, March 17, 1768. No. 1099. Printed by Henry Baldwin, at the Printing-Office, White Friars, Fleet Street."

The author had seen nothing wrong with praying, reading, expounding the Scriptures and singing hymns. And, after reading Hill's *Pietas Oxoniensis*, he was inspired to take up lay preaching. Shaver desired to prove that preaching was not only for the elite. As his pseudonym indicates, he was not a gentleman, nor is it likely that he was educated. He claimed to see "the honours of my family cast down into the puddle by the arrogance of Oxonian priests" and decided to defend his family's honor by taking up the very activities that led to the Oxford expulsions. This response to the classist nature of the trail and its accusations against the students was not common but indicates one of the many ways in which the trial far exceeded the expectations of its prosecutors.[35]

According to evangelical authors, the trial was a circus.[36] Different reports of the behavior of the spectators and treatment of the accused during the trail, however, describe seemingly separate events. Regardless, a full public trial at Oxford was a unique spectacle in the late eighteenth century.

Initially, there was to be no trial. The head of the hall, Dr. Dixon, resolved on "mild measures" against the irregularities of the six students. One of them, Thomas Jones, had been called before the vice principal months before for preaching in the fields and appears to have been unaware that he was in violation of any laws. He asked the vice principal at some point whether there was any harm in preaching. The vice principal is said to have claimed that "God knows; I don't know that there is any harm in it; it is very well for people to instruct their neighbours, provided there is no enthusiasm in it."[37] The vice principal would later claim to have been deceived by the nature of Mr. Jones's meetings.[38] At the trial John Higson asserted that the six students were not only incapable of passing the language requirements of the hall but had been insubor-

---

[35]Ibid., iv.

[36]See especially Hill's *Pietas Oxoniensis*, 18.

[37]Ibid., 23-24.

[38]Ollard, *Six Students of St. Edmund Hall*, 8-9. And see Hill's *Pietas Oxoniensis*, 23; and Thomas Nowell, *An Answer to a Pamphlet, Entitled Pietas Oxoniensis, in a Letter to the Author. Wherein the Grounds of the Expulsion of Six Members from St. Edmund-Hall Are Set Forth; and the Doctrines of the Church of England, and Its First Reformers, Fully Considered, and Vindicated. By Thomas Nowell, D. D. Principal of St. Mary Hall, and Public Orator of the University of Oxford. Occasioned by the Reply of the Same Author* (Oxford: 1769), 146.

dinate. Higson's relationship to the students is complicated. Personality seems to have had as much to do with its breakdown as did any break in university policy.

Following Hill's suggestion in *Goliath Slain*, Ollard believed the trial was ordered by outside influences, presumably from Bishop Hume. Hill claimed that "certain intimations of what was wished to be done were received from a certain quarter."[39] Ollard interprets this "malign influence here hinted" as Bishop Hume, "the Bishop of Salisbury (formerly of Oxford), an ardent anti-Methodist."[40] Hume, the same bishop who had removed Haweis from St. Mary Magdalene, had left Oxford in 1766. In his work on Charles Simeon, Charles Smyth also says that episcopal pressure was asserted to make an example of the evangelicals at St. Edmund Hall.[41] Thomas Nowell, in his reply to *Pietas Oxoniensis*, implicates Jones and Middleton for the rumor, and in defense of the university writes, "I am fully persuaded that the Vice-Chancellor was not pushed on by the violence of others, but urged by an affectionate regard for the honour and welfare of the University."[42]

The possibility of episcopal involvement aside, Ward argues that the significance of the trial and its judgment was the influence of the newly ascendant Tories. He argues that the "significance of the judgment was that all the judges (apart from the vice-chancellor, but including Nowell) were prominent among the growing body of Oxford courtiers of Tory origin."[43] The Tories and their high church allies during the reign of George III were behind efforts described earlier to rein in dissent, irregularity and liberalism on a national scale. Interestingly, the prosecutors of the trial were of the same political ilk as John and Charles Wesley.

THE STUDENTS

For all the attention that the trial drew, the six students were pawns of larger political and theological debates brewing around the issues of

---

[39]Ollard, *Six Students of St. Edmund Hall*, 16.
[40]Ibid.
[41]Smyth, *Charles Simeon and Church Order*, 211.
[42]Nowell, *An Answer to a Pamphlet*, 196.
[43]*Works* 22:164n13.

church loyalty, dissent and irregularity. Samuel Johnson was not impressed with the students. He said of the students that "a cow is a very good animal in the field, but we turn her out of the garden."[44] Among modern interpreters, Ollard is the most interested in the lives of the students themselves. His summary statement on the students says much about the place of irregularity within the church as the century progressed. He claims that, unlike their judges, "the paths of the Six Students did not lead to positions of dignity and ease."[45] Only three of the students had successful careers after the expulsions; one because he was a man of means by birth, and the other two, Erasmus Middleton and Thomas Jones, as the only students who were ordained and had a regular ministry within the Church.

Most of the students were associated with leading figures in the Evangelical Revival, both Calvinist and Arminian. Jones was closely connected to John Newton beginning in 1765. In Newton's early letters to Jones, he attempted to convey the importance of a regular ministry. Newton's style was nonconfrontational, and he appeared open to the possibility that Jones would have an irregular ministry, but one outside the Church. Newton wrote, "If you have a desire to enter into the Established Church, endeavour to keep your zeal within moderate bounds, and avoid every thing that might unnecessarily clog you admission with difficulties."[46] Newton specifically points out to Jones the need to "avoid what looks like preaching."[47]

There are five letters to Jones from Newton from 1765 to 1772. Both before and after his time at Oxford, Jones made Olney his home. Likely through the influence of Lord Dartmouth, Newton's patron, Jones was ordained and became a curate in Buckinghamshire at Clifton Raynes, a village a mile from Olney. He was ordained by the bishop of Lincoln, John Green, who had also ordained Newton. Jones's curacy at Clifton Raynes was uneventful, and it appears that Newton and his experience at Oxford

---

[44]Ollard, *Six Students of St. Edmund Hall*, 31.
[45]Ibid.
[46]John Newton, *Cardiphonia: Or, the Utterance of the Heart; in the Course of a Real Correspondence in Two Volumes* (London: 1798), 51.
[47]Ibid.

impressed on him the importance of regularity. He is said to be one of the earliest proponents of Sunday school.[48] And unlike his earlier staunch disdain for Arminians, he maintained a friendship with both Calvinist and Arminian Evangelicals even after the controversies that erupted following the publication of Wesley's 1770 Conference Minutes.

James Matthews was connected to John Fletcher of Madeley, a staunch Arminian and defender of Wesley, and after his expulsion from Oxford he and Joseph Shipman were "received by Lady Huntingdon in a house just taken by her on Mount Ephraim at Tunbridge Wells."[49] Shortly after their arrival Huntingdon sent them to her newly founded school at Trevecca. Rack notes that after the events at St. Edmund Hall in 1768, both "Wesley and Lady Huntingdon had increasing difficulty placing their protégés in Oxford."[50] Kingswood and Trevecca were their response.

Huntingdon's Trevecca College became a symbol of irregular evangelicalism. Its establishment spoke of the divide then taking place in the Church as political challenges forced irregulars further from the center of ecclesiastical life. Every student at Trevecca was required to preach in the nearby towns "without holy orders," including the two of the St. Edmund six who were sponsored by Lady Huntingdon to attend her new school.

Aaron C. Hobart Seymour recounts a story about Matthews and Shipman after their arrival at Lady Huntingdon's home at Tunbridge Wells. Those wedded to irregular methods, primarily from the earlier generation of leadership, seemed either incapable of interpreting the political situation or obstinate in their refusal to follow regular means.

> It occurred to Lady Huntingdon that, as she had two ministers in her house, one of them should preach. Notice was accordingly sent round that on such an evening there would be preaching before her door. At the appointed time a great many people had collected together, which the young men seeing, inquired what it meant. Her Ladyship said: "As I have two preachers in my house, one of you must preach to the people." In reply

---

[48]Ollard, *Six Students of St. Edmund Hall*, 38-39.
[49]Ibid., 36.
[50]Rack, *Reasonable Enthusiast*, 453.

they said they had never preached publicly, and wished to be excused. Mr. Shipman was a ready speaker, but Mr. Matthews was remarkably diffident. Lady Huntingdon, therefore, judged it best for Mr. Shipman to make the first attempt. While he hesitated she put a Bible into his hand, insisting upon his appearing before the people, and either tell them he was afraid to trust to God or do the best he could. On the servants opening the door, her Ladyship thrust him out with her blessing, saying, "The Lord be with you—do the best you can."[51]

Shipman continued to preach for Lady Huntingdon as an itinerant lay preacher. He is the only one of the six that is known to have gone into an irregular ministry. He died within three years of his expulsion from Oxford at the age of twenty-four, reportedly from a broken blood vessel, having "overworked" himself.[52]

Benjamin Kay and Thomas Grove are the most difficult to trace. Kay's career after the expulsions is not known. He came from Yorkshire, a hotbed of Evangelical piety in the eighteenth century and the home of a sizeable number of Evangelical clergymen. Grove is noted by Ollard for his Calvinist views on grace and free will.

Of the six Erasmus Middleton was the only member of the group to have made a lasting impression on Anglican Evangelicalism. Middleton went to Cambridge, where he studied at Clare College.[53] Although he studied with Joseph Townsend, an Evangelical who as rector of Pewsey itinerated for Lady Huntingdon, Middleton appears to have taken a regular ministry after his ordination. A. S. Wood writes that Middleton's ministry was "unusually effective."[54] Middleton served in numerous capacities as a part of the Evangelical fraternity. His first two curacies were under leading Evangelicals, Romaine in London and William Cadogan in Chelsea. His assistantship at St. Margaret's, Westminster, was under Evangelical John Davies. He would later publish a history of international evangelicalism.[55]

[51]Seymour, *Life of Lady Huntingdon*, 2:126.
[52]Ollard, *Six Students of St. Edmund Hall*, 37.
[53]Ollard notes that Erasmus went to King's College, but the *DEB* lists Clare.
[54]*DEB* 1117.
[55]See Erasmus Middleton, *Biographia Evangelica: Or, an Historical Account of the Lives and Deaths*

THE AFTERMATH

Four of the students were said to have preached "without holy orders" and participated in "methodistical behaviour." It is clear, however, that the students themselves were the vulnerable casualties of larger political and theological realities. The aftermath of the trial saw the advent of a propaganda war. Whitefield wrote, "So severe a sentence, in an age when almost every kind of proper discipline is held with so lax a rein, hath naturally excited a curiosity in all that have heard it."[56] Gibson describes it as an explosion that "released a flood of debate on the importance of academical subscription to the Thirty-Nine Articles on matriculation or graduation."[57] With the propaganda war, the trial and evangelicalism were plunged into the political controversies of the day, some of which only remotely related to the events at the hall. All of these political controversies, however, fed the machine that led to the expulsions.

Dissenters had always been against full subscription by their very nature as dissenters. The connections between Evangelicals as standard-bearers of the Old Divinity and their Calvinist colleagues who dissented from the established Church became more apparent with the subscription controversy. Yet not all Evangelicals of a Calvinist bent were in favor of discarding the subscription requirement. Some, like Hill, were fully committed to the idea of subscription to the Thirty-Nine Articles as they had been interpreted by Calvinists. Commenting on the interpretation of the article on predestination, Hill wrote: "Surely whoever candidly reads over the article itself, taking it in the *plain literal grammatical sense*, and *not drawing it aside any way* (according to the royal declaration prefixed,) must needs be astonished that any man of common understanding should ever suppose it capable of an Arminian construction."[58] Many Evangelicals, in line with Hill, felt that they were

---

of the Most Eminent and Evangelical Authors or Preachers, Both British and Foreign, in the Several Denominations of Protestants from the Beginning of the Reformation, to the Present Time* (London: 1779).

[56]George Whitefield, *A Letter to the Reverend Dr. Durell, Vice-Chancellor of the University of Oxford: Occasioned by a Late Expulsion of Six Students from Edmund Hall* (London: Printed for J. Millan, E. and C. Dilly and M. Folingsby, 1768), 8.

[57]Gibson, *Church of England 1688–1832*, 140.

[58]Richard Hill, *A Gross Imposition upon the Public Detected: or, Archbishop Cranmer Vindicated from*

reviving the original intent of the Reformers. Ward notes that "the evangelicals maintained that no one who did not accept the doctrine of predestination in their sense was loyal to the seventeenth article of the
Church," and, joining the fray, Unitarians and other heterodox within
the Church "now claimed that they asked for no more latitude in subscribing trinitarian Articles than the Arminians habitually obtained in
subscribing articles Calvinist in colour."[59]

The subscription controversy, according to J. C. D. Clark, was distinctly connected to heterodoxy within the Church, particularly anti-
trinitarians. Clark writes that "the cause of heterodox theology and the
abolition of subscription within the Church was associated, above all,
with Newcastle's henchman in Cambridge University politics, Edmund
Law."[60] Taking the Protestant notion of *sola Scriptura* to its logical conclusion within an extreme individualism, Law wrote:

> We should beware of having any other Gospel preached unto us, or any
> other articles propounded to us for Gospel: we neither should ourselves
> attempt to fix, nor, so far as in us lieth, suffer others to fix any standards,
> or criterions of faith separate from this gospel, as containing some au-
> thentic exposition of it; and these of such authority, that the text itself
> must bend to them upon occasion, and be determined by them, as they
> are proved again by that in a circle. Such a proceeding constitutes the
> worst part of the whole Popish system.[61]

Both the antisubscription evangelicals and the heterodox ultimately
demanded an end to subscription to the Articles, with the Scriptures
as the sole rule of faith. As such, the politics of the antisubscription
league may have had similar goals, but their theological views and the

---

the Charge of Pelagianism, Being a Brief Answer to a Pamphlet Entitled 'A Dissertation on the Sev-
enteenth Article of the Church of England, Wherein the Sentiments of the Compilers and Other
Contemporary Reformers on the Subject of the Divine Decrees Are Fully Deduced from Their Own
Writings'; In a Letter to the Dissertator by the Author of Pietas Oxoniensis (Shrewsbury: Printed by
J. Eddowes, 1774), 14-15.

[59] Works 22:164n13.

[60] J. C. D. Clark, *English Society, 1660–1832: Religion, Ideology, and Politics During the Ancien Régime*
(New York: Cambridge University Press, 2000), 368.

[61] Edmund Law, *Considerations on the Propriety of Requiring a Subscription to Articles of Faith*, 2nd
ed., corrected and enlarged (London: 1774), 14-15.

ways in which they might interpret that "sole rule of faith" produced strange bedfellows.

These Unitarians, like the irregular evangelicals of St. Edmund Hall, did not escape persecution at Oxford or even relegation as the Church became increasingly high church during the 1760s and '70s. Isolation felt by one group was felt by the other, as both were considered to be fringe movements. Unlike the persecuted evangelicals, the loudest proponents of Unitarianism were found at Cambridge, especially at Peterhouse. Clark notes that during Law's mastership at Peterhouse there was "produced a remarkable string of graduates whose reformist and even revolutionary proclivities in public life had its roots in religious heterodoxy, including Jebb, Disney and Lofft."[62] Peterhouse had produced antisubscription politicians, including Lord John Cavendish, Augustus Fitzroy and Sr. James Lowther, all of the Whig Party.[63] Law's antisubscription argument, promoted by his students, tapped into latent anti-Catholicism. His claim was that the subscription requirement was Papism, a coercive force and a vestige of pre-Reformation England. This was not quite the line taken by Evangelicals but would have inspired dissenters convinced that the reforms of the English Church had not gone far enough. What these strange political alliances point to is the future of political debate in England. The arguments over the expulsion of the six students present in smaller detail the later battles that would be waged between a dissenting/low church bloc within the Whig Party and the high church bloc within the Tories.

Nowell's 1772 sermon for the Feast Day of Charles I, given before Parliament at St. Margaret's, Westminster, provides a glimpse of the high church Tory mindset. Ollard interprets the sermon as a comparison of George III to Charles I and the Whigs as opponents of the latter king.[64] George III, while not opposed to the Whigs necessarily, thought very highly of Charles. Linda Colley's description is apt when she writes about his early reign: "Those radicals on both sides of the Atlantic who claimed

---

[62]Clark, *English Society*, 369-70.
[63]Ibid.
[64]Ollard, *Six Students of St. Edmund Hall*, 29.

to detect in the new reign a return to Stuart principles may have seen more clearly into the royal mind than they knew."[65]

One can see in Nowell's description of those who overthrew Charles I how he might have viewed eighteenth-century dissent and irregularity. James Sack, in his work on the rise of an English Right, comments that "the attitude of the Right towards their fellow Protestants in the English dissenting churches was above all an attitude steeped in a peculiar view of history."[66] This view was that the dissenters "were engaged in a nefarious conspiracy" and thus "hated in the seventeenth (or even the sixteenth) century" as those out to destroy the English monarchy and Church.[67] Nowell's words encapsulate these sentiments:

> When men consider themselves placed in their several subordinate stations . . . by the will of Him who is the fountain of government, the supreme Lord of heaven and earth; when they consider that all authority, dominion, and power, are his prerogative, and derived from him to those, whom his Providence has delegated to be his representatives upon earth; cheerful duty, and willing obedience, will be the natural result of such reflections. To minds under this persuasion, the ordinance of man will recommend themselves to be . . . the ordinances of God. So close is the connection between government and religion . . . that without this sacred band, all civil union would be dissolved; and mankind, given over to their own misrule, uncontrouled [sic] by that Almighty Power which called them into being, and order, would by perpetually warring with one another reduce all things into a state of anarchy and confusion.[68]

Such was the view held by Jacobites who had refused to bow to the House of Orange earlier in the century. Until George III, this connection between Church and state had been less explicitly promoted. It is no surprise that George III would reinstitute Parliament's celebration of the

---

[65]Linda Colley, *Britons: Forging the Nation, 1707–1837*, 2nd ed. (New Haven, CT: Yale University Press, 2005), 207.

[66]James Sack, *From Jacobite to Conservative: Reaction and Orthodoxy in Britain, c. 1760–1832* (New York: Cambridge University Press, 1993), 199.

[67]Ibid.

[68]Thomas Nowell, *A Sermon Preached Before the Honourable House of Commons, at St. Margaret's, Westminster, on Thursday, January XXX, 1772* (London: 1772), 10.

Feast Day of King Charles I as a nod to his political supporters, although he himself never actually attended the service.

While Nowell was in London describing the connection between Church and state, the Feathers Tavern petition to end subscription was in circulation, even among some of the Evangelical clergy. The Feathers Tavern petition sought relaxation of the canonical requirements of the Church of England.[69] Many Evangelicals were against the petition, but there was an obvious split in the movement over the issue since the expulsion of the students. The move was defeated in Parliament. It was little different from Bishop Hoadly's earlier attempts as a bishop of the Church to deny that Christ had left any authority in the Church and to say that all Christians were then free to interpret the Scriptures according to their consciences.[70] This perspective corresponded with the politics of extreme Protestantism held by dissenters, theological liberals and some of the Evangelicals, Newton among them.[71]

Nigel Yates notes that "such views completely undermined the ability of the Church of England to determine and require subscription to a particular doctrinal stance, and gave power to the state to regulate religion as it saw fit."[72] The arguments made on both sides of the subscription controversy, the antitrinitarian controversy at Cambridge, and by Bishop Hoadley and his supporters can be seen as the continued settlement of the Toleration Act, which in some respects had already unsettled the Church of England. The debate, however, promoted continued Anglican isolation and further relegation of groups such as the Evangelicals.

John Wesley—an Oxonian till his dying breath—was according to Ward "delighted by the theological line" taken by the university "and the government backing it received."[73] Unlike Whitefield, Wesley

---

[69]See Rack, *Reasonable Enthusiast*, 461-64.

[70]For a modern assessment of Hoadly, see William Gibson, *Enlightenment Prelate: Benjamin Hoadly 1676–1761* (Cambridge: James Clark, 2004).

[71]See Newton, *Cardiphonia*.

[72]Nigel Yates, *Eighteenth-Century Britain: Religion and Politics 1714–1815* (New York: Longman, 2008), 19.

[73]*Works* 22:164n13.

showed no apparent interest in the expulsions themselves but rather in the aftermath and the propaganda war.[74] Wesley wrote in his *Journal* in November 1768:

> Sat. 19. I read Dr. Nowell's *Answer* to Mr. Hill, concerning the expulsion of the students at Oxford. He has said all that could be said for that stretch of power, that instance of *summum ius* [supreme law]; and he says quite enough to clear the Church of England from the charge of predestination—a doctrine which he proves to be utterly inconsistent with the Common Prayer, the Communion Service, the Office of Baptism, the Articles, the Homilies, and the other writings of those that compiled them.[75]

What Wesley failed to see were the connections between the actions of the six students and his cadre of lay preachers roaming the English countryside. It can be argued that his reference to Hill and Nowell's debate had little to do with the actual reasons for the expulsions. Unlike Whitefield, Wesley refused publicly to admit the actual expulsions had any bearing on his ministry. Wesley's founding of Kingswood can be seen as a reaction to the expulsions, but no explicit connection was made by Wesley himself.

The six students were expelled for more than just field preaching. The Conventicle Act of 1664 outlawed all meetings of more than five persons to gather for worship, apart from that which was prescribed in the 1662 Book of Common Prayer. Forsaith notes that the Conventicle Act was "repealed by the Toleration Act (1689) although elements of it remained in force." The 1689 act was not entirely clear, and ecclesiastical authorities applied it inconsistently.[76]

The Evangelicals were well aware of the Conventicle Act. Fletcher went to Martin Madan, an Evangelical and a lawyer, for his opinion on the act.

---

[74]For Whitefield's immediate response to the expulsions, see George Whitefield, *A Letter to the Reverend Dr. Durell, Vice-Chancellor of the University of Oxford: Occasioned by a Late Expulsion of Six Students from Edmund Hall* (1768). Eliciting the common fear that Evangelicals would be unable to procure ordinations in the Church, Whitefield wrote: "But alas! how is this general joy damped, and the pleasing prospect almost totally eclipsed, by a late melancholy scene exhibited in that very place from whence, as from a fountain, many of their preachers frequently and expressly pray, that pure streams may for ever flow to water the city of God?" (7-8).

[75]*Works* 22:164-65.

[76]See chapter four for a discussion of Methodist conventicles.

He also sought the opinion of John Henshaw, a lawyer in Shropshire, who wrote that the law was enforceable as the meetings in question were held "in other Manner than according to the Liturgy & Practice of the Church of England."[77] In Fletcher's case, where he had a small gathering in his own parish, the meeting was led by an ordained clergyman within the parish bounds. The meetings that the six students attended were not led by clergy.

Nowell's arguments, supported by the vice chancellor of Oxford, backed the Evangelicals and their lead propagandist into a corner. Nowell challenged Hill's understanding of church history and specifically that of the Church of England. He wrote, "Had you the least degree of candor, you would not have been guilty of so shameful a misinterpretation, nor have had the confidence to impose it on the reader."[78] The Evangelicals appeared to hold a distinctly narrow historiographical view of English religious history after the Reformation that excluded the majority of eighteenth-century churchmen. As a high churchman, Wesley would have been pleased with Nowell's arguments. Although not held by all Evangelicals, Hill's widely read arguments for a purely Calvinistic interpretation of the Articles made the Evangelicals look out of touch with their orthodox Anglican colleagues.

Hill's venom against any Arminian interpretation of the seventeenth article was met with the sarcastic recommendation that he read the Caroline divines and come to better appreciate the breadth of his own Anglican tradition.[79] Nowell was not the only author to take Hill to task for his reading of the Articles; one Academicus continued to argue that Hill was unaware of his own Church's history writing: "I hope to make it evidently appear to the satisfaction of every fair enquirer, that not only a latitude of interpreting these articles was allowed from the beginning,

---

[77]See Peter Forsaith, ed., *Unexampled Labours: Letters of the Revd John Fletcher to Leaders in the Evangelical Revival* (London: Epworth, 2008), 166n123.

[78]Nowell, *An Answer to a Pamphlet*, 82.

[79]Academicus, *The Church of England Vindicated from the Rigid Notions of Calvinism; or, Some Observations on a Letter from the Author of Pietas Oxoniensis to the Revered Doctor Adams of Shrewbusy. To which is added, A Letter to the Revered Mr. Romaine, in Answer to his Letter to Dr. Adams* (London: Printed for B. White, in Fleet-Street; and T. Cadell, in the Strand, 1770), 37-39.

but moreover that many of the most pious and learned divines of the English church have always subscribed them in a sense totally different from the rigid ideas of Calvin's theology."[80]

IRREGULAR CASUALTIES

The Church would emerge from the challenges to its hegemony more securely settled. Not until the 1830s did challenges to the Church bring drastic changes to its dominance. With the decline of that hegemonic monopoly, a high church movement would arise out of Oxford to decry that loss and ultimately shape the ecclesiastical landscape of Anglicanism.

The casualties from these shifts were those who, for theological and political reasons, placed themselves on the outskirts of the mainstream of eighteenth-century Anglicanism. Because of them, the Evangelicals and the Methodists had to face the stark costs of irregularity. Evangelicals within the Church had to turn from irregularity or face increasing opposition fueled by an ascendant high churchmanship. What happened to the six students could also happen to them. For anyone who wished to remain within the bounds of the Church, opposition to the Restoration establishment was politically and socially dangerous and undermined the long-term project of an Evangelical presence within the Church. Connection to Wesley and his irregular system was becoming too costly to maintain.

---

[80]Ibid., 18-19.

8

VISION AND DIVERGENCE

A New Anglican Historiography

PREDESTINATION AND PERFECTIONISM have long dominated discussion of the divide between Wesley and the Evangelicals. The importance of these two theological issues should not be discounted. They were highly controversial. Outside the revival, both Wesleyan perfectionism and a Calvinist understanding of predestination were seen as extremist. Within the historiography of Methodism, it has become commonplace to designate entire decades to controversies surrounding these two doctrines: the 1760s to perfectionism and the following decade to predestination. The standard line is that the great debate between the Calvinists and the Arminians over these theological issues caused a split in the revival between Calvinist and Arminian branches. The argument is that this division took place after the Calvinist controversies of the 1770s. The one book-length study of John Wesley's relationship to the Evangelical Anglicans, Albert Brown-Lawson's *John Wesley and the Anglican Evangelicals of the Eighteenth Century*, takes up this line and argues that these theological issues were at the root of the eventual split. To be fair to Brown-Lawson's work, he does include polity and politics in his larger argument, but theology remains supreme, and particularly the Calvinist/Arminian divide that culminated in the 1770s.[1]

---

[1] Albert Brown-Lawson, *John Wesley and the Anglican Evangelicals of the Eighteenth Century: A Study in Cooperation and Separation with Special Reference to the Calvinistic Controversies* (Edinburgh: Pentland, 1994), xvi.

My argument here is that though theological differences were apparent between Wesley and many of the Evangelicals, the divide that took place must be seen in a broader context. The trajectories of these various men were set well before the infamous fights of the 1770s. Wesley's sermon "On Free Grace" and his brother's distinctly Arminian hymns published with it in the late 1730s were well known among revival participants.[2] Among evangelicals the theological debate over free will and predestination had spanned the century and existed within the Church of England for much longer. Had the divide between Wesley and the Evangelicals been over theological issues, the divide would have taken place much earlier than 1770. Polity and its social repercussions were the driving force behind the division that ultimately took place.

Theology should not be overlooked. The issues discussed so far have been related to theology, if not explicitly. Yet the historiographical methodology used to describe Wesley and the Evangelicals cannot be overlooked either. In this chapter I will attempt to outline a larger-scaled historiography of English Christianity that places Wesley and the bulk of the Evangelical clergy—those known by their moderate Calvinism—on different sides of the Anglican via media. In a sense the purpose of the current chapter is to place these divergent theologies within an overarching Anglican model, acknowledging their common English roots while at the same time identifying their distinct trajectories within English Christianity.

The Anglican via media has been used as a propaganda piece to place the Anglican tradition snugly between Roman Catholicism and hyper-Calvinism. Yet it might be more accurate to describe Anglicanism as a ship comprising both a high church starboard and a Reformed port. For the sake of clarity, the term *high church* in this chapter describes those traditional elements common to Anglican, Roman Catholic and Orthodox Christianity. These elements would include an emphasis on the centrality of communion, ancient forms of liturgy, emphasis on apostolic

---

[2]Wesley, sermon 110, "On Free Grace," *Works* 3:542-63.

succession, the threefold clerical orders of bishop, priest and deacon, and belief in the efficacy of the sacraments. At the heart of eighteenth-century high church thought was a restorationist project focused on the writings of the early church fathers.

Throughout the history of English Christianity after the Reformation, the ship has rocked back and forth.[3] A tradition that includes Stephen Gardiner and Thomas Cranmer, William Laud and Oliver Cromwell, John Wesley and William Romaine, is bound to teeter between supposedly divergent theologies. The English Reformers, the Caroline divines, the Puritans and the nonjurors were all part of the English Church. They are all represented on the Anglican ship. Even the Tractarians of the nineteenth century fit on this ship, although on one side of it. By the time the Evangelical Revival came on the scene, John Wesley and the Evangelical Anglicans simply represented different sides of that ship, thus ultimately working separately, albeit it within the same ecclesiastical space.[4]

As with other models, such as the Wesleyan Quadrilateral, this metaphor of an Anglican ship will break down if pressed too far.[5] John Wesley was influenced by Protestant reform movements and by the Puritans. The Evangelicals were influenced by the larger catholic tradition. William Gibson rightly argues that doctrinal divisions between high and low churchmanship were "permeable" and that within this scope a churchman could hold a range of views.[6] The stark difference appears in that Wesley was much more influenced by and used the lens of the early church and the Caroline divines (high church Christianity), and the Evangelicals the English Reformers and Puritanism. The two looked back to these different

---

[3]In fact, it could be argued that the English Reformation itself lasted much longer than is usually thought, extending through the Civil War period up to the Restoration of the monarchy in 1660.

[4]While not using the model of a ship, Archbishop Ramsey describes the Anglican Church as "committed not to a vague position wherein the Evangelical and Catholic views are alterations, but to the scriptural faith wherein both elements are of one." See A. M. Ramsey, *The Gospel and the Catholic Church* (London: Longmans, Green, 1936), 208-9.

[5]See Hempton's critique of the Wesleyan Quadrilateral in David Hempton, *Methodism: Empire of the Spirit* (New Haven, CT: Yale University Press, 2005), 56.

[6]William Gibson, "Samuel Wesley's Conformity Reconsidered," in *Methodist History* 47, no. 2 (January 2009): 75.

periods of church history to define their ministries and theological perspectives. The bases on which they formed their theological outlooks were of a different hue and even a different trajectory.

This difference is seen when the nonjuror-influenced Wesley and the Puritan-influenced Evangelicals are placed next to each other. Walsh writes:

> If evangelicals themselves had been asked what their Revival intended to revive, they would have had a ready answer. It was a restatement of the "good old divinity" of English Puritans and Reformers, a resurgence of that ancient tradition of Augustinian spirituality which evangelical historians like Joseph Milner attempted ingeniously, but not absurdly, to trace back through the medieval centuries to the primitive church itself.[7]

Hindmarsh similarly argues that the early Evangelicals used the New Testament as their principal source, "filtered through the theology of the magisterial Reformation."[8] This lens, or filter, was distinctly different from that used by Wesley. Comparing Wesley's historical writings to Milner's provides a glimpse into this distinction. While both men used a theologically informed methodology to produce their various works, Milner traced evangelicalism through church history, highlighting the Reformers. He wrote at the beginning of his history:

> It is certain, that from our Saviour's time to the present, there have ever been persons whose dispositions and lives have been formed by the rules of the New Testament; men, who have been real, not merely nominal Christians; who believed the doctrines of the Gospel, loved them because of their divine excellency, and suffered gladly the loss of all things that they might win Christ and be found in him. It is the history of these men which I propose to write.[9]

Wesley's historical writing is explicitly theocentric and shows deference not only to the Reformation as a means of overthrowing Roman

---

[7]J. D. Walsh, "The Anglican Evangelicals in the Eighteenth Century," in *Aspects de L'Anglicanisme.* Travaux du Centre D'Etudes Supérienures Spécialisé D'Historie des Relgions de Stausbourg (Paris: Presses Universitaires de France, 1974), 87.

[8]D. Bruce Hindmarsh, *The Evangelical Conversion Narrative: Spiritual Autobiography in Early Modern England* (New York: Oxford University Press, 2005), 13.

[9]See Joseph Milner, *The History of the Church of Christ, Volume the First: Containing the First Three Centuries,* new ed. (London: Luke Hansard and Sons for T. Cadell, in the Strand, 1827), A2.

Catholic influence but also to the high church "martyr" Charles I.[10] Additionally, he had immense respect for the nonjurors, especially Bishop Thomas Ken. Ward claims Wesley's upbringing instilled in him deference for the high church and the Jacobites.[11] He writes that Wesley was "born into a Jacobite milieu" and the "younger brother of a (non-Methodist) collaborator of Bishop Atterbury," a bishop with striking high church sympathies and who ended his days exiled and in service to the dethroned Stuarts. According to Ward, "Wesley did not adopt the world as his parish; indeed his one substantial trip abroad was to a nest of Jacobites in Georgia, headed by General Oglethorpe, who had been christened James Edward for the Old (Jacobite) Pretender."[12]

In this paradigm Wesley, representing a high church Anglicanism focused on the early church fathers, and the Evangelicals, representing Reformed/Puritan Anglicanism, could not suffer each other long. Their politics, their polity and their theology would guide them to diverge. This model provides a context in which to understand broadly the issues and personalities that drove the Wesleyans and the Evangelicals apart. The battles between high church and Reformed Anglicanism stretch back to the sixteenth and seventeenth centuries, were represented within the Evangelical Revival, and appear in the nineteenth century with the rise of both an Evangelical party and the Oxford Movement battling for the soul of the Church of England. They were not determined, however, simply by the doctrine of predestination. John Wesley's theological vision grew out of the context of this larger struggle for Anglican identity.

WESLEY THE TORY

The lenses through which Wesley and the Evangelicals saw their work and theological outlook can be seen almost to separate Wesley from the

---

[10]See John Wesley, *Concise History of England, from the Earliest Times to the Death of George II* (London: 1775).

[11]Given the success of Methodism in Cornwall, it is interesting to note that Cornwall was also a stronghold of Tory high churchmanship and nonjurors. See H. Miles Brown, *The Church in Cornwall* (Truro, UK: Oscar Blackford, 1964), 64.

[12]W. R. Ward, *The Protestant Evangelical Awakening* (New York: Cambridge University Press, 2004), 119.

Evangelical Revival itself. In the fights for "the real Wesley" in the nineteenth century between Methodists and high church ritualists, some of the polemical works of the high church party implied that Wesley was not an Evangelical at all.[13] Recently, in an attempt to balance the view of institutional Methodism promoted by Luke Tyerman and John Telford, Ward highlighted Wesley's connections to the nonjurors and the Tories. He writes, "Wesley, in short, was born into a rabidly Tory circle which damned foreigners, foreign religions and foreign entanglements," adding that Wesley did not throw these sentiments overboard after his Aldersgate experience but "kept up Jacobite sentiment far down the eighteenth century."[14] For this group the Restoration was the reconstruction of the Church of England, a "revival of morality" and "a cosmic event modelled on the resurrection."[15]

The revival of morality was not based on the Puritan divines but on high church Anglicanism. William Law and Jeremy Taylor represent this "holy living" tradition within Anglicanism. Wesley's debt to these two authors and especially Law's *A Serious Call to a Devout and Holy Life* and Taylor's *Holy Living* and *Holy Dying* is widely acknowledged. Wesley's famous *Journal* is an outgrowth of this tradition of spiritual discipline. He read the works of these Caroline divines while at Oxford, that seat of restorationist movements.

Taylor was a favorite of Restoration England. He had served with Laud and been chaplain ordinary to Charles I. After the Restoration, Taylor was made bishop of Down and Connor in Ireland and chancellor of the University of Dublin.[16] The drive toward moral revival, or "primitive Christianity," was a reaction to what Ward described as the "crass di-

---

[13]Both Harrington William Holden's, *John Wesley in the Company of High Churchmen* (London: 1870) and Richard Denny Urlin's *The Churchman's Life of Wesley* were written in the heat of an ecclesiastical firestorm and seem almost to make Wesley an outright high churchman devoid of evangelical convictions.

[14]Ward, *Protestant Evangelical Awakening*, 296.

[15]Ibid.

[16]Taylor's Catholicism is seen in his works, including *On the Reverence Due to the Altar* (London[?]: 1649); *An Apologie for Authorized and Set Forms of Liturgie* (London[?]: 1649); and *The Golden Grove, or, A Manuall of Daily Prayers and Letanies, Fitted to the Days of the Week . . . Also, Festival Hymns, According to the Manner of the Ancient Church* (London[?]: 1655).

chotomy in Restoration England between official and public confession and private conduct," as seen in the formation of the Society for the Reformation of Manners, among others.[17]

Wesley's high churchmanship is evident in his reverence for Charles I. Charles remains the only saint canonized by the Church of England. His sainthood after the Restoration was a rejection of the Puritans and also a brilliant public relations scheme launched shortly after the king's execution, or martyrdom, in 1649 with the publication of *Eikon Basilike*. This royalist propaganda, published ten days after the death of the king, was purported to be have been written by Charles himself.[18] Although it is hard to tell what Wesley said, his *Journal* indicates that he preached regularly on January 30, Charles's feast day.

Wesley twice visited Carisbrooke Castle on the Isle of Wight where Charles was held prisoner between his trial and execution. His reflections on these visits are telling in that they display a shift in his perspective. In both accounts Wesley notes seeing the window through which the king attempted to escape. In the first account Wesley describes "poor King Charles."[19] In the second the visit inspired him to ponder "that whole train of occurrences wherein the hand of God was so eminently seen."[20] It is not clear from his later comment whether it should be taken as pro-royalist or pro-parliamentarian. Given Wesley's royalist proclivities, especially after the American Revolution, when the visit was made, it is not unlikely that the "whole train of occurrences" included the restoration of the Church and monarchy under Charles II in 1660.[21] This interpretation of the events of the Civil War, Commonwealth and Restoration was explicit in the prayers appointed for Evening Prayer on January 30.[22]

---

[17]Ward, *Protestant Evangelical Awakening*, 34-35.

[18]See Paul Kléber Monod, *The Power of Kings: Monarchy and Religion in Europe, 1589–1715* (New Haven, CT: Yale University Press, 1999), 184-91.

[19]*Works* 20:467 (July 11, 1753).

[20]*Works* 23:372 (Aug. 10, 1785).

[21]*Works* 23:372-73n21.

[22]One of the collects appointed for evening prayer on January 30 in the Book of Common Prayer reads: "Blessed God, just, and powerful, who didst permit thy dear servant, our late dread Sovereign, to be this day given up to the violent out-rages of wicked men, to be despightfully used,

A *Journal* entry for January 30, 1785, describes Wesley preaching on Psalm 119:137, a text not appointed for the feast day. Wesley claimed to have "endeavoured to point out those sins which were the chief cause of that awful transaction we commemorate this day." The chief sin, however, was the king's persecution of "the real Christians."[23] By persecution of "the real Christians," Charles drove them "into the hands of designing men" and brought about the end of his reign. This interpretation of the events Ward describes as "an ingenious adjustment of the Jacobitism of his early milieu to the respect for Puritan vital religion which he had acquired."[24] Wesley had found a place for Puritan vital religion, although distinctly contained within a celebration of one of high church Anglicanism's principal saints.

Wesley displayed his affection for the high church and especially for nonjurors in his admiration for the writings of Charles Leslie. Leslie, an Irish Anglican nonjuror, was known for his support of the Stuarts and high church theology, especially of a high sacramentalist sort. Leslie, like Atterbury, spent time abroad with the Stuarts, but he tired of Roman Catholicism and returned to Ireland, where he died in 1722. Wesley read and republished many of Leslie's works. He donated many of them to the Kingswood library. These books display Leslie's high churchmanship but specifically his disdain for heresy, deism and liturgical innovation.[25] One, *The History of Sin and Heresy Attempted, from*

---

and at last murthered by them; Though we cannot reflect upon so foul an act but with horrour and astonishment; yet do we most greatly commemorate the glories of thy grace, which then shined forth in thine Annointed, whom thou wert pleased, even at the hour of death, to endue with an eminent measure of exemplary patience, meekness, and charity, before the face of his cruel enemies. And albeit, thou didst suffer them to proceed to such a height of violence against him, as to kill his person, and take posession of his throne; yet didst thou in great mercy preserve his son, whose right it was, and at length by a wonderful providence bring him back, and set him thereon, to restore thy true Religion, and to settle peace among us: For which, we glorifie thy Name, through Jesus Christ our blessed Saviour. *Amen.*"

[23] *Works* 23:342 (Sunday, Jan. 30 [1785]).

[24] Ibid., n. 85.

[25] Special thanks to Randy Maddox for providing this information. The books include Leslie's *The History of Sin and Heresy Attempted, from the First War They Raised in Heaven . . . [to] Their Final Condemnation in Hell* (London: H. Hindmarsh, 1698), §XIII.2, "Of Foreknowledge and Freedom"; *A Religious Conference between a Minister and Parishioner; concerning the practice of our orthodox Church of England, in baptizing infants by pouring water on their faces or sprinkling them, and in confirming them afterwards by the bishop, proving all three lawful by good reasons and the authority*

the First War They Raised in Heaven . . . [to] Their Final Condemnation in Hell (1698), Wesley republished in his *Arminian Magazine* in 1778 as "Thoughts on Absolute Predestination."[26]

Wesley inherited a strong Tory tradition from his parents, who, Hempton notes, "were nevertheless divided on the legitimacy of the Hanoverian regime." According to Hempton, Wesley "flirted with Jacobitism (later vigorously denied) in his early Oxford days and in the surprisingly Jacobite circles in which some of the early leaders of the evangelical revival were located."[27] Susanna Wesley's commitment to nonjuring interests caused a rift in the Wesley home in 1702 that lasted six months.[28] Her influence on all of her children is undeniable. Wesley's early Jacobite associations would expand, however, and include Oxford Methodist John Clayton, who was raised in the Jacobite stronghold of Manchester. It was Clayton who influenced Wesley to study the early church and to see the importance of a theology of works.[29] Walsh describes Wesley's theology as "strongly eudaemonic," claiming that Wesley understood the ideal Christian life as "a life of ceaseless, cheerful, activism."[30]

Hempton argues that Wesley, "as with many erstwhile Jacobites," finally came to accept the Hanoverian regime because he came to believe

---

of Holy Scripture; with a vindication of the lawfulness of godfathers and godmothers, and of the sacred order of bishops and their being spiritual lords (London: Charles Brome et al., 1698); A Short and Easy Method with the Deists, wherein the Certainty of the Christian Religion is Demonstrated by Infallible proof from Four Rules . . . To which is added, a second part to the Jews . . . with an answer to the most material of their objections, and prejudices against Christianity, published by Wesley as A Preservative Against Unsettled Notions in Religion (1758); The Snake in the Grass; or, Satan Transformed into an Angel of Light, 2nd ed. (London: Charles Brome, 1697); and The Socinian Controversy Discussed (London: G. Strahan, 1708), published by Wesley as "Extract of Preface," in Arminian Magazine 10 (1787): 491-93, 542-45, 593-96, 643-45.

[26]See *Arminian Magazine* 1 (1778): 356-63.

[27]David Hempton, "Wesley in Context," in *The Cambridge Companion to John Wesley*, Randy L. Maddox and Jason E. Vickers, eds. (New York: Cambridge University Press, 2009), 70.

[28]See Geordan Hammond, *John Wesley in America: Restoring Primitive Christianity* (New York: Oxford University Press, 2014), 16-17.

[29]See Rack's description of Wesley's theology in Henry D. Rack, *Reasonable Enthusiast: John Wesley and the Rise of Methodism*, 3rd ed. (Philadelphia: Trinity Press International, 2002), as well as Randy L. Maddox's *Responsible Grace: John Wesley's Practical Theology* (Nashville: Kingswood Books, 1994).

[30]John Walsh, *John Wesley 1703-1791: A Bicentennial Tribute* (London: Friends of Dr. William's Library, 1993), 7.

that the Glorious Revolution "had ushered in an unprecedented era of civil and religious liberty." However, this peace with the Hanoverians did not mean peace with Robert Walpole.[31] Wesley's Jacobite sentiments were clear in his staunch opposition to the policies of the Whig government. He was following the footsteps of his father, a strident Tory whose ecclesiastical career had been stunted by Whig politics. Even after Walpole, Wesley's Toryism is seen in his cries of God and king during the American Revolution.[32] This Toryism and flirtation with Jacobitism do not set Wesley apart from every leader of the revival—the Huntingdons were, as Clark argues, "dangerously overt" in their Jacobitism, and so were some early members of Whitefield's tabernacle in London—but they do mark him out as noticeably different from the moderate Calvinists who came to define the Evangelical Party.[33] Wesley was connected to political movements that were distinctly aligned with high church Anglicanism.

The holy living tradition of high church Anglicanism was not foreign to the Evangelical Revival. Although most Evangelicals in the period would undergo conversion experiences as a reaction to fears of being outside the "elect," Whitefield's experience was connected to the holy living tradition. Hindmarsh notes that although Whitefield "would move in an increasingly Calvinist direction in his own theology," the "spiritual anxiety that prompted his conversion was induced in 1735 more by the high-church piety of William Law and the 'holy living' tradition than by any introspective doubts that came with a high predestinarian theology."[34]

These varied approaches to a conversion experience match well the diverse nature of the revival. The revival was more than the renewal of the "old theology" represented by English dissent. While not exclusively

---

[31]Hempton, "Wesley in Context," 70.

[32]See Wesley's *Calm Address to Our American Colonies* (London: 1775). For a recent study see Theodore R. Weber, *Politics in the Order of Salvation: Transforming Wesleyan Political Ethics* (Nashville: Kingswood Books, 2001).

[33]See J. C. D. Clark's chapter in William J. Abraham and James E. Kirby, eds., *The Oxford Handbook of Methodist Studies* (New York: Oxford University Press, 2009), 6, and Boyd Stanley Schlenther, *Queen of the Methodists: The Countess of Huntingdon and the Eighteenth-Century Crisis of Faith and Society* (Durham: Durham Academic Press, 1997), 27-31.

[34]Hindmarsh, *Evangelical Conversion Narrative*, 107-8.

a revival of Puritanism—Adam recommended nonjuror Bishop Ken's devotional materials in his catechism, for example—the "old theology" was held in various degrees by the majority of Evangelicals.[35] So while Bebbington has claimed that the revival represented "an expansion of the Puritan experience in the seventeenth century," he also claims that the evangelical experience of the eighteenth century was distinct from the seventeenth because of the "extensive connectedness of local revival to revival elsewhere, to a world that transcended the local milieu of parish, denomination, or sect."[36]

Ironically, Wesley's conversion was of a distinctly pietistic flavor. His conversion was part of an evangelical sweep that included persons from diverse places and varying degrees of churchmanship. Regardless, the majority of the leaders of the revival were of a moderate Calvinist outlook. Wesley, among this group, was still the odd man of the revival regardless of conversion experiences, parish boundaries or lay preachers.

There is no doubt that Wesley promoted aspects of the "Old Divinity"; his frequent citation of the Homilies and his republication of Puritan divines, however edited, in his Christian Library make that plain. Wesley held a strong doctrine of original sin, believed in the need for repentance and the New Birth, and emphasized justification by faith alone.[37] As Walsh notes, however, "there was another side to the medal."[38]

> Victorian High Anglicans striving to win back errant Methodists to the priestly fold in which their founder had lived and died pointed to dimensions of Wesley's mature faith and practice which were hard to square with the image of Wesley as godfather of the Evangelical Alliance, or as Dwight Moody in a tricorn hat and knee breeches.[39]

---

[35]Thomas Adam, *Practical Lectures on the Church-Catechism. By Thomas Adam, The Fifth Edition. To Which Is Now Added, an Exercise, by Way of Question and Answer, Preparatory to Confirmation* (London: 1767), 120.

[36]David Bebbington, *Evangelicalism in Modern Britain: A History from the 1730s to the 1980s* (London: Unwin Hyman, 1989), 70.

[37]Fred Sanders's *Wesley on the Christian Life: The Heart Renewed by Love* (Wheaton, IL: Crossway, 2013) is, in part, an attempt to make Wesley amenable to a Reformed audience by highlighting these various doctrinal emphases.

[38]Walsh, *John Wesley 1703–1791*, 10.

[39]Ibid.

High church Anglicans of the Victorian era would latch onto this Wesley, while contemporary Methodists strove to ignore the high church facet of the man as much as possible. While Wesley held to some of the distinctly Protestant elements of the Anglican tradition, he was also a strong sacramentalist. He believed in the doctrine of the Real Presence and baptismal regeneration, and he prayed for the faithful departed. Wesley also emphasized "constant" communion and the use of ancient patterns of prayer and fasting more reminiscent of monasticism. Roman Catholic eccentrics such as Gaston de Renty and Gregory Lopez were role models he promoted among the Methodist societies. His admiration for these two men lasted throughout much of his life.

There is a sharp difference, however, between Wesley's admiration for Catholic saints and his opinion of the Roman Catholic Church. Eamon Duffy begins his essay on Wesley and the Counter-Reformation with the words "John Wesley detested Roman Catholicism."[40] Wesley was distinctly anti-Roman. He was distrustful of the political institution called the Roman Catholic Church. Duffy writes that Wesley "thought that in pursuit of its own interests the Catholic Church would not hesitate to 'burst all the ties of truth, justice and mercy,' and he believed that no government— whether it be 'Protestant, Mahometan or Pagan'—should tolerate Roman Catholics."[41] Wesley's distrust for Roman Catholic political aspirations in England resulted in his connection to the Protestant Association and through them to the notorious Gordon Riots of the 1780s. These political feelings, however, did not detract from Wesley's insistence on theological propositions that were a part of the larger high church tradition.[42]

This combination of Roman Catholic disdain and Anglican high churchmanship was common. As the century wore on, the Tories became

---

[40]Eamon Duffy, "Wesley and the Counter-Reformation," in *Revival and Religion Since 1700: Essays for John Walsh*, ed. Jane Garnett and Colin Matthew (Rio Grande, OH: Hambledon, 1993), 1.

[41]Ibid. Duffy describes Lopez and de Renty in his essay—Lopez as "an eccentric Spanish hermit who died in Mexico in 1596" and de Renty as "a French nobleman best known for his philanthropic and religious activities, and in particular for his part in the development of a sort of seventeenth-century *Opus Dei*, the powerful secret society of wealthy devout lay people known as the Company of the Blessed Sacrament" (1).

[42]See Aelred Burrows's chapter "Wesley the Catholic," in John Stacey, ed., *John Wesley: Contemporary Perspectives* (London: Epworth, 1988).

the party of the Church of England. They combined nationalism with a distinct bigotry for the established Church. James Sack describes Toryism of this period as constituting the "normative example of right-wing political groupings throughout Europe and her off-shoots beyond the seas in the nineteenth and twentieth centuries."[43] The amalgamation of a religious group with a political party was not new, but it was pronounced in the Tory's combination of high churchmanship, loyalty to the establishment and its Church, and political conservatism.

Sack's description of the Methodists' place within this political climate is worth noting. He describes the "Arminian Methodists" as having had "a strangely self-conscious relationship with the High Church."[44] Establishment Tories were not keen of Methodism's irregularity. Regardless of this tension, Wesley was firm in this political-religious perspective. In a 1775 letter to the earl of Dartmouth, Wesley penned the words, "I am a High Churchman, the son of a High Churchman." Sack writes:

> John Wesley, to the end of his long life, called himself a High Churchman— which he presumably meant in a political sense, as he coupled it with his belief in passive obedience and non-resistance, and he had given up any belief in the apostolic succession as early as 1746. Wesley strongly admired Horne, Jones, and Johnson ("that great man") and supported Dr. Nowell at the time of the expulsion of the six predestinarian Oxford students in 1769 [sic]. In return Johnson approved of Wesley; Jones of Nayland thought him a "wonderful man in his way;" and Bishop Horne as late as 1790 allowed him to preach from a pulpit in his diocese.[45]

Wesley's Tory connections seem at odds with his maverick evangelicalism. What they provide is a key distinction from the majority of Evangelicals, who saw their role in the Church as a restoration of the principles of the English Reformation.

One area where differing lenses caused theological debate was the idea of Christian perfectionism. Wesley's admiration for the holy living

---

[43]James Sack, *From Jacobite to Conservative: Reaction and Orthodoxy in Britain, c. 1760–1832* (New York: Cambridge University Press, 1993), 35.

[44]Ibid., 196.

[45]Ibid.

tradition of the Caroline divines and his affection for the lives of Catholic saints point to his doctrine of Christian perfection. The holiness tradition within Anglicanism, inspired by the church fathers, primarily Eastern, runs through the high church wing of the Church.[46] The idea that one could be "perfected in love" was controversial and often seen as rank enthusiasm. However, Wesley's views on perfection, like his views on predestination, were well known by the early 1740s. The most damaging repercussion of the doctrine to Wesley's relationship with the Evangelicals sprang from its abuse. Some of Wesley's followers pushed Wesley's claims further than he ever intended and bathed them in apocalyptic fervor.

Encouraged by Wesley's insistence that perfection was possible instantaneously, perfectionist revivals broke out among Wesleyan Methodists in the late 1750s and early 1760s. Thomas Maxfield and John Bell led revivals in London that included claims of sinless perfection and, at least on Bell's part, the ability to name the date on which Jesus would return: February 28, 1763. These excesses caused great confusion within Wesleyan Methodism, were condemned by Wesley after a time and also raised concerns among Evangelicals, including Grimshaw and Fletcher.[47] The concerns of these friends of Wesleyan Methodism were based on an aversion to enthusiasm. They were not the only Evangelicals to notice. Newton was alarmed by these claims made by some of Wesley's vested preachers, and the claims did help to place a wedge between him and Wesley that lasted for a few years, until Wesley reached out to Newton in 1765.[48] What the perfectionist controversy highlights is a volatile amal-

---

[46]See especially Geoffrey Rowell, Kenneth Stevenson and Rowan Williams, eds., *Love's Redeeming Work: The Anglican Quest for Holiness* (New York: Oxford University Press, 2001). The editors provide writings from Anglican divines both before and after Wesley that show the distinctive emphasis on holy living within Anglicanism, and especially the Caroline divines, that fueled Wesley's thought.

[47]For an in-depth discussion of the perfectionist controversy, see W. Stephen Gunter, *The Limits of 'Love Divine': John Wesley's Response to Antinomianism and Enthusiasm* (Nashville: Kingswood Books, 1999), 215-26. See also *Works* 21:240-41 and *Letters* (Telford) 4:10. The greatest damage from the controversy was probably that done to the London society after the followers of Maxfield and Bell separated from them.

[48]D. Bruce Hindmarsh, *John Newton and the English Evangelical Tradition: Between the Conversions of Wesley and Wilberforce* (Grand Rapids: Eerdmans, 2001), 127-32.

gamation of issues discussed earlier, including theology, but also social pressures on the Evangelicals, the eighteenth-century avoidance of enthusiasm and the challenges brought about by the work of lay ministers.

THE OLD DIVINITY

The Evangelical Revival was seen by many of its participants as a renewal, or restoration, of the "Old Divinity," the theology of the English Reformers and the Puritans. One critic of the Church argued that the writings of the Protestant martyrs Hugh Latimer and Nicholas Ridley would be unacceptable within early eighteenth-century Anglicanism.[49] John Newton, challenging the charge of evangelical dissent, argued that the Evangelicals were simply promoting the doctrines and methods of the Church of England. If incumbents who followed these Evangelicals held to the same standards, Newton claimed, their congregations would not "wholly forsake their favourite church."[50]

Evangelical congregations did dissent from the Church. It has been noted that Samuel Walker's congregation left the Church after his death. Henry Venn's church did the same thing after he left. These departures were caused by a lack of Evangelicals to fill vacant pulpits, but Newton's justification for the departures is telling. Evangelicals promoted a distinct vision of Anglicanism that did not fit well within either the high church wing or with the latitudinarian majority. Hindmarsh claims that "while Calvinism never recovered the prominence it had had in public and religious discourse during the seventeenth century, there was nevertheless a significant return to Reformed theology in the context of the Evangelical Revival."[51] They promoted a Calvinist vision of Anglicanism, dominant among the Reformers and the Puritans in the two previous centuries but more at home in the dissenting meetinghouse than in the

---

[49]Robert Seagrave, *A Letter to the People of England. Occasion'd by the Falling Away of the Clergy from the doctrines of the Reformation* (London: 1735), 28.

[50]John Newton, *Memoirs of the Life of the Late Rev. William Grimshaw, A. B., Minister of Haworth, in the West-Riding of the County of York; With Occasional Reflections* (London: W. Baynes and Son, 1825), 102-3.

[51]Hindmarsh, *John Newton and the English Evangelical Tradition*, 50.

Anglican parish church by the eighteenth century.[52] This is the reason why David Lyle Jeffery writes in his volume on the spiritual life of the revival of the "affection and respect evangelical Anglicans felt toward Independents and Puritans" when he describes the role of dissenting literature on the conversion of Evangelical layman William Wilberforce.[53]

The "Old Divinity" was based on a Reformed reading of the standards of Anglican theology. For example, in the controversy following the expulsion of Calvinist Methodists from St. Edmund Hall, outlined previously, Toplady, much like Hill, argued for a strict Calvinist reading of the Articles of Religion that left little room for most Anglicans. Toplady argued that "the principles commonly termed *Calvinistic*, are *plainly* and *repeatedly* delivered in the authentic declarations" of the Church of England. His goal was to "vindicate the best of visible churches" from the charge that they were anything otherwise.[54] While most Evangelicals, and especially Newton, would not have argued for such an exclusivist reading, Toplady used the lens through which most Evangelicals viewed these foundational documents. The Articles, Homilies and liturgy of the Church were, apart from traces of a high church past, Reformed documents. This is why Elliott-Binns, in his history of the early Evangelicals, describes the theology of the Evangelicals as simply "those of the Church of England as contained in the Articles, Prayer Book, and Homilies." The Evangelicals differed from their fellow priests, according to Elliott-Binns, by placing special emphasis on "certain doctrines" and "reviving them and bringing out their true meaning."[55]

Evangelical Anglicans saw themselves as promoting a moderate form of Calvinism. Bebbington describes the Evangelicals as moderate Calvinists in that they "rejected stronger views of God's control of human destiny." Evangelicals, Wesley included, left room for human agency.

---

[52]Ibid., 236-37.

[53]David Lyle Jeffrey, *English Spirituality in the Age of Wesley* (Grand Rapids: Eerdmans, 1987), 38.

[54]See Augustus Toplady, *The Church of England Vindicated from the Charge of Arminianism* (Holborn, UK: Joseph Gurney, 1769), A2.

[55]L. E. Elliott-Binns, *The Early Evangelicals: A Religious and Social Study* (London: Lutterworth, 1953), 382.

Humans, "they emphatically taught, [were] responsible agents."[56] This moderate Calvinism is seen in Newton's comment that Calvinism, like sugar in tea, should only be served "mixed and diluted."[57] Likewise, Walker has been called a moderate Calvinist, although Davies questioned Walker's Reformed credentials. One of Walker's sermons gives a striking place for human will and agency: "For as in a reconciled God he proposes to our reason or understanding the most suitable and convincing argument into our obedience, so thereby he stirs up our wills in the most deliberate manner, with the freest consent, and without the least constraint or violence to choose the holy way of God's commandments."[58] The role of human agency and the English proclivity to read the doctrine of total depravity in a more generous way than their Continental counterparts may have influenced the Evangelicals.

Bebbington describes this moderation principally in relation to the doctrine of reprobation—the doctrine that God had destined certain persons for damnation. He argues that the Evangelicals generally rejected this traditional Calvinist doctrine and instead insisted that human disobedience was the root of any failure to respond to the gospel.[59] In his sermon "The Characters of Those from Whom Gospel Doctrines Are Hid," Newton blamed the distraction of the world, riches and human wisdom for deterring the grace of God. While content to believe that God was the author of salvation, Newton did not think it necessary to conclude that God had predetermined those who are thus distracted.[60]

What drew most Evangelicals to Calvinism was not the logical system of the Swiss reformer. They saw Calvinism, and its emphasis on divine agency, as the best description of their conversion experiences. And these conversion experiences were common to the Puritans of the seventeenth century. Hindmarsh writes that "the Puritans fostered spiritual autobiography in part by

---

[56]Bebbington, *Evangelicalism in Modern Britain*, 64.

[57]Hindmarsh, *John Newton and the English Evangelical Tradition*, 168.

[58]G. C. B. Davies, *The Early Cornish Evangelicals 1735–60: A Study of Walker of Truro and Others* (London: SPCK, 1951), 155.

[59]Bebbington, *Evangelicalism in Modern Britain*, 64.

[60]John Newton, *Letters and Sermons, Including Cardiphonia and the Messiah; A Review of Ecclesiastical History, Hymns, and Miscellaneous Pieces. By John Newton, Rector of St. Mary Woolnoth, London. In Nine Volumes* (Edinburgh: 1798), 4:123-32.

their stress upon religious experience."[61] In Hindmarsh's reading of early evangelical conversion narratives, he argues not only that the international Evangelical Revival was "constituted chiefly by the repeated experience of evangelical conversion," but also that there was an "irreducibly religious element in this experience that was in continuity with seventeenth-century Puritanism and related traditions."[62] This direct connection between the Puritans and the Evangelical Revival was acknowledged by the Evangelicals. James Hervey asked in a letter in 1748, "Is it Puritanical?" to which he answered, "Be not afraid of the name."[63] The Puritans, while not always accurate in their view of the Church, had simply taken the reforms of the sixteenth century to their logical conclusion.

A Calvinist in post-Restoration England was, however, as Walsh describes it, "a rare bird." By 1720 the Anglican Calvinist was almost extinct: "after the Restoration of Charles II in 1660, the Calvinism which had dominated the Church for much of a century fell into decline."[64] The political aftermath of the seventeenth-century Puritanism experiment created a context in which Calvinism was suspect. Walsh writes:

> Puritan doctrines seemed too closely associated with Puritan politics. Calvinism had acquired deep psychological associations with the Civil War and Commonwealth, the antinomianism of sectaries, the dismemberment of the Church, the killing of the king. These folk memories dogged it like a kind of political original sin for more than a century to come.[65]

---

[61]Hindmarsh, *Evangelical Conversion Narrative*, 35.

[62]Ibid., 80.

[63]James Hervey, *The Works of the Late Rev. James Hervey, A. M.* (London: 1807), 6:11 (letter of Jan. 12, 1748).

[64]Walsh, "Anglican Evangelicals," 87. For a different understanding of the decline of Calvinism in the Church of England, see Stephan Hampton, *Anti-Arminians: The Anglican Reformed Tradition from Charles II to George I* (New York: Oxford University Press, 2008). Hampton's fluid application of the term *Reformed* makes it possible to argue for a stronger Calvinist presence within the church after the Restoration of the monarchy. Hampton notes, "It is necessary to adopt a broad and flexible understanding of Reformed theology, if we are to identify any post-Restoration Anglicans as a Reformed writer" (269). See Hampton's argument for the effects of his historiographical approach to the rise of the Evangelical Revival (272). Walsh's description better describes the effects of anti-Calvinist sentiment during the period, as does Dewey D. Wallace's description in *Shapers of English Calvinism 1660–1714: Variety, Persistence, and Transformation* (New York: Oxford University Press, 2011). Wallace provides a wider lens with a more discernible definition of the terms *Calvinist* and *Reformed*.

[65]Walsh, "Anglican Evangelicals," 87.

Robert Seagrave, in his *A Letter to the People of England* (1735), supplied a contemporary account of the void left in English religious life following the collapse of Anglican Calvinism. He wrote vehemently that "learning and oratory, it must be owned, are arrived at great perfection; but our true *Old Divinity* is gone."[66] Evangelical William Romaine bewailed the loss of this "vital religion," which he claimed in 1775 was lost "more than a century ago."[67] This "Old Divinity," as Wallace describes it, was a form of Calvinism that had dominated the Church of England under the influence of Thomas Cranmer, Martin Bucer, Richard Baxter and Thomas Owen.[68] Apart from the chapels royal, Calvinism held sway over the theology and liturgy of the newly formed Church of England beginning in the Elizabethan era and extending to the Restoration.[69] Seagrave described this Calvinist Anglicanism as at one point the "universal belief amongst Protestants at the Reformation" and claimed that the pulpits of England "know no other language" than faith only as "the genuine method of salvation." This language of *sola fide*, explicitly rejecting works, was common among the Evangelicals. It is easily seen in such contemporary works as Elliot's *Encouragement for Sinners; or, Righteousness Attainable Without Works.*[70]

---

[66]Seagrave, *A Letter to the People of England*. Robert Seagrave Jr., an Evangelical clergyman, would work with both Wesley and Whitefield (see p. 6).

[67]William Romaine, *An Essay on Psalmody* (London: 1775), 104.

[68]See Dewey D. Wallace Jr., *Puritans and Predestination: Grace in English Protestant Theology, 1525–1695* (Eugene, OR: Wipf and Stock, 2004).

[69]The divisions of earlier periods were distinctly present in the Restoration period, as another example of the long historical memory of the English people. Dewey Wallace writes, "Restoration England was a deeply divided society and strong currents ran against those who sought to create a more inclusive established church or allow greater religious toleration. Thus the religious divisions which had been a key factor in the political life of England before the civil war and Interregnum continued to disrupt the nation after the Restoration" (*Shapers of English Calvinism 1660–1714*, 21). See also Tim Harris, Paul Seaward and Mark Goldin, eds., *The Politics of Religion in Restoration England* (Oxford: Basil Blackwell, 1990); and Muriel C. MacClendon, Joseph P. Ward and Michael MacDonald, eds., *Protestant Identities: Religion, Society, and Self-Fashioning in Post-Restoration England* (Stanford, CA: Stanford University Press, 1999).

[70]Rack highlights the tension among Calvinists over the doctrine of justification by faith alone, arguing that the Presbyterians spoke out against the Evangelical emphasis on the doctrine. See Henry D. Rack, "Survival and Revival: John Bennet, Methodism, and the Old Dissent," in *Protestant Evangelicalism: Britain, Ireland, Germany and America c. 1750–c. 1950, Essays in Honour of W. R. Ward*, ed. Keith Robbins (New York: Basil Blackwell, 1990), 1-23. He writes, "Presbyterians, like Anglicans in the 1740s, were very distrustful of teachers of justification by faith for fear that this would mean devaluing good works, and the risk of antinomian breaches of the moral law" (3).

According to Seagrave, the "Old Divinity" began to recede in England during the reign of Charles I. He noted that "it is observable, since the Time of *Archbishop Laud*," that the clergy "have taken up a *different* Language." This language, he argued, was different from that contained in the article "Of Free-Will" in the Thirty-Nine Articles.[71] Therefore it was counter to the English Reformers. What he provides in his letter to the people of England is a history of the decline of what he considered authentic Anglicanism.

> It is observable, these *Old* Principles are still to be found amongst Dissenters, in a good Measure; which, I fear, may be Part of the Reason why the *Clergy* have drop'd the Use of them. In regard these Doctrines [of the Reformation] were the Principles and Language of the *Dissenters*, and others, who follow'd the Standard of the Parliament against King CHARLES the First; . . . yet, at the *Restoration* of King CHARLES the Second, the Resentment which took Place against the Persons of the *Dissenters*, and ran high, I apprehend, led the Church *Clergy*, not only to be angry with the *Men*, but to forsake their *Principles* too, though right and innocent in themselves, and afore-time held in common amongst all Protestants.[72]

Although correct in terms of a rising latitudinarianism after the Civil War, the above description, like the description provided more recently by Wallace, misses the Catholic or high church elements within the Church of England that not only existed before Henry VIII but remained an integral part of Anglican theology and practice in varying degrees.

RESTORATIONISTS OF A DIFFERENT SORT

Richard Hooker, in his seminal work on the English Church, the *Laws of Ecclesiastical Polity*, wrote in the sixteenth century that "it is out of doubt that the first state of things was best, that in the prime of Christian religion faith was soundest." This primitivist principle, or affection for the early church as a pristine period of Christian faith, is what motivated Hooker to argue that "therefore it must needs follow, that custom, laws, and ordinances devised since are not so good for the Church of Christ,

---

[71]Seagrave, *A Letter to the People of England*, 19.
[72]Ibid., 26-27.

but the best way is to cut off later inventions, and to reduce things unto the ancient state wherein at the first they were."[73] This attempt to return to an "ancient state" of purity marked the Augustan Age as much as it did the Reformers. The eighteenth century was an attempt to return to "a better state." In Wesley and the Evangelicals we see two views of what that ancient state might have looked like.

The Augustan Age has been described as an age of classicism. The desire to revive an ancient culture was ubiquitous both inside and outside the Church. Forsaith writes that "in art and architecture, politics and physic, society frequently looked over its shoulder to some past and primitive golden age."[74] For Forsaith, the biblicism of the Evangelical Revival was an outgrowth of this concern.

Ted Campbell, in *John Wesley and Christian Antiquity*, describes a religious context desiring to revive an age of ancient purity:

> English theologians of this period stressed the revival of "classical" early Christian practices and theology. Conservative Anglicans claimed to have revived the polity of ancient episcopalianism and the theology of the earliest ecumenical councils. Latitudinarians appealed to early Christianity for models of diversity in religious establishments.[75]

Even the Neo-Arians and the deists joined the restorationist parade and, as Campbell describes, "tried to show that the most primitive Christians either regarded Jesus as a lesser divine figure, or as a merely human teacher."[76] The restorationist impulse was pervasive.

Robert Ingram argues that Secker, archbishop of Canterbury, was at heart a restorationist reformer. His reforms, however, have been overlooked, driven by the modern assumption that reform meant progress rather than restoration. According to Ingram, Secker should be seen as

---

[73]Richard Hooker, *The Works of That Learned and Judicious Divine Mr. Richard Hooker with an Account of His Life and Death by Isaac Walton. Arranged by the Rev. John Keble MA, 7th edition revised by the Very Rev. R. W. Church and the Rev. F. Paget* (Oxford: Clarendon, 1888), 1:ii.2.

[74]Peter Forsaith, ed., *Unexampled Labours: Letters of the Revd John Fletcher to Leaders in the Evangelical Revival* (London: Epworth, 2008), 21.

[75]Ted A. Campbell, *John Wesley and Christian Antiquity: Religious Vision and Cultural Change* (Nashville: Kingswood Books, 1991), 2.

[76]Ibid.

one of the key restorationist reformers of the eighteenth century, implementing reforms of the clergy, restoring orthodoxy to a place of dominance and attempting to move the parochial system of England toward efficiency.[77] Secker placed heavy emphasis on biblical knowledge and orthodox teachings. In 1762 he delayed an ordination because the applicant could not answer questions "that the average parishioner should already know about the scriptures."[78] According to Secker, "promoting religious knowledge and practice is not only the express design of all church-government, but a matter (would God it were well considered) of great importance to the state."[79]

This restorationist impulse, pervasive as it was, was not uniform in its application. Nor was there agreement as to what historic periods should take precedence over others. Debates were had as to the definition of "primitive Christianity." Reformed, Arminian, high church, low church and others packaged the concept differently.[80] Wesley argued for the use of pre-Constantinian Christianity. The majority of Evangelicals would have been happy to use a vision of Christianity inspired by Augustine of Hippo.

Wesley's restorationist impulse ran through the high church and its commitment to the church fathers.[81] Campbell writes that Wesley "believed the earlier Christian writers to have had greater piety and holiness than later ones, and thought that for that reason God had given the earlier Christians more aid in avoiding delusions."[82] This is seen in his sermon "On Laying the Foundation of the New Chapel" (1777), in which Wesley described Methodism as "the *religion of the primitive church*, of the whole church in the purest ages," and argued that this primitive church was "clearly expressed in the small remains of Clemens Romanus, Ignatius, and Polycarp, . . . seen more at large in the writings of Tertullian,

[77]See Robert G. Ingram, *Religion, Reform and Modernity in the Eighteenth Century: Thomas Secker and the Church of England*, Studies in Modern British Religious History 17 (Woodbridge, UK: Boydell, 2007), 45.

[78]Ibid., 78-79.

[79]Thomas Secker, *Lectures on the Catechism of the Church of England; with a Discourse on Confirmation*, ed. Beilby Porteus and George Stinton (London: 1799), 7-8.

[80]Hammond, *John Wesley in America*, 20.

[81]Ibid., 13.

[82]Campbell, *John Wesley and Christian Antiquity*, 47.

Origen, Clemens Alexandrinus, and Cyprian." Even in the fourth century this purity was "found in the works of Chrysostom, Basil, Ephrem Syrus, and Macarius."[83] Apart from the omission of Irenaeus, this was Wesley's standard roster of church fathers from the purest age of the church and provides a key connection to the continuing influence of high church Anglicanism on Wesley.[84]

As a high churchman, Wesley would refer to the Anglican standards and in the next breath the church fathers.[85] Robert Cornwall describes this high church fascination with the early church fathers and the scholarship that it produced as "as a bridge between the Caroline divines of the early and mid-seventeenth century and the Oxford Movement of the nineteenth century."[86] The primitive church was the "authoritative interpreter of scripture, the final arbitrator in doctrinal disputes, and as a model of Christian piety and discipline."[87] High churchmen looked to the early church and the early church fathers to find a truly universal pattern.

In his debate with Cambridge don Conyers Middleton, Wesley defended Christian antiquity and its necessity for understanding the Christian faith. Middleton attempted to undermine the credibility of the church fathers.[88] Wesley's strong support for the early church as arbiter came through loudly in his reply, as did his anti-Romanism.

> (1.) The Scriptures are a complete rule of faith and practice; and they are clear in all necessary points. And yet their clearness does not prove, that they need not be explained; nor their completeness, that they need not be enforced. (2.) The esteeming the writings of the first three centuries, not

---

[83] *Works* 3:586.

[84] Ibid. See n. 31.

[85] For an example, see the same sermon, *Works* 3:582, 586.

[86] Robert D. Cornwall, "The Search for the Primitive Church: The Use of Early Church Fathers in the High Church Anglican Tradition, 1680–1745," *Anglican and Episcopal History* 59, no. 3 (1990): 303.

[87] Ibid.

[88] See Conyers Middleton, *A Free Enquiry in to the Miraculous Powers, which are Supposed to have Existed in the Christian Church, from the Earliest Ages, through Several Successive Centuries. By which it is shown that we have no sufficient reason to believe, upon the authority of the Primitive Fathers, that any such powers were continued to the church after the days of the Apostles* (London: 1747).

equal with, but next to, the Scriptures, never carried any man yet into dangerous errors, nor probably ever will. But it has brought many out of dangerous errors, and particularly out of the errors of Popery.[89]

Wesley's sentiments sound very similar to those of Thomas Brett, whose work on liturgy Wesley is known to have read.[90] Brett, a high churchman of the period, wrote two books on the necessity of tradition for understanding the Scriptures, *Tradition Necessary to Explain and Interpret the Holy Scriptures* (1718) and *A Farther Proof of the Necessity of Tradition, to Explain and Interpret the Holy Scriptures* (1720). While Wesley did not agree with Brett's insistence that the Scriptures alone do not contain everything necessary to salvation, the influence of Brett comes through in Wesley's writings, as seen in his letter to Conyers Middleton.

On Monday, January 2, 1749, Wesley wrote, "I had designed to set out with a friend for Rotterdam. But being much pressed to answer Dr. Middleton's book against the Fathers, I postponed my voyage and spent almost twenty days in that unpleasant employment."[91] During that "unpleasant employment" Wesley read the work of Jean Daillé, a seventeenth-century French Protestant pastor whose treatise, written first in French and translated into English in 1651 as *A Treatise concerning the Right Use of the Fathers in the Decision of the Controversies that are at This day in Religion*, was very much like Middleton's. Daillé's treatise, according to Ward, did not encourage respect for the fathers but was congenial to much eighteenth-century opinion.[92] Having read Daillé, Wesley wrote: "I soon saw what occasion that good man had given to the enemies of God to blaspheme, and that Dr. Middleton in particular has largely used that work in order to overthrow the whole Christian system."[93]

Wesley's own *A Letter to the Reverend Doctor Conyers Middleton Occasioned by his late "Free Inquiry"* uses an arsenal of early church fathers

---

[89] *Works* (Jackson) 10:14.
[90] Special thanks to Randy Maddox for providing information on Wesley's reading lists.
[91] *Works* 20:262.
[92] Ibid., n. 15. Ward refers to C. J. Abbey and J. H. Overton's *The English Church in the Eighteenth Century* (London: 1878), 1:165.
[93] Ibid.

to combat Middleton, from Hermas to Irenaeus to Justin Martyr. His primary concern was to challenge Middleton's denial of the continuation of spiritual gifts in the postapostolic age. Middleton claimed that the continuation of such gifts would give credence to Roman Catholics. What the letter provides is a glimpse into Wesley's attachment to liturgical practices of a high church bent.

Based on early church practice, Wesley argued for the high church custom of mixing water with the wine at the sacrament.[94] He also insisted on the benefits of prayers for the dead, although in an attempt to separate himself from the Roman doctrine of purgatory he claimed that "it is far from certain that, 'the purpose of this was to procure relief and refreshment to the departed souls in some intermediate state of expiatory pains;' or that 'this was the general opinion of those times.'"[95] He argued that by means of prayers for the dead, "God would shortly accomplish the number of his elect and hasten his kingdom," and anointing the sick with oil "you will not easily prove to be any corruptions at all."[96] Even in Wesley's most "Protestant" period his high church views are evident.

One high churchman with whom Wesley found greater affinity was William Beveridge, bishop of St. Asaph and a student of the early church. Beveridge "grounded his doctrinal formulations in scripture, 'consonant with right reason' and confirmed by belief and practice of the primitive church."[97] His theology, however, was nuanced. In his sermon "Christ's Resurrection the Cause of Our Justification," Beveridge sounded liked a good Calvinist, arguing that no one could "merit or deserve to be accounted righteous before God" and rejecting any notion that salvation is found in good works. Beveridge argued, "we are accounted righteous before God, not for our own works or deservings; and it is as contrary to the plain and express words of scripture, where it is said once and again,

---

[94] *Works* (Jackson) 10:8-9.
[95] Ibid., 9.
[96] Ibid., 10.
[97] See William Beveridge, *Ecclesia Anglilcana Ecclesia Catholic; or the Doctrine of the Church of England Consonant to Scripture, Reason, and the Fathers in a Discourse upon the Thirty-Nine Articles Agreed upon in the Convocation Held at London MDLXII* (Oxford: Oxford University Press, 1847).

by the works of the law there shall no flesh be justified."[98] Upon a cursory reading, it is easy to place Beveridge within the Reformed Anglicanism of the Evangelicals. Yet, what Beveridge had written was not a treatise on justification by faith alone but a treatise against the ancient heresy of Pelagianism. Similarly, Wesley would provide in his soteriology, or Way of Salvation, a way to similarly dodge the extremes of faith alone or works-righteousness much like Beveridge.

Wesley's debates with Evangelicals over predestination and perfectionism show his debt to the high churchmen of the late seventeenth and early eighteenth centuries. There are direct connections between his arguments against predestination in the eighteenth century and those of the English "Arminians" of the early seventeenth. Wesley's avowal that the doctrine of reprobation cannot be separated from predestination, or supported by Scripture and tradition, along with insistence that the doctrine of predestination makes God into a tyrant, has direct correlations to his seventeenth-century predecessors.

Wallace describes the increase of "a more moderate theology of grace than that enshrined in Reformed scholasticism" arising at the end of the sixteenth century in England "partly under revived humanist impulses emanating from the Continent and partly from a renewed patristic interest."[99] This more moderate theology was simply a part of the eventual unraveling of Reformed hegemony over the Church of England and would include such leaders as Lancelot Andrewes and John Donne. Andrews and Donne, along with Hooker, represent for Wallace a new "emerging 'Anglican' school of theology." Under Charles I and Laud, this moderate Anglican school would turn into outright opposition to Calvinism.

There are similarities between Wesley's views and this Arminian assault. Wesley's "responsible grace" corresponds with the theology of Richard Montague (whom Charles I made bishop of Chichester) in *A Gag for the New Gospell? No: A New Gagg for an Old Goose* (1624). Philip

---

[98]William Beveridge, "Christ's Resurrection the Cause of our Justification," sermon LXXIV in *The Works of the Right Reverend Father in God, Dr. William Beveridge, . . . Containing [sic] All His Sermons, as Well [as] Those Publish'd by Himself* (London: 1729), 1:615.

[99]Wallace, *Puritans and Predestination*, 72.

Benedict argues that the publication of Montague's treatise during the reign of James I "implies that the balance may have already have been tipping toward the Laudians by the last years of James's reign."[100]

While Reformed Anglicans attempted to label their opponents as followers of Arminius, Benedict argues that these opponents of predestination, who by the turn of the seventeenth century included Richard Neile, Lancelot Andrewes, John Overall, John Buckridge, John Cosin and William Laud, were influenced more by native antipredestinarians such as Peter Baro.[101] These native antipredestinarians, representing a Catholic vision of the Reformation or a rejection of it, provide continuity for a high church stream within Anglicanism. It is well known that Bishops Stephen Gardiner, Cuthbert Tunstall and Edmund Bonner welcomed the reign of Mary because they thought that the Reformation had gone too far.[102]

Archbishop Laud declared that the "doctrine of universal atonement was the 'constant doctrine of the Catholic Church in all ages, and no error of Arminius,'" adding that the idea that "God reprobated from eternity the greater part of mankind" was an "opinion my very soul abominates."[103] Likewise, Thomas Jackson, an Oxford theologian connected with Laud, declared his belief in the possibility of falling from grace and referred to the doctrine of reprobation as "an idolatrous and blasphemous imagination," asserting that Christ died for all.[104]

Throughout his life Wesley would make claims identical to those of Laud and Jackson. In his "Thoughts Concerning Gospel Ministers," Wesley wrote:

> Let it be particularly observed, if the gospel be "glad tidings of great salvation which shall be unto all people," then those only are, in the full sense,

---

[100]Philip Benedict, *Christ's Churches Purely Reformed: A Social History of Calvinism* (New Haven, CT: Yale University Press, 2002), 388.

[101]Ibid., 386.

[102]See Lacey Baldwin Smith, *Tudor Prelates and Politics, 1536–1558* (Princeton, NJ: Princeton University Press, 1953).

[103]William Laud, *The History of the Troubles and Tryall of the Most Reverend Father in God and Blessed Martyr, William Laud, Lord Arch-Bishop of Canterbury, Wrote by Himself During His Imprisonment in the Tower; to Which Is Prefixed the Diary of His Own Life* (London[?]: 1694), 14.

[104]Wallace, *Puritans and Predestination*, 91. See Thomas Jackson's *Commentaries on the Apostles' Creed* (London[?]: 1627).

Gospel Ministers who proclaim the "great salvation;" that is, salvation from all (both inward and outward) sin, into "all the mind that was in Christ Jesus;" and likewise proclaim offers of this salvation to every child of man. This honourable title is therefore vilely prostituted, when it is given to any but those who testify "that God willeth all men to be saved," and "to be perfect as their Father which is in heaven is perfect."[105]

Wesley would never back down from his belief in the universal reach of God's saving work. Neither would he accept that belief in predestination could be separated from reprobation. He claimed that "if you narrowly observe, unconditional election cannot appear without the cloven foot of reprobation."[106]

Wesley argued vehemently in *Predestination Calmly Considered* (1752) that to believe in predestination is to believe in reprobation, that one ensures the other and that they stand or fall based on the acceptance of both. He was writing to "my brethren," an unnamed group who have an uncanny resemblance to many of the Evangelical Anglicans, such as John Newton, who in an attempt to describe their evangelical conversions used the language of election because it best fit their understanding of the impotence they felt in the face of converting grace.[107]

In Wesley's view, the Scriptures did not support the doctrine of reprobation and could be used to refute the doctrine with a cursory reading of the biblical text. He provided a list of biblical references that he claimed countered the understanding of an eternal divine decree that designated the saved and the damned, and wrote that "you are sensible, these are but a very small part of the scriptures which might be brought on each of these heads. But they are enough; and they require no comment: Taken in their plain, easy, and obvious sense, they abundantly prove, that there is not, cannot be, any such thing as unconditional reprobation."[108]

In an attempt to undermine the doctrine of predestination, Wesley not only chose a target that was opprobrious to the broader public but

---

[105] *Works* (Jackson) 10:456.
[106] Ibid., 10:209.
[107] Hindmarsh, *John Newton and the English Evangelical Tradition*, 160.
[108] Ibid., 215-16.

at the same time steered his argument away from a direct attack on Evangelicals. It is not surprising, however, to see the Oxford logician challenge what he saw as the weakest link in a Calvinist-inspired chain in order to overthrow the doctrine of predestination. He appears to have little concern whether his opponents were full Calvinists or moderate ones with "warmed hearts" much like his own. At the center of Wesley's argument was his understanding of God. Hempton notes, "Wesley could not conceive of a God who had determined everything in advance or of human spirituality that was mere acquiescence."[109] The doctrine of predestination simply countered everything that Wesley knew about God. Wesley, it appears, had been schooled well in the theology of the Caroline divines.

DIVERGENT VISIONS

At the heart of the divide between Wesley and the Evangelicals was a vision for the restoration of "vital religion" in the Church of England, a divergence of theological and historical outlook. The attempt on the part of the Evangelicals to revive the "Old Divinity" did not sit well with the strange amalgamation of high churchmanship and Pietism found in Wesley. The Calvinist controversy of the 1770s would explode on the scene after the publication of Wesley's 1770 Conference Minutes, but this explosion took place within an already divided revival. The arguments of the 1770s had already been heard as early as the 1730s. Whitefield's death just before the publication of Wesley's Minutes exacerbated the situation, as Wesley's friendship with Whitefield had often smoothed over theological spats in the past. The Calvinist controversy took place well after the Evangelical Anglicans had begun to form themselves into a distinctly regular element within the Church. Issues of polity had already separated these two groups.

Theologically, what these two groups represented at a fundamental level were divergent streams within the Church of England itself. The Evangelicals, as a group, represented a Reformed vision of Christianity

---

[109]Hempton, *Methodism*, 57.

stemming back to the Puritans and the English Reformers, while Wesley represented a restorationist vision based on the church fathers as read through high church Anglicanism and the Caroline divines. These visions provided the lenses through which each came to understand the very heart of the revival itself, the definition of conversion. In the next century these visions would continue to dominate the Church of England. Through English missionary efforts, these divergent visions would expand well beyond the British Isles.

CONCLUSION

Constrained to Deviate

The complexities of Wesley's relationship with Evangelical Anglicans are many. The relationship of this one maverick Anglican with a whole host of Evangelicals each attempting to find his way in the eighteenth-century Church was bound to be multifaceted. There is not one particular reason why Wesley and his Evangelical colleagues did not unite their work, nor one reason why they silently diverge after 1770. No one issue, whether the use of lay preachers, political and ecclesiastical pressure, theological controversy or parochial boundaries, provides the key to answering this question. They are all necessary to see the broader picture of a complex relationship that led to division.[1] With differing trajectories, both theological and practical, against the backdrop of ecclesiastical and political pressure, a united evangelical work faced numerous hardships that it simply could not overcome.

Regardless of previous setbacks to unite the Evangelical clergy, Wesley did not lose hope in a unified Evangelical work until the end of the 1760s. For that reason, the focus of this study culminates at 1770. Wesley's last push toward union began early in the decade, in 1764, with a letter that

---

[1]For a description of the commitment to unity among many leaders of the revival, see James L. Schwenk, *Catholic Spirit: Wesley, Whitefield, and the Quest for Evangelical Unity in Eighteenth-Century British Methodism*, Pietism and Wesleyan Studies 26 (Lanham, MD: Scarecrow, 2008). Schwenk steers clear of many of the hot-button theological issues known to have caused divergence among these leaders.

he sent to "forty or fifty clergymen" outlining a united Evangelical effort. Howell Harris had apparently spearheaded the effort the year before. Baker notes that Harris "spent the better part of three months touring England 'striving for universal union and for the [Evangelical] clergy to meeting each other.'"[2]

Wesley met in spring 1764 with Evangelical Richard Conyers of Helmsley and with Lady Huntingdon to discuss his dream of a union, and despite the insistence of Conyers that his efforts to unite the clergy were impractical, Wesley took up the charge with renewed energy.[3] After reading the words of Thomas á Kempis—which in 1735 he had translated, "Wait upon the Lord, do manfully, be of good courage, do not despair, do not fly, but with constancy expose both *body* and *soul* for the glory of God"—he was convinced he was called to bring about an Evangelical union.[4]

The list of the clergy Wesley addressed included a "who's who" of the Evangelical clergy.[5] It is not clear, however, that the letter was sent to all of them at the same time. Telford's edition of the *Letters* indicates that Newton may not have received his copy until 1766.[6] Writing from Scarborough, Wesley noted in his journal entry for April 19, 1764, "I wrote a letter today, which after some time I sent to forty or fifty clergymen." He provided not only the preface to the letter but the letter he had written and three responses to his proposal when he published the journal extract four years later.[7]

Wesley proposed a loose confederation of Evangelicals agreeing to meet together for mutual benefit. At its core, it was a plea to end intraevangelical fighting. He desired the clergy to unite in the face of

[2]Frank Baker, *John Wesley and the Church of England* (Nashville: Abingdon, 1970), 189-90.
[3]See *Works* 21:458. Wesley mentions Conyers's hesitancy in his letter to the clergy. He describes Conyers as "objecting the impossibility of ever effecting such a union."
[4]Ibid.
[5]The list of clergy is provided in Curnock's edition of the *Journal* and supplemented in Ward and Heitzenrater's volumes of the *Journal and Diaries* in the bicentennial edition of the *Works*. Nehemiah Curnock, ed., *The Journal of the Rev. John Wesley, Standard Edition, 8 Volumes* (London: Epworth, 1905–1916).
[6]See *Letters* (Telford) 4:236n1 (April 19, 1764).
[7]*Works* 21:454.

rising ecclesiastical challenges to "*speak* respectfully, honourably, kind of each other; *defend* each other's character; speak all the good we can of each other; recommend each other where we have influence" and, most controversially, to "help the other on in his work and *enlarge* his influence by all the honest means he can."[8] It appears from the proposal that Wesley himself would be the foundation on which the union would be secured. This aspect by itself would have discouraged the participation of most of the regular clergy. The Methodists under Wesley's care had caused great headaches for those wishing to work within the regular practices of the established Church. The Methodists were suspected of schismatic tendencies, the lay preachers roamed unwelcomed in Evangelical parishes, and Walker's admonition to "be very civil to the Methodists, but have nothing to do with them" seemed, as Baker notes, the typical attitude of most of the Evangelical clergy.[9]

Wesley's letter, originally sent to Lord Dartmouth, begins with a historical sketch of the revival that places him and his brother at its center. He wrote, "Some years since, God began a great work in England, but the labourers were few. At first those few were of one heart, but it was not so long. First one fell off, then another, and another, till not two of us were left together in the work beside my brother and me."[10] This history of the revival, much like the history he provided in his sermon "On Laying the Foundations" and in his letter to the father of William Morgan at the very beginning of the movement, is distinctly and yet surprisingly centered on the work of Wesleyan Methodism. Wesley appears entirely oblivious to the Evangelical fraternity that through common connections, clergy associations and shared controversy had grown organically to unite the Evangelicals and give them a network of support within the Church.

Wesley continued the letter by stating that "as labourers increased, disunion increased," such that "at length those who are not only brethren

---

[8]Ibid., 21:457.
[9]Baker, *John Wesley and the Church of England*, 189.
[10]*Works* 21:456.

in Christ, but fellow-labourers in his gospel, had no more connection or fellowship with each other than Protestants have with Papists."[11] He asks, "But ought this to be?" It should be noted that Wesley made this claim just months before the 1764 conference in Bristol, discussed in a previous chapter, where many Evangelicals came to discuss the use and purpose of lay preachers and to ask Wesley to remove them from their parishes.[12] His insistence that Evangelical cooperation had waned may indicate the impact that the deaths of both Walker and Grimshaw had made on him, together with his brother's continued withdrawal from the work of the Methodist connexion.

Wesley names thirty-six of the likely recipients of the proposal within the letter itself. His list includes both regular and irregular clergy, although it is dominated by regular clergymen. The list includes Evangelicals of various theological stripes. Wesley includes Perronet and Sellon, with whom he cooperated on a regular basis, as well as Adam and Romaine, who were known to have reservations about Methodism and its trajectory. What Wesley outlines are the three doctrines that he claims should unite the Evangelicals: original sin, justification by faith and holiness of heart and life, to which he adds "provided their life be answerable to their doctrine."[13]

The heart of the letter describes what Wesley's proposed Evangelical union would look like:

> "But *what union* would you desire among these?" Not an union in *opinions*. They might agree or disagree touching absolute decrees on the one hand and perfection on the other. Not an union in *expressions*. These may still speak of the "imputed righteousness," and those of the "merits" of Christ. Not an union with regard to *outward order*. Some may still remain *quite regular* and *partly irregular*. But these things being as they are, as each is persuaded in his own mind, is it not a most desirable thing. . . . This is the *union* which I have long sought after.[14]

---

[11]Ibid.
[12]See chapter six.
[13]*Works* 21:456.
[14]Ibid., 21:457.

Wesley had desired this unification of the Evangelical clergy for years. In a letter to Samuel Furley in May 1762, Wesley not only discussed Venn's book "concerning gospel ministers" but also declared that he thought it "high imprudence for any of those who preach the essential gospel truths to stand aloof from each other," adding that "there ought to be the most cordial and avowed union between them."[15] He admits that the shyness had never been on his part, and this was true. Although some Evangelicals, such as Haweis and Romaine, met with Wesley to discuss union earlier, the Evangelicals were united by this time in their local clerical associations, or through Lady Huntingdon and Lord Dartmouth. They were increasingly united in their passion to serve faithfully their respective parishes.

The power that both Huntingdon and Dartmouth yielded to influence nervous bishops to ordain Evangelicals or to secure parish incumbencies for unemployed "gospel ministers" made them essential to the work of the early revival within the Church and a unifying force at least until Huntingdon herself dissented. As a sign of their loyalty to the Church, the Evangelicals connected to Huntingdon, except for a very few, remained in the parish structure of the Church when she left. Apart from Wesley, it was Lady Huntingdon who attempted a more formal union of those involved in the revival. As early as 1742 Whitefield approached the countess about the possibility of backing a proposal to unify the Calvinist and Wesleyan arms of the revival.[16] She almost pulled off a "great coup," as Fletcher noted in a letter to Charles Wesley, for attempting to unite the Evangelical clergy after the disastrous 1764 conference of the Wesleyan Methodists.[17]

Lord Dartmouth, as a powerful politician under George III and secretary of state for the American Department, was instrumental in "securing ordination and important appointments for the early Evangelical clergy."[18] Davies notes that it was through Lord Dartmouth's efforts that

---

[15]Ibid., 27:293-95 (Wesley to Samuel Furley, May 21, 1762).
[16]See Faith Cook, *Selina, Countess of Huntingdon* (Carlisle, UK: Banner of Trust, 2001), 73–74.
[17]Peter Forsaith, ed., *Unexampled Labours: Letters of the Revd John Fletcher to Leaders in the Evangelical Revival* (London: Epworth, 2008), 197 (Fletcher to Charles Wesley, Aug. 22, 1764).
[18]See G. C. B. Davies, *The Early Cornish Evangelicals 1735–60: A Study of Walker of Truro and Others*

"John Newton was ordained, Henry Venn went to Huddersfield, Robinson to Leicester, Stillingfleet to Hotham, and later Newton to Olney."[19]

Richard Conyers's caution to Wesley of the impractical nature of his proposal was more prophetic than Wesley wanted to admit. Yet the issues that divided Wesley and the Evangelicals were explicitly named in the letter. Wesley attempted to brush over issues of regularity and irregularity, yet these issues—"opinions," "expressions" and "outward order"— were at the heart of Evangelical reluctance to be associated with Wesley and his movement. With their own place in the Church so often questioned, it is surprising that they continued to entertain his proposal for union at all. Wesley, as one of the leading irregular figures of the revival and head of an expanding network of societies, was too much of a liability for the already marginalized Evangelicals to form such a public bond. His waning friendship with Venn and the subsequent dissolution of their Huddersfield agreement was likely fresh on the minds of many Evangelicals, as was the continuing struggle to train and ordain Evangelicals for the work within the Church. If the Evangelicals can be said to have united behind any clergyman, they would have seen themselves united by clergy such as Walker, Newton and finally Charles Simeon.

By the end of the decade, as described earlier, the political force of rising Tory influence under George III, the reaction against dissent and irregularity caused by the Feather's Tavern petition, and the very public expulsion of six Methodists from Oxford for irregular activity would pressure the Evangelicals to prove their loyalty to the establishment. Fletcher, a keen observer of the political scene, although not a native Englishman, wrote to Charles Wesley just one month after the ascension of George III: "I suppose by the proclamation which I have just seen in the Gazette that our young King will really deserve the title of Josiah! What happiness for the nation even though it seems an accidental misfortune for the M[ethodists]!"[20]

(London: SPCK, 1951), 178; and G. R. Balleine, *A History of the Evangelical Party in the Church of England* (London: Longmans, Green, 1909), 58. Dartmouth's seventh son, Edward Legge, would be made bishop of Oxford in 1816.

[19]Ibid.

[20]Forsaith, *Unexampled Labours*, 122 (Fletcher to Charles Wesley, Nov. 7, 1760).

The Evangelicals would continue their efforts to be seen as a regular part of the Church and her parochial system. Although most of them in this early period of the revival would never ascend the ladder of ecclesiastical preferment, the Evangelicals of this period would carve out niches that in the next century would serve as strongholds of an Evangelical party. By the first part of the next century, the Evangelicals would continue in their loyalty to the Church such that, as Bebbington notes, they would become loyal to the institution itself.[21]

Against the rising tides of regularity, loyalty and a vision of evangelicalism as a movement for the renewal of the Church through its own structures, Wesley's vision of renewal through irregularity and an ecclesial substructure became less convincing. His movement, centered so strongly on personality, was thought to reside on the cusp of dissent. Many, such as Adam, believed that it already had.

The three responses that Wesley received to his letter seeking an evangelical union were from Richard Hart, vicar of St. George's, Bristol; Walter Sellon of Breedon on the Hill, Leicestershire; and Vincent Perronet of Shoreham. Hart, the vicar of an Evangelical parish that had been created to minister to the coal miners of Kingswood, sought the unity of evangelical groups throughout his ministry.[22] Both Sellon and Perronet worked closely with the Wesley brothers, and their responses reflect that personal connection. Two of Perronet's sons served as lay itinerant ministers within Wesley's connexion. None of the leading figures of the revival within the Church responded in writing to Wesley's proposal, and neither do we have evidence that they approached him in person to discuss it.

As the decade wore on and responses to Wesley's overtures toward union met a silent response, his own attitude toward the Evangelicals began to sour. Throughout the period he tried to coax Fletcher out of his Madeley parish, arguing that Fletcher would be more effective in irregularity. Wesley never seems to have felt that the parish system provided a

---

[21]David Bebbington, *Evangelicalism in Modern Britain: A History from the 1730s to the 1980s* (London: Unwin Hyman, 1989), 97.

[22]See *DEB* 1:527.

proper context in which to fully promote the gospel. In a letter to Adam
in the fall of 1755, Wesley argued that only one regular Evangelical had
been successful working in the parish system of the Church, Samuel
Walker. He wrote that he knew of Piers, Perronet, Manning "and several
other regular clergymen who do preach the genuine gospel, but to no
effect at all."[23] Expecting pushback on his assertion, he wrote: "If it be
said, 'Has not Mr. Grimshaw and Mr. Baddeley?' No, not one, till they
were *irregular*; till both the one and other formed irregular societies, and
took in laymen to assist them. Can there be a stronger proof that God is
pleased with *irregular* even more than with *regular* preaching?"[24] Wesley
never seemed to stray from this negative view of the efficacy of a regular
ministry. His reaction in 1767 to the suggestion that the real work of the
revival was being done by the "awakened clergy" is significant. It shows
a growing impatience for regular Evangelicalism. He wrote to Evangelical Joseph Townsend: "How many has any one of them convinced or
converted since Whitsuntide I fear, when we come to particulars, there
will be small room to boast. If you put things on this issue, 'Whose word
does God now bless?' the matter will soon be determined."[25]

By 1768 Wesley's impatience for Evangelical regularity was seen in his
sardonic letter to Thomas Adam, as well as another that same year to
Fletcher.[26] In his letter to Fletcher he nearly scolds him for his connections to Evangelicals Madan, Romaine and Whitefield, and declares that
"the conversing with these I have rarely found to be profitable to my soul.
Rather it has damped my desires, it has cooled my resolutions, and I have
commonly left them with a dry, dissipated spirit." Wesley was losing patience with those whom he designated "the genteel Methodists."[27] Finally, at the conference of 1769, he had given up on his plans for an

---

[23] *Works* 26:610-11 (Wesley to Thomas Adam, Oct. 31, 1755). Baker notes that Manning had attended
conferences in both 1747 and 1748 (611n14).

[24] Ibid., 611.

[25] *Letters* (Telford) 5:59 (Wesley to Joseph Townsend, Aug. 1-3, 1767). Ironically, Townsend was a
very effective Anglican clergyman in Pewsey, Wiltshire, where he served from 1764 until his
death in 1816.

[26] For the letter to Adam, see *Letters* (Telford) 5:97-99 (July 19, 1768); for Fletcher, 5:82-85 (March
20, 1768).

[27] *Letters* (Telford) 5:83 (Wesley to John Fletcher, March 20, 1768).

evangelical union. In an address to the Methodist conference, he called the Evangelicals a "rope of sand" and declared, "I can do no more."[28] His attention turned from the Evangelical clergymen to the continuing work of his lay preachers and the connexion that he had built. From that point on his focus would not waver.

The history of evangelicalism in the latter part of the eighteenth century can be seen as a period of institutional adjustment and alignment. By 1770 the Evangelical clergy and John Wesley's Methodism had diverged. The controversies of the 1770s simply highlight the theological divides of an already divided group. With Huntingdon's departure for dissent in 1779, the Evangelicals remained within the Church as the arbiters of the revival with a renewed emphasis on regularity. Wesley's ordinations for America in 1784 represented the next logical step in his own gradual move from conventional Anglican practice. The year 1770 does not represent a date after which Wesley and Evangelical Anglicans cease to speak; it represents a point after which it is clear that the Evangelicals and the Wesleyan Methodists have taken different paths. The Evangelicals would go on to become one of the strongest parties within the Church of England. Methodism after the death of the Wesleys became a worldwide movement.

The Evangelical Anglicans were an untamable group that Wesley tried to convert to his revivalistic vision, and, as with other groups that he attempted to amalgamate to Methodism, his attempt met varied success for various reasons. What sets the Evangelical Anglicans apart from these other groups, which would have included the local preachers, dissenters, Moravians and others, is the fact that the Evangelical Anglicans served as Wesley's closest link to the broader Church of England that he claimed to love so much. It is within this group, as an ordained clergyman of the Church of England, that Wesley rightly belonged. The gradual loss of contact with the Evangelicals, with all of its various nuances, can be seen as the beginning of Wesleyan Methodism's parting from the Church it had been designed to reform.

---

[28] *Works* 10:377.

APPENDIX

Evangelical Anglican Clergy in the Church of England During the Life of John Wesley (1703–1791)

Name of Clergy	Incumbency/Appointment	Active Dates During Period
Abdy, William Jarvis (1755–1823)	Staines, Middlesex, curate St. John's Horsley Down, Southwark	1778–1780 1782–
Adam, Thomas (1701–1784)	Wintringham, Lincolnshire	1724–1784
Andrews, John (ca. 1730–?)	Stinchcombe, Glouchestershire Marden, Kent	1767–
Atkinson, Christopher	Thorp Arch, Yorkshire	1749–1774
Atkinson, Miles (1741–1811)	Leeds Parish Church Walton-on-the-Hill, Lancashire Kippax Leek	1764–1767 1780–1788 1783– 1785–
Baddelley, George	Markfield, Leicestershire, rector	
Baddeley, John (1706–1764)	Hayfield, Derbyshire, rector	1748–1764
Barnard, Thomas[1] (d. 1750)	Leeds Grammar School	1712–1750
Bassett, Christopher (d. 1784)	St. Anne's, Blackfriars, London, curate[2] St. Fagan's near Cardiff, Wales[3]	1775–1778 1778–1784
Bateman, Richard Thomas[4] (1712–1760)	Lylsfrau, Dyfed (then Pembrokeshire) St. Bartholomew the Great, London	

---

[1]"Barnard's evangelical credentials are questioned by some historians. It is clear that he became a close friend of Lady Elizabeth Hastings and assisted her in her charitable work. Her nephew, George Hastings, became his pupil and boarded with him. George's mother, Lady Hastings, consulted Barnard about her spiritual well-being, and he played an important part in her conversion to Methodism in July 1739. He wrote several long letters of advice to her. Despite this, when he came to write his *Historical Character of . . . Lady Elizabeth Hastings* in 1742 he attacks the Methodists and denied that she had ever been one. His change of heart can possibly be attributed to the marriage of Benj. Ingham and Lady Margaret Hastings, which was unpopular in Yorkshire" (*DEB* 60).

[2]Curate to William Romaine in London.

[3]"Here he established a Welsh Methodist meeting house, and itinerated with the Methodists throughout Wales. These activities caused him to be passed over for the vicarage of Cardiff, even though it was in the patronage of his father's employers" (*DEB* 66).

[4]Attended Oxford with John Wesley, Charles Wesley and George Whitefield.

Name of Clergy	Incumbency/Appointment	Active Dates During Period
Bayley, Cornelius (1751–1812)	Madeley, curate[5] Deptford, curate[6] St. James's, Manchester	1787–
Beale, Thomas	Pershore, Worcestershire	
Bennet, John (1715–1759)	North Tamerton, Cornwall Tresmere, Cornwall Laneast, Cornwall	1731–1750 1731–1750 1731–1750
Bentley, Roger[7] (c. 1734–1795)	St. Giles, Camberwell in Surrey, vicar	1769–1790
Berridge, John[8] (1716–1793)	Stapleford, curate Everton	1749–1755 1758–1793
Biddulph, Thomas (1735–1790)	Collwall, Herefordhsire, curate Worcester Bengeworth, incumbent Padstown, Cornwall	1760– –1770 1769–1770 1770–1790
Biddulph, Thomas Tregenna[9] (1763–1838)	Padstow, curate Ditcheat St. Mary-le-Port Wansborough (Wiltshire) St. Mary-le-Port	1785– 1786 1787 1788 1789
Bliss, Thomas R. (1739–1802)	Broadwoodwidger, Devon, curate[10] Ashford and Yarnscomb, vicar	1760–1766 1770–
Bridges, Nathaniel (1750–1834)	Magdalen College, Oxford, fellow Toot Bladen, Oxford, vicar[11] North Moreton, Berkshire Wadenhoe, Northamptonshire Orlingbury, Northamptonshire	1775– 1778 1783– 1783–
Broughton, Thomas[12] (1712–1777)	SPCK, secretary Wotton, Surrey All Hallows, Lombard St., London	1743–1777 1752–1777 1755–1777
Brown, James[13] (1730–1791)	Bradford-upon-Avon, curate Bristol Grammar School St. Nicholas, lecturer Westharptree, Somerset, rector Portishead, rector Kinston near Taunton Chaplain to the Duke of Athol	1752–1759 1759–1763 1763–1765 1761– 1764/5 1764/5 1771–

[5]Curate to John Fletcher.

[6]Curate to Richard Conyers.

[7]"Bentley was ordained 20 September 1760 in York. John Thornton, a wealthy friend of early Methodists and evangelicals, attempted to find livings for several of Bentley's contemporaries. Thornton first attempted to place Bentley in the parish of Cottingham near Hull, in 1767. The Bishop of Chester, patron of the living, wrote to the Archbishop of York, enquiring whether there was 'anything of a methodistical cast' about Bentley. The bishop was anxious not to present 'an improper' person under which the category of 'methodistical' clergy evidently fell. Bentley did not get the living" (*DEB* 85).

[8]Evangelical conversion in 1757. Began to itinerate two years later.

[9]Educated at Truro under George Conon.

[10]Curate to William Grimshaw.

[11]"Between 1775 and 1783, Bridges was Oxford's most influential evangelical" (*DEB* 139).

[12]Oxford Methodist.

[13]Leading evangelical among Bristol and Somerset Anglican clergy.

Name of Clergy	Incumbency/Appointment	Active Dates During Period
Browne, Moses (1704–1787)	Weston Favell, curate Olney	1753–1764
Buckley, Edward (1743–1783)	Kippax and Hunslet, curate[14] Kippax, vicar[15]	1767–1770 1770–83
Burnett, George (1734–1793)	Padstow, curate Huddersfield, curate[16] Slaithwaite, perpetual curate Elland, vicar[17]	1759 1759–1761 1761–
Cadogan, William Bromley (1751–1797)	St. Giles, Reading[18] St. Luke's, Chelsea	1771– 1775–
Cecil, Richard (1748–1810)	St. Thomas's and All Saints Lewes St. John's Bedford Row, London Held lectureships at: Orange Street, Leicester Friells, Long Acres, St. Margaret's Lothburg and Christ Church, Spitalfields	1777– 1797/98 1780–
Chaplainman, Walter[19] (1711–1791)	Master of St John's Hospital, Bath Bristol Cathedral, canon Bradford-upon-Avon, Wiltshire	1735–1745 1745–1754 1754–1791
Clark, Thomas	Chesham Bois, Buckinghamshire	1766–1793
Coetlogon, Charles Edward de (1746–1820)	Marden, Kent, curate Lock Hospital Chaplain, assistant[20] Lord Mayor's chaplain	1770–1772 1772–1789 1789
Colley, Benjamin (?–1767)		
Collins, Brian Bury[21] (1754–1807)	Christ Church, Macclesfield, curate	1781–1782
Conon, George[22] (1698–1775)	Truro Grammar School	1728–1775

[14]Was nominated as curate by Henry Crooke.

[15]Helped to provide a meetinghouse for the Methodists at Pontefract.

[16]Curate to Henry Venn.

[17]"In his vicarage the EIS was formed in 1777 to raise funds for the education of evangelical candidates for the ministry" (*DEB* 171).

[18]Fired his evangelical curate at Reading, John Hallward, before his conversion. Later had Erasmus Middleton, one of the six "Methodists" kicked out of Oxford in 1768, as his curate.

[19]Oxford Methodist.

[20]Assistant to Martin Madan.

[21]"A number of bishops refused him orders because of his field-preaching for John Wesley, but he was eventually accepted and became curate to David Simpson at Christ Church. . . . He continued, however, to exercise an itinerant ministry for both Wesley and Lady Huntingdon, a work in which he could more freely indulge after inheriting the estate of his uncle, Thomas Irwin Bury at Blankney (Lincolnshire) whose name he then assumed." *Proceedings of the Wesley Historical Society* 9.2 (1913): 25-35. See also Bury's *An Address to the Higher Ranks of People in the Parish of St. Mary, Hull* (1778).

[22]Instrumental in the conversion of Samuel Walker. George Burnett was his assistant at one point and Thomas Haweis his pupil.

Name of Clergy	Incumbency/Appointment	Active Dates During Period
Conyers, Richard[23] (1725–1786)	Kirby Misperton, curate Helmsley, rector Kirby Misperton, rector Deptford	1745–1750 1756–1762 1763–1768 1785–1786
Cooper, Edward (b. 1739)	Bengeworth, perpetual curate	
Coulthurst, Henry William[24] (1753–1817)	St. Sepulchre's, Cambridge Yelling[25] Halifax	1782–1790 1784 1790–
Creighton, James (1739–1819)	Dublin Cathedral, curate Swanlimbar London with Wesley	1765–1769 1769–1783 1783–
Crooke, Henry[26] (1708–1770)	Huddlesfield, Kirk Sandal and Kippax, curate Hunslit, rector	1735–1745 1740–1770
Crosse, John[27] (1739–1816)	Wiltshire, curate Lock Hospital, chaplain Chapleries of Todmorden, Halifax, minister Whitechapel, Leeds, minister Bradford, Vicar	1762–1765 1762–1765 1768– 1774– 1784–
Crouch, Isaac[28] (1756–1835)	St. Martin's, Worcester, curate[29] Winkfield, Wiltshire, curate Billericay, Essex, curate Chiselhampton and Stadhampton, Oxfordshire, curate	1778–1779 1779–1781 1781/3 1783–
Crowther, Samuel		
Cuthbert, Edward[30] (1746–1803)	Wolingworth, Suffold, curate Slifford, Essex Longacre Chapel, London, joint-minister	1768– 1772–1784 1780–
Davies, Edward	Bengeworth, Worcestershire Coychurch Batheaston, curate	1765/1767[31]

---

[23]Friend of Venn, Madan and Wesley. His funeral sermon was given by Thomas Scott.

[24]Came to know Charles Simeon and was a member of the Elland Society.

[25]Served with Henry Venn.

[26]"He met John Wesley in 1755, and both he and Charles Wesley preached for Crook. John preached for Crook on July 30, 1769. Crook, however, always saw the importance of church order and objected to the increasing exlusiveness of Methodist connexions and to the Wesley's encouragement of lay preachers" (*DEB* 271).

[27]See *Memoir of Rev. John Crosse* (London: 1844). Crosse considered leaving the Church of England to join Wesley because of opposition to his ministry within the Church.

[28]"Crouch was appointed (by Principal Dixon, who was already inclined to countenance evangelicals), vice-principal and bursar at St. Edmund Hall 1783. From 1783 to 1797 he served as curate to Dr. J.W. Peers (another evangelical), at Chiselhampton and Stadhampton, Oxfordshire, as chaplain of Merton College 1796–1817, and as a city lecturer, St. Martin's Carfax, Oxford from 1805" (*DEB* 275).

[29]Curate to James Stillingfleet.

[30]One of the founders of the Christian Missionary Society.

[31]A letter from John Fletcher to Charles Wesley indicated that Davies was at Bengeworth in 1765; however, the register at Bengeworth does not include his name until 1767. See Peter Forsaith, ed., *Unexampled Labours: Letters of the Revd John Fletcher to Leaders in the Evangelical Revival*

Name of Clergy	Incumbency/Appointment	Active Dates During Period
Davy, William (1743–1826)	Moretonhampstread, curate Drewsteighton, curate	1760s? 1785–
De Courcy, Richard (1743–1803)	Loughrea, curate Shawbury, Shropshire, curate Chaplain to Lady Glenorchy Crown living of St. Alkmund, Shrewsbury	1768 1771 1770 1774–
Dickenson, Peard (1758–1802)[32]	Shoreham, curate Radcliffe-on-Trent, Nottinghamshire, curate	1783 1785
Downing, George (ca. 1729–1803?)	Ovington, Essex, rector	
Duchè, James[33] (1737–1798)	Chaplain at the Asylum for Female Orphans, London	
Dykes, Thomas[34] (1761–1847)	Cottingham, curate Barwick-in-Elmet St. John's, Hull, rector and builder	1778 1789–1791 1791–
Easterbrook, Joseph[35] (1751–1791)	Holy Cross (Temple) Church, Bristol	1779
Eastwood, Jonas (d. 1772)	Dewsbury, assistant curate Cleckheaton, curate Whitechapel, Leeds	1755 1757
Elton, Sir Abraham (1755–1842)	Leicester, curate[36]	1783
Farish, William[37] (1759–1837)	Magdalene College, Cambridge, tutor and fellow	
Farrer, John (1735–1808)	Escomb, curate Bishop Auckland Grammar School, Master Witton le Wear, perpetual curate	1759
Fawcett, James (1752–1831)	St. John's, Cambridge, fellow St. John's, Leeds, curate to Father St. Sepulchre, Cambridge, vicar	1777– 1776 1791–
Featherstone, Francis		

(London: Epworth, 2008), 210, and George May, *The History of Evasham: Its Benedictine Monastery, Conventual Church, Existing Edifices, Municipal Institutions, Parliamentary Occurrences, Civil and Military Events* (Evasham, UK: 1834), 148.

[32] Curate to Vincent Perronet at Shoreham. Assisted John Wesley in the ordination of Henry Moore and was one of Wesley's executors. Was a "reader" at City Road, London, from 1786. See *Proceedings of the Wesley Historical Society* 33.1 (March 1961): 13.

[33] In London as an exile from the United States from 1778–1793.

[34] Connected to William Farish, Henry Jowett, John Venn and Robert Jarrett. See J. King, *Memoir of the Reverend Thomas Dykes* (1849).

[35] Easterbrook was connected to both Fletcher and Wesley. According to A. S. Wood, "He regarded the Methodists as useful auxiliaries to the Establishment and attached his converts to classes" (*DEB* 342).

[36] Ordained in 1783. Curate to Thomas Robinson.

[37] "He was senior wrangler and became fellow and tutor of Magdalene and thereby played an important part in making the college pre-eminently evangelical" (*DEB* 378).

Name of Clergy	Incumbency/Appointment	Active Dates During Period
Fletcher, John William (1729–1785)	Madeley, vicar	1760–1785
Foster, Henry (1745–1814)	St. Anne's, Blackfriars, London, curate[38] Long Acre proprietary chaplain	1768– 1780–
Franks, James (1760–1829)	Haddenham, Cambridgeshire, curate	1787
Furley, Samuel (1732–1795)	London, curate Kippax, Yorshire, assistant[39] Slaithwaite, perpetual curate[40] Roche, Cornwall	1758 1759(?)–1762 1762–1766 1766
Garden, James[41] (d. 1772)	Slingsby, Yorkshire, rector Hovingham, curate	
Gauntlett, Henry (1762–1834)	Tilshead and Imber, Wiltshire, curate	1786
Gisborne, Thomas (1758–1846)	Barton-under-Needwood, perpetual curate	1783
Glascott, Cradock (ca. 1743–1831)	Preached for Lady Huntingdon Trevecca College Hatherleigh, Devon, vicar	1766–1781 1781–
Glazebrook, James (1744–1803)	Smisby, Derbyshire (now Leicestershire) Rowley Regis, Staffordshire, curate Latchford, near Warrington, curate	1773 1779
Goode, William, Sr. (1762–1816)	Abbots Ladgley, curate King's Langley St. Andrew-by-the-Wardrobe and St. Anne's, Blackfriars, London, curate[42]	1784–1786 1785 1786–
Graces, Charles Casper (1717–1787)	Ockbrook, Derbyshire, vicar	
Graham, John (1765–1844)		
Gurdon, Philip (1746–1817)	Magdalen College, Oxford, fellow Cookham, Berkshire, curate Family estates in Suffolk, Asslington Hall	1770–1778 1771–1777 1777
Hall, Westley[43] (1711–1776)	Wooten Rivers, Wiltshire	1735
Hallward, John[44] (1749–1826)	St. Giles, Reading, curate Worcester College, Oxford, fellow Shawbury, Shropshire, vicar Milden, Suffolk, rector Asington, Suffolk, vicar	1773–1775 1775 1775–1780 1779– 1779–

---

[38]Curate to William Romaine.

[39]Assistant to Henry Crooke.

[40]Appointed through the influence of Henry Venn.

[41]See S. T. Kimbrough Jr. and Kenneth G. C. Newport, *The Manuscript Journal of the Reverend Charles Wesley, M. A.* (Nashville: Kingswood Books, 2007), 2:370; and *Works* 19:330.

[42]Curate to Romaine.

[43]Westley was an Oxford Methodist and one of John Wesley's students at Lincoln College. He eventually converted to Moravianism.

[44]Evangelical at Oxford in the 1760s with connections to the St. Edmund Hall six.

Name of Clergy	Incumbency/Appointment	Active Dates During Period
Harmer, John	Said to have worked with Wesley[45] St. James's, Warrington, assistant Butlers Marson, Warwickshire, vicar	1766–1772 1777– 1779–1784
Hart, Richard (1727–1808)	Warminster, curate St. George's, Kingswood, Bristol, vicar[46]	1756–1759 1759–
Hartley, Richard (1746–1836)	The Bournes, Kent, curate	1786
Hartley, Thomas (1709–1784)	Chiswick, curate Winwick, Huntingdon	1737–1744 1744–1770
Haweis, Thomas (1734–1820)	St. Mary Magdalene, Oxford, curate[47] Lock Hospital, assistant chaplain All Saints, Aldwincle, Northamptonshire Trustee and executor and chaplain to Lady Huntingdon	1757–1758 1758–1764 1764–
Hawker, Robert (1753–1827)	St. Martin, near Looe, Cornwall, curate Charles, near Plymouth, curate Charles, near Plymouth, rector	1778–1779 1779–1784 1784–
Hervey, James[48] (1714–1758)	Dummer, Hampshire, curate Stoke Abbey, Devon, chaplain Bideford, curate Weston Favell, curate Collingtree, curate[49] Weston Favell, rector Collingtree, rector	1736–1737 1737–1739 1740–1743 1743–1752 1752–1758
Hervey, Thomas (1741–1806)	Chapel of Rampside, curate Underbarrow near Kendal, perpetual curate	ca. 1770–?
Hey, Samuel (1745–1828)	Steeple Aston, vicar	1787–
Hicks, William	Wrestlingworth, Bedfordshire	
Hill, Charles[50] (ca.1727–1801)	Fremington, Devon, curate Tawstock (Tawslock?), rector	1752–1756 1756–
Hill, Rowland[51] (1744–1833)	Roving preacher Kingston, near Taunton, curate	1769–1773 1773–

---

[45]There is no record of Harmer having been stationed within Wesleyan Methodism, but he is said to have worked with Wesley. See William Myles, *Chronological History, 3rd ed.* (London: 1803), 301.

[46]Hart was born into a well-connected Bristol mercantile and clerical family with Tory, and perhaps even Jacobite, affiliations. St. George's parish was "created to offer Anglican care to the coal-mining community which had attracted so much early evangelical preaching. He held this post to his death, reporting by 1766 that Methodism was declining in the parish" (*DEB* 527).

[47]Curate to Joseph Jane when he was run out of Oxford.

[48]Oxford Methodist.

[49]Collingtree had been Hervey's father's church.

[50]Converted under the preaching of George Thomson of St. Genny's, Cornwall, at his father's church in Devon.

[51]Hill still faced opposition to his desire for holy orders. Alan Munden notes, "Though he was diligent in his parish duties, he would not be confined by the parochial system and continued to itinerate. The Bishop of Carlisle had agreed to ordain him priest (on letters dimissory from

Name of Clergy	Incumbency/Appointment	Active Dates During Period
Horne, Melville[52] (ca. 1761–1841)	Madeley, curate	1786
Housman, Robert (1759–1838)	Gargrave, Yorkshire, curate St. John's Chapel, Lancaster, curate Langton, Leicestershire, curate[53] St. Mary's, Leicestershire, curate Markfield, curate St. Martin's, Leicester, lecturer	1781–1785 1785 1786–1787 1787–1788 1788–
Hutchings, John[54] (ca. 1716–?)	Dummer, Hampshire, curate[55]	1738
Jane, Joseph (1716–1795)	Cowley, curate St. Thomas, Oxford, vicar St. Mary Magdalene, Oxford Iron Acton, Glouchestershire, rector	1737(?) 1748–1763 1763–1788
Jesse, William[56] (ca. 1739–1815)	Chigwell, Essex, curate Itinerated for Lady Huntingon Hutton Cranswick, near Driffield in Yorkshire, vicar West Bromwich, perpetual curate	1765 1766–1781 1767–1780 1790–
Johnson, Samuel (ca. 1727–1784)	Cirencester, Gloucestershire, perpetual curate	1753–1778
Jones, John[57] (1721–1785)	Wesley's assistant Dovercourt and Harwick with Ramsey, curate, later vicar	1746–1748 post-1767
Jones, Thomas (1729–1762)	Collegiate Church of St. Saviour, Southwark Chaplain to bishop of London, Thomas Sherlock[58]	
Jones, Thomas[59]	Dunton, Bucks, Advent, curate Clifton Reynes, curate	1771–1772 1772–
Jones, William (1755–1821)	Broxbourne and Hoddesdon, Hertfordshire, curate	1781–

the Bishop of Bath and Wells) but the Archbishop of York intervened and for the rest of his ministry Hill remained in deacon's orders" (*DEB* 553). Hill was known to found chapels in non-Evangelical parishes but closed them when Evangelicals were appointed to the parishes in which they resided.

[52]Worked with Wesley just as had Fletcher, but had a later falling-out with Jabez Bunting.

[53]Curate to Thomas Robinson.

[54]Oxford Methodist but eventually converted to Moravianism.

[55]Curate to Charles Kinchin.

[56]Was of aristocratic stock and influenced by Thomas Haweis and Lady Huntingdon.

[57]"He had been refused episcopal ordination several times in his early years, because, presumably, of his Methodism" (*DEB* 621).

[58]For a long time Jones was the only beneficed Evangelical in London.

[59]Jones was one of six students expelled from St. Edmund Hall in 1768. He eventually served at Clifton Reynes, a mile from Olney. He had been tutored before going to Oxford by John Newton. Eventually he was ordained deacon in 1771 and priest in 1772 by John Green of Lincoln, who had ordained Newton in 1765.

Name of Clergy	Incumbency/Appointment	Active Dates During Period
Jowett, Henry (1756–1830)		
Kinchin, Charles[60] (1711–1742)	Dummer, Hampshire, rector	1735–1742
King, John (ca. 1724–1812)	Pertonhall, Bedfordshire	1752–1800
"Mr. King"[61]	Hull (Bristol) Middleton	
Kirkham, Robert[62] (1708–1767)	Stanway, Gloucestershire, curate to Uncle Stanton and Snowhill, rector, family living	1731 1739–1766
Knight, Samuel (1759–1827)	Witherington, curate[63]	1783–
Madan, Martin (1726–1790)	All Hallows, Lombard St., London Lock Hospital, London	1750– ca. 1755–1780
Maxfield, Thomas[64] (?–1784)	Wesley's Foundry, London	?–1763
Mayor, John (1755–1826)	Shawbury[65]	1781–
Mead, Henry[66] (1745–1806)	Ram's Chapel, Hackney St. John's Wapping, lecturer St. Pancras, lecturer	1777–
Meriton, John[67] (1698–1753)		
Michell, Thomas (d. 1773)	Most likely of St Mewan, Cornwall Vicar of Veryan	1743

[60]He was assisted by a succession of Evangelical curates, including George Whitefield and James Hervey. He was a constant companion of Charles Wesley and then emerged as the leader of the Oxford Methodists after the brothers had left.

[61]See Bryan Bury Collins, *An Address to the Higher Ranks of People in the Parish of St. Mary, Hull* (1778).

[62]Oxford Methodist, brother of Varanese, i.e., Sarah (Sally) Kirkham.

[63]First year of curacy under Thomas Adam.

[64]Maxfield, one of the first Methodist lay preachers, was ordained at Bath by the bishop of Derry on John Wesley's recommendation. After his split from Wesley, Maxfield worked with both John Fletcher and John Berridge.

[65]Was successor at Shawbury to James Stillingfleet and presented by Sir. Richard Hill. The parish was geographically close to Fletcher and de Courcy.

[66]Early student at Lady Huntingdon's college, Trevecca.

[67]See Charles Wesley's *Manuscript Journal* for Sunday, July 3, 1743, 2:356, and also his *Funeral Hymns* (1759), 28-29.

Name of Clergy	Incumbency/Appointment	Active Dates During Period
Middleton, Erasmus[68] (1739–1805)	Blackfriars, London, curate[69] Chelsea, curate[70] St. Benet's, Gracechurch St., lecturer St. Helen's, Bishopsgate St. Margaret's, Westminster, assistant Chaplain to dowager countess of Crawford and Lindsey	1783–?
Milner, Isaac (1750–1820)	President of Queen's College, Cambridge Dean of Carlisle	
Milner, John[71] (1710–1777)	Vicar of Chipping	1739–1771
Milner, Joseph[72] (1744–1797)	Hull Grammar School Holy Trinity, lecturer North Ferriby, curate North Ferriby, vicar	1767 1768–1786 1768–1786 1786–
Newell, Jeremiah (1756–1803)	Knightwick, Doddington, and St. John's Worcester, curate Missendon and Lea[73]	1771– 1787–
Newton, John (1725–1807)	Olney, Lincoln, curate City Living of St. Mary Woolnoth at St. Mary Woolchurch, Lombard Street	1764–1780
Nicholson, Isaac (1761–1807)	Cheshire Coddington, curate	ca. 1784 1785
Ogden, Joseph (1760–1839)	Sowerby Bridge, Halifax, curate[74] St. John's, Bacup	1785–1788 1788–
Pattrick (also Patrick), George (1746–1800)	St. Michael, Myland, Colchester, curate Aveley, Essex, rector Wennington, curate Chaplain to Lord Dacre of Aveley Chaplain at Morden College, Blackheath	1770 1772–1787 1773–1787 1780 1787–1790
Peckwell, Henry (1746–1787)	Bloxham-cum-Digby, Lincolnshire, rector	1782–
Penrose, John[75] (1713–1776)	St. Gluvias, Penryn vicar with Budock, Cornwall	1741–1776

[68]One of six students ejected from St. Edmund Hall in 1768. Middleton was the author of *Biographica Evangelica* (1769–1786), a history of Evangelicalism.

[69]Curate to Romaine after 1768.

[70]Curate to Cadogan.

[71]"In 1748 he was appointed as one of the King's preachers with opportunity to spread the gospel throughout the country" (*DEB* 775-76). Friend of both Grimshaw and Wesley. He may have been present at the 1753 conference at Leeds.

[72]Critical of Wesleyan Methodist theology.

[73]Under the patronage of Lord Stillingfleet.

[74]Dismissed from curacy as "Methodistical."

[75]One of the seven original members of Samuel Walker's clerical club. According to Hindmarsh he "remained suspicious of Methodism, advocating instead a vigorous but regular parochial ministry" (*DEB* 873). He was a friend of Walker, Thomas Adam and Haweis.

Name of Clergy	Incumbency/Appointment	Active Dates During Period
Pentycross, Thomas[76] (1747–1808)	Horley, Surrey, curate St. Mary's, Walingford, Berkshire, rector	1771–1774 1774–
Perronet, Vincent[77] (1693–1785)	Shoreham, vicar	
Piercy, William[78] (1744–1819)	West Bromwich, curate Lock Hospital, chaplain[79]	
Piers (also Pierce), Henry[80] (1694–1770)	Bexley, vicar	1737–1770
Powley, Mathew (1740–1806)	Wivenhoe, Northants, curate Slaithwaite, Cornwall, curate[81] Dewsbury, vicar[82]	1767–1777 1777–
Pugh, John[83] (1744–1799)	Raunceby and Cranwell, Lincolnshire, vicar	1771(?)–
Ramsey, James (1733–1789)	St. Kitts Teston, Kent	1762(?) 1781–1789
Rawlings, William (1761–1836)	Padstow, Cornwall[84]	1790–
Richardson, John[85] (1733–1792)	Cheddleston, Staffordshire, curate Leek, Stafforshire, curate[86] Battle, Sussex Ewhurst Methodist	1756(?) 1759 1762
Richardson, William[87] (1745–1821)	Kirby Morrside, near Pickering, curate York Minster, vicar-choral Incumbent of St. Michael-le-Belfrey and St. Sampon	1768–1771 1771– 1771–
Riland, John (1736–1822)	Sutton Coldfield, curate Huddersfield, curate St. Mary's (Anglican) chapel Sutton Coldfield, rector	1773 1774 1790–
Roberson, Hammond (1757–1841)	Dewsbury, curate[88]	1779–1778
Robinson, Thomas (1749–1813)	Wicham and Wichford, Isle of Ely, curate St. Martin and All Saints, Leicester, curate St. Mary's, Leicester, vicar	1771–1774 1774–1778 1778–

[76]Connected to Lady Huntingdon and for a time a Baptist.

[77]Longtime friend of the Wesleys.

[78]Connected to Lady Huntingdon.

[79]Chaplain with Madan, perhaps in the 1770s.

[80]Friend of Methodism and member of the first conference in 1744.

[81]Succeeded Samuel Furley.

[82]Gained Dewsbury through the influence of Lord Dartmouth.

[83]Influenced by George Whitefield at Oxford.

[84]Followed Thomas Biddulph.

[85]Preached John Wesley's funeral sermon.

[86]Dismissed from his curacy for evangelical leanings.

[87]No university education but was a founding member of the Elland Society.

[88]Curate to Matthew Powley.

Name of Clergy	Incumbency/Appointment	Active Dates During Period
Rogers, Thomas	Norton-cum-Galby, Leicester, curate Ravenstone, Derbyshire, curate St. Mary's, Leicester, curate	Most likely 1778–?
Romaine, William (1714–1795)	Lewtrenchard, Devon, curate Banstead, Surrey, curate Chaplain to Lord Mayor of London St. Dunston's-in-the-West, lecturer St. George's, Hanover Square, London, assisted in morning St. Olave's, Southwark, assistant in preaching and curate St. Bartholomew the Great in Smithfield, assistant minister of preaching and curate St. Anne's Blackfriars, annexed to St. Andrews-by-the-Wardrobe	1736–1738 1738–1741 1741–? 1749–? 1750–1756 1756–? 1759–1761 1766–
Rose, William (1750–1829)	Carshalton and Beckenham, Surrey and Kent, rector	1776–
Rouquet, James (1730–1776)	Kingswood, Bristol, Gloucestershire West Harptree, vicar West Werburgh's, Bristol, curate[89]	1765–1769 1769–
Salmon, Matthew[90] (1713–1797)		
Scott, Thomas (1747–1821)	Stoke Goldington and Gayhurst, Buckinghamshire, curate Weston Underwood, curate Ravenstone, curate (?) Olney, curate Lock Hospital, London, joint chaplaincy	1773–1775 1775–1786 1781– 1785
Sellon, Walter[91] (1715–1792)	Donative of Smisby, Derbyshire Breedon on the Hill, Leicestershire Ledsham, Yorkshire	1754– 1770
Sheppard, Edward[92]	Bath	1765–1789
Shirley, Walter, Sr. (1725–1786)		
Simeon, Charles (1759–1836)	St. Edwards, Cambridge, curate Holy Trinity, Cambridge	1782–1783 1783–
Simpson, David (1745–1799)	Ramsden Bellhouse, Essex, curate Buckingham, curate[93] St. Michael, Macclesfield, curate[94] Christ Church, Macclesfield, first incumbent	1769–1771 1771–1772 1772–1779 1779–

---

[89]Under Richard Symes.

[90]Was an Oxford Methodist. Never held a clerical post and was later critical of Methodism.

[91]Walter Sellon was one of Wesley's first preachers and a master at Kingswood. He was ordained and settled at Smithsby, near Ashby-de-la-Zouch. He became vicar of Ashby and was one of Wesley's chief supporters in the controversy with Toplady. See *Works* 22:223.

[92]Itinerated occasionally for Lady Huntingdon.

[93]Suspended by the bishop of Chester for "methodistical bias."

[94]Allowed John Wesley to preach in his church.

Name of Clergy	Incumbency/Appointment	Active Dates During Period
Simpson (also Sympson), John[95] (1709/10–?)		
Smith, William (1706–1765)	Combe, Oxfordshire, curate in charge	1737–1765
Spencer, Edward (1739–1819)	Bradford-on-Avon, curate[96] South Stoke, vicar Wingfield	1768–1769 1769–1771 1775–
Stillingfleet, Edward (ca. 1732–1795)	Prebendary, Worcester Cathedral West Bromwich, Staffordshire, vicar	1757–1782
Stillingfleet, James (1729–1817)	Merton, fellow Wolvercote, curate Coychurch, Glamorgan, rector Prebendary of Worcester St. Martin's, Worcester Knighttwick at Doddenham, Worcestershire	1752–1767 1765–1767 1767–1772 1772– 1775–1779 1775–
Stillingfleet, James (1741–1826)	Bierley Hall, near Bradford, chaplain[97] Hotham, East Yorkshire, rector	1766 1771–
Stonehouse, George (1714–1793)	St. Mary's, Islington, vicar	1738–1740
Stonehouse, James (Sir) (1716–1795)	Little Cheverell, Wiltshire, rector Great Cheverell, Wiltshire, curate[98]	1764– 1779–
Storry, Robert (1751–1814)	Hovingham, Yorkshire, curate[99] Winteringham, curate[100] St. Peter's, Colchester[101]	1781–1814
Symes, Richard[102] (ca. 1722–c. 1794)	St. Werburgh's, Bristol, rector	1754–
Talbot, William[103] (ca. 1719–1774)	Kineton, Warwickshire, vicar St. Giles, Reading, vicar	1740–1768 1768–1774
Tandy, William (1750–1832)	High Ham, Somerset, curate Portishead, curate[104] St. Mary-le-Port, curate	after 1773/4 1784–

[95]Held a living in Leicestershire after graduating from university but is not mentioned after the 1740s.

[96]Curate to Walter Chapman. Wood writes that Spencer's "attachment to the Established Church was such that he declined to become one of Lady Huntingdon's chaplains" (*DEB* 1039). Spencer left St. Edmund Hall in 1768 without a degree.

[97]Chaplain to Richard Richardson. Cousin to James Stillingfleet of previous entry.

[98]Curate to Thomas Stedman.

[99]Prepared for holy orders by Milner.

[100]Curate to Thomas Adam.

[101]Presented to St. Peter's by William Wilberforce's aunt.

[102]"Both John Wesley and the Samuel Walker identified him as one of Bristol's evangelical clergy, but distrusted his mystical tendencies" (*DEB* 1074).

[103]Itinerated for Lady Huntingdon.

[104]Curate to James Brown.

Name of Clergy	Incumbency/Appointment	Active Dates During Period
Taylor, Samuel[105] (1710–1772)	Quinton, vicar	1738–1772
Thomson, George (1698–1782)	St. Genny's, Cornwall	1732–1782
Toplady, Augustus Montague (1740–1778)	Blagdon, Somerset, curate Taleigh, Hungerford, near Bath Harpford, vicar Fen Ottery, Devonshire Broadhembury, Devonshire, rector	1756 1762–1764 1766–1768 1766–1768 1768–1778
Townsend, Joseph (1739–1816)	Pewsey, Wiltshire	1764–
Townshead, Edward (1760–1822)	Henley-on-Thames, rector Stewkley, Buckinghamshire, vicar Bray, vicar	1784– 1785–1788 1787–
Trelawny, Henry (Sir) (1756–1834)	Prebandery of Exeter	1789–
Venn, Henry[106] (1725–1797)	Clapham Parish Church, curate Huddersfield, Yorkshire, vicar Yelling, Cambridgeshire, rector	1754–1759 1759–1771 1771–
Vivian, Thomas (1722–1793)	Truro, curate Redruth Cornwood, vicar	1747–
Vowler, James[107] (c. 1727–1758)	St. Agnes, Cornwall, curate	1754–1758
Walker, Samuel (1714–1761)	Doddiscombsleigh, Devonshire, curate Lanlivery, Cornwall, curate Truro, curate Talland, vicar	1737–1738 1740–1746 1746–1761 1747–1752
Waltham, John (1750–1814)	Roche and Darlaston, Cornwall	ca. 1784–
Waterhouse, Thomas	Wroot	1734–1769
Wilkinson, Watts (1755–1840)	Little Horwood, Buckinghamshire, curate St. Mary Aldermary with St. Thomas the Apostle in Bow Laver Lane, lecturer Aske's (Haberdasher's) Hospital, chaplain	1779 1779– 1780–
Williams, Daniel (1749–1807)	Romsey, Hampshire, curate and later rector	1774–
Williams, John (1762–1802)	Burton and Williamstown, Dybed, curate	
Woodd, Basil (1760–1831)	St. Peter's, Cornhill, London, lecturer Bentinck Chapel, Marylebone	1784 1785–

[105]The Wesleys preached regularly at Quinton. Taylor met much opposition for his Methodist tendencies.

[106]Founded Yorkshire Clerical Club, later Elland Society.

[107]"He was concerned that Wesleyan societies should not be formed in evangelical parishes" (*DEB* 1147).

BIBLIOGRAPHY

PRIMARY SOURCES

Academicus. *The Church of England Vindicated from the Rigid Notions of Calvinism; or, Some Observations on a Letter from the Author of Pietas Oxoniensis to the Revered Doctor Adams of Shrewbusy. To which is added, A Letter to the Revered Mr. Romaine, in Answer to his Letter to Dr. Adams*. London: Printed for B. White, in Fleet-Street; and T. Cadell, in the Strand, 1770.

Adam, Thomas. *Posthumous Works of the Rev. Thomas Adam, Late Rector of Wintringham. In Three Volumes. Containing His Private Thoughts on Religion, and Sermons on Different Subjects. To Which Is Prefixed a Short Sketch of His Life and Character, Volume 1*. York: 1786.

———. *Practical Lectures on the Church-Catechism. By Thomas Adam, The Fifth Edition. To Which Is Now Added, an Exercise, by Way of Question and Answer, Preparatory to Confirmation*. London: 1767.

Anderson, George. *A Reinforcement of the Reasons Proving That the Stage Is an Unchristian Diversion*. Edinburgh and London: 1733.

Anonymous. *An Address to the Right Honourable —: With Several Letters to the D— of —, from the L—, in Vindication of Her Conduct, on Being Charged with Methodism*. London: Printed for W. Sandby, 1761.

Anonymous. *The Christian History, Containing Accounts of the Revival and Propagation of Religion in Great-Britain & America. For the Year 1743*. Boston: 1744–1745.

Anonymous. *A Letter to the Revd. Mr. John Wesley; Occasioned by His Address to the Clergy, February 6, 1756. By One of That Clergy*. London: Printed for M. Cooper, 1756.

Anonymous. *The Question Whether It Be Right to Turn Methodist Considered: In*

a Dialogue Between Two Members of the Church of England. London: Printed
for M. Cooper, 1745.

Anonymous. *The Ruin of Methodism*. London: Printed for the author and sold
by J. Dodsley and the booksellers of Oxford and Cambridge, 1776.

Anonymous (A Gentleman Late of the Temple). *The Mitre and Crown; or, Great
Britain's True Interest: In Which Our Constitution in Church and State will be
Explain'd and Defended, and a Short Account of Most Valuable Books Given,
with Some Original Pieces, and Law-Cases. . . .* London: printed for the author,
and sold by J[ohn] Fuller in Ave-Maria Lane, and by all the booksellers in
town and country, [1749].

Anonymous (Impartial Hand). *A Brief Account of the Late Persecution and Bar-
barous Usage of the Methodists at Exeter: Wherein the Characters of the Rioters,
their Aiders, and Abettors, are Fully Described, their Reasons and Pretensions
Fairly Examined, and Fully Refuted . . . : With a Vindication to Which are
Prefixed Some Arguments to Prove that Popery is a Religion in its Own Nature
More Detestable . . . than Mahometism or Pagan Idolatry, The Third Edition,
Corrected and Amended*. Exon: Printed by Andrew and Sarah Brice for Aaron
Tozer, 1746.

Beckerlegge, Oliver A., ed. "The Lavington Correspondence." In the Proceedings
of the Wesleyan Historical Society, XLII, part 4, May 1980.

Bennet, John. *John Bennet's Copy of the Minutes of the Conferences of 1744, 1745,
1747, and 1748; with Wesley's Copy of Those of 1746*. Publication of the Wesley
Historical Society 1. London: Wesley Historical Society, 1896–1904.

Berridge, John. *The Christian World Unmasked. Pray Come and Peep. By John
Berridge, A. M. Vicar of Everton, Bedfordshire; Late Fellow of Clare-Hall, Cambridge*. London: 1773.

Beveridge, William. *Anglilcana Ecclesia Catholic; or the Doctrine of the Church
of England Consonant to Scripture, Reason, and the Fathers in a Discourse
upon the Thirty-Nine Articles Agreed upon in the Convocation Held at London
MDLXII*. Oxford: Oxford University Press, 1847.

———. "Christ's Resurrection the Cause of Our Justification," sermon LXXIV. In
*The Works of the Right Reverend Father in God, Dr. William Beveridge, Con-
taining All His Sermons, as Well [as] Those Publish'd by Himself*. 2 vols. London:
1729.

*The Book of Common Prayer and Administration of the Sacraments and other
Rites and Ceremonies of the Church according to the use of The Church of
England together with the Psalter or Psalms of David pointed as they are to be*

sung or said in Churches and the form or manner of making, ordaining and consecrating of Bishops, Priests and Deacons. London: 1662.

Broughton, Thomas. *The Christian Soldier: Or, The Duties of a Religious Life Recommended to the Army, from the Example of Cornelius: in a Sermon.* London: 1738.

———. *Christianity Distinct from the Religion of Nature, In Answer to a Late Book, Entitled, Christianity as Old as the Creation.* London: 1732.

———. *A Defense of the Commonly-Received Doctrine of the Human Soul.* Bristol: 1766.

———. *The Inspiration of the New Testament Asserted: The Integrity of the Sacred Writers Vindicated.* London: 1739.

Browne, William. *A Vindication of the Proceedings Against the Six Members of E— Hall, Oxford by a Gentleman of the University.* London: Printed for M. Hingeston in the strand near Temple-Bar, S. Bladon in Pater Noster-Row, and sold by D. Prince at Oxford, 1768.

Bull, Patrick. *A Wolf in Sheep's Cloathing: Or, An Old Jesuit Unmasked. Containing an Account of the Wonderful Apparition of Father Petre's Ghost, in the Form of the Rev. John Wesley . . .* Dublin and London: 1775.

Buller, James. *A Reply, to the Rev. Mr. Wesley's Address to the Clergy.* Bristol: Printed by S. Farley, 1756.

Charles II. *1670: An Act to Prevent and Suppresse Seditious Conventicles. Statutes of the Realm: Volume 5: 1628-80.* 1819.

Christophus. *A Serious Inquiry Whether a Late Epistle from the Rev. Mr. Charles Wesley to the Rev. Mr. John Wesley Be Not an Evident Mark of Their Being Unhappily Fallen into One of the Most Crafty and Most Dangerous Wiles of the Devil, for the Delusion of Many Innocent, Unthinking Christians; by Inducing Their Hearers to Have Too High an Opinion of Them, as the Peculiar Servants of God, and Apostles Sent by Him to Have an Apostate, Sinking Church, and Encouraging Them Utterly to Contemn Their Own Regular Pastors, Set over Them by the Providence of God, Whom They by Their False Insinuations Represent as Apostates from the Church of England, and the True Church of Christ.* England and Wales: Printed for the author, 1755.

Clapham, Samuel. *How Far Methodism Conduces to the Interests of Christianity, and the Welfare of Society: Impartially Considered, in a Sermon, Preached at the Visitation, of . . . William, Lord Bishop of Chester, holden at Boroughbridge, in Yorkshire, September 2, 1794.* Leeds: Printed by J. Binns, and sold by J. Johnson and J. Deighton, London; J. and J. Merrills, Cambridge; and J. Fletcher, Oxford, 1794.

Crooke, Henry. *The Church of England a Pure and True Church: Attempted in a Sermon, Preached at the Parish Church of Leeds, in Yorkshire, on Wednesday the 12th Day of March, Being the 5th Wednesday in Lent. By Henry Crooke.* London: 1755.

———. *Extracts from the Diary of the Reverend Henry Crooke: Curate of Hunslet and Vicar of Kippax,* The Frank Baker Collection of Wesleyana and British Methodism, Box 22. David M. Rubenstein Rare Book & Manuscript Library, Duke University.

Downes, John. *Methodism Examined and Exposed, or, The Clergy's Duty of Guarding Their Flocks Against False Teachers: A Discourse Lately Delivered in Four Parts.* London: Printed for John Rivington, 1759.

Edwards, Jonathan. A *Faithful Narrative of the Surprising Work of God in the Conversion of Many Hundred Souls in Northampton, Massachusetts, A. D. 1735.* London: 1737.

Fawcett, Richard. *An Expostulatory Letter to the Rev. Mr. Wesley: Occasioned by His Address to the Clergy.* London: Printed for J. Wilkie, 1757.

Fernell, John. *Essay on the Origin of What is Called Methodism, and its Moral and Political Advantages: Addressed to Men of Reason and Religion, In reply to a Sermon, Preached and Published by a Clergyman of Liverpool.* Liverpool: Printed by Nuttall, Fisher and Dixon, 1806.

Fielding, Henry. *A Serious Address to the People of Great Britain: In Which Certain Consequences of the Present Rebellion, are Fully Demonstrated: Necessary to be Perused by Every Lover of His Country, at This Juncture.* London: Printed for M. Cooper, 1745.

Filmer, Robert. *The Anarchy of a Limited or Mixed Monarchy. Or, A Succinct Examination of the Fundamentals of Monarchy, Both in This and Other Kingdoms, as Well About the Right of Power in Kings, as of the Originall or Naturall Liberty of the People: A Question Never Yet Disputed.* Oxford: 1648.

———. *The Necessity of the Absolute Power of Kings, and in Particular, the King of England.* 1648.

———. *Patriarcha, Or the Natural Power of Kings.* 1680.

Fletcher, John. *Checks on Antinomianism in a Series of Letters to Rev. Mr. Shirley and Mr. Hill.* New York: Hunt and Eaton, 1770–1775, 1889.

Fletcher, Nathaniel. *A Vindication of the Methodist Dissected, or, The Methodists Writings Briefly Examined.* Halifax: Sold by Mrs Swale in Leeds, Mr Richard Whip, at Halifax, and by the author at Ovenden, 1750.

Forsaith, Peter S., ed. *Unexampled Labours: Letters of the Revd John Fletcher to Leaders in the Evangelical Revival*. London: Epworth, 2008.

Fox, John. *An Earnest Persuasive to the Manly Defense of Our Happy Constitution in Church and State; a Sermon, Preached in the Parish-Church of Kildwick-Piercy, in the County of York, on Friday, February 17, 1758*. York: 1758.

Gibson, Edmund. *The Case of the Methodists Briefly Stated: More Particularly in the Point of Field-Preaching*. London: Printed for Edward Owen, 1744.

———. *A Caution Against Enthusiasm: Being the Second Part of the late Bishop of London's Fourth Pastoral Letter, A New Edition*. London: Printed for F. and C. Rivington, booksellers to the S.P.C.K. by Bye and Law, 1801.

———. *The Charge of Edmund, Lord Bishop of London, to the Clergy of His Diocese, in His Visitation Begun in the Year 1741, and Finish'd in the Year 1742*.

———. *The Charge of the Right Reverend Father in God, Edmund Lord Bishop of London. At the Visitation of His Diocese in the Years 1746 and 1747*. London: 1747.

———. *Codex Juris Ecclesiastici Anglicani*. 1713.

———. *Observations Upon the Conduct and Behaviour of a Certain Sect, Usually Distinguished by the Name of Methodists*. London: Printed by Edward Owen, 1743 or 1744.

J. H. and A. B. *Gratitude to God the Surest Defence Against Future Dangers. A Sermon Preached to a Selected Audience, on Thursday October 9, 1746. Being the Day Appointed for a General Thanksgiving for Our Happy Deliverance from the Miseries of the Late Unnatural Rebellion*. London: 1746.

Hardy, Richard. *A Letter from a Clergyman to One of His Parishioners Who Was Inclined to Turn Methodist: With an Appendix, Concerning the Means of Conversion, and the Imputation of Righteousness*. London: Printed for the author and sold by J. Hinxman, 1753 [i.e., 1763].

Haweis, Thomas. *The Communicant's Spiritual Companion. Or, an Evangelical Preparation for the Lord's Supper. In which I. The Nature of the Ordinance is Shewn. II. The Dispositions Requisite for a Profitable Participation Thereof. Wherein, The Careless Sinner is Admonished, The Formalist Detected and Reproved, The Feeble-Minded Comforted, The Doubting Relieved, The Sincere Assisted, and The Faithful Confirmed. With Meditations and Helps for Prayer, Suitable to the Subject. By the Reverend Thomas, Haweis, Rector of Aldwinckle, Northamptonshire; And Chaplain to the Right Hon. the Earl of Peterborow*. 6th ed. London: 1770.

———. *The Life of William Romaine, M. A.: Late Rector of St. Ann's, Blackfriars, and Lecturer of St. Dunstan's*. London: 1797.

———. *A Supplement; Or, the Second Part of an Epistolary Correspondence Relative to the Living of Aldwinkle. Containing Several Important Letters, Now Forced to Be Made Public to Vindicate Injured Characters, and to Undeceive the Friends of Religion.* London: Printed for J. Wilkie and J. Walker, 1768.

Hervey, James. *Eleven Letters from the late Rev. Mr. Hervey, to the Rev. Mr. John Wesley; Containing an Answer to that Gentleman's Remarks on Theron and Aspasio. Published from the Author's Manuscript, Left in the Possession of his Brother W. Hervey. Second Edition.* London: J. F. and C. Rivington, 1789.

———. *The Works of the Late Rev. James Hervey, A. M.* Vol. 6. London: 1807.

Hill, Richard. *Goliath Slain, Being a Reply to the Reverend Dr. Nowell's Answer to 'Pietas Oxoniensis': Wherein the False Glosses of that Gentleman's Pamphlet are Removed, His Great Misrepresentations Detected, the Ancient Doctrines of the Reformation and of the Church of England Defended, and the Sentence Against the Expelled Young Men Proved from His Own Words to be More Severe, Arbitrary and Illegal than it Hath Hitherto Been Represented; With a Dedication to Every Particular Member of the University by the author of Pietas Oxoniensis.* London: Printed for G. Keith, E. and C. Dilly, M. Folinsby, and Mr. Fletcher at Oxford, 1768.

———. *A Gross Imposition upon the Public Detected: or, Archbishop Cranmer Vindicated from the Charge of Pelagianism, Being a Brief Answer to a Pamphlet Entitled 'A Dissertation on the Seventeenth Article of the Church of England, Wherein the Sentiments of the Compilers and Other Contemporary Reformers on the Subject of the Divine Decrees Are Fully Deduced from Their Own Writings'; In a Letter to the Dissertator by the Author of Pietas Oxoniensis.* Shrewsbury: Printed by J. Eddowes and sold by E. and C. Dilly and J. Matthews in London, also by Mr. Prince in Oxford, 1774.

———. *A Letter to the Rev. Dr. Adams of Shrewsbury: Occasioned by the Publication of His Sermon, Preached Against the Rev. Mr. Romaine, Entitled a Test of True and False Doctrines, to Which is Now Added a Dedication . . . with an Appendix by the Author of Pietas Oxoniensis, Second Edition revised, corrected, and very much enlarged.* London: Printed for E. and C. Dilly, M. Folingsby, and sold by Mr. Eddowes, at Shrewsbury, 1770.

———. *A Letter to the Reverend Dr Nowell: Containing Some Remarks on Certain Alterations and Additions in the Second Edition of His Answer to 'Pietas Oxoniensis' by the author of Pietas Oxoniensis.* London: Printed for G. Keith, E. and C. Dilly, M. Folinsby and Mr. Fletcher at Oxford, 1769.

———. *Monthly Review* (November 1772).

————. *Pietas Oxoniensis: or, A Full and Impartial Account of the Expulsion of Six Students from St. Edmund Hall, Oxford; With a Dedication to the Right Honourable the Earl of Litchfield, Chancellor of that University by a master of arts of the University of Oxford.* London: Printed for G. Keith, J. Millan, E. and C. Dilly, M. Folingsby, Mr. Mills [in] Bath, Mr. Eddowes at Shrewsbury, Mr. Collins at Salisbury, Mr. Fletcher at Oxford, and Mr. Merrill at Cambridge, 1768.

Hill, Rowland. *Imposture Detected, and the Dead Vindicated: In a Letter to a Friend: Containing Some Gentle Strictures on the False and Libellous Harangue, Lately Delivered by Mr John Wesley, Upon Laying the First Stone of his New Dissenting Meeting-House, Near City-road, The Second edition with a postscript.* London: Printed for T. Vallance; sold also by G. Keith and J. Mathews, 1777.

Hooker, Richard. *Of the Laws of Ecclesiastical Polity.* New York: Cambridge University Press, 1989.

————. *The Works of That Learned and Judicious Divine Mr. Richard Hooker with an Account of His Life and Death by Isaac Walton. Arranged by the Rev. John Keble MA. 7th edition revised by the Very Rev. R. W. Church and the Rev. F. Paget.* Oxford: Clarendon, 1888.

Horne, George. *The Christian King: A Sermon Preached Before the University of Oxford, at St Mary's on Friday, January 30, 1761.*

Hough, John. *The Pastor: Addressed to the Rev. John Wesley, by J. Hough, of the Inner Temple; in Which the Character of that Fallacious Casuist is Accurately Delineated.* London: Published by Mr. Williams, bookseller, near St. Dunstan's-Church, Fleet Street [ca. 1765].

Ingram, Robert Acklom. *The Causes of the Increase of Methodism and Dissension, and other Popularity of what is called Evangelical Preaching, and the Means of Obviating Them, considered in a Sermon, preached at the Visitation of the Rev. the Archdeacon of Leicester, held at Melton Mowbray, June 20, 1805.* London: Stanhope and Tilling, 1807.

Jackson, Thomas. *Commentaries Upon the Apostles' Creed, by the Rev. Thomas Jackson, D. D., Sometime Vicar of Newcastle-Upon-Tyne, President of Corpus Christi College, Oxford; Prebendary of Winchester and Dean of Peterborough.* London: John Goodwin, 1627.

Late member of the University of Oxford, *Remarks Upon the Reverend Mr. Whitefield's Letter to the Vice-Chancellor of the University of Oxford: In a Letter to the Rev. Mr. Whitefield by W. C. (a late member of the University of Oxford).* Oxford: Printed at the Theatre for J. Fletcher and sold by J. Fletcher and Co. in London, 1768.

272 WESLEY AND THE ANGLICANS

Laud, William. *The History of the Troubles and Tryall of the Most Reverend Father in God and Blessed Martyr, William Laud, Lord Arch-Bishop of Canterbury Wrote by Himself During His Imprisonment in the Tower; to Which Is Prefixed the Diary of His Own Life.* London: Printed for Ri. Chiswell, 1694.

Lavington, George. *The Bishop of Exeter's Answer to Mr. J. Wesley's Late Letter to His Lordship.* London: Printed for John and Paul Knapton, 1752.

———. *The Enthusiasm of Methodists and Papists Compared, Part II; Second Edition.* London: Printed for J. and P. Knapton, 1752.

———. *The Enthusiasm of the Methodists and Papists Compared, The Third Edition.* London: J. and P. Knapton, in Ludgate-Street, 1752.

Law, Edmund. *Considerations on the Propriety of Requiring a Subscription to Articles of Faith.* 2nd ed., corrected and enlarged. London: 1774.

Lawson, George. *Politica Sacra & Civilis: or, A Modell of Civil and Ecclesiastical Government.* London: 1660.

Leslie, Charles. *The History of Sin and Heresy Attempted, from the First War They Raised in Heaven . . . [to] Their Final Condemnation in Hell.* London: H. Hindmarsh, 1698.

———. *A Religious Conference between a Minister and Parishioner; concerning the practice of our orthodox Church of England, in baptizing infants by pouring water on their faces or sprinkling them, and in confirming them afterwards by the bishop, proving all three lawful by good reasons and the authority of Holy Scripture; with a vindication of the lawfulness of godfathers and godmothers, and of the sacred order of bishops and their being spiritual lords.* London: Charles Brome et al., 1698.

———. *A Short and Easy Method with the Deists, wherein the Certainty of the Christian Religion is Demonstrated by Infallible proof from Four Rules . . . To which is added, a second part to the Jews . . . with an answer to the most material of their objections, and prejudices against Christianity.* Published by John Wesley as *A Preservative Against Unsettled Notions in Religion.* London: 1758.

———. *The Snake in the Grass; or, Satan Transformed into an Angel of Light.* 2nd ed. London: Charles Brome, 1697.

———. *The Socinian Controversy Discussed.* London: G. Strahan, 1708.

Locke, John. *Two Tracts on Government.* Edited by Philip Abrams. New York: Cambridge University Press, 1967.

MacGowan, John. *A Further Defence of Priestcraft: Being a Practical Improvement of the Shaver's Sermon on the Expulsion of Six Young Gentleman from the University of Oxford, for Praying, Reading, and Expounding the Scriptures;*

Occasioned by a Vindication of that Pious Act by a Member of the University; inscribed to Mr. V— C— and the H—ds of H—s by their humble Servant the Shaver [i.e. John MacGowan], Fifth Edition. London: Printed for G. Keith, in Gracechurch-street, and J. Johnson and J. Payne, in Pater-noster-row, 1768.

Madan, Martin. *Account of the Triumphant Death of F. S. A Converted Prostitute, Who Died April 1763, Aged Twenty-Six Years*. London: 1763.

———. *An Answer to a Pamphlet, Intitled, a Faithful Narrative of Facts Relative to the Late Presentation of Mr. H—s, to the Rectory of Al— W—le, in Northamptonshire*. London: Printed for E. & C. Dilly, J. Robson and J. Matthews, 1767.

———. *A Funeral Sermon on the Much Lamented Death of the Rev. Mr. Thomas Jones, M. A.* London: 1762.

———. *Justification by Works: and Not by Faith Only, Stated, Explained, and Reconciled with Justification by Faith, Without Works. Being the Substance of a Sermon on James ii.24. Preached at St. Vedast's Church, Foster-Lane, February 8, 1761*. London: 1761.

———. *Letters on Thelyphthora: With an Occasional Prologue and Epilogue*. London: 1782.

———. *A Scriptural Comment upon the Thirty-Nine Articles of the Church of England*. London: 1772.

———. *Thelyphthora; or, a Treatise on Female Ruin, in its Causes, Effects, Consequences, Prevention, and Remedy*. London: 1780.

———. *A Treatise on Christian Faith, Extracted and Translated from the Latin of Hermannus Witsius*. London: 1761.

Manners, Nicholas. *A Dialogue, Between a Methodist Preacher, and a Minister of the Church of England, Second Edition*. London[?]: 1778.

Mason, William. *Methodism Displayed, and Enthusiasm Delected: Intended as an Antidote Against, and a Preservative from the Delusive Principles and Unscriptural Doctrines of a Modern Set of Seducing Preachers: and as a Defence of our Regular and Orthodox Clergy, from their Unjust Reflections by a member of the Church of England*. Liverpool: Printed by H. Forshaw, 1813.

Middleton, Conyers. *A Free Enquiry in to the Miraculous Powers, which are Supposed to have Existed in the Christian Church, from the Earliest Ages, through Several Successive Centuries. By which it is shown that we have no sufficient reason to believe, upon the authority of the Primitive Fathers, that any such powers were continued to the church after the days of the Apostles*. London: 1747.

Middleton, Erasmus. *Biographia Evangelica: or, an Historical Account of the Lives and Deaths of the Most Eminent and Evangelical Authors or Preachers, Both*

British and Foreign, in the Several Denominations of Protestants from the Beginning of the Reformation, to the Present Time. London: 1779.

Milner, Joseph. *The History of the Church of Christ, Volume the First: Containing the First Three Centuries, New Edition*. London: Luke Hansard and Sons for T. Cadell, in the Strand, 1827.

More, Henry. *Enthusiasmus Triumphatus: Or, a Discourse of the Nature, Causes, Kinds, and Cure of Enthusiasme*. London[?]: 1662.

Mortimer, Thomas. *Die and Be Damned: or, An Antidote Against Every Species of Methodism and Enthusiasm, Second Edition*, rev. and enl. London: Printed for S. Hooper and A. Morley, 1758.

Myles, William. *The Life and Writings of the Late Reverend William Grimshaw, Second Edition*. London: Printed at the Conference Office, by Thomas Cordeaux, 1813.

Newport, Kenneth, ed. *The Sermons of Charles Wesley: A Critical Edition, with Introduction and Notes*. New York: Oxford University Press, 2001.

Newton, John. *Cardiphonia: Or, the Utterance of the Heart; in the Course of a Real Correspondence in Two Volumes*. Vol. 2. London: 1798.

———. *Letters and Sermons, Including Cardiphonia and the Messiah; A Review of Ecclesiastical History, Hymns, and Miscellaneous Pieces. By John Newton, Rector of St. Mary Woolnoth, London. In Nine Volumes*. Vol. 4. Edinburgh: 1798.

———. *Memoirs of the Life of the Late Rev. William Grimshaw . . . : With Occasional Reflections; in Six Letters to the Rev. Henry Forster*. London: Printed for T. Hamilton (W. Flint, printer), 1814.

No Methodist. *Strictures on an Answer to the Pietas Oxoniensis: by Thomas Nowell, D.D., principal of St. Mary-Hall and Professor of Oratory in the University of Oxford by No Methodist*. London: S. Bladon, 1769.

Nowell, Thomas. *An Answer to a Pamphlet, Entitled Pietas Oxoniensis: or, A Full and Impartial Account of the Expulsion of Six Students from St. Edmund-Hall, Oxford in a Letter to the Author*. Oxford: Clarendon, 1768.

———. *An Answer to a Pamphlet, Entitled Pietas Oxoniensis, in a Letter to the Author. Wherein the Grounds of the Expulsion of Six Members from St. Edmund-Hall Are Set Forth; and the Doctrines of the Church of England, and Its First Reformers, Fully Considered, and Vindicated. By Thomas Nowell, D. D. Principal of St. Mary Hall, and Public Orator of the University of Oxford. Occasioned by the Reply of the Same Author*. Oxford: 1769.

———. *A Sermon Preached Before the Honourable House of Commons, at St. Margaret's, Westminster, on Thursday, January XXX, 1772*. London: 1772.

Orton, Job. *Diotrephes Re-Admonished, or, Some Remarks on the Second Edition of a Letter from the Author of Pietas Oxoniensis to the Rev. Dr. Adams of Shrewsbury Occasioned by His Sermon Entitled A Test of True and False Doctrines: Wherein Dr. Adams, the Church of England and Some Evangelical Doctrines are Vindicated from the Misrepresentations of the Letter-writer by a parishioner of St. Chad's and author of Diotrephes Admonished.* London: Printed for B. White and T. Cadell, 1770.

Parkhurst, John. *A Serious and Friendly Address to the Reverend Mr. John Wesley: In Relation to a Principal Doctrine Advanced and Maintained by Him and His Assistants.* London: Printed for J. Withers, 1753.

Pawson, John. *An Affectionate Address to the Members of the Methodist Societies, Containing an Account of the State of their Temporal Affairs, Namely, the Preachers Fund, the Yearly Collection, Kingswood Collection, and the Back-Room. In Which Some Notice is Taken of the False Accusations of Alexander Kilham.* London: 1795.

Philadelphus. *Remarks on a Pamplet, Intitled, A Dialogue Between a True Methodist and an Erroneous Methodist.* London: 1751.

Romaine, William. *An Essay on Psalmody.* London: 1775.

Ryves, Bruno. *Mercurius Rusticus: Or, the Country's Complaint of the Barbarous Outrages Begin in the Year 1642, by the Sectaries of this Late Flourishing Kingdom, Fifth Edition.* London: 1685, 1732.

Sanderson, Robert. *Lectures on Conscience and Human Law: Delivered in the Divinity School at Oxford.* Lincoln, UK: James Williamson, 1615, 1877.

Scott, Thomas. *Force of Truth: An Authentic Narrative.* London[?]: 1778.

Seagrave, Robert. *A Letter to the People of England. Occasion'd by the Falling Away of the Clergy from the Doctrines of the Reformation.* London: 1735.

Secker, Thomas. *Lectures on the Catechism of the Church of England; with a Discourse on Confirmation.* Edited by Beilby Porteus and George Stinton. London: 1799.

A Shaver. *Priestcraft Defended, A Sermon Occassioned by the Expulsion of Six Young Gentlemen from the University of Oxford, for Praying, Reading, and Expounding the Scriptures.* London and Boston: 1771.

Smith, George. *The Notions of the Methodists Fully Disprov'd, by Setting the Doctrine of the Church of England, Concerning Justification and Regeneration, in a True Light: In Answer to their Earnest Appeal, &c. with a Vindication of the Clergy of the Church of England from their Aspersions in Two Letters to the Reverend Mr. John Wesley.* London: Printed for Jacob Robinson, 1744.

Swathe, George. *Enthusiasm No Novelty, or, The Spirit of the Methodists in the Year 1641 and 1642.* London: Printedr [sic] for T. Cooper, 1739.

Taylor, Jeremy. *An Apologie for Authorized and Set Forms of Liturgie.* London[?]: 1649.

———. *The Golden Grove, or, A Manuall of Daily Prayers and Letanies, Fitted to the Days of the Week . . . Also, Festival Hymns, According to the Manner of the Ancient Church.* London[?]: 1655.

———. *On the Reverence Due to the Altar.* London[?]: 1649.

Toplady, Augustus. *A Caveat Against Unsound Doctrines: Being the Substance of a Sermon Preached in the Parish Church of St. Ann, Blackfryars [sic], on Sunday, April 29, 1770.* London: Printed for Joseph Gurney, 1770.

———. *The Church of England Vindicated from the Charge of Arminiamism.* Holborn, UK: Joseph Gurney, 1769.

———. *Historic Proof of the Calvinism of the Church of England.* London: 1774.

Towgood, Micaiah. *A Dissent from the Church of England, Fully Justified, and Proved to be the Genuine and Just Consequence of the Allegiance Which is Due to Christ, the Only Lawgiver in the Church: Being the Dissenting Gentleman's Three Letters and Postscript, in Answer to the Letters of the Rev. Mr. John White, on that Subject; Also a Letter to the Bishops, on the Present State of Religion in this Kingdom, and the Opinions of Three Eminent Lawyers, on the Question, Whether an Action can be Maintained Against a Clergyman, for Refusing to Admit a Notorious Evil-liver to the Sacrament, who Demands it as a Qualification for an Office, Eighth edition.* Cambridge: Printed by and for B. Flower: and for S. Woolmer, Exeter; J. Reed, Bristol; C. Sutton, Nottingham; T. Conder, Bucklersbury; W. Button and M. Gurney, London, 1800.

Trapp, Joseph. *The True Spirit of the Methodists, and Their Allies, (Whether Other Enthusiasts, Papists, Deists, Quakers, or Atheists) Fully Laid Open: in an Answer to Six, of the Seven Pamphlets, (Mr. Law's Being Reserv'd to be Consider'd by Itself) Lately Publish'd Against Dr. Trapp's Sermons Upon Being Righteous Over-Much.* London: Printed for Lawton Gilliver and sold by T. Cooper, 1740.

Tyson, John R., ed. *Charles Wesley: A Reader.* New York: Oxford University Press, 1989.

University of Oxford. *Pietas Universitatis Oxoniensis in Obitum Augustissimi & Desideratissimi Regis Caroli Secundi.* Oxonii: E Theatro Sheldoniano, 1685.

Venn, Henry. *Correspondence: The Letters of Henry Venn with a Memoir by John Venn.* Carlisle, UK: Banner of Truth Trust, 1993.

————. *The Duty of a Parish-Priest; His Obligations to Perform It; and the Incomparable Pleasure of a Life Devoted to the Care of Souls: A Sermon Preached at a Visitation of the Clergy, Held at Wakefield, July 2, 1760, Third Edition.* London: Printed for G. Keith, 1761.

Venn, John. *Memoir of the Rev Henry Venn.* London: John Hatchard and Son, 1834.

Walker, Samuel. *The Christian. Being a Course of Practical Sermons. Sermon I. The Sinfulness and Misery of Man. Sermon II. The Helplessness of Man. Sermon III. The Power and Love of Christ. Sermon IV. Faith in Christ. Sermon V. VI. Vii. Viii. IX. X. The Believer a New Creature; Wherein that Character is Largely Described—Opposed to that of a Careless Sinner—and Contradistinguished from that of a Formalist. Sermon XI. An Earnest Address to the Careless—the Formal -the New Creature. By Samuel Walker, A. B. Curate of Truro in Cornwall, and formerly of Exeter-College in Oxford.* London: 1755.

————. *Fifty Two Sermons, on the Baptismal Covenant, the Creed, the Ten Commandments, and Other Important Subjects, To Which Is Prefixed a Preface.* 2 vols. London: 1763.

Wesley, Charles. Charles Wesley to The Revd Mr. [Samuel Jr.] Wesley/Schoolmaster of Tiverton, Devon; Dated March 25, 1735, from Ch[rist] Church. In Wesley Historical Society Library at Oxford Brookes University.

————. *An Epistle to the Reverend Mr. John Wesley, by Charles Wesley, Presbyter of the Church of England.* London: 1755.

————. *The Manuscript Journal of the Reverend Charles Wesley, M. A.* 2 vols. Edited by S. T. Kimbrough and Kenneth Newport. Nashville: Kingswood Books, 2007.

Wesley, John. *The Bicentennial Edition of the Works of John Wesley.* General eds. Frank Baker and Richard P. Heitzenrater. Nashville: Abingdon, 1976–.

————. *Calm Address to Our American Colonies.* London: 1775.

————. *Concise History of England, from the Earliest Times to the Death of George II.* 4 vols. London: 1775.

————. *The Letters of the Rev John Wesley.* 8 vols. London: Epworth, 1931.

————. *Minutes of the Methodist Conferences, from the first, held in London, by the late Rev John Wesley, A.M., in the year 1744.* London: John Mason at the Wesleyan Conference Office, 1862–1864.

————. *Reasons Against a Separation from the Church of England, by John Wesley, Printed in the Year 1758; with Hymns for the Preachers Among the Methodists (so called) by Charles Wesley.* 2nd ed. London: Printed by W. Strahan, and sold at the Foundery in Upper-Moorfields, 1760.

———. *A Second Letter to the Lord Bishop of Exeter: In Answer to His Lordship's Late Letter.* 2nd ed. London: Printed by H. Cock, and sold at the Foundery, near Upper-Moorfields, by J. Robinson, by T. Trye, Holborn, by T. James and G. Englefield, 1752.

Whitefield, George. *The Almost Christian: A Sermon Preached to a Numerous Audience in England.* London: 1739.

———. *An Answer to the First and Second Part of an Anonymous Pamphlet, Entitled, Observations upon the Conduct and Behaviour of a Certain Sect Usually Distinguished by the Name of Methodists. In Two Letters to the Right Reverend the Bishop of London, and the Other the Right Reverend the Bishops Concern'd in the Publication Thereof.* London: 1744.

———. *George Whitefield's Journals: A New Edition Containing Fuller Material Than Any Hitherto Published.* London: The Banner of Truth Trust, 1960.

———. *A Letter to the Reverend Dr. Durell, Vice-Chancellor of the University of Oxford: Occasioned by a Late Expulsion of Six Students from Edmund Hall.* London: Printed for J. Millan, E. and C. Dilly and M. Folingsby, 1768.

Woodward, Josiah. *An Account of the Societies for the Reformation of Manners, in London and Westminster, and other Parts of the Kingdom. With a Persuasive to Persons of all Ranks, to be Zealous and Diligent in Promoting the Execution of the Laws against Prophaness and Debauchery, for the Effecting A National Reformation, Published with the Approbation of a Considerable Number of the Lords Spiritual and Temporal.* London: Printed for B. Aylmer, at Three Pigeons in Cornhill, 1699.

SECONDARY SOURCES

Abbey, C. J., and J. H. Overton. *The English Church in the Eighteenth Century.* 2 vols. London: 1878.

Abraham, William J., and James E. Kirby, eds. *The Oxford Handbook of Methodist Studies.* New York: Oxford University Press, 2009.

Anderson, Misty G. *Imagining Methodism in Eighteenth-Century Britain: Enthusiasm, Belief, and the Borders of the Self.* Baltimore: Johns Hopkins University Press, 2012.

Axtell, James. *The Invasion Within: The Contest of Cultures in Colonial North America.* New York: Oxford University Press, 1985.

Ayling, Stanley. *John Wesley.* Nashville: Abingdon, 1979.

Baines-Griffiths, David. *Wesley the Anglican.* London: Macmillan, 1919.

Baker, Frank. *Charles Wesley as Revealed by His Letters.* London: Epworth, 1948.

———. *John Wesley and the Church of England.* Nashville: Abingdon, 1970.

————. *William Grimshaw, 1708–1763*. London: Epworth, 1963.

Balleine, G. R. *A History of the Evangelical Party in the Church of England*. New York: Longmans, Green, 1909, 1933.

Bebbington, David W. *Evangelicalism in Modern Britain: A History from the 1730s to the 1980s*. Boston: Unwin Hyman, 1989.

Benedict, Philip. *Christ's Churches Purely Reformed: A Social History of Calvinism*. New Haven, CT: Yale University Press, 2002.

Best, Gary. *Charles Wesley: A Biography*. Werrington, UK: Epworth, 2006.

Binns, Leonard Elliott. *The Early Evangelicals: A Religious and Social Study*. London: Lutterworth, 1953.

————. *The Evangelical Movement in the English Church*. London: Methuen, 1928.

Black, Jeremy. *Eighteenth-Century Britain, 1688–1783*. 2nd ed. New York: Palgrave Macmillan, 2001, 2008.

Borgen, Ole E. *John Wesley on the Sacraments: A Definitive Study of John Wesley's Theology of Worship*. Grand Rapids: Francis Asbury, 1972, 1985.

Bowmer, John C. *The Sacrament of the Lord's Supper in Early Methodism, with Four Plates*. Westminster, UK: Dacre, 1951.

Brown, H. Miles. *The Church in Cornwall*. Truro, UK: Oscar Blackford, 1964.

Brown-Lawson, Albert. *John Wesley and the Anglican Evangelicals of the Eighteenth Century: A Study in Cooperation and Separation with Special Reference to the Calvinistic Controversies*. Edinburgh: Pentland, 1994.

Burch, Maxie B. *The Evangelical Historians: The Historiography of George Marsden, Nathan Hatch, and Mark Noll*. Lanham, MD: University Press of America, 1996.

Burdon, Adrian. *Authority and Order: John Wesley and His Preachers*. Burlington, VT: Ashgate, 2005.

Burrows, Aelred. "Wesley the Catholic," in *John Wesley: Contemporary Perspectives*, edited by John Stacey, 54-66. London: Epworth, 1988.

Campbell, Ted A. *John Wesley and Christian Antiquity: Religious Vision and Cultural Change*. Nashville: Kingswood Books, 1991.

————. "John Wesley as Diarist and Correspondent," in *The Cambridge Companion to John Wesley*, edited by Randy L. Maddox and Jason E. Vickers, 129-43. New York: Cambridge University Press, 2010.

Campbell, Ted A., and Kenneth Newport, eds. *Charles Wesley: Life, Literature, and Legacy*. London: Epworth, 2008.

Carus, William. *Memoirs of the Life of the Rev. C. Simeon*. London: J. Hatchard and Son, 1846.

Chilcote, Paul Wesley. *John Wesley and the Women Preachers of Early Methodism*. Metuchen, NJ: Scarecrow, 1991.

Clark, J. C. D. *English Society, 1660–1832: Religion, Ideology, and Politics During the Ancien Régime*. New York: Cambridge University Press, 2000.

Clark, Stanley Charles. *Unity, Uniformity and the English Church*. London: A. R. Mowbray, 1961.

Colley, Linda. *Britons: Forging the Nation, 1707–1837*. 2nd ed. New Haven, CT: Yale University Press, 2005.

Collins, Kenneth J. *The Theology of John Wesley: Holy Love and the Shape of Grace*. Nashville: Abingdon, 2007.

Collins, Kenneth J., and John H. Tyson. *Conversion in the Wesleyan Tradition*. Nashville: Abingdon, 2001.

Collinson, Patrick. *From Cranmer to Sancroft*. New York: Hambledon Continuum, 2006.

Cook, Faith. *Selina, Countess of Huntingdon*. Carlisle, UK: Banner of Truth Trust, 2001.

Cornwall, Robert D. "The Search for the Primitive Church: The Use of Early Church Fathers in the High Church Anglican Tradition, 1680–1745." *Anglican, Episcopal History* 59, no. 3 (1990): 303-29.

Cruickshank, Joanna. *Pain, Passion, and Faith: Revisiting the Place of Charles Wesley in Early Methodism*. Toronto: Scarecrow, 2009.

Davies, G. C. B. *The Early Cornish Evangelicals 1735–60: A Study of Walker of Truro and Others*. London: SPCK, 1951.

Davies, Rupert. *Methodism*. London: Epworth, 2003.

Ditchfield, G. M. *The Evangelical Revival*. Bristol: UCL Press, 1998.

Duffy, Eamon. *Stripping of the Altars: Traditional Religion in England c. 1400–c. 1500*. New Haven, CT: Yale University Press, 1992.

———. "Wesley and the Counter-Reformation," in *Revival and Religion Since 1700: Essays for John Walsh*, edited by Jane Garnett and Colin Matthew, 1-19. Rio Grande, OH: Hambledon, 1993.

Field, Clive D. *Anti-Methodist Publications of the Eighteenth Century: A Revised Bibliography*. Manchester, UK: John Rylands Library, 1991.

Forsaith, Peter S. *A Kindled Fire: John and Charles Wesley and the Methodist Revival in the Leeds Area*. Leeds, UK: Peter S. Forsaith, 1988.

———. "Moorfields, Mollies, and Methodists: The Co-Incidence of Two Divergent Sub-Cultures in Eighteenth-Century England." Paper given at the 12th Oxford Institute of Methodist Theological Studies, Christ Church, Oxford, 2007.

Forsaith, Peter S., and Geordan Hammond. *Religion, Gender, and Industry: Ex-*

ploring Church and Methodism in a Local Setting. Eugene, OR: Wipf and Stock, 2011.

Garnett, Jane, and Colin Matthew, eds. *Revival and Religion Since 1700: Essays for John Walsh*. Rio Grande, OH: Hambledon, 1993.

Gay, J. D. *The Geography of Religion in England*. London: Duckworth, 1971.

Gibson, William. *The Church of England 1688–1832: Unity and Accord*. New York: Routledge, 2001.

———. *Enlightenment Prelate: Benjamin Hoadly 1676–1761*. Cambridge: James Clark, 2004.

———. "Samuel Wesley's Conformity Reconsidered." *Methodist History* 47, no. 2 (January 2009): 68-83.

Gillies, John. *Historical Collections Relating to Remarkable Periods of the Success of the Gospel*. Kelso, UK: John Rutherford, 1845.

González, Justo L. *The Story of Christianity*. Vol. 2, *The Reformation to the Present Day*. New York: HarperCollins, 1985.

Gregory, Jeremy. "The Long Eighteenth Century," in *The Cambridge Companion to John Wesley*, edited by Randy L. Maddox and Jason E. Vickers, 13-39. New York: Cambridge University Press, 2010.

Gregory, Jeremy, and John Stevenson. *The Routledge Companion to Britain in the Eighteenth Century, 1688–1820*. New York: Routledge, 2007.

Gunter, Stephen W. *The Limits of 'Love Divine': John Wesley's Response to Antinomianism and Enthusiasm*. Nashville: Kingswood Books, 1999.

Hain, David, and Gardiner H. Shattuck Jr. *The Episcopalians*. New York: Church Publishing, 2004.

Hammond, Geordan. *John Wesley in America: Restoring Primitive Christianity*. New York: Oxford University Press, 2014.

Hampton, Stephan. *Anti-Arminians: The Anglican Reformed Tradition from Charles II to George I*. New York: Oxford University Press, 2008.

Harding, Alan. *The Countess of Huntingdon's Connexion: A Sect in Action in Eighteenth-Century England*. New York: Oxford University Press, 2003.

———. *Selina: Countess of Huntingdon*. London: Epworth, 2008.

Harris, Tim, Paul Seaward and Mark Goldin, eds. *The Politics of Religion in Restoration England*. Oxford: Basil Blackwell, 1990.

Haykin, Michael A. G., and Kenneth J. Stewart, eds. *The Emergence of Evangelicalism: Exploring Historical Continuities*. Nottingham, UK: Apollos, 2008.

Hefling, Charles, and Cynithia Chattuck, eds. *The Oxford Guide to The Book of Common Prayer: A Worldwide Study*. New York: Oxford University Press, 2006.

Heitzenrater, Richard P. *The Elusive Mr. Wesley*. Nashville: Abingdon, 2003.

———. *Mirror and Memory: Reflections on Early Methodism*. Nashville: Kingswood Books, 1989.

———, ed. *The Poor and the People Called Methodists*. Nashville: Kingswood Books, 2002.

———. "Purge the Preachers: The Wesleys and Quality Control," in *Charles Wesley: Life, Literature, and Legacy*, edited by Ted A. Campbell and Kenneth Newport, 486-514. London: Epworth, 2008.

———. *Wesley and the People Called Methodists*. 2nd ed. Nashville: Abingdon, 1995, 2013.

Hempton, David. *The Church in the Long Eighteenth Century*. I. B. Taurus History of the Christian Church. New York: I. B. Taurus, 2011.

———. *Methodism and Politics in British Society, 1750–1850*. Stanford, CA: Stanford University Press, 1984.

———. *Methodism: Empire of the Spirit*. New Haven, CT: Yale University Press, 2005.

———. *Religion and Political Culture in Britain and Ireland: From the Glorious Revolution to the Decline of Empire*. New York: Cambridge University Press, 1996.

———. *The Religion of the People: Methodism and Popular Religion c. 1750–1900*. New York: Routledge, 1996.

———. "Wesley in Context." In *The Cambridge Companion to John Wesley*, edited by Randy L. Maddox and Jason E. Vickers. New York: Cambridge University Press, 2009.

Hempton, David, and Myrtle Hill. *Evangelical Protestantism in Ulster Society 1740–1890*. New York: Routledge, 1992.

Hill, Christopher. *The World Turned Upside Down: Radical Ideas During the English Revolution*. London: Temple Smith, 1972.

Hindmarsh, D. Bruce. *The Evangelical Conversion Narrative: Spiritual Autobiography in Early Modern England*. New York: Oxford University Press, 2005.

———. *John Newton and the English Evangelical Tradition: Between the Conversions of Wesley and Wilberforce*. Grand Rapids: Eerdmans, 2001.

Hinton, Michael. *The Anglican Parochial Clergy: A Celebration*. London: SCM Press, 1994.

Holden, Harrington William. *John Wesley in the Company of High Churchmen*. London: Church Press, 1870.

Hopkins, Hugh Evan. *Charles Simeon of Cambridge*. Grand Rapids: Eerdmans, 1977.

Horn, James. "British Diaspora", in *The Oxford History of the British Empire*, vol. 2, *The Eighteenth Century*, edited by P. J. Marshall, 28-52. New York: Oxford University Press, 1998.

Hylson-Smith, Kenneth. *Evangelicals in the Church of England, 1734–1984*. Edinburgh: T&T Clark, 1989.

Ingram, Robert G. *Religion, Reform and Modernity in the Eighteenth Century: Thomas Secker and the Church of England*. Studies in Modern British Religious History 17. Woodbridge, UK: Boydell, 2007.

Jackson, Thomas. *Life of the Rev. Charles Wesley*. Rev. and enl. London: Wesleyan Methodist Book Room, 1900.

———. *The Lives of the Early Methodist Preachers, Chiefly Written by Themselves*. 6 vols. London: Wesleyan Conference Office, 1876.

Jeffrey, David Lyle. *English Spirituality in the Age of Wesley*. Grand Rapids: Eerdmans, 1987.

Jones, David Ceri. *'A Glorious Work in the World': Welsh Methodism and the International Evangelical Revival, 1735–1750*. Cardiff: University of Wales Press, 2004.

Kidd, Thomas. *George Whitefield: America's Spiritual Founding Father*. New Haven, CT: Yale University Press, 2014.

Kimbrough, S. T., Jr., ed. *Charles Wesley: Poet and Theologian*. Nashville: Kingswood Books, 1992.

Kirkham, Donald Henry. "Pamphlet Opposition to the Rise of Methodism; the Eighteenth-Century English Evangelical Revival Under Attack." PhD diss., Duke University, 1973.

Klein, Milton M. *An Amazing Grace: John Thornton and the Clapham Sect*. New Orleans: University Press of the South, 2004.

Knight, Henry H., III. *The Presence of God in the Christian Life: John Wesley and the Means of Grace*. Pietist and Wesleyan Studies 3. Lanham, MD: Scarecrow, 1992.

Knox, Ronald A. *Enthusiasm: A Chapter in the History of Religion with Special Reference to the Seventeenth and Eighteenth Centuries*. New York: Oxford University Press, 1961.

Langford, Paul, ed. *The Eighteenth Century, 1688–1815*. Oxford: Oxford University Press, 2002.

Lean, Gareth. *John Wesley, Anglican*. London: Blandford, 1964.

Lenman, Bruce P. "Colonial Wars and Imperial Instability," in *The Oxford History of the British Empire*, vol. 2, *The Eighteenth Century*, edited by P. J. Marshall, 151-68. New York: Oxford University Press, 1998.

Lenton, John. *John Wesley's Preachers: A Social and Statistical Analysis of the British and Irish Preachers Who Entered the Methodist Itinerancy Before 1791.* Paternoster Studies in Evangelical History and Thought. Eugene, OR: Wipf and Stock, 2011.

Lloyd, Gareth. *Charles Wesley and the Struggle for Methodist Identity.* Oxford: Oxford University Press, 2007.

———. "'Croakers and Busybodies': The Extent and Influence of Church Methodists in the Late 18th and Early 19th Centuries." *Methodist History* 42 (2003): 20-32.

Loane, Marcus L. *Oxford and the Evangelical Succession.* London: Lutterworth, 1950.

Lovegrove, Deryck. *Established Church, Sectarian People: Itinerancy and the Transformation of English Dissent, 1780–1830.* New York: Cambridge University Press, 1988.

Lowery, Ralph. "William Grimshaw." *Proceedings of the Wesley Historical Society* 34 (March 1963): 2-4.

Luckock, Herbert Mortimer. *Who Are Wesley's Heirs? A Reply to the Challenge of Rev. E. T. Carrier, Wesley's Minister.* New York: Longmans, Green, 1891.

Macaulay, Thomas Babington. *The Complete Works of Lord Macaulay.* 12 vols. New York: G. P. Putnam's Sons, 1898.

MacClendon, Muriel C., Joseph P. Ward and Michael MacDonald, eds. *Protestant Identities: Religion, Society, and Self-Fashioning in Post-Restoration England.* Stanford, CA: Stanford University Press, 1999.

Maddox, Randy L., ed. *Aldersgate Revisited.* Nashville: Abingdon, 1990.

———. *Responsible Grace: John Wesley's Practical Theology.* Nashville: Kingswood Books, 1994.

Maddox, Randy L., and Jason E. Vickers, eds. *The Cambridge Companion to John Wesley.* New York: Cambridge University Press, 2010.

Marsden, George M. *Jonathan Edwards: A Life.* New Haven, CT: Yale University Press, 2003.

Marshall, P. J., ed. *The Oxford History of the British Empire.* Vol. 2, *The Eighteenth Century.* New York: Oxford University Press, 1998.

Matthew, H. C. G., and Brian Harrison, eds. *Oxford Dictionary of National Biography.* 60 vols. New York: Oxford University Press, 2004.

May, George. *The History of Evasham: Its Benedictine Monastery, Conventual Church, Existing Edifices, Municipal Institutions, Parliamentary Occurrences, Civil and Military Events.* Evasham, UK: 1834.

McGovern, Terrence Xavier. "The Methodist Revival and the British Stage." PhD diss., University of Georgia, 1978.

McInelly, Brett. *Textual Warfare and the Making of Methodism.* New York: Oxford University Press, 2014.

Messer II, Glen Alton. "Restless for Zion: New England Methodism, Holiness, and the Abolitionist Struggle, Circa 1789–1845." ThD thesis, Boston University School of Theology, 2006.

Monod, Paul Kléber. *The Power of Kings: Monarchy and Religion in Europe, 1589–1715.* New Haven, CT: Yale University Press, 1999.

Moorman, J. R. H. *A History of the Church in England.* 3rd ed. London: A&C Black, 1980.

Moule, H. C. G. *Charles Simeon.* London: Methuen, 1892.

Mursell, Gordon. *English Spirituality: From 1700 to the Present.* Louisville, KY: Westminster John Knox, 2001.

Myles, William. *A Chronological History of the People Called Methodists, Of the Connexion of the Late Rev. John Wesley; From Their Rise, in the Year 1729, to Their Last Conference, in 1812.* London: Printed at the Conference Office, 1813.

Nelson, William H. *The American Tory.* Oxford: Clarendon, 1961.

Newport, Kenneth, and Ted A. Campbell. *Charles Wesley: Life, Literature and Legacy.* Peterborough, UK: Epworth, 2007.

Nockles, Peter. "Church Parties in Pre-Tractarian Church of England, 1750–1833: The 'Orthodox'—Some Problems of Definition and Identity," in *The Church of England, c. 1689–c. 1833: From Toleration to Tractarianism*, edited John Walsh, Colin Haydon and Stephen Taylor, 334-59. New York: Cambridge University Press, 1993.

Noll, Mark A. *The Rise of Evangelicalism: The Age of Edwards, Whitefield, and the Wesleys.* Downers Grove, IL: InterVarsity Press, 2010.

Noll, Mark A., David W. Bebbington and George A. Rawlyk, eds. *Evangelicalism: Comparative Studies of Popular Protestantism in North America, the British Isles, and Beyond, 1700–1900.* New York: Oxford University Press, 1994.

O'Brien, Susan. "A Transatlantic Community of Saints: The Great Awakening and the First Evangelical Network, 1735–1755." *The American Historical Review* 91 (October 1986): 811-32.

Oden, Thomas C., and Leicester R. Longden. *The Wesleyan Theological Heritage: Essays of Albert C. Outler.* Grand Rapids: Zondervan, 1991.

O'Gorman, Frank. *The Long Eighteenth Century: British Political and Social History, 1688–1832.* New York: St. Martin's, 1997.

Oh, Gwang Seok. *John Wesley's Ecclesiology: A Study in Its Sources and Development*. Lanham, MD: Scarecrow, 2008.

Ollard, S. L. *The Six Students of St. Edmund Hall Expelled from the University of Oxford in 1768 with a Note on the Authorities for Their Story*. London: A. R. Mowbray, 1911.

Outler, Albert, ed. *John Wesley*. New York: Oxford University Press, 1964.

Overton, J. H. *Evangelical Revival in the Eighteenth Century*. London: Longmans, 1900.

Overton, J. H., and F. Relton. *The English Church from the Accession of George I to the End of the Eighteenth Century*. New York: Macmillan, 1906.

Pawlyn, John S. *Bristol Methodism in John Wesley's Day: With Monographs of the Early Methodist Preachers*. Bristol: W. C. Hemmons, 1877.

Pearce, Edward. *The Great Man: Sir Robert Walpole: Scoundrel, Genius and Britain's First Prime Minister*. London: Jonathan Cape, 2007.

Pestana, Carla Gardina. *Protestant Empire: Religion and the Making of the British Atlantic World*. Philadelphia: University of Pennsylvania Press, 2009.

Pocock, W. W. *History of Wesleyan Methodism in Some of the Southern Counties of England*. London: Wesleyan Conference Office, 1885.

Podmore, Colin. *The Moravian Church in England, 1728–1760*. Oxford: Clarendon, 1998.

Pollard, Arthur, and Michael Hennell. *Charles Simeon (1759–1836): Essays Written in Commemoration of His Bi-Centenary by Members of the Evangelical Fellowship for Theological Literature*. London: SPCK, 1959.

Porter, Andrew. *Religion Versus Empire? British Protestant Missionaries and Overseas Expansion, 1700–1914*. New York: Manchester University Press, 2004.

Prichard, Robert. *A History of the Episcopal Church*. Rev. ed. New York: Morehouse, 1999.

Rack, Henry D. *Reasonable Enthusiast: John Wesley and the Rise of Methodism*. 3rd ed. Philadelphia: Trinity Press International, 2002.

———. "Religious Societies and the Origins of Methodism." *Journal of Ecclesiastical History* 38 (1987): 582-95.

———. "Survival and Revival: John Bennet, Methodism, and the Old Dissent," in *Protestant Evangelicalism: Britain, Ireland, Germany and America c. 1750–c. 1950, Essays in Honour of W. R. Ward*, edited by Keith Robbins, 1-23. New York: Basil Blackwell, 1990.

Ramsbottom, John D. "Presbyterians and 'Partial Conformity' in the Restoration Church of England." *Journal of Ecclesiastical History* 43 (April 1992): 248-70.

Ramsey, A. M. *The Gospel and the Catholic Church*. London: Longmans, Green, 1936.

Rattenbury, J. Ernest. *The Conversion of the Wesleys*. London: Epworth, 1938.

———. *The Eucharistic Hymns of John and Charles Wesley, to Which Is Appended Wesley's Preface Extracted from Brevint's Christian Sacrament and Sacrifice Together with Hymns on the Lord's Supper*. American ed. Edited by Timothy J. Crouch, OSL. Cleveland: OSL Publications, 1990.

———. *Wesley's Legacy to the World: Six Studies in the Permanent Values of the Evangelical Revival*. London: Epworth Press, 1928.

Reynolds, John Stewart. *The Evangelicals at Oxford, 1735–1871: A Record of an Unchronicled Movement with the Record Extended to 1905 and an Essay on Oxford Evangelical Theology by J. I. Packer*. Oxford: Marcham Manor, 1975.

Rigg, James H. (James Harrison). *Is Modern Methodism Wesleyan Methodism?, or, Wesleyan Methodism and the Church of England: Being a Sequel to "Was John Wesley a High Churchman?": a Dialogue for the Times*. London: Wesleyan-Methodist Book-Room, 1891.

Rivers, Isabel, ed. *Books and Their Readers in Eighteenth-Century England*. Leicester, UK: Leicester University Press, 1982.

———. *Books and Their Readers in Eighteenth-Century England: New Essays*. New York: Continuum, 2001.

Robbins, Keith, ed. *Protestant Evangelicalism: Britain, Ireland, Germany and America c. 1750–c. 1950: Essays in Honour of W. R. Ward*. Oxford: Published for the Ecclesiastical History Society by Basil Blackwell, 1990.

Rogal, Samuel J. *A Biographical Dictionary of 18th Century Methodism*. Lewiston, UK: E. Mellen, 1997–1999.

Rowell, Geoffrey, Kenneth Stevenson and Rowan Williams, eds. *Love's Redeeming Work: The Anglican Quest for Holiness*. New York: Oxford University Press, 2001.

Rubenhold, Hallie. *The Harlot's Handbook: Harris's List*. Stroud, UK: Tempus, 2007.

Rupp, Gordon. *Religion in England, 1688–1791*. Oxford: Clarendon, 1986.

Sack, James. *From Jacobite to Conservative: Reaction and Orthodoxy in Britain, c. 1760–1832*. New York: Cambridge University Press, 1993.

Samuel, D. N., ed. *The Evangelical Succession in the Church of England*. Cambridge: J. Clarke, 1979.

Sanders, Fred. *Wesley on the Christian Life: The Heart Renewed by Love*. Wheaton, IL: Crossway, 2013.

Schlenther, Boyd Stanley. *Queen of the Methodists: The Countess of Huntingdon and the Eighteenth-Century Crisis of Faith and Society.* Durham, UK: Durham Academic Press, 1997.

Schwenk, James L. *Catholic Spirit: Wesley, Whitefield, and the Quest for Evangelical Unity in Eighteenth-Century British Methodism.* Pietism and Wesleyan Studies 26. Lanham, MD: Scarecrow, 2008.

Selen, Mats. *The Oxford Movement and Wesleyan Methodism in England 1833–1882: A Study in Religious Conflict.* Bibliotheca Historico–Ecclesiastica Lundensis 30. Lund, Sweden: Lund University Press, 1992.

Seymour, Aaron C. Hobart. *The Life and Times of Selina, Countess of Huntingdon, By a Member of the Houses of Shirley and Hastings, Volume 2.* London: William Edward Painter, 1840.

Shenton, Tim. *A Cornish Revival: The Life and Times of Samuel Walker of Truro.* New York: Evangelical Press, 2003.

———. *Forgotten Heroes of Revival: Great Men of the 18th Century Evangelical Awakening.* Leominster, MA: Day One Publications, 2004.

———. *An Iron Pillar: The Life and Times of William Romaine.* Webster, NY: Evangelical Press, 2004.

Shoemaker, Robert. *The London Mob: Violence and Disorder in Eighteenth-Century England.* New York: Hambledon Continuum, 2007.

Sidney, Edwin. *The Life and Ministry of the Rev. Samuel Walker, Formerly of Truro, Cornwall.* London: Seeley, 1838.

———. *The Life of Sir Richard Hill.* Oxford: Oxford University Press, 1839.

Simon, J. S. "The Conventicle Act and Its Relation to the Early Methodists." *Proceedings of the Wesley Historical Society* 11 (1918): 82-93.

Smith, Lacey Baldwin. *Tudor Prelates and Politics, 1536–1558.* Princeton, NJ: Princeton University Press, 1953.

Smyth, Charles. *Simeon and Church Order: A Study of the Origins of the Evangelical Revival in Cambridge in the Eighteenth Century.* Cambridge: Cambridge University Press, 1940.

Stacey, John, ed. *John Wesley: Contemporary Perspectives.* London: Epworth, 1988.

Steer, Roger. *Church on Fire: The Story of Anglican Evangelicals.* London: Hodder and Stoughton, 1998.

Stout, Harry S. *The Divine Dramatist: George Whitefield and the Rise of Modern Evangelicalism.* Grand Rapids: Eerdmans, 1991.

Sutherland, L. S., and L. G. Mitchell, eds., *History of the University of Oxford: The Eighteenth Century.* Oxford: Clarendon, 1986.

Swift, Wesley, F. "Headingley Papers." *Proceedings of the Wesley Historical Society* 28 (1951–1952).

Sykes, Norman. *Edmund Gibson, Bishop of London 1669–1748*. New York: Oxford University Press, 1926.

Sykes, Stephen, John Booty and Jonathan Knight. *The Study of Anglicanism*. Rev. ed. Minneapolis: Fortress, 1998.

Taylor, S. "Sir Robert Walpole, the Church of England and the Quaker Tithe Bill of 1736." *Historical Journal* 28 (1985): 51-77.

Thompson, E. P. *The Making of the English Working Class*. New York: Vintage, 1963.

Trevor-Roper, Hugh. *Archbishop Laud*. 2nd ed. London: Phoenix, 1962.

Turner, John Munsey. *Conflict and Reconciliation: Studies in Methodism and Ecumenism in England, 1740–1982*. London: Epworth, 1985.

———. *John Wesley: The Evangelical Revival and the Rise of Methodism in England*. Peterborough, UK: Epworth, 2002.

Tyerman, Luke. *The Life and Times of the Rev. John Wesley, M.A., Founder of the Methodists*. 2nd ed. New York: Harper & Brothers, 1872.

———. *Wesley's Designated Successor: The Life, Letters and Literary Labours of the Rev John William Fletcher*. London: Hodder and Stoughton, 1882.

Tyson, John R., with Boyd S. Schlenther. *In the Midst of Early Methodism: Lady Huntingdon and Her Correspondence*. Lanham, MD: Scarecrow, 2006.

Urlin, Richard Denny. *The Churchman's Life of Wesley*. New York: The Society for Promoting Christian Knowledge, 1880.

Wainwright, Geoffrey. "Charles Wesley and Calvinism," in *Charles Wesley: Life, Literature, and Legacy*, edited by Kenneth G. C. Newport and Ted A. Campbell, 184-203. Peterborough, UK: Epworth, 2007.

Wallace, Dewey D., Jr. *Puritans and Predestination: Grace in English Protestant Theology, 1525–1695*. Eugene, OR: Wipf and Stock, 2004.

———. *Shapers of English Calvinism 1660–1714: Variety, Persistence, and Transformation*. New York: Oxford University Press, 2011.

Walsh, John. "The Anglican Evangelicals in the Eighteenth Century," in *Aspects de L'Anglicanisme: Travaux du Centre D'Etudes Supérienures Spécialisé D'Historie des Relgions de Stausbourg*, 87-102. Paris: Presses Universitaires de France, 1974.

———. *John Wesley 1703–1791: A Bicentennial Tribute*. London: Friends of Dr. William's Library, 1993.

———. "Methodism and the Mob in the Eighteenth Century." *Studies in Church History* 8 (1972): 213-28.

————. "'Methodism' and the Origins of the English-Speaking Evangelicalism," in *Evangelicalism: Comparative Studies of Popular Protestantism in North America, the British Isles, and Beyond, 1700–1990*, 19-37. New York: Oxford University Press, 1994.

————. "Religious Societies, Methodist and Evangelical: 1738–1800," in *Voluntary Religion: Papers Read at the 1985 Summer Meeting and the 1986 Winter Meeting of the Ecclesiastical Historical Society*, edited by W. J. Shields and Diana Wood, 279-302. London: 1986.

————. "The Yorkshire Evangelicals of the Eighteenth Century: With Especial Reference to Methodism." PhD diss., University of Cambridge, 1956.

Walsh, John, Colin Haydon and Stephen Taylor, eds. *The Church of England, c. 1689–c.1833: From Toleration to Tractarianism*. New York: Cambridge University Press, 1993.

Ward, W. Reginald. *Christianity Under the Ancien Régime, 1648–1789*. New York: Cambridge University Press, 1999.

————. *Early Evangelicalism: A Global Intellectual History, 1670–1789*. New York: Cambridge University Press, 2006.

————. *Faith and Faction*. London: Epworth, 1993.

————. *Georgian Oxford: University Politics in the Eighteenth Century*. Oxford: Clarendon, 1958.

————. *The Protestant Evangelical Awakening*. New York: Cambridge University Press, 2004.

Watson, David Lowes. *The Early Methodist Class Meeting*. Nashville: Discipleship Resources, 1985.

Watson, Kevin M. *Pursuing Social Holiness: The Band Meeting in Wesley's Thought and Popular Methodist Practice*. New York: Oxford University Press, 2014.

Watts, Michael R. *The Dissenters*. 3 Volumes. New York: Oxford University Press, 1985–2015.

Weber, Theodore R. *Politics in the Order of Salvation: Transforming Wesleyan Political Ethics*. Nashville: Kingswood Books, 2001.

Willard, Margaret Wheeler, ed. *Letters on the American Revolution, 1774–1776*. Boston: Houghton Mifflin, 1925.

Wood, A. Skevington. *Brothers in Arms: John Wesley's Early Clerical Associates*. Wesley Historical Society Publishing Office, 1992.

————. *The Burning Heart: John Wesley, Evangelist*. Minneapolis: Bethany Fellowship, 1967, 1978.

Yates, Nigel, ed. *Bishop Burgess and His World: Culture, Religion and Society in*

Britain, Europe and North America in the Eighteenth and Nineteenth Centuries. Cardiff: University of Wales Press, 2007.

―――. *Eighteenth-Century Britain: Religion and Politics, 1710–1815.* New York: Longman, 2008.

Zabriskie, Alexander C., ed. *Anglican Evangelicalism.* Church Historical Society 13. Philadelphia: Church Historical Society, 1943.

Zahl, Paul F. M. *The Protestant Face of Anglicanism.* Grand Rapids: Eerdmans, 1998.

AUTHOR INDEX

Subject Index

Finding the Textbook You Need